The Imperial Underbelly

The volume introduces a new analysis of interconnected labour and economic history of colonial India and Scandinavia. From a recently found archive of a railway contractor's private and business papers, the studies revise both Indian labour history and Scandinavian modern history, and ties south Sweden into the British Empire. With deep insights into everyday work practices of Indian and European contractors and manual labourers, the book establishes a bridge across the globe, between two poor regions as sites of extraction and industrial transformation, resulting from global migration and capital flows. Drawing on rich archival sources such as the Joseph Stephens Archive, Maharashtra State Archives, the National Archives of India, and the British Library, the book offers deep insights into everyday business practices of European contractors in India, which were rarely documented and have remained largely inaccessible so far.

A unique look into the labour and entrepreneurship practices under British colonial rule in India, as well as its impact on the most transformative years of modern southern Scandinavia, the book will be of great interest to students, academics, and teachers of history, labour studies, subaltern studies, colonialism, imperialism, economic history, railways, economics, and Scandinavian and South Asian studies.

Gunnel Cederlöf is Professor of History, Linnaeus University, Sweden, and member of the Linnaeus University Centre for Concurrences in Colonial and Postcolonial Studies. She specializes in the environmental, legal, and colonial history of India and South Asia. She has taught at Uppsala University and KTH Royal Institute of Technology. She is the author of *Founding an Empire on India's North-Eastern Frontiers, 1790–1840: Climate, Commerce, Polity* (2014), *Landscapes and the Law: Environmental Politics, Regional Histories, and Contests over Nature* (2008, 2019), *Bonds Lost: Subordination, Conflict and Mobilisation in Rural South India c. 1900–1970* (1997, 2020), *At Nature's Edge: The Global Present and Long-Term History* (2018 with M. Rangarajan), *Subjects, Citizens and Law: Colonial and Independent India* (2017 with S. Das Gupta), and *Ecological Nationalisms: Nature, Livelihoods, and Identities in South Asia* (2006, 2014 with K. Sivaramakrishnan).

The Imperial Underbelly

Workers, Contractors, and Entrepreneurs in Colonial India and Scandinavia

Edited by Gunnel Cederlöf

Routledge
Taylor & Francis Group
LONDON AND NEW YORK

First published 2023
by Routledge
4 Park Square, Milton Park, Abingdon, Oxon OX14 4RN

and by Routledge
605 Third Avenue, New York, NY 10158

Routledge is an imprint of the Taylor & Francis Group, an informa business

British Library Cataloguing-in-Publication Data
A catalogue record for this book is available from the British Library

Library of Congress Cataloging-in-Publication Data
Names: Cederlöf, Gunnel, editor.
Title: The imperial underbelly : workers, contractors, and entrepreneurs in colonial India and Scandinavia / edited by Gunnel Cederlöf.
Description: Abingdon, Oxon ; New York, NY : Routledge, 2023. | Includes bibliographical references and index. |
Identifiers: LCCN 2022033742 (print) | LCCN 2022033743 (ebook) | ISBN 9781032320922 (hbk) | ISBN 9781032328928 (pbk) | ISBN 9781003317227 (ebk)
Subjects: LCSH: Labor—India. | Labor—Scandinavia. | Contractors—India. | Contractors—Scandinavia. | Economic history.
Classification: LCC HD8686.5 .I43 2023 (print) | LCC HD8686.5 (ebook) | DDC 331.0948—dc23/eng/20220916
LC record available at https://lccn.loc.gov/2022033742
LC ebook record available at https://lccn.loc.gov/2022033743

ISBN: 978-1-032-32092-2 (hbk)
ISBN: 978-1-032-32892-8 (pbk)
ISBN: 978-1-003-31722-7 (ebk)

DOI: 10.4324/9781003317227

Typeset in Sabon
by Apex CoVantage, LLC

Contents

List of Illustrations vii
List of Contributors ix

1 Circular Migrations, Capital, and Opportunity: A Global History of Scandinavia and India at the Industrial Turn, an Introduction 1
GUNNEL CEDERLÖF

2 The Life of Contract Capitalism and the Building of the Colonial Railway 26
ARUN KUMAR

3 Bureaucracy and Ideologies of Control in British India: Social and Professional Networks and the 'Contract System' in Railway Building 56
RADHIKA KRISHNAN

4 Social Capital and Its Limits in Fortune Making: Joseph Stephens' Enterprises in India and Scandinavia, 1859–69 72
DHIRAJ KUMAR NITE

5 Labour Practices and Well-Being: Construction Workers in 1860s Western India 101
DHIRAJ KUMAR NITE

6 Circulation of Knowledge, Capital, and Goods: Scandinavia and the British Empire 135
ELEONOR MARCUSSEN

7 Colonial Entrepreneurial Capital in the Industrialization of Southern Sweden: The Huseby Estate under Joseph Stephens 161
ERIK WÅNGMAR

8 Doing One's Duty, Making a Future: The Ironmaster's Daughters and the Unceasing Project of Rearing a Family 181
MALIN LENNARTSSON

Bibliography 204
Publications From Research Related to the Huseby Estate and Joseph Stephens Archives 219
Index 222

Illustrations

Figures

1.1 Joseph Stephens 4
1.2 Weighing cotton on the Colaba Island, Bombay 10
1.3 The manor house at the Huseby Estate, 1870 14
2.1 Mhow-ke-Mullee Viaduct, 3,000 men employed, Khumnee Hill, 1856 33
2.2 Part I, A copy of Stephens' contract in Modi script dating from 1865 35
2.3 Original copy of the contract between Stephens and Reembhy Casseembhy 36
2.4 Contract with lime supplier, with a third-party guarantor contract 42
2.5 List of tools and tent and with Yemma Muccadam, January 1865 45
3.1 Engineers, contractors and other visitors to the Bhor Ghat works on the Great Indian Peninsular Railways, 1856 62
4.1 The contractor Mr. Clowser at his workshop at Oonee village. Constructions at Bhor Ghat 86
5.1 Railway workmen's quarters at the Great Ravine near Rajmachi Fort, 1856 117
6.1 Joseph Stephens (left) in a meeting at Huseby together with regional timber merchants, most prominently M. M. Warburg (next to Stephens) of Bark & Warburg, Gothenburg, and Robert Ternström (sitting with arms crossed) of Schmidt & Co, Karlshamn, 1870 148
7.1 At the entrance of the Huseby manor house, from left, Joseph Stephens, his daughter Florence, two unknown men, daughter Maggie, Elisabeth Stephens, daughter Mary, unknown woman, circa 1900 167
8.1 Florence, Mary, and Maggie Stephens, mid-1890s 182

Graphs

5.1 Real wages in terms of price of subsistence living basket in 1861 108
5.2 Wage inequality or distribution ratios: Skill premium 110
5.3a Subsistence or welfare ratios 115
5.3b Subsistence ratios (bare-bones subsistence basket) 115
5.4 Trend in price of subsistence basket, jowar, and rice 121

Tables

4.1 Profitability situation in rupees (Rs.) 82
4.2 Monthly share (Rs.) in the monetary value of output: An indicative estimate (around the Bhusawal—Nagpur railway) during 1862–7 90
5.1 Occupational pattern 104
5.2 Wages (Rs.-As-Pies). (1 Re = 16 As, 1 As =12 Pies) 106
5.3 Wages 107
5.4 Real wages in terms of the price of monthly subsistence in base year 1861 (Pb) [MW/(Pt/Pb). MW—Money wage. Pt—price in current year. Pb—price in base year] 107
5.5 Real wages in terms of the price of monthly subsistence in 1861 (Pb). (MW/(Pt/Pb)) 108
5.6 Wage distribution (inequality) ratios: Skill premium (mason/ coolie, writer/mason) 110
5.7 Subsistence basket 114
5.8 The cost of subsistence (Rs.). (Family size of 4.5 persons, corresponding to 3.5 adult consumers) 114
5.9 Subsistence ratios: Annual earnings for 264 days/cost of subsistence basket 116

Maps

0.1 Railway Lines in India circa 1870 xii
0.2 Berar and Khandesh circa 1870 xiii
0.3 Southern Scandinavia, Railway lines of interest, circa 1874 xiv

Contributors

Arun Kumar is Assistant Professor of British Imperial and Colonial History, University of Nottingham, UK. His studies on the social, economic, and labour history of modern India have appeared in the journals South Asia: Journal of South Asia, Past and Present, and Journal of South Asian Development. He has been a research fellow at the Linnaeus University, Sweden, the International Institute of Social History Amsterdam and the Merian-Tagore International Centre for Advanced Studies (ICAS) New Delhi. His current book project on working-class education, based on his award-winning PhD thesis of Göttingen University, explores the dreams and aspirations of Indian workers. Among his publications are 'Letters of the Labouring Poor: Letter Writing in Colonial India' (2020), The 'Untouchable School': American Missionaries, Hindu Social Reformers and Educational Dreams of Labouring Dalits in Colonial North India' (2019), and 'Skilling and its Histories: Labour Market and the Making of Skilled Workers in Colonial India (1880–1910)' (2018).

Dhiraj Kumar Nite is Assistant Professor, Ambedkar University, Delhi, India, and Senior Research Associate at University of Johannesburg, South Africa. He specializes in the history of well-being, labour relations, and entrepreneurship. His PhD in History, Jawaharlal Nehru University, New Delhi, is titled 'Work and Culture on the Mines: Jharia Coalfields 1890s-1970'. He was Postdoctoral Fellow at the Linnaeus University, Sweden, and at the University of Johannesburg. Among his publications are 'Employee Benefits, Migration and Social Movement: An Indian Coalfield, 1895–1970'(2019), 'Negotiating the Mines: The Culture of Safety in the Indian Coalmines, 1895–1970'(2019), 'Consenting to Labour Appropriation?': The Mineworker on South African Gold and Coalmines, 1951–2011' (2017, with Paul Stewart), and 'Worshiping the Colliery-Goddess: An Exploration of the Religious View of Safety in Indian Coalminers (Jharia), 1895–2009,' (2016).

Eleonor Marcussen is Research Fellow in History at the Linnaeus University, Sweden, and member of the Linnaeus University Centre for Concurrences in Colonial and Postcolonial Studies. She was a MWK-COFUND

Fellow at The Max Weber Centre for Advanced Cultural and Social Studies (Max Weber Kolleg, University of Erfurt, Germany), a postdoctoral fellow at the Linnaeus University, and Assistant Professor of History at North South University, Dhaka, Bangladesh. Her PhD in South Asian History from Heidelberg University was published as a monograph with Cambridge University Press in 2022, titled *Acts of Aid: Politics of Relief and Reconstruction in the 1934 Bihar-Nepal Earthquake*. Among her publications are 'Cooperation and Pacifism in a Colonial Context: Service Civil International and Work Camps in Bihar, 1934–1937' (2018), 'Town Planning after the 1934 Bihar-Nepal Earthquake: Earthquake-Safety, Colonial Improvements and the Restructuring of Urban Space in Bihar' (2017), and 'Explaining the 1934 Bihar-Nepal Earthquake: The Role of Science, Astrology, and "Rumours" ' (2017).

Erik Wångmar is Associate Professor of History and Senior Lecturer in Political Science at the Linnaeus University, Sweden. He specializes in the history of local government, politics, crime, and the individual, and in historiography. Among his publications are 'How Coerced Municipal Amalgamations Thwart the Values of Local Self-Government' (2020 with G. Erlingsson and J. Ödalen), *Historians and Their Sources: The Use of Unpublished Source Material in Swedish Doctoral Theses in History, 1959–2015, and in Student Bachelor's and Master's Theses, 2010–2015* (2018 with M. Lennartsson, in Swedish), Understanding Large-Scale Institutional Change: Social Conflicts and the Politics of Swedish Municipal Amalgamations, 1952–1974 (2015 with G. Erlingsson and J. Ödalen), and *Husebyfröken: En studie om Florence Stephens 1881–1979* (2020, The Huseby Ma'am: A Study of Florence Stephens 1881–1979)

Gunnel Cederlöf is Professor of History, Linnaeus University, Sweden, and Member of the Linnaeus University Centre for Concurrences in Colonial and Postcolonial Studies. She specializes in the environmental, legal, and colonial history of India and South Asia. She has taught at Uppsala University and KTH Royal Institute of Technology. She is the author of *Founding an Empire on India's North-Eastern Frontiers, 1790–1840: Climate, Commerce, Polity* (2014), *Landscapes and the Law: Environmental Politics, Regional Histories, and Contests over Nature* (2008, 2019), *Bonds Lost: Subordination, Conflict and Mobilisation in Rural South India c. 1900–1970* (1997, 2020), *At Nature's Edge: The Global Present and Long-Term History* (208 with M. Rangarajan), *Subjects, Citizens and Law: Colonial and Independent India* (2017 with S. Das Gupta), and *Ecological Nationalisms: Nature, Livelihoods, and Identities in South Asia* (2006, 2014 with K. Sivaramakrishnan).

Malin Lennartsson is Associate Professor and Senior Lecturer in History, Linnaeus University, Sweden. Her work focuses on the early modern and nineteenth-century history of culture, law, and gender. Among her publications are 'Falken och liksvepningen: auktoritet och makt

I Tudordynastin' (2018, 'The falcon and the winding sheet: authority and power in the Tudor Dynasty'); *Historians and their Sources: The Use of Unpublished Source Material in Swedish Doctoral Theses in History 1959–2015, and in Student Bachelor's and Master's Theses, 2010–2015'* (2018 with E. Wångmar); 'Barnhustrur eller mogna brudar? Nya perspektiv på giftermålsmönster i svensk stormaktstid' (2012, 'Child wives or adult brides? New perspectives on marriage patterns in Sweden's age of greatness');'Hävdande och hustrubröst: Sexualitet, kropp och identitet i det tidigmoderna Sverige' (2009, 'Carnal knowledge: Sexuality, Body, and Identity in Early Modern Sweden') and *I säng och säte: Relationer mellan kvinnor och män i 1600-talets Småland* (1999, *Bed and Board. Relationships between women and men in seventeenth century Småland*, PhD thesis, Lund University 1999).

Radhika Krishnan is Assistant Professor of Humanities at the International Institute of Information Technology, Hyderabad, India. Her field of research includes the interactions between technological regimes, communities, and local ecologies. She was Postdoctoral Fellow at the Linnaeus University and Fellow at the Indian Institute of Advanced Study in Shimla, India. She is the author of 'The Environment and Civil Society in India' (2017), 'The Industrial Project and Organised Labour: The (Im)possibility' 'The Industrial Project and Organised Labour: The (Im)possibility of "Red" and "Green" Imaginations?' (2017), 'Red in the Green: Forests, Farms, Factories and the Many Legacies of Shankar Guha Niyogi (1943–1991)' (2016), and '"Ecological Warriors" versus "Indigenous Performers": Understanding State Responses to Resistance Movements in Jagatsinghpur and Niyamgiri in Odisha' (2017 with Rama Naga).

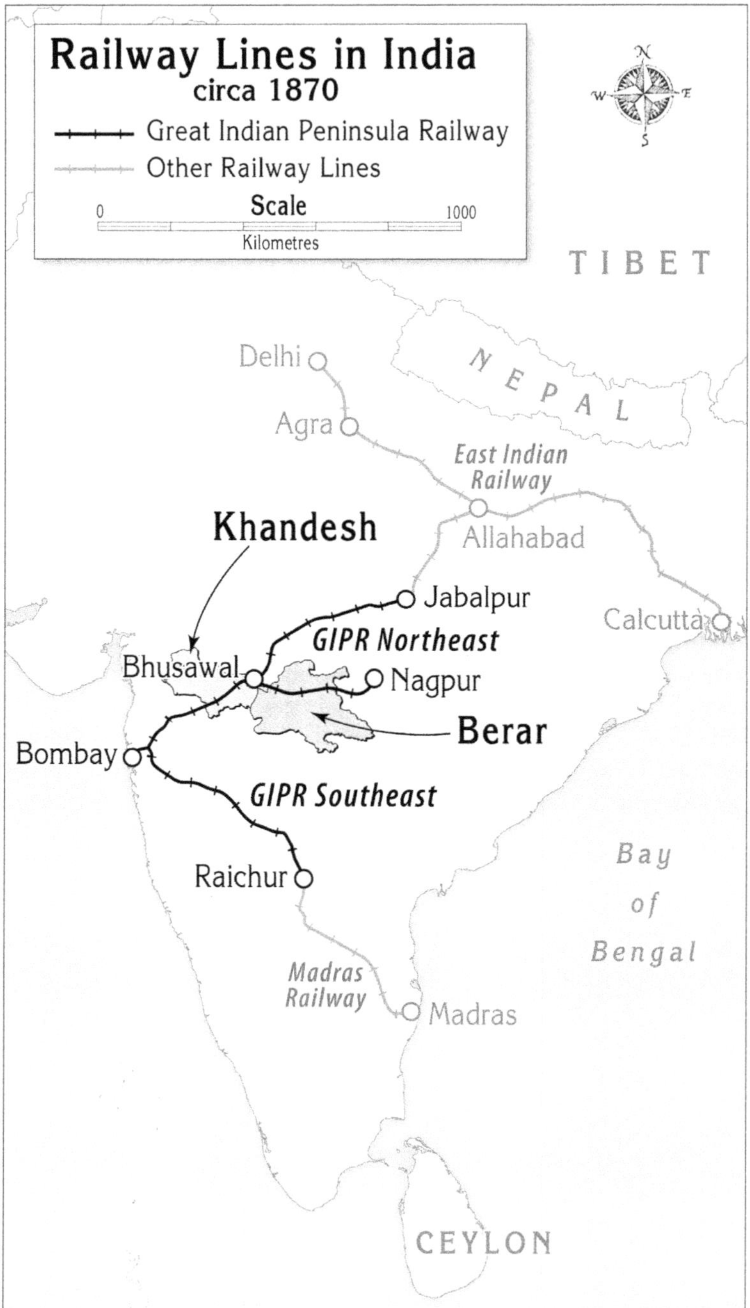

Map 0.1 Railway Lines in India circa 1870

Source: Map drawn by Laurie Whiddon, Map Illustrations.

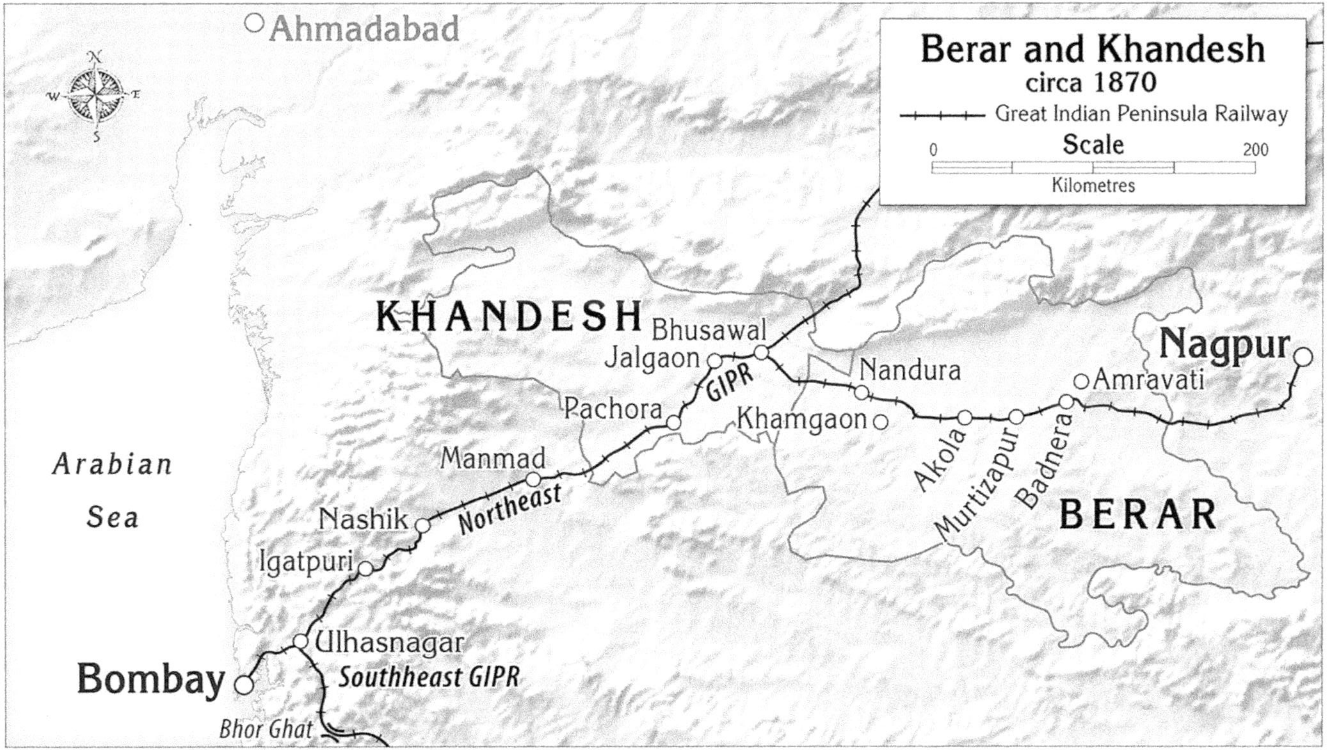

Map 0.2 Berar and Khandesh circa 1870

Source: Map drawn by Laurie Whiddon, Map Illustrations.

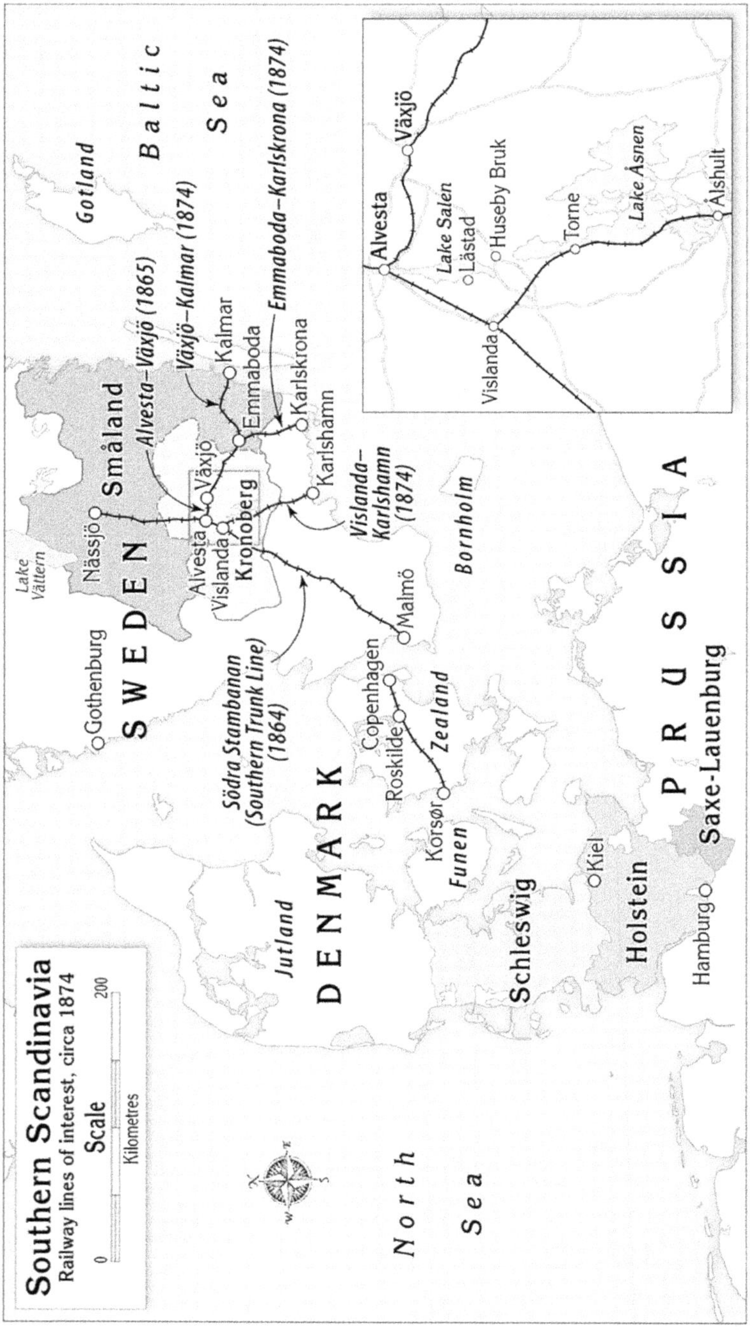

Map 0.3 Southern Scandinavia, Railway lines of interest, circa 1874

Source: Map drawn by Laurie Whiddon, Map Illustrations.

1 Circular Migrations, Capital, and Opportunity

A Global History of Scandinavia and India at the Industrial Turn, an Introduction

Gunnel Cederlöf

Most of the research published in this volume would not have been carried out if a box of documents from the 1860s from western India had not surfaced in the attic of a manor house in Sweden in 2008. Careful study of the contents of this box has given us access to the lives of the lowest levels of contractors and workers involved in the extension of a large and complex infrastructure of railway, roads, and administration into Berar in the northern Deccan Plateau of central India. Historians working in other parts of the world discuss such projects in terms of a technical or socio-technical mega-system constructed to efficiently extract the natural resources required in industrial production. In Berar, the Nagpur Extension was the spine of a huge technical and societal change. The documents in the box reveal the activities undertaken and the consequences for people on the ground as the British imperial government made plans to draw cotton from the fields to the Bombay ports and on to England as rapidly and efficiently as possible. The project or the system, if we prefer to see it as such, depended on a weak underbelly. With the evidence of people's experiences of breaking stones and carrying rails, we can see the harsh realities of those who rarely benefited from the 'system' put in place. At the same time, the documents also show us life in the bottom layers of the infrastructure project, the low-level contractors, a few of whom were successful. Joseph Stephens was one of them, and his documents are now kept as the Joseph Stephens Archive (JSA) at Linnaeus University in Sweden.[1]

The story of how the private and business documents of one of the lower-level contractors ended up on an ironmaking estate in the southern Swedish uplands reveals linkages and mobility in Europe, outside the British imperial realms. It not only reveals non-English and non-British involvement in the construction of large imperial grids across the Indian subcontinent in the years following the Great Uprising (1857–8). It also traces the mid-nineteenth-century reconstruction of regional economies in Scandinavia and the role of global capital and skills. On the one hand, the chapters in this volume allow us to follow a young man from Copenhagen who travelled to Bombay to seek professional training and profit. On the other hand, they

DOI: 10.4324/9781003317227-1

enable us to trace the rapid social and economic transformations in which he played a small part. To find his point of entry, we first need to see the larger framework.

As has often been acknowledged, the American Civil War (1861–5) both caused a crisis for English textile producers and became a window of opportunity for cotton merchants operating in Egypt and India. When the North American ports of export blocked cotton from the southern states, Britain turned to long-established Asian and African places of production, where growers massively expanded their output. British eyes had been on Berar cotton even before the war; now both demand and production were scaled up. Within just a few years, Indian short-staple cotton, less valuable than the Egyptian long-staple variety, was growing in more fields in west and south India. In the Berar district on the Deccan Plateau, north-east of Bombay, the acreage under cotton doubled in the war years. Getting cotton from the fields to the Bombay ports on such an industrial scale completely transformed both social and natural landscapes. Laxman D. Satya characterizes these changes as a deskilling of labour, a deindustrialization of the economy, and a complete destruction of domestic textile production. While the small Berar district alone produced as much cotton as Egypt, 'half the population went naked' when all the cotton cultivated was exported to England and textiles imported from Britain were far too expensive for the growers and labourers in Berar.[2]

Such an enterprise could only be achieved using the most advanced technology. At a frenetic pace, within one decade, an imperial grid was laid across Berar's savannah landscape for the purpose of efficiently transporting the cotton to the coast. A railway from Bombay to Nagpur, with a new line connecting Nagpur to the main Bombay—Allahabad line, was rapidly put in place. New metalled roads connected cotton-producing villages with the railway, and a telegraph line was put up along the embankment, linking all the stations with Bombay and the merchants in England. Their correspondence was handled at the many new post offices along the 165-mile-long Nagpur Dak Line. As a result, new cotton market towns emerged along the railway line, serving to draw economic activities away from old market centres in the north and south of the district. Such an enormous infrastructure operation required a massive workforce. Contractors recruited skilled and unskilled labourers, both of which were drawn from the villages during agricultural low seasons and arrived in Berar as migrant workers. The contractors operated by bidding for specific contracts in the hands of private companies and their engineers and the Government of India's Public Works Department. The largest actor was the Great Indian Peninsula Railway (GIPR), a private company put in charge of the entire operation by the government. Like railway companies in other parts of the world, the GIPR was guaranteed a 5 per cent return on its capital by the government, whether it made a profit or not.[3]

The contractors were mostly young men, many of whom had come from Europe in search of an income and, hopefully, a fortune. One of them was Joseph Stephens. Joseph's family had made a long journey across two generations before Joseph left for India. From the mines of Cornwall and from Liverpool, they moved via Stockholm to Copenhagen in geographical and socio-economic leaps. We could say that this was a typical imperial family that made a better future for itself by migrating within Europe or moving to North America or Australia. Joseph's uncles settled as missionaries and businessmen in the United States and Australia, while his father, George, moved with his wife and their three children to the Scandinavian hub of colonial commerce, Copenhagen. This town was open to the world, a characteristic that came to mark Joseph's journey to adulthood.[4]

When the Stephens family arrived in Copenhagen in 1851, the town had experienced a troubled and transformative half-century.[5] In the mid-1790s, first the royal palace of Christiansborg and thereafter one-third of the town itself went up in flames in devastating fires. A decade later, during the Napoleonic Wars, Britain sought control of the Danish fleet. After three days' bombardment of Copenhagen, leaving about a thousand buildings in ruins, Denmark yielded. The kingdom was a small player in the European wars, but it controlled the bottleneck passage between the North and the Baltic Sea—to which the British now gained access. They also eliminated a hostile alliance. In the wake of this trauma for Denmark, economic recession followed. The fact that the town was fairly soon rebuilt reflected the colonial wealth that supported its merchant aristocracy. The dual monarchy uniting Denmark and Norway that dated back to the sixteenth century had opened up to Denmark the old Norwegian possessions in Greenland, Iceland, and the Faroes. In the late seventeenth and eighteenth centuries, when Denmark secured shares in the West Indies, the Gold Coast, Tranquebar and Serampore in India, and the Nicobar Islands, wealth from these colonies enriched the country's merchants. In spite of the disastrous start to the 1800s, therefore, colonial capital supported the restoration of Copenhagen, promoting modern urban development and city planning. Displayed in prominent ways in the architecture of the new and monumental buildings was an abundance of oriental ornamentation. The royal capital held a great attraction for people across the country, giving rise to continuous immigration, since all the state, commercial, and religious institutions of importance were here. When the Stephens family arrived in the city, Copenhagen had 150,000 inhabitants, more than one-tenth of Denmark's population. Significantly, the first half of the nineteenth century is known as the Danish Golden Age. It was a time when Romanticism blossomed and the expanding bourgeoisie enjoyed culture and the arts. The close of this period is associated with the end of absolutist monarchy and with territorial wars.[6]

Joseph's father George was a philologist. He studied Scandinavian runic inscriptions, folk songs, and tales, and the linguistic and historical

Figure 1.1 Joseph Stephens.

Source: Courtesy Huseby Bruk AB.

relationship between Old Norse and Old and Middle English. In Copenhagen, he was employed as a lecturer and, before long, a professor of English language. His move to Copenhagen put him right at the centre of trade in old Nordic artefacts, and he added many items from Greenland, Iceland, and the Sami regions of northern Scandinavia to his collection. Over the years, he built his own cabinet of curiosities with objects from all over the world.[7] His thinking about a common Scandinavian cultural past had a close affinity to the political ideas of Scandinavianism that thrived in Denmark, and his work helped to strengthen that movement. There were calls for a union of the Scandinavian countries, which were particularly strong in Denmark in response to efforts to unify the many German states. Nationalist movements grew on both sides of the border, in support of a Danish nation and a united Scandinavia, on the one hand, and unification of the German states, on the other. George arrived in Copenhagen immediately after the first of two wars with Prussia and her allies over the southernmost duchies under Danish control: Schleswig, Saxe-Lauenburg, and Holstein. The majority population of Schleswig was Danish, whereas in the other two duchies people were ethnically German. Winning the war in 1851 further strengthened Danish nationalism. More importantly, it played a part in ending absolutism and ushering in a new constitution. The Stephens family arrived in an atmosphere of promising opportunities.[8]

Joseph's sister, Ingeborg, married a railway engineer by the name of John Hallen Abbott. He had trained in Birmingham as an apprentice to Sir Charles Fox, a civil engineer. In 1852, Fox sent him to Denmark to work for the Zealand Railway Company, which was when he met Ingeborg. The Zealand Company constructed the first railway line in Denmark between Roskilde and Copenhagen, with the aim of connecting Kiel in the southern duchies with the Baltic Sea. Engineering skills and technology came from England, a frontrunner in engineering in Europe. Britain's engineers were proud not to have trained at educational institutions, but in apprenticeships to senior civil engineers and under the auspices of the Institution of Civil Engineers. This was not an educational establishment: its members were senior engineers, and new ones were elected by those already belonging to the institution. At this time, most countries in Europe were setting up institutions of higher education. In Denmark, the Polytechnic Institute emphasized theoretical training from the outset. Since there was little industrial need for professionals highly trained in engineering, the early cohorts who passed through the institute were employed in government or the military establishment. However, they were few and the institute got off to a slow start. John worked on the connection between Roskilde and Korsør. When an opportunity arose for employment on the largest infrastructure project in the world—the construction of the main lines in British India—John joined the operation and he and his wife travelled to Bombay in 1857, the year of the large uprising in north India. He started out as a third-class assistant engineer for the GIPR in Nashik, before going on to make quite a rapid career. After his third promotion, when he was made District Engineer, he was elected a member of the Institution of Civil Engineers in England, and in 1870 he became Chief Engineer, twice officiating as Chief Resident Engineer, in charge of the entire railway. He did not leave India for England until 1884, dying there soon after his arrival.[9]

Ingeborg, by contrast, could not stand living in India and did not spend more than four years there across a period of 11. She returned to Denmark for good in 1868, long before her husband left India. The letters between the family members provide somewhat meagre accounts of the couple's everyday life in Bombay and on the construction sites—John from the engineer's perspective and Ingeborg in an increasingly miserable tone from her isolated life as a European, non-British woman. Margareta Petersson describes how, after starting out in a tent, they moved to a house in Nashik, and how Ingeborg occasionally fled boredom for the still restricted social life of Bombay. George planned for Joseph to join his brother-in-law and, in the English engineering tradition, train under him. John in turn tempted him with the rich bird life of India. The reason for going was of course not the birds, but the prospect of being trained on site to become an engineer and earn more money than Joseph would ever do in Denmark. He landed in Bombay in 1860, 19 years old, and came to spend 10 years in western India, mainly in the Berar district. During that time, he made only one trip to Scandinavia, to inspect the ironmaking estate of Huseby in southern Sweden which his father and godfather had suggested that he purchase. Joseph was one of the few in the lower ranks of railway construction who actually earned a fortune from working as a contractor. In 1867, he put all this money into the estate.[10]

We know very little about life on the lowest echelons of infrastructure construction in mid-nineteenth-century India. Contractors like Joseph did not keep the documents after work on a contract had been completed. This group of fairly untrained young men in their twenties, from a mix of lower social backgrounds, had no reason to keep their administrative paperwork once they had done their job. If they earned a profit, they would take the money and destroy the documents. Not so Joseph. Carefully mentored by his father, who was a collector of sorts, when he left India in 1869 Joseph packed his business papers and correspondence into a wooden box and shipped them to Scandinavia. The still unopened box with the documents inside was found in the attic of the manor house at Huseby in 2008. They have opened a window onto life and work along the railway line in 1860s Berar. In a unique way, these documents give detailed evidence of the many specialized trades of manual labourers—in the wage accounts, even down to the individual labourer, whose name, gender, occupation, pay, and signature are all recorded. Joseph's contracts with labourers, his own descriptions of labour conflicts, notes on 'cherimerry' given to workers, and on negotiations with them after accidents occurred, bring flesh and personality to our knowledge of a group of people otherwise referred to collectively and facelessly as 'labourers'. They also give voice to the mostly hidden and disliked class of small contractors and subcontractors, via Joseph's diaries, correspondence, notes, accounts, drawings, sketches, and maps.

Joseph's relationship to the GIPR and its engineers, when tendering for and securing contracts, or fending off complaints about construction failures, allows us an insight into the contractors' lives. His correspondence with his brother-in-law, in particular, illustrates the advantage to a contractor like Joseph of having such intimate connections with the GIPR engineers. The contractors' work was part of a social economy. Six of the eight chapters in this volume investigate different aspects of the contractors', subcontractors', and workers' realities based on this collection of papers, read in relation to documents in the Maharashtra State Archives, the National Archives of India, and the British Library. Arun Kumar explores the central place of contract laws in regulating the labour-capital relationship at infrastructural sites in the colonial capitalist economy. He shows how the penal and economic punishment clauses of the contracts added an extra layer of exploitation and inequality in contract laws that subordinated and disciplined labour. Radhika Krishnan investigates the very same contracts but from the perspective of social and professional networks which, she argues, retained the system long after the economic advantages had begun to fade away. Dhiraj Kumar Nite contributes two studies, one of which investigates the business network shared by the contractors as 'merchant intermediaries'. They shared business attitudes and aspirations that worked through partnerships. He emphasizes Stephens' capacity to generate his own social and cultural resources, which made social mobility possible. In his second study, Nite makes a detailed analysis of the information gained from the pay sheets that Stephens kept. He shows the intricate working of the contractual employment and commercialized economy, which controlled the workforce. His study also provides an insight into the diversified welfare return for different groups of workers, based on task, gender, and age. These four chapters make important contributions in the fields of labour and economic history.

Eleonor Marcussen's work establishes a bridge between western India and southern Sweden that gives an insight into how Joseph made use of the experiences and skills gained from the most formative years of his life when he became the owner of the largest estate in the southern Sweden province of Småland. In this way, she is able to show that regions beyond the colonizers and the colonized, such as Sweden and Denmark, had a key role in realizing the ambitions of imperial expansion. The last two chapters discuss life on the Huseby Estate from the perspective of Joseph's work to revive the estate's economy from the 1870s onwards and of Joseph's three daughters when he was an old man. Erik Wångmar discusses the ways in which Stephens rebuilt and invested in the estate and places its progression in view of the long-term development of the economy of Sweden. Malin Lennartsson penetrates deeply into the relationships within the Stephens family and, especially, the troubled road to adulthood for the daughters. In Lennartsson's study, Joseph is a widower and an old man, and memories of his years as a young man in India has turned into family anecdotes. Yet his social climb into the Swedish economic higher echelons, without gaining the social acceptance of the aristocracy for his daughters, reflects a socially transformative society with wealth and status out of joint. Family history is here made to show how the global transformations and Joseph's own social and economic upward mobility materialized in his responsibilities as the patriarch of both an estate and a family with three daughters. Lennartsson investigates in particular how his ambitions for Huseby and for his daughters influenced their individual circumstances and lives.

The journeys of Joseph and his family across the globe at a time of large-scale mobility and change were both uniquely personal and representative of myriads of similar initiatives to benefit from the openings which the British Empire provided for an upcoming social class in Europe. The following gives a brief introduction to society and environmental and socio-economic change in western India and the Berar district, where Joseph was working at the time the infrastructural grid was constructed. It also shows how capital and skills gained in British India made their way into an impoverished part of southern Sweden. This, too, was simultaneously unique to Joseph's life and part of a major transformation of a Scandinavian regional economy.

Extractive Processes Eroding a Regional Economy

Berar was a small region in the northern part of the large Deccan Plateau. These parts of the Deccan geology formed at the end of the Cretaceous Period, around 66.25 million years ago, and are today one of the earth's largest formations of volcanic basalt. This has resulted in the mineral-rich black soil that holds water in spite of dry conditions and was a precondition for successful cotton cultivation in Berar. Rainfall is plentiful along the coast and in the western parts of the steep, rocky, and jagged hills entering the plateau. These hills are part of the long Western Ghats range that runs along the western side of the Indian subcontinent. Further inland, in Berar, the country is in a rain shadow, with the plains receiving on average only 660 mm of annual rainfall. Further east, at slightly higher locations, the Nagpur district received on average 1,170 mm of rain, compared with 1,900 mm at Bombay on the coast. Natural conditions here permitted a cover of moist or dry tropical deciduous or tropical thorn forest. However, as Sumit Guha observes, long-term human intervention in the form of lopping, shifting cultivation, grazing, and burning of forests and grass had turned this part of the plateau into open savannah grassland and thorny shrub. Guha concludes that the process was far advanced by the time the region was surveyed by the British in the 1820s.[11]

The ecology and landscape varied from the place where the Nagpur extension line branched off the main line at Bhusawal, immediately east of the Western Ghats, across the open dry grasslands to Nagpur, the subcontinent's geographical centre. Bhusawal was located at the eastern extreme of the otherwise hilly Khandesh district. Because of its location immediately east of the Western Ghats, Bhusawal was a dry area, with rainfall as low as in Berar. In spite of the dry conditions, in years with a normal monsoon the quality of the soil still made for good harvests.

Cotton has a long history in Berar. The unsafe years following the British victory in the last of the three Maratha Wars (1817–18) opened up the region to speculation in cotton cultivation and exporting. Berar was within the Hyderabad state territories, and its government utilized the potential for cotton and farmed out land to Bombay- and Hyderabad-based private companies and moneylenders. By making large loans to growers and levying charges on the various transport routes, the private actors profited, while corruption was rampant, producers benefited little, and quite a lot of cotton remained in Berar for the local manufacture of cloth owing to poorly functioning transport. In the early 1850s, the British were in search of cotton supplies for the textile factories in England, which was one of the reasons they entered into a treaty with Hyderabad in 1853 that gave them de facto control of Berar. The district, acquired by Hyderabad on the fall of the Maratha states, was now 'assigned' to the British, who thereby gained control of the revenues from the higher yielding districts. From 1861, the year when the American Civil War began, the British resident in Hyderabad was put in charge of all of Berar's administration. By that time, a railway line had begun to be built. The operation included far more than the tracks and the station buildings. Thousands of workers, recruited by a large number of contractors and subcontractors, worked to secure the entire infrastructure required for the railway to function as an artery for the flow of cotton from the growers to the Bombay ports.[12]

When John Hallen Abbott arrived in Nashik to start work on the GIPR, the technically advanced construction of lines, bridges, and reversing stations to bring the trains up and down the steep hillsides and across the chasms and gorges at Bhor Ghat had been completed. Construction work on the undulating plains, where Joseph would soon also work, was technically much less challenging. However, in the territories where the rails were laid, they encroached significantly on society and people's livelihoods. They not only changed life along the new tracks but also had an impact on old established markets and nodal points of communication routes away from the railway line. According to Satya, the cotton economy and the system of rail transport in combination 'wiped out the fine urban—rural balance of pre-colonial Berar'. Like Berar, Guha shows, Khandesh also experienced a gravitation of economic centres away from once important market towns to those where the new railway stations were constructed.[13]

Satya's seminal work on cotton and famine in Berar provides a good deal of knowledge about the imperial cotton economy and its effects on the agricultural economy and society of the district. He shows that when

Figure 1.2 Weighing cotton on the Colaba Island, Bombay, photograph by William Johnson and William Henderson, The Indian Amateur's Photographic Album, 1858.

Source: Courtesy Huseby Bruk AB.

intensive cotton production and British administration arrived in the region, the population had a mix of settled and mobile livelihoods. The caste-based specialization of crafts was also reflected in the region's textile production, in the ginners, spinners, weavers, and dyers. The business of redirecting the export of cotton, away from existing markets in India towards the mills of England, was undertaken by far deeper colonial penetration into the region's economy than simply placing a railway track across its plains. Revenue surveys, based on a preference for individual landholdings, led to the introduction of the *ryotwari* revenue system. This is often argued to have introduced private property in land without diluting the power of the state as the ultimate landholder. Satya argues that, without overthrowing existing land relations, controlled by dominant families, the British government would not have been able to gain control of crops and revenues. That is, they would not have been capable of introducing cotton production for the global market in Berar. He summarizes the process thus: '[c]otton under colonialism became the curse of Berar'.[14]

Reading Satya's work in relation to Sumit Guha's study of what he calls the margins of agriculture in central and western India, with a focus on the medieval to modern periods, provides a broader perspective on the radical transformation of nature, economy, and livelihoods. Guha's main focus is on the mountain regions to the north, the west, and the south-west of Berar—as seen from the viewpoint of our study. These large tracts had an earlier interdependent relationship with Berar through markets and trade, warfare and raiding, natural calamities causing large flows of migrants, and polities that both separated and integrated the plain, forest, and hill ecologies. Guha explains how, in the nineteenth century, British administration and resource extraction in Khandesh upset the system of political relations between the forest-based polities and the open country.[15]

The increased clearance of forest played a crucial role in the radical shift that followed. Extensive cutting of forests was not unique to the British government. Many earlier rulers had made excessive use of timber. They had also cut down large numbers of trees as a security measure, pacifying a country by opening up the landscape, or to promote production of crops for export. The pressure these policies placed on swidden and settled cultivators also reduced the forest cover. The British did all this and, in addition, introduced an industrial scale and speed to the operations. The colonial state's apparent indifference to the consequences not only demolished the influence of the former rural elite but also introduced a system of extraction that tailored the social fabric to the new system of operation. By all the means available to the state, settled cultivation was given priority over itinerant livelihoods. In Guha's words: 'agrarianisation was an overriding priority'. Many specialized crafts disappeared and itinerant communities were forced into settled livelihoods. Many of them left Khandesh for Berar to work as landless labourers. Some people refused employment that circumscribed their 'freedom to move'. Guha explains how the latter were often termed 'criminal' on account of their unsettled lives.[16]

Railway construction became a huge consumer of hardwood timber for sleepers. One mile of broad-gauge track required 1,800–2,000 sleepers. By 1878, two million sleepers had been used for the railways.[17] The Conservator of Forests in the Madras Presidency, Hugh Cleghorn, argued in 1861 for restrictions on forest felling and suggested setting up plantations exclusively for the railways in order to keep a check on supply and demand. However, the Khandesh forests were not spared. Here, private timber agents purchased timber directly from the Bhil population. The Bombay Forest Reports showed a profit from duties on timber sold in the market in the early 1860s, when the GIPR was building the main line across eastern Khandesh. When profits fell, the Bombay government tried to reduce the influence of the contractors, but large private supplies of timber continued to drive the government out of the market. As Mahesh Rangarajan observes, '[t]he crisis in the supply of timber for the railways led to the consolidation of existing initiatives for conservation. The Forest Department was set up only in

1864.'[18] We are given a view of the ultimate transformation of Berar in the *Imperial Gazetteer of India* of 1908:

> The scenery of the Payanghat [*sic*, the central valley of Berar] is monotonous and uninteresting. The wide expanse of black cotton soil, slightly undulating, is broken by few trees except babuls and groves near villages. In the autumn the crops give it a fresh and green appearance; but after the harvest the monotonous scene is unrelieved by verdure, shade, or water, and the landscape is desolate and depressing.[19]

Joseph was one of the small players when the large grid of infrastructure technology fell on Berar. Many contractors were big firms that had secured large contracts after submitting tenders. Less acknowledged is the fact that the firms in question subcontracted in bits and pieces to young men like Joseph. These small contractors were essential cogs in the machinery. The contract was the device used to get the work done. It enabled the state to avoid risk and responsibility by transferring them to a contractor. The contract set the rules to which both parties agreed. When subcontracts were entered into, the risk was transferred by the new contracts to the subcontractors. As explained by Prabhu Mohapatra, 'the amount of pressure put on the contract chain will trickle down.'[20] What may have looked chaotic was in fact highly structured. At a time immediately after the Great Uprising, when the British rulers were making massive efforts to strengthen their administration, rebuild the Bengal army, and scale up the extraction, appropriation, and export of natural resources from India to Britain, these young men were in great demand. They were the link between the engineers' plans and sketches and the manual labourers. They also competed with the cotton producers and with each other for labourers. As these contractors operated with little political capital or economic clout, in a disadvantaged position, the situation gave labourers and their foremen an opportunity to bargain for better wages.

Most of the low-level contractors had poor training and barely any knowledge of the geology and climate of the regions where the railway infrastructure was expected to stand firm and forever. They were willing to take risks, jumped on every invitation to tender on the market, and cut corners to finish projects at speed. Sometimes they cut too many corners, the work was shoddy, and structures collapsed, which gave contractors collectively a bad reputation. Race and class also intersected to influence their repute among Europeans in India. Whereas racial separation put European contractors above their Indian colleagues, the strict class hierarchies placed them low on social scales and near the bottom among the Europeans in railway construction operations. The government wanted to get rid of the subcontractors and have them replaced with engineers who had received training in educational institutions. In contrast to the practice in Britain, where engineers trained as apprentices, in 1872 the India Office in London set up the Royal

Indian Engineering College in Surrey in England. The aim was to train engineers already in England to work in the Public Works Department in India. The 1860s were a gold-rush period for Joseph and his fellow contractors. By the time he left for good, this window of opportunity had closed.[21]

The lower-level contractors, such as Joseph, depended on remaining within social and business networks. As Radhika Krishnan explains, his career was bolstered by such informal networks. For example, through contacts of this kind, he managed to get a worker whose skill he required out of jail, lobby against competing contractors, and manipulate wage payments to keep labourers available and in place. Dhiraj Kumar Nite has made a close reading of Josephs' pay sheets, which represent an extremely rare historical source. He can show that, in general, the real income of workers improved, but that in the case of sweat labourers total income compared to the cost of subsistence remained below unity. Only by increasing the supply of family labour could workers provide for their basic household needs. Women and children—an important part of the workforce—received a far smaller increase in wages than male workers. Nite emphasizes that the contract was the means by which the contractor-worker relationship was constrained. Arun Kumar digs deep into the logic of the contracts between the low-level contractor and the workers. He concludes that Joseph and his fellow contractors feared the workers not finishing projects on time—a failure that would put Joseph in breach of his own contracts. At any given time, he had about 400–500 labourers tied into different contracts, working on different minor contracts under him. He used pecuniary measures, both 'carrots and sticks', to keep the workers in place. The large demand for labourers within this massive operation also opened up rare opportunities for workers to negotiate their agreements, absenting themselves from work, working more slowly, or refusing a work contract if the pay was too low and the particular skill asked for was protected within their community. In this regard, too, the JSA holds very rare documents such as Joseph's contracts with his labourers, written in the language of the workers and signed by their foremen.[22]

Indian Colonial Capital Into a Peripheral Scandinavian Region

Joseph returned to Scandinavia, first in 1867 when he purchased the Huseby Estate in Kronoberg county in the province of Småland, and then, after a couple of more years in India, in 1869 when he settled at Huseby for good. He considered it pointless to stay on in India, since the work he was putting in had become unremunerative. It was no longer worth it. Nite observes how Joseph's profits from his method of hiring labour began to fall as he gradually turned to subcontractors. In 1867–8, competition between contractors had increased, resulting in lower quotes in tenders from other contractors. And in spite of his attempts, Joseph never succeeded in securing a contract from the Bombay office.[23]

Figure 1.3 The manor house at the Huseby Estate, 1870.
Source: Photograph by Kirchoff, courtesy Huseby Bruk AB.

Globally speaking, Scandinavia seems like a small region, but when Joseph moved in at Huseby, Kronoberg in Sweden was a world away from Copenhagen. Joseph knew only one man living here—his godfather, Gunnar Olof Hyltén-Cavallius. Joseph was an immigrant through and through. This was a region of smallholders, tenants, and crofters. The crofters were landless agricultural labourers, paid in kind and given a small cottage to live in. Hard-broken glacial till made cultivation of the soil back-breaking work. In 1860, Kronoberg county had the lowest regional GDP per capita in Sweden, reaching only 0.57 on a national index of 1. The year 1867 was the first of a number of years with failed, though not completely lost, harvests. The spring was particularly cold, making the growing season impossibly short. The following two years were even colder, and the poor replaced flour with the inner bark of pine, leaves, and straw. Småland is known for large-scale emigration from the mid-nineteenth to the early twentieth century, when many farms were auctioned off and people either left for the towns and factories or moved to Denmark or Germany or overseas to North America. The area may have appeared hostile to Joseph as he arrived during the first of the hunger years, but on the other hand he was able to buy Huseby at about half its value. After 10 years as a contractor on the railways in British India, he was able to take a step or two up the ladder to become the owner of a large estate in northern Europe, with an iron furnace and workshop and 6,000 hectares of farmland and forest.[24]

Today, the nineteenth-century flow of migrants leaving Sweden forms a core of national historical narratives that have given rise to important literature, plays, and films.[25] However, the JSA is evidence of a counter-flow of migration. This consisted of foreign citizens who purchased the farms and estates and added to the minor flow of returning migrants who arrived back in Sweden with new earnings or failed dreams. These migration flows were part of the large and intricate global mobility of people who searched for opportunities to make a living or who speculated in making a fortune from the growing industrial and capital markets. Joseph's global travels show the complexity of the migration currents as he moved from one economically peripheral region in India to another in Europe and thereby increased his opportunities for creating wealth. Studies about the global migration strategies among the lower social groups in Europe were long overshadowed by a focus on elite migration in the British Empire. Many biographically oriented studies have investigated the imperial careers of governors, high commissioners, and members of the nobility. The opportunities for Scots and Irish to make a career within the Empire, which was not possible in the British Isles, generated a new field of historical research. Martha McLaren chose to focus on the Scottish highest orders, making careers in India, whereas Jonathan Hyslop gives us an insight into how men from 'humble backgrounds' benefitted from good village schools and apprenticeships and made a career from opportunities in the colonies. Migration among the emerging European middleclass has also prominently been studied within the organized frames of missionary societies.[26] However, the broader migration flows of poor or middle-class Europeans outside the imperial heartlands remain to be investigated. Joseph was one among these migrants who put his imperial earnings into landed property in southern Sweden. To the foreign investors in the southern Swedish uplands, the new national Southern Main Line inaugurated in 1865, which made possible large-scale exports of heavy goods from Småland province, coincided with a slump in land prices that helped make holdings attractive for speculation and investment. When an extension from the main line was built from Alvesta to Kalmar in the south of the province in 1874, and two further extensions branched out from this line to the southern ports on the Baltic Sea, economic activity in the large province gravitated towards the south. The many new owners from Denmark and Germany saw their purchases either as an investment opportunity or as an opportunity to cultivate land of their own, and exports of timber especially increased. The year Joseph bought Huseby, 20 landholdings in the vicinity of his estate went to new owners from Denmark. These immigrants to Småland were fewer than those who left, but they made a difference to the province. They arrived with capital and skills in a province that was hard hit by natural disaster and whose economy was under strain. They brought with them work practices and social and business networks, the effects of which have still to be investigated.

Joseph invested capital in the Huseby Estate that he had accumulated from profits gained from British imperial infrastructure operations in India. The historian Lars-Olof Larsson has calculated the number of farms in Kronoberg county sold to foreign citizens, arriving at a figure of 250 between 1867 and 1882. To this day, however, that knowledge has not spread beyond the confines of academic study, and it has left only a small imprint even in scholarly works. In his chapter in this volume, Erik Wångmar qualifies this representation of immigration when he notes that most of the properties in question were small, whereas Joseph's was one of the largest that ended up in the hands of foreign owners. The combination of a slump in prices and the construction of the railways, which enabled forest products to be exported on a large scale, played a part in making these holdings attractive. Some of the new owners, like Stephens, considered clear-cutting their forests for the export market. Towards the turn of the century, large-scale felling causing significant landscape changes and the Swedish government was taking legal measures for securing regrowth and for draining wetlands by ditches to delay the effect of frost on the young saplings. Two decades into the twentieth century, spruce monoculture covered larger acreages of land, resulting in ecological change and an increasingly industrial forest production.[27]

Eleonor Marcussen traces the process of immigration in more detail by studying Joseph's investment in the Huseby Estate and his intentions in making the purchase. She turns the searchlight on southern Sweden to ask why and how economic and social conditions created a lucrative market for private interests and business investments deriving from wealth generated in British India. Again, social and family networks played an important part in securing private property far beyond Joseph's expectations. By analysing circumstances, intentions, and acts, Marcussen provides a better understanding of how colonialism and private entrepreneurs contributed to socio-economic change in Småland province. Future research in this field promises to reveal the broader networks within the south of Scandinavia, in particular those that linked economically disadvantaged regions to each other as a result of the immigration of people who brought with them global capital, skills, and networks.[28]

The Huseby ironworks had its heyday in the seventeenth century, during the Thirty Years War (1618–48), when cannon and cannonballs were sold to the navy and shipped to the Baltic Sea. More than two centuries later, Joseph bought a run-down estate and put all his energy into putting it back on its feet. Ironworks in Småland used lake ore, derived from iron-rich sediment at the bottom of shallow, nutrient-poor lakes. The iron formed into small flat plates and was collected through the winter ice. Since this was a more fragile material than the iron ore produced from mines in central and northern Sweden, from the mid- to the late-nineteenth-century either

Småland's ironworks closed down or the estates switched to producing glassware.[29] From 1850 to 1899, 45 glass factories began production in Småland, 12 of which were built in 1850–75. With the competence in place of handling the melting of material at high temperatures, this made good use of workers' skills where there had been an old workshop, and skilled artisans arrived in Småland from Denmark and England. The final decades of the iron mills in Kronoberg were dramatic. Production peaked in 1860, when the eight mills in use produced more than they had ever done in their 230 years of existence. They were subsequently closed between 1877 and 1886. Only the Huseby Estate remained, with Joseph persisting in using iron from the lakes on his estate and developing Huseby into a workshop for iron stoves and agricultural and household tools.[30]

An upward social leap did not automatically follow from an economic leap. Joseph spent a decade hectically building up the Huseby Estate and placing its products firmly on the market. With a growing workforce, he extended the estate, drained the wetlands for more agricultural land, renovated the workshop, and was a leading figure in an initiative to build a small railway line connecting Huseby with the southern coastal port town of Karlshamn, to make for easy access to the Baltic. It is clear from the way Joseph established his enterprise at Huseby that his connections towards the south were stronger than those to the north. From the viewpoint of this and similar estates, it makes more sense to study the turnaround of southern Sweden in the perspective of a southern Scandinavian region rather than one primarily or solely oriented towards the north and defined by the political centre of the Swedish nation state. Outside the immediate realms of Kronoberg county, Joseph cultivated his economic ties within the networks connecting him to Copenhagen, England, and the British Empire, whereas later in life he became a conservative member of the Swedish parliament, arguing in favour of protectionist policies. After 13 years at Huseby, Joseph married Elisabeth Kreüger, the daughter of a high-ranking naval officer, and they soon had three daughters. From his training, Elisabeth's father knew the king of Sweden well, and Elisabeth had been a lady-in-waiting to the queen. This connection with high society opened doors for Joseph; however, membership of that social class did not automatically follow. Furthermore, neither Joseph nor his wife seems to have had the tools to bring up and educate their daughters for a society where middle-class women could do better if they knew how to handle finances and run a business.[31]

When Elisabeth died far too early, the oldest of the daughters, Florence, began to assist her father on the estate. Wångmar observes how Joseph allowed her into the running of the business. As he himself had once done, now Florence learnt from watching her father closely and training at his side. During her father's lifetime, she became increasingly involved in practical and legal matters. However, Malin Lennartsson finds that the three sisters seem to have entered adulthood poorly equipped to fend for themselves. Schooling under governesses seems to have been a waste, and the ambition for the daughters appears to have been to marry them off to well-situated men. This would confirm the family's social advancement from the dusty Berar plains to high society in the kingdom of Sweden in only two generations. Only one of them married, however. Lennartsson traces the life of the youngest of the three, Maggie, describing a very unstable and insecure path. Paradoxically, only after her father's death, when she inherited a small estate, did she succeed in setting up a business of her own, remaining unmarried and legally independent. She came also to be supported in the running of her business by a manager who left Huseby and joined Maggie's estate Ålshult.[32]

Work on the Joseph Stephens Archive has changed historical perspectives. The best thing that can happen to a newly discovered collection of historical documents is for research to open up knowledge about the life hidden within them. A growing body of research is now developing, based on Stephens' documents from his time in India. The studies published up to now are listed at the back of this volume, and more are yet to come. Margareta Petersson's work on the family history of the Stephenses, and especially on Joseph's sister Ingeborg, lends a dense texture to the social family connections, aspirations, and experiences in which Joseph grew up. Five postdoctoral researchers have each dedicated a year to the work. Alexander Bubb, now a scholar of literature at the University of Roehampton, the United Kingdom, spent 2013–14 at Linnaeus University. Four of the authors in this volume—Radhika Krishnan, Dhiraj Kumar Nite, Arun Kumar, and Eleonor Marcussen—worked in the archives from 2015 to 2019. Ingemar Gunnarsson has written a licentiate thesis[33] and he and Per Johansson at the Linnaeus University Library have spent a good deal of time taking care of the documents, which are now preserved in the university's central archives, located within the large Huseby Archives.

All of this research has been made possible by generous funding from Linnaeus University and its centre of excellence, the Centre for Concurrences in Colonial and Postcolonial Studies, and from the Crafoord Foundation. The project *Huseby in the World*, funded by the Kamprad Family Foundation, has made both scholarly and cultural work possible in a unique collaboration with the Huseby Estate, which is today open to the public. We are grateful both to the funder and to the estate's director, Sofie Magnusson, and her colleagues for the creative environment that grew out of this collaboration. The photographs from the 1860s India, published in this volume are all brought from India by Joseph Stephens and John Hallen Abbott and held in trust by the Huseby Estate, Huseby Bruk AB. A special thank you to Henrik Chetan Aspengren, historian and member of the *Huseby in the World* project, for coming up with the ideas behind the title of this volume. He is now a research fellow at the Swedish Institute of International Affairs in charge of its South Asia Initiative. Janaki Nair, Jawaharlal Nehru University, New Delhi in India, and Ravi Ahuja, Georg-August-Universität Göttingen, Centre for Modern Indian Studies in Germany, have given important support and feedback throughout the work. Over the years, research related to this work has benefited from discussions and collaboration at conferences and workshops. I would especially like to acknowledge the Centre for Historical Studies at Jawaharlal Nehru University in New Delhi, India, and the Division of History of Science, Technology, and Environment at KTH Royal Institute of Technology in Stockholm, Sweden.

Notes

1 I am grateful for assistance and comments on this chapter from Maria Ågren, Peter B. Andersen, Björn Hakon Lingner, K. Sivaramakrishnan, and Rolf Torstendahl. See Staffan Hansson, 'Tekniken som samhällsomdanare: Exemplet Norrbottens teknologiska megasystem', in Eva Landberg, Karin Rönnbäck, and Per Moritz (eds), *Norrbotten: Årsbok 2007* (Luleå: Norrbottens hembygdsförbund, 2007), pp. 26–41.

2 From 1860/1 to 1865/6, cotton cultivation in Berar expanded from 629,000 to 1,238,966 acres. Laxman D. Satya, *Cotton and Famine in Berar, 1850–1900* (New Delhi: Manohar, 1997), pp. 143, 180, 183–5, 192; Henrik Chetan Aspengren, 'Bombay—möjligheternas stad', in Margareta Petersson (ed.), *Från Brittiska Indien till Huseby bruk: Järnvägen som arena för modernitet och kolonialism under lycksökaren och järnvägsentreprenören Joseph Stephens tid i Indien 1860–69* (Lund: Arkiv förlag, 2018), pp. 57–60.

3 Satya, *Cotton and Famine*, pp. 58, 179; Ian J. Kerr, *Building the Railways of the Raj, 1850–1900* (New Delhi; New York: Oxford University Press, 1995), p. 25.

4 Margareta Petersson, 'Joseph Stephens—Familjen och arkivet', in Petersson (ed.), *Från Brittiska Indien*, pp. 15–20; Margareta Petersson, 'A Danish Family in India: Gendered Colonial Upbringing, Everyday Life, and Cultural Encounters', in Kristina Myrvold (ed.), *India: Research on Cultural Encounters and Representations at Linnaeus University* (Gothenburg; Stockholm: Makadam, 2017), p. 74.

5 I am grateful to Dr. Peter B. Andersen and Dr. Björn Hakon Lingner for their generous assistance and conversations with me on the situation in Denmark and Copenhagen in the mid nineteenth century.

6 Henriette Steiner, *The Emergence of a Modern City: Golden Age Copenhagen 1800–1850* (Burlington: Ashgate Publishing Company, 2014), pp. 19, 39, 43–7; Aksel Lassen, 'The Population of Denmark, 1660–1960', *Scandinavian Economic History Review*, 14/2 (1966), pp. 134, 143, table 2. Steiner bases her information about the population of Copenhagen on C. Bjørn, 'Fra reaktion til grundlov', in Olaf Olsen (ed.), *Gyldendal og Politikens Danmarkshistorie* (Copenhagen: Gyldendalske boghandel Politikens forlag, 1988), p. 84; and Michael Bregnsbo and Kurt Villads Jensen, *Det danske imperium: Storhed og fald* (Viborg: Aschehoug Banks Forlag, 2005), pp. 162–3, 168–70.

7 Petersson, 'Joseph Stephens—Familjen och arkivet', p. 16; Svend Cedergreen Bech, *Dansk biografisk leksikon*, 3rd ed., 16 vols (København: Gyldendal, 1983), pp. 99–100.

8 In the Second Schleswig War of 1864, Denmark lost the duchies to Prussia, a loss confirmed at the Peace of Prague in 1866. William Carr and Harry Hearder, *The Wars of German Unification 1864–1871* (Boca Raton, FL: Taylor & Francis Group, 1991), pp. 34–40; Benedikte Brincker, 'A "Small Great National State": An Analysis of the Cultural and Political Factors that Shaped Danish Nationalism 1760–1870', *Journal of Historical Sociology*, 16/4, December (2003), pp. 417–18; Alexander Bubb, 'Class, Cotton, and "Woddaries": A Scandinavian Railway Contractor in Western India, 1860–69', *Modern Asian Studies*,

51/5 (2017), pp. 1377–8; Bregnsbo and Villads Jensen, *Det danske imperium*, pp. 184–5.

9 The Institution of Civil Engineers in England was founded in 1818, and new members were elected by the existing ones. The Polyteknisk Læreanstalt was established in 1829. The Roskilde—Copenhagen line was opened in 1847. Kulturministeriet, Slots- og kulturstyrelsen, Fredede og bevaringsværdige bygninger, www.kulturarv.dk/fbb/sagvis.pub?sag=7396535, 23 April 2020. 'Obituary Notice', Institution of Civil Engineers, Minutes of Proceedings, London, Institution of Civil Engineers, 1885, Vol. 79, pp. 360–1. Henrik Harnow, *Den danske ingeniørs historie 1850–1920: Danske ingenrørers uddannelse, professionalisering og betydning for den danske moderniseringsproces* (Århus: Systime, 1998), pp. 44–7; Rolf Torstendahl, *Engineers in Western Europe: Ascent—and Decline? A Profession Torn Between Technology and Economy, 1850–1990, with Outlooks to the Present* (Berlin and Heidelberg: Springer-Verlag, forthcoming), pp. 68, 80–1.

10 Bubb, 'Class, Cotton, and "Woddaries"', pp. 1377–8; Petersson, 'A Danish Family', pp. 80, 84–5; Ingemar Gunnarsson, 'Från lärling till "ingenjör"', in Petersson (ed.), *Från Brittiska Indien*, p. 68.

11 Deccan, or Dakhan in more recent transcription. 660.18 mm of annual rainfall was measured for Akola as an average for the years 1869–1906. Sumit Guha, *Environment and Ethnicity in India, 1200–1991*, Cambridge Studies in Indian History and Society, 4 (New York: Cambridge University Press, 1999), pp. 33–5; A. E. Nelson, *Central Provinces District Gazetteers, Akola District, Volume B, Statistical Tables (1891–1907)* (Nagpur: Government Press, 1909), pp. 4–5, table 1; William Stevenson Meyer, Richard Burn, James Sutherland Cotton, and Herbert Hope Risley, *The Imperial Gazetteer of India* (Oxford: Clarendon Press, 1908), Vol. 7, p. 365, Vol. 8, p. 277, and Vol. 18, p. 306.

12 Satya, *Cotton and Famine*, pp. 137–40; Eric Lewis Beverley, *Hyderabad, British India, and the World: Muslim Networks and Minor Sovereignty, c. 1850–1950* (Cambridge: Cambridge University Press, 2015), pp. 66–7.

13 Meyer et al., *Imperial Gazetteer of India*, Vol. 8, p. 153; Guha, *Environment and Ethnicity*, p. 148; Kerr, *Building the Railways*, pp. 55–6; Satya, *Cotton and Famine*, p. 179.

14 Satya, *Cotton and Famine*, pp. 25, 48, 60–1, 87, ch. 4.

15 Guha, *Environment and Ethnicity*, pp. 1, 135.

16 Ibid., pp. 65, 71–2, 136, 168–9, 172; Bubb, 'Class, Cotton, and "Woddaries"', p. 1388.

17 Mahesh Rangarajan, *Fencing the Forest: Conservation and Ecological Change in India's Central Provinces, 1860–1914*, Studies in Social Ecology and Environmental History (New Delhi: Oxford University Press, 1996), p. 29. The calculation is from Dietrich Brandis, 'Memorandum on the Supply of Railway Sleepers of the Himalayan Pines Impregnated in India', *Indian Forester*, 4 (1879), p. 366. Dietrich Brandis was Inspector General of Forests in India 1864–83. S. Ravi Rajan, *Modernizing Nature: Forestry and Imperial Eco-Development 1800–1950*, Oxford Historical Monographs (Oxford; New York: Clarendon Press; Oxford University Press, 2006), p. 83.

18 Rajan, *Modernizing Nature*, p. 71. Rajan refers to Hugh F. C. Cleghorn, *The Forests and Gardens of South India* (London: W. H. Allen & Co., 1861), p. 32; Guha, *Environment and Ethnicity*, pp. 165–6; Rangarajan, *Fencing the Forest*, p. 30; Madhav Gadgil and Ramachandra Guha, *This Fissured Land: An Ecological History of India* (New Delhi; New York: Oxford University Press, 1992), p. 120.

19 Meyer et al., *Imperial Gazetteer of India*, Vol. 7, p. 362.

20 Prof. Prabhu Mohapatra, at the conference 'The Underbelly of the Empire: Workers, Contracts, and the Social Economy of the Industrial Turn', jointly organized

by Jawaharlal Nehru University, Centre for Historical Studies, and Linnaeus University, Centre for Concurrences in Colonial and Postcolonial Studies, 11–12 December 2019, notes by the author. See also Arun Kumar, Chapter 3, in this volume.

21 Dhiraj Kumar Nite, 'En lycksökares liv och affärer i Indien och Skandinavien', in Petersson (ed.), *Från Brittiska Indien*, pp. 145–52; Alexander Bubb, 'An Element of Risk: The Corrupt Contractor in Indian Fiction and Film, 1886–1983', *Cambridge Journal of Postcolonial Literary Inquiry*, 4/1 (2017), p. 113. The first engineering college in India was opened as early as 1847 at Roorkee, and three more soon followed. Arun Kumar, 'Colonial Requirements and Engineering Education: The Public Works Department, 1847–1947', in Roy M. Macleod and Deepak Kumar (eds), *Technology and the Raj: Western Technology and Technical Transfers to India, 1700–1947* (New Delhi; Thousand Oaks: SAGE, 1995), pp. 216–18; *Account of Roorkee College, Established for the Instruction of Civil Engineers, with a Scheme for Its Enlargement* (Agra: Secundra Orphan Press, 1851), pp. 4–5, paras 14–16; Harald Fischer-Tiné, 'Hierarchies of Punishment in Colonial India: European Convicts and the Racial Dividend, c. 1860–1890', in Harald Fischer-Tiné and Susanne Gehrmann (eds), *Empires and Boundaries: Rethinking Race, Class, and Gender in Colonial Settings* (New York: Routledge, 2009), pp. 43–44.

22 Radhika Krishnan, Chapter 2; Arun Kumar, Chapter 3; and Dhiraj Kumar Nite, Chapters 4 and 5 in this volume.

23 Nite, 'En lycksökares liv', pp. 150, 159–61, tables 2 and 3.

24 Kerstin Eneflo and Joan Ramón Rosés, 'Coping with Regional Inequality in Sweden: Structural Change, Migrations, and Policy, 1860–2000', *Economic History Review*, 68/1 (2015), p. 196, table 1; Harald Runblom and Hans Norman, *From Sweden to America: A History of the Migration*, Acta Universitatis Upsaliensis, Studia historica Upsaliensia, 74 (Minneapolis: University of Minnesota Press, 1976); Ingvar Svanberg, 'The Use of Wild Plants as Food in Pre-industrial Sweden', *Acta Societatis Botanicorum Poloniae*, 81/4 (2012), https://doi.org/10.5586/asbp.2012.039, pp. 322–3.

25 The foremost of the novels to narrate the long history of Swedish migration to the USA from the experience of a single family from Småland province was the trilogy *The Emigrants* by Vilhelm Moberg. It was published in Swedish in 1949 and in English 1951. The novel was made into the two films 'The Emigrants' and 'The Good Land' in 1971, directed by Jan Troell, and the musical 'Kristina from Duvemåla' by Benny Andersson and Björn Ulvaeus in 1995.

26 Martha McLaren, *British India and British Scotland, 1780–1830: Career Building, Empire Building, and a Scottish School of Thought on Indian Governance* (Akron: University of Akron Press, 2001); Lambert and Alan Lester, 'Introduction: Imperial Spaces, Imperial Subjects', in Lambert and Alan Lester (eds), *Colonial Lives across the British Empire: Imperial Careering in the Long Nineteenth Century* (Cambridge: Cambridge University Press 2006), pp. 1–31; Hyslop, Jonathan, 'Making Scotland in South Africa: Charles Murray, the Tranvaal's Aberdeenshire Poet', in David Lambert and Alan Lester (eds), *Colonial Lives Across the British Empire: Imperial Careering in the Long Nineteenth Century* (Cambridge: Cambridge University Press, 2006), pp. 310–11.

27 Rune Ahlander, 'Skogsvårdsstyrelsen i Kronoberg: Frostdikning och emigration tidigt på agendan', in *Skogshistoriska Sällskapets Årsskrift 2015* (Ödeshög: Danagård LiTHO, 2015), pp. 34–43, 35–37, 40.

28 Lars-Olof Larsson, *Historia kring Huseby* (Grimslöv: Skatelövs Hembygdsförening, 1978), p. 83; Ulf Beijbom, 'Från utvandrar- till invandrarlän', in Lennart Johansson (ed.), *Landen kring sjöarna: En historia om Kronobergs län i mångtusenårigt perspektiv; Kronobergsboken 1999–2000* (Växjö: Grafiska

Punkten, 1999), pp. 375–6. Erik Wångmar, Chapter 7, and Eleonor Marcussen, Chapter 6, in this volume.

29 Lake ore and bog ore are forms of limonite. This source of iron has high proportions of phosphorus, making it comparatively fragile. In Lake Åsnen, part of which belonged to the Huseby Estate, the ore contained 32–36 per cent iron. Lake ore can assume different forms. In Lake Åsnen it formed into plates which could be harvested every 30 years. If not removed, it would cover the bottom of the lake. Lars-Olof Larsson, 'Studier kring järnhantering i södra Småland fram till det industriella genombrottet', in Lars-Olof Larsson and Leif Rubensson (eds), *Från blästbruk till bruksdöd*, Jernkontorets bergshistoriska skriftserie (Jönköping: Järnkontoret, 2000), pp. 130–2.

30 Olle Krantz, 'Järnbruket som blev glasbruk: Ägarskap, tillverkning, konkurrens', in Kerstin Wickman, Hans Cogne, Gunnel Holmér, and Denise Grünstein (eds), *Orrefors: Glasbrukets historia 1898–1998* (Stockholm: Byggförlaget-Kultur, 1998), p. 16; Olof Nordström, 'Förteckning över glasbruk och hyttor i Sverige 1150–2000', *Glasteknisk tidskrift*, 54/3 (1999), pp. 78–80; Larsson, 'Studier kring järnhantering, pp. 213–14.

31 The railway line connected Vislanda and Karlshamn, stopping at Huseby on the way. Nite, 'En lycksökares liv', pp. 144–5.

32 Malin Lennartsson, Chapter 8, in this volume.

33 Gunnarsson, Ingemar, *En skandinavisk järnvägskontraktörs karriär i Indien 1860–1867: Ackumulering av socialt och kulturellt kapital som framgångsstrategi i en kolonial kontext*, Lnu Licentiate No. 31, Department of Cultural Sciences, Linnaeus University, Sweden (Växjö: Linneaus University Press, 2020).

References

Account of Roorkee College, Established for the Instruction of Civil Engineers, with a Scheme for Its Enlargement (Agra: Secundra Orphan Press, 1851).

Aspengren, Henrik Chetan, 'Bombay—möjligheternas stad', in Margareta Petersson (ed.), *Från Brittiska Indien till Huseby bruk: Järnvägen som arena för modernitet och kolonialism under lycksökaren och järnvägsentreprenören Joseph Stephens tid i Indien 1860–69* (Lund: Arkiv Förlag, 2018).

Beijbom, Ulf, 'Från utvandrar- till invandrarlän', in Lennart Johansson (ed.), *Landen kring sjöarna: En historia om Kronobergs län i mångtusenårigt perspektiv; Kronobergsboken 1999–2000* (Växjö: Grafiska Punkten, 1999), pp. 365–90.

Beverley, Eric Lewis, *Hyderabad, British India, and the World: Muslim Networks and Minor Sovereignty, c. 1850–1950* (Cambridge: Cambridge University Press, 2015).

Bjørn, C., 'Fra reaktion til grundlov', in Olaf Olsen (ed.), *Gyldendal og Politikens Danmarkshistorie* (Copenhagen: Gyldendalske Boghandel Politikens Forlag, 1988).

Brandis, Dietrich, 'Memorandum on the Supply of Railway Sleepers of the Himalayan Pines Impregnated in India', *Indian Forester*, 4 (1879).

Bregnsbo, Michael, and Kurt Villads Jensen, *Det danske imperium: Storhed og fald* (Viborg: Aschehoug Banks Forlag, 2005).

Brincker, Benedikte, 'A "Small Great National State": An Analysis of the Cultural and Political Factors that Shaped Danish Nationalism 1760–1870', *Journal of Historical Sociology*, 16/4, December (2003), pp. 407–31.

Bubb, Alexander, 'An Element of Risk: The Corrupt Contractor in Indian Fiction and Film, 1886–1983', *Cambridge Journal of Postcolonial Literary Inquiry*, 4/1 (2017), pp. 109–26, https://doi.org/10.1017/pli.2016.33.

Bubb, Alexander, 'Class, Cotton, and "Woddaries": A Scandinavian Railway Contractor in Western India, 1860–69', *Modern Asian Studies*, 51/5 (2017), pp. 1369–93, https://doi.org/10.1017/S0026749X16000251.

Carr, William, and Harry Hearder, *The Wars of German Unification 1864–1871* (Boca Raton, FL: Taylor & Francis Group, 1991).

Cedergreen Bech, Svend, *Dansk biografisk leksikon*, 3rd ed., 16 vols (København: Gyldendal, 1983).

Cleghorn, Hugh F. C., *The Forests and Gardens of South India* (London: W. H. Allen & Co., 1861).

Eneflo, Kerstin, and Joan Ramón Rosés, 'Coping with Regional Inequality in Sweden: Structural Change, Migrations, and Policy, 1860–2000', *Economic History Review*, 68/1 (2015), pp. 191–217.

Fischer-Tiné, Harald, 'Hierarchies of Punishment in Colonial India: European Convicts and the Racial Dividend, c. 1860–1890', in Harald Fischer-Tiné and Susanne Gehrmann (eds) *Empires and Boundaries: Rethinking Race, Class, and Gender in Colonial Settings* (New York: Routledge, 2009), pp. 41–65.

Gadgil, Madhav, and Ramachandra Guha, *This Fissured Land: An Ecological History of India* (New Delhi; New York: Oxford University Press, 1992).

Guha, Sumit, *Environment and Ethnicity in India, 1200–1991*, Cambridge Studies in Indian History and Society, 4 (New York: Cambridge University Press, 1999).

Gunnarsson, Ingemar, *En skandinavisk järnvägskontraktörs karriär i Indien 1860–1867: Ackumulering av socialt och kulturellt kapital som framgångsstrategi i en kolonial kontext*, LNU Licentiate No. 31, Department of Cultural Sciences, Linnaeus University, Sweden (Växjö: Linnaeus University Press, 2020).

Gunnarsson, Ingemar, 'Från lärling till "ingenjör"', in Margareta Petersson (ed.), *Från Brittiska Indien till Huseby bruk: Järnvägen som arena för modernitet och kolonialism under lycksökaren och järnvägsentreprenören Joseph Stephens tid i Indien 1860–69* (Lund: Arkiv Förlag, 2018), pp. 65–82.

Hansson, Staffan, 'Tekniken som samhällsomdanare: Exemplet Norrbottens teknologiska megasystem', in Eva Landberg, Karin Rönnbäck, and Per Moritz (eds), *Norrbotten: Årsbok 2007* (Luleå: Norrbottens hembygdsförbund, 2007), pp. 26–41.

Harnow, Henrik, *Den danske ingeniørs historie 1850–1920: Danske ingenrørers uddannelse, professionalisering og betydning for den danske moderniseringsproces* (Århus: Systime, 1998).

Hyslop, Jonathan, 'Making Scotland in South Africa: Charles Murray, the Tranvaal's Aberdeenshire Poet', in David Lambert and Alan Lester (eds), *Colonial Lives Across the British Empire: Imperial Careering in the Long Nineteenth Century* (Cambridge: Cambridge University Press 2006), pp. 309–34.

Kerr, Ian J., *Building the Railways of the Raj, 1850–1900* (New Delhi; New York: Oxford University Press, 1995).

Krantz, Olle, 'Järnbruket som blev glasbruk: Ägarskap, tillverkning, konkurrens', in Kerstin Wickman, Hans Cogne, Gunnel Holmér, and Denise Grünstein (eds), *Orrefors: Glasbrukets historia 1898–1998* (Stockholm: Byggförlaget-Kultur, 1998).

Kumar, Arun, 'Colonial Requirements and Engineering Education: The Public Works Department, 1847–1947', in Roy M. Macleod and Deepak Kumar (eds), *Technology and the Raj: Western Technology and Technical Transfers to India, 1700–1947* (New Delhi; Thousand Oaks: SAGE, 1995), pp. 216–32.

Lambert and Alan Lester, 'Introduction: Imperial Spaces, Imperial Subjects', in Lambert and Alan Lester (eds), *Colonial Lives Across the British Empire: Imperial Careering in the Long Nineteenth Century* (Cambridge: Cambridge University Press, 2006), pp. 1–31.
Larsson, Lars-Olof, *Historia kring Huseby* (Grimslöv: Skatelövs Hembygdsförening, 1978).
Larsson, Lars-Olof, 'Studier kring järnhantering i södra Småland fram till det industriella genombrottet', in Lars-Olof Larsson and Leif Rubensson (eds), *Från blästbruk till bruksdöd*, Jernkontorets bergshistoriska skriftserie (Jönköping: Järnkontoret, 2000), pp. 11–252.
Lassen, Aksel, 'The Population of Denmark, 1660–1960', *Scandinavian Economic History Review*, 14/2 (1966), pp. 134–57.
McLaren, Martha, *British India and British Scotland, 1780–1830: Career Building, Empire Building, and a Scottish School of Thought on Indian Governance* (Akron, OH: University of Akron Press, 2001).
Meyer, William Stevenson, Richard Burn, James Sutherland Cotton, and Herbert Hope Risley, *The Imperial Gazetteer of India* (Oxford: Clarendon Press, 1908).
Moberg, Vilhelm, *The Emigrants: A Novel* (New York: Simon and Schuster, 1951).
Moberg, Vilhelm, *Utvandrarna* (Stockholm: Bonniers Förlag, 1949).
Nelson, A. E., *Central Provinces District Gazetteers, Akola District, Volume B, Statistical Tables (1891–1907)* (Nagpur: Government Press, 1909).
Nite, Dhiraj Kumar, 'En lycksökares liv och affärer i Indien och Skandinavien', in Margareta Petersson (ed.), *Från Brittiska Indien till Huseby bruk: Järnvägen som arena för modernitet och kolonialism under lycksökaren och järnvägsentreprenören Joseph Stephens tid i Indien 1860–69* (Lund: Arkiv Förlag, 2018), pp. 135–65.
Nordström, Olof, 'Förteckning över glasbruk och hyttor i Sverige 1150–2000', *Glasteknisk tidskrift*, 54/3 (1999), pp. 77–84.
Petersson, Margareta, 'A Danish Family in India: Gendered Colonial Upbringing, Everyday Life, and Cultural Encounters', in Kristina Myrvold (ed.), *India: Research on Cultural Encounters and Representations at Linnaeus University* (Gothenburg; Stockholm: Makadam, 2017), pp. 74–99.
Petersson, Margareta, 'Joseph Stephens—Familjen och arkivet', in Margareta Petersson (ed.), *Från Brittiska Indien till Huseby bruk: Järnvägen som arena för modernitet och kolonialism under lycksökaren och järnvägsentreprenören Joseph Stephens tid i Indien 1860–69* (Lund: Arkiv Förlag, 2018), pp. 15–43.
Rajan, S. Ravi, *Modernizing Nature: Forestry and Imperial Eco-Development 1800–1950*, Oxford Historical Monographs (Oxford; New York: Clarendon Press, Oxford University Press, 2006).
Rangarajan, Mahesh, *Fencing the Forest: Conservation and Ecological Change in India's Central Provinces, 1860–1914*, Studies in Social Ecology and Environmental History (New Delhi: Oxford University Press, 1996).
Runblom, Harald, and Hans Norman, *From Sweden to America: A History of the Migration*, Acta Universitatis Upsaliensis, Studia Historica Upsaliensia, 74 (Minneapolis: University of Minnesota Press, 1976).
Satya, Laxman D., *Cotton and Famine in Berar, 1850–1900* (New Delhi: Manohar, 1997).
Steiner, Henriette, *The Emergence of a Modern City: Golden Age Copenhagen 1800–1850* (Burlington: Ashgate Publishing Company, 2014).

Svanberg, Ingvar, 'The Use of Wild Plants as Food in Pre-industrial Sweden', *Acta Societatis Botanicorum Poloniae*, 81/4 (2012), https://doi.org/10.5586/asbp.2012.039.

Torstendahl, Rolf, *Engineers in Western Europe: Ascent—and Decline? A Profession Torn Between Technology and Economy, 1850–1990, with Outlooks to the Present* (Berlin; Heidelberg: Springer-Verlag, forthcoming).

2 The Life of Contract Capitalism and the Building of the Colonial Railway

Arun Kumar

Capitalism thrives on contracts via the backdoor of a state-led legal regime. Contract laws that guarantee a free exchange of goods, and property laws that ensure the private ownership of assets and public resources, had been the pillars of the capitalist system. The modern state ensured that these laws were not only created but also implemented to protect the interests of the propertied class. However, how these laws came to favour the bourgeois class over the feudal lords and the customary rights of the poor was a conflictual process, and as Tigar and Levy remark, the landed gentry and bourgeois required the state to institute their powers.[1] They argue that contractarian ideology, though a powerful ally of the capitalist system, required courts, judges, and the state on its side to be effective.[2] From recruiting workers and employees to transacting everyday business with various agents and selling commodities, contracts have become an absolute necessity for capitalism to function and regulate the employer-employee relationships.[3] They ensure a regime of secure and trustworthy business, and above all the regime of the 'free market'.

Within the classical political economy that safeguarded and advocated the capitalist system, contracts acquired a prominent place because of their capability of making transactions smooth between two individuals. Adam Smith, an advocate of capitalism and the Scottish Enlightenment, believed that economic prosperity was fuelled when commodities were transacted freely in a market and the actions of the participants were voluntary. Contracts thus combined the essence of two systems: the Enlightenment, which propagated the notion of reason and individualism, and classical political economy, which argued for individual self-interest and free exchange of commodities. It would be unfair to say that contracts were just legal and economic documents, because on those documents lay the burden of a 'free, equal, and rational' society. Although they were to check and punish the crooked, dishonest, and fraudulent behaviours of humans, their role in the post-slavery abolition world gave them a significant meaning which idealized contracts as symbols of freedom.[4]

In 1861, Henry Maine, a Victorian jurist and lawmaker in India, published his now-classic *Ancient Laws* and propounded the theory of

DOI: 10.4324/9781003317227-2

progressive societies moving from 'status' to 'contract'.[5] Contracts as agreements between two free individuals/parties appeared as harbingers of free wage labour, which liberated society from the 'inhuman vestiges of the past'—slavery, bonded labour, and other coerced labour. The idea of contracts, which classical political economists and jurists put forward in the nineteenth century, was premised on the 'will theory' or the 'consensus' of the two contracting parties. The two parties had obligations that they promised to meet in the future, and because the agreement was between two 'free' individuals, the terms and conditions of the contract were bound by the law.[6] As a result, laws, economic debates, legal inquiries, and government reports consolidated wage labour as the dominant form of labour relation under capitalism.[7]

This classical liberal framework of the capitalist system operating on the basis of the 'free will' of individuals was questioned by Karl Marx. The production of 'free' wage labour through primitive accumulation (the process of separating people from their means of production) was, Marx argued, achieved by means of 'terroristic' and cruel laws. Marx wrote that 'capital comes dripping from head to toe, from every pore, with blood and dirt'.[8] Employment contracts, considered essential in producing free wage labour regimes, covered the violent and unequal nature of capitalism with the disguised language of freedom, individuality, and equality. Michel Foucault also talked about how a 'formally egalitarian juridical framework' of the eighteenth century entailed a dark history of disciplinary mechanisms.[9]

A much sharper critique of contracts and contract laws came from legal scholars and practitioners, first from the legal realism school and then from critical legal studies.[10] The realism school challenged the supposed 'equal status' of contracting parties, which they argued was not the case as employment contracts involved the powerless labouring poor.[11] By the 1960s and 1970s, a highly critical legal tradition began to emerge, in contrast to the consensus school, which highlighted the role of contracts in economic growth and prosperity. Its representatives argued that through laws, including contract laws, judges and lawyers pushed the interests of the bourgeois/propertied class to the forefront while dismantling traditional rights.[12] This close link between capitalist classes and law was further taken up by legal historians.[13] Robert Steinfeld's influential work *Coercion, Contract, and Free Labor in the Nineteenth Century* argued that free wage labour was not really 'free'. Wage labour relations in rural and urban England until 1875 operated under contract laws that criminalized a breach of contract by workers and forced them to remain in contract or face prison until the contract was completed.[14] Steinfeld argued that employers used contract laws not so much to punish workers, as to enforce the specific performance of agreed contracts and extract labour. Employers did, though, punish workers when they wanted to set an example and when workers did not complete their terms even after the threat.[15] It is this particular feature of contracts in producing unfree and coercive labour relations within the capitalist system that has been picked up by Indian historians who have studied the relationship between law, labour, and colonialism. We will deal with this historiography as we progress with Joseph Stephens' contracts—a contractor who worked on the construction of the railway line from Bhusawal to Nagpur in the 1860s. But at the outset, it would be useful to point out the salient features of these scholarly studies.

First, the colonial state made heavy use of contract laws to govern labour relations, despite Henry Maine characterizing India as a 'traditional', 'status', and community-based society.[16] These laws, influenced by the British Master and Servant Acts, were implemented from the very beginning (from the late eighteenth century) to acquire labour for state-managed projects and for European capitalists doing business in or from India. Second, despite contracts being civil matters, criminal breach of contracts and penal punishment remained an essential component of the contract laws until the late 1920s, whereas in England the criminal breach clause was abolished in 1875 leading to the 1875 Employers and Workmen Act. The colonial contractarian ideology appears in these studies to have been evolved as a tool to subordinate 'native' labourers, create unfree labour relations, and protect the economic interests of employers. Third, a variety of general and industry-specific contract laws were established by the colonial state that competed with each other but supported specific industries or labour regimes, such as tea plantations, offshore sugar plantations, domestic servants, indigo peasants, and construction workers. Finally, our understanding of the contractarian ideology and employer-workman relationship in colonial India is derived from contract laws rather than actual contracts. It is here that this essay makes a departure from the existing studies, in terms of both the material analysed and the arguments made.

Labour and the Contractarian Ideology

The Joseph Stephens Archive (JSA) offers a number of contracts between Stephens and artisans, coolies, and labour headmen that nuance our understanding of the power of contracts and the labour-legal history of India. We will see that he uses contracts as a powerful tool to create a disciplined labour force for himself in a very new, uncertain, rural, but competitive labour market. We will also see that workers found various openings and closings of their bargaining power vis-à-vis employers in the light of contracts and an expanding labour market. Contract laws (and implicitly contracts) in India have principally been studied as mechanisms to produce unfree labour regimes and structure the overall labour-capital relationship. Actual copies of contracts from the railway construction sites tell us that they had a wider role in managing everyday work relations and work processes. Their usefulness lay not only in their ability to punish workers through the punitive clauses of the laws but also in their ability to function as self-acting legal tools which, to some extent, governed the issues of delayed work, usurpation of advanced money, withholding of wages, costs of damage, monetary fines, satisfactory work, and guarantees. Stephens' contracts also articulated significant universal concerns of employers, particularly the assumed dishonesty, laziness, and carelessness of workers—what can be called the capitalist's distrust of the labour class.

Joseph Stephens reached India in 1860 and, after completing his apprenticeship with John Abbott, he began working as an assistant (with the duties of inspection, surveying, and accounting combined) to a small contractor named E. W. Winton and moved to the north-eastern region of Nashik to work on viaducts. During his apprenticeship and early career, Stephens not only learned mathematics, Hindustani, English, letter writing, and engineering, but he also learned how to become a European colonial master. Hunting, playing cricket, employing servants, and writing a daily journal were part of this conditioning.[17] He built his career through the social and political connections of Abbott, whose employment records at the British Library show that he was among the earliest cohorts of assistant engineers of the GIPR, and whose colleagues later supervised, passed, and inspected Stephens' works and contracts.[18] In 1862, Stephens became a subcontractor under a bigger contracting firm named Wythes and Jackson (who were working on Contract No. 12, Chalisgaon to Bhusawal line, 72 miles), and later under Lee, Watson, and Aiton, who were working on the Nagpur extension line (Bhusawal to Nagpur). These jobs pushed Stephens deep into the countryside of the cotton belt in Khandesh region, where he remained until 1869.

In the early years, Stephens worked in Jalgaon, in particular building a small viaduct at Alasana, currently in Buldana district of Maharashtra. Subcontracting generated substantial profits and gave Stephens the required practical experience to be able to submit tenders for irrigation work in Satara district in early 1864 and get some work at Nandgaon, Sheagaon, and Kajgaon stations.[19] He formed his own construction firm, Joseph Stephens Construction Company, with G. B. Peck as his agent, and sent in tenders for the building of bridges, ginning factories, pump houses, viaducts, stations, and irrigation tanks in Poona, Khandesh, and Berar.[20] By 1865, Stephens had emerged as a small contractor working directly on the GIPR's Contract No. 13. Over the years, he commanded hundreds of Indian labourers, artisans, muccadams (the headmen of Indian labourers), and lower European staff, and supervised the construction of arches, railway lines, stations, pump houses, and fencing.[21] When dealing with Indian workers and artisans, Stephens and his company generally, but not always, relied on contracts to hire workers and services.[22]

Alexander Bubb points out that Stephens relied heavily on Vaddars ('Woodaries' or Odde) and Beldars for artisanal and coolie labour. These castes, usually associated with earthwork and tank construction, became the go-to labourers for railway construction in western India.[23] They formed what Ian Kerr calls circulating labour because of their ability to move as families along the railway construction line, which suited contractors.[24] Railways involved about 400,000 construction workers in the early 1860s, and a significant number of this workforce were tribes like the Vaddars, Beldars, Maugs, and Dalits (the 'ex-untouchables').[25] Because the railway line was being laid down on a large scale in the Bombay Presidency, and particularly in Khandesh region, labour was a scarce commodity, especially skilled and docile labour. And incidents of native labour contractors, headmen, and workers being poached by competing contractors were not unknown. Bubb argues that Stephens and Peck had to placate workers by rewarding hard-working, loyal, and docile workers/headmen with cherimerry (small gifts), brandy, and bonuses.[26] We will discuss some instances of labour scuffles as we move on to locate the place of contracts in Stephens' business. In such a tense labour market, contracts came to play a key role in controlling and disciplining labour and shaping the contractor-labour relationship at the railway construction sites.[27]

Stephens arrived in India in the midst of profound legal controversies over the labour laws. On the one hand, there were officials who wanted to criminalize all breaches of contract with imprisonment, and on the other, officials who saw it as contrary to the liberal ideology and the policy of laissez-faire and wanted to criminalize only the fraudulent practice of taking an advance and not fulfilling the contract.[28] The latter camp won, and the Workmen's Breach of Contract Act XIII was passed in 1859 to regulate the relationship between employers and artisans/domestic labour/contract hires. This act, initially applied in presidency towns and by the 1870s extended to all parts of colonial India, formed the pinnacle of the contractarian ideology in colonial labour policy. For a long time, historians maintained that the colonial state had no clear-cut labour policy to begin with in the eighteenth century and relied on caste and kinship networks (Indigenous social structures) to recruit, control, and discipline the labour force.[29] The implication was that colonial/Western laws and interventions had little effect on the actual labour regime, which was dominated by 'the persistence of status relations based on caste'.[30]

A number of labour historians have rejected this reductionist understanding of labour relationships in colonial India. Ravi Ahuja, in the context of the late eighteenth and nineteenth centuries, argued that the East India Company state not only had a formidable labour policy by the end of the eighteenth century, produced through colonial regulations, police, and the justice system, but also developed powerful employer-employee contract regulations by the beginning of the nineteenth century, drawing their inspiration from the English Master and Servant laws. These regulations, particularly the Police Regulations of 1811, made the 'misconduct' of servants, workmen, and lascars punishable by a combination of monetary fines, corporal punishment, and imprisonment with hard labour, while their masters merely needed to meet their contractual 'obligations'. Failure to do so invited only monetary fines, leaving the sacrosanct body of the master intact.[31] Ahuja argues that there was nothing laissez-faire as such in the labour relations of the company with Indian labourers; in fact, they produced, on the one hand, contract laws and wage regulations and, on the other, the powers of local caste headmen and intermediaries who helped to procure, manage, and discipline labour.[32]

A much sharper critique came from labour historian Prabhu Mohapatra, who looked at the variety of contract laws (in the weaving industry, tea plantations, and indigo cultivation), including the 1859 Workmen's Breach of Contract Act. Mohapatra argued that the contracting ideology based on the idea of 'free' labour and 'consent' was inherently contradictory in this period. Once 'consent' was given by any means, 'theoretically there was nothing to prevent the most blatant form of servitude'.[33] The customary practice of taking an advance came to be seen as 'consent' by the worker. However, exiting from the contract produced tensions and violence. Breach of a civil contract by workers was penalized through criminal proceedings by the state. The 1859 Act punished the 'fraudulent' behaviour of workmen (the fraudulent intention was deduced from workers deserting work after taking an advance) by sentencing them to up to three months' imprisonment. Mohapatra remarks that the act not only gave employers an upper hand over labour but also converted the customary power of workers to demand an advance into a legal means of binding them.[34]

A number of scholars have shown that contracts were used by the colonial state and employers to resolve specific problems of labour supply and discipline and, more importantly, to create a large 'unfree' labour market to produce commercial commodities such as textiles, indigo, sugar, and tea.[35] They were also used to subordinate and discipline service groups such as servants, boatmen, palanquin bearers, and dak runners.[36] Railway construction, especially in the interiors, required a large labour force which not only had to be recruited from local and distant areas, but also needed to be kept content and settled at the construction site. Penal contract laws were so important in these rural areas that a separate law, by the name of Regulation 7 of 1819, came into being in the Bengal Presidency to regulate the work of artisans and workmen. According to that law, workers could be sent to jail for a month for breaching their contracts, and for two months for repeating the offence.[37] Rural Bengal was by this time dotted with the presence of various European planters, landowners, and merchants, who produced commodities such as indigo, silk, and tea with the labour of Indians. A similar regulation was introduced in the Bombay Presidency in 1827.

However, this law was repealed in 1862 with the passing of the Indian Penal Code, rendering employers in the countryside powerless. Among those who protested were the railway contractors, who argued that civil actions against deserting and negligent workers were useless as it was a waste of employers' money pursuing lawsuits against workers who had little money or property to pay any damages. Penal punishment was the only effective solution.[38] Railway contractors Messrs. Burn and Co. made a similar argument, adding to it their personal experience of dealing with fraudulent Indian workers. They reported that workers had taken about one lakh of rupees in advance for the work that they had not done, and there was little hope of recovering even one-twentieth of this money through the civil courts. They described the case of a Noonea worker who owed about Rs. 500 to the company, but the case had been going on for 17 months now and nothing was known about the worker's whereabouts.[39]

A year after the 1859 Breach of Contract Act, whose reach at the time extended only to presidency towns, a new act, specifically intended for railway construction and other public works, was passed. The Employers' and Workmen's Disputes Act IX was passed in 1860, regulating employment relationships between contractors/employers and workers and service providers at construction sites, including railway-, canal-, and bridge-building sites, throughout colonial India.[40] Such industry-specific contract laws to meet the demands and problems of particular employers remained a key feature of the colonial state, reflecting its direct interest in creating and disciplining labour markets. In the case of tea plantations in Assam, the Assam Contract Act of 1865 overshadowed the general Bengal Native Labour Act III of 1863. While the latter act allowed criminal prosecution of tea workers in the case of refusal or abandonment of their contract, the 1865 Contract Act gave European plantation managers the power to arrest absconding workers. Nitin Varma argues that penal labour laws were made to ensure that workers, once contracted, had no bargaining power, accepted lower wages and poor and unhealthy working conditions, and remained settled on the plantations.[41] The act affirmed what Nitin Varma articulates as the private control of labour by European plantation owners.[42] Tirthankar Roy and Anand V. Swamy propose that the penal laws in tea plantations were a solution to a specific 'contractual' problem, which was the practice of giving advances to workers in order to recruit them. Where costs of recruitments were significantly higher in terms of bringing workers from northern and central India to Assam, such as in the Brahmaputra Valley and the Surma Valley in Assam, employers used penal laws to minimize the risk of losing upfront recruitment costs. The authors assert that planters in the Dooars region of North Bengal never used penal labour-laws as their costs of recruiting workers from Chota Nagpur were significantly lower.[43]

Ian J. Kerr, who studied the making of the 1860 Act in great detail, argued that this act, like that of 1859, derived its spirit from the British Master and Servant laws, under which servants could be prosecuted for breaches of contract.[44] While under the 1859 Act fraudulent behaviour *after taking an advance* was punished, under the 1860 Act, workers could be prosecuted even if no advance had been paid to them. It gave more powers to railway authorities, engineers, and contractors to subordinate workers. Kerr shows that the 1860 Act was a direct response to a wage dispute between workers and contractors building the GIPR railways at Bhor Ghat in 1859.[45] On the one hand, it allowed the settlement of wages between workers and contractors, and on the other, it gave contractors the power to prosecute workers who had entered into a voluntary contract to provide goods, labour, and other services, but *neglected* or *refused* to meet the specific predetermined terms, or *absconded*. A magistrate could impose a fine of Rs. 20, or in lieu of a fine compel *specific performance* of the contract by the worker, and in the case of non-compliance could send the worker to prison for up to two months.[46]

Kerr pointed out that additional features of the 1860 Act were the use of special magistrates to settle disputes, summary administration of the law, and a clause barring any appeal against a magistrate's decision. He suggested that while the act might have provided some relief to workers in wage disputes, its purpose was to strengthen the hold of capital over labour and criminalize defiance by workers. However, he found hardly any evidence of this act being invoked at railway construction sites, other than at canal construction sites in Punjab, and even there, the 1859 Act was invoked more.[47] Mohapatra argues that the effect of these laws lays not so much in their actual implementation, but in their use as a threat to coerce workers into accepting unfavourable and unfree work conditions.[48]

Figure 2.1 Mhow-ke-Mullee Viaduct, 3,000 men employed, Khumnee Hill, 1856.
Source: Photograph by Alice Tredwell, courtesy Huseby Bruk AB.

Joseph Stephens' Contracts

Stephens signed several contracts for services (for the supply of stones, baskets, lime, etc.) and for hire (of workmen and artisans). From the very beginning, he was aware of the implication of the laws described earlier and of the power of contracts. He himself had served under an apprenticeship contract with his brother-in-law and was under contract to various large contractors, and later directly to the GIPR. The whole railway construction operation relied on a series of hierarchical contracts—between the colonial state and the GIPR, between engineers, surveyors, inspectors, skilled railway workers, and the GIPR, between contractors, between contractors and European subcontractors and the GIPR, between European contractors and subcontractors and native worker headmen or goods suppliers.[49] Contracts ensured that railways were built in a stipulated time, and the work done was accountable in the courts. We find several unsigned contracts and various drafts of contracts in English and the vernacular, suggesting that Stephens wrote these contracts himself and later corrected them. His contracts highlight the role of stamps, bond papers, witnesses, clear terms and obligations, signatures, and dates of contract and delivery of services in shaping the labour-capital relationship at construction sites.

Let us begin by analysing Stephens' earliest contracts with stone suppliers and masons while he was constructing a bridge for the Nagpur extension line near Alasana village in Shegaon Taluka in 1862. The first contract that we find was with a mason headman, Reembhy Casseembhy (dated 16 September 1862).[50] The contract, on a Re. 1 government-stamped paper, reads as follows (Figure 2.3):

> I, Reembhy Casseembhy, hereby agree to complete for Messrs. J. S. Wells and J. S. F. Stephens the masonry in the 7–30 ft girder bridge at 53–23 Nagpoor Extension by the 31st January 1863 at the following rates.

Rubble with coursed face work	Rs. 8 and 5 annas per cubic yard
Blocking course	Rs. 16 per cubic yard
Ashlar	Rs. 1 and 4 annas per cubic yard

> I Reembhy Casseembhy also agree to have the work taken out of my hand at any time if it should not proceed with sufficient rapidity to give satisfaction to Messrs. J. S. Wells and J. S. F. Stephens.
>
> In case the above mentioned work should not be completed by me by the 31st January 1863 I forfeit 20 Rupees per day for every day exceeding that time.
>
> Witness, L. Pereira (signed by both parties)

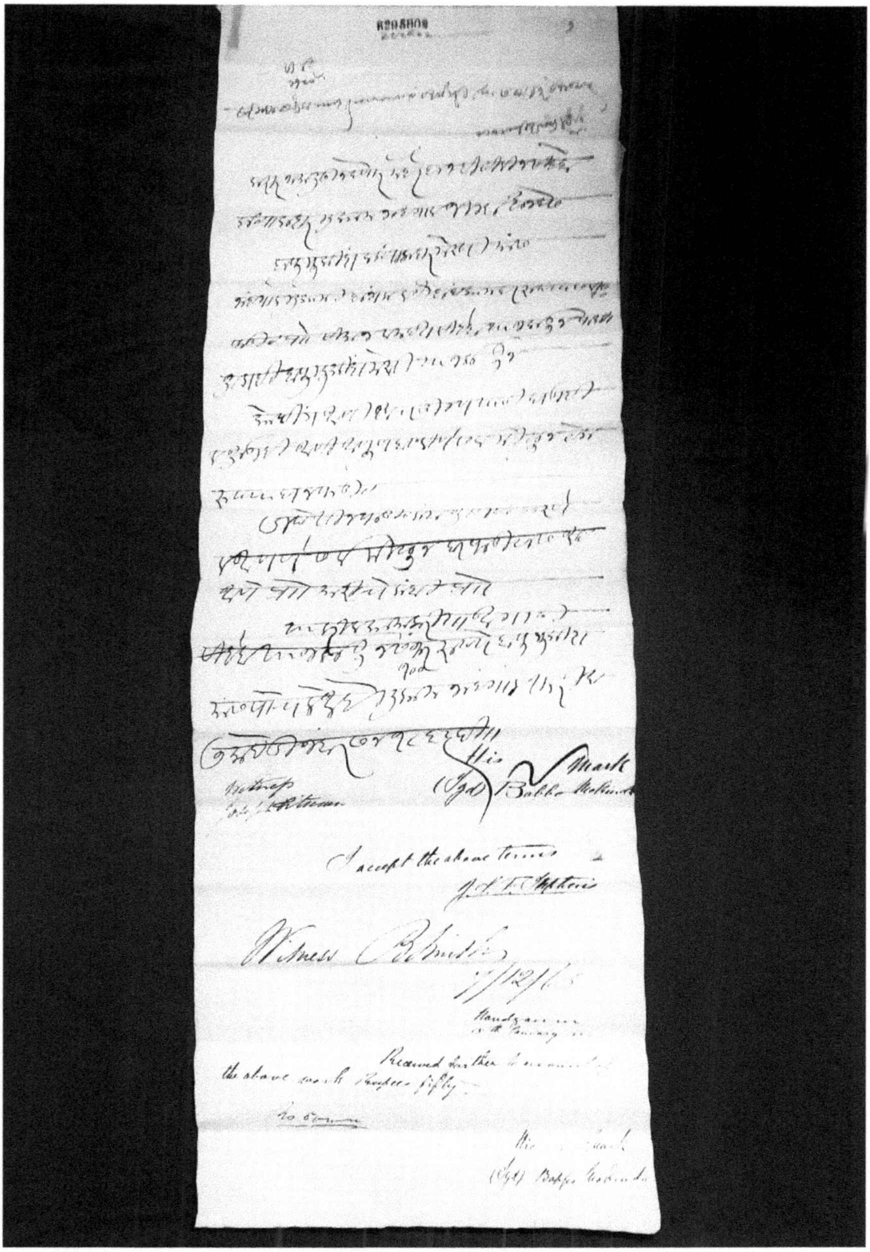

Figure 2.2 Part I, A copy of Stephens' contract in Modi script dating from 1865.

Source: LNU, HA, JSA, Box F1B:1.

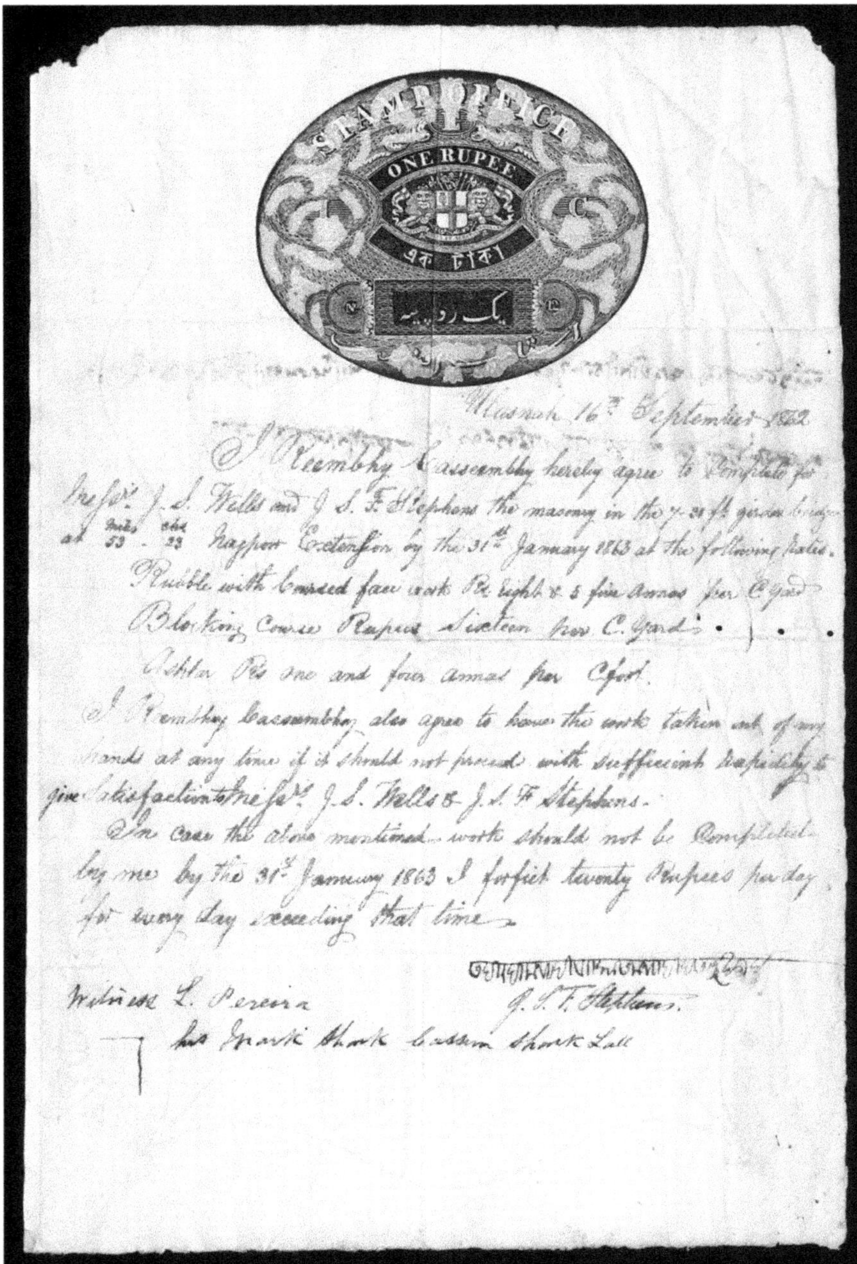

Howrah 16th September 1862

I Reembhy Casseembhy hereby agree to Complete for Messrs J. S. Wells and J. S. F. Stephens the masonry in the 7-31 ft girder bridge at Mile 53 - chs 23 Nagpore Extension by the 31st January 1863 at the following Rates.

Rubble with Coursed face work Rs eight & 5 five Annas per C yard

Blocking Course Rupees Sixteen per C. Yard

Ashlar Rs one and four annas per C foot.

I Reembhy Casseembhy also agree to have the work taken out of my hands at any time if it should not proceed with sufficient Rapidity to give Satisfaction to Messrs J. S. Wells & J. S. F. Stephens.

In case the above mentioned work should not be Completed by me by the 31st January 1863 I forfeit twenty Rupees per day for every day exceeding that time.

Witness L. Pereira

J. S. F. Stephens

his Mark Sheik Cassim Sheik Lall

Figure 2.3 Original copy of the contract between Stephens and Reembhy Casseembhy.

Source: LNU, HA, JSA, F1B:1.

Although contracts on a simple sheet of paper or by word of mouth were also contracts in the eyes of the law, Stephens showed more legal awareness.[51] Most of his contracts involved not only the terms and dates of contracts but also names and signatures of witnesses, body marks as marks of identification, signatures and names of both the parties, exact dates, and sometimes stamp paper and validation of the contract by a clerk.

The earlier contract is a classic example of subcontracting at the lowest level between a European and an Indian worker. Stephens' archive answers Kerr's complaint about the difficulty of locating archival material at the lowest level of railway construction. We should remember that these contracts were not a replacement for Indigenous forms of labour control and recruitment; rather, contractarian ideology supplemented and harnessed these power structures.[52] By subcontracting portions of works to different native mason maistries (gang headmen), Stephens was able to relieve himself of the direct responsibility for recruiting and entering into contracts with individual workers. Rather than reducing dependence on intermediaries, contracts strengthened the position and role of intermediaries vis-à-vis workers and contractors. Subcontracting reduced Stephens' task more to that of a supervisor, inspector, designer, and facilitator. In such a work setup, contracts assumed a significant role, as the actual work depended on the subcontractor's ability to finish the job or provide finished material on time.

The contract presented here reflected Stephens' anxiety about Casseembhy's (in)ability to complete the expected fixed task on the bridge on time and for the pre-agreed wages. The first term in the contract was that in the event that Stephens found the work of Casseembhy [and his workers] slow, he had the right to remove Casseembhy. In such a situation, we get no sense of what would have been the terms of his removal. The second condition was an extension of the first concern of the employer, which was about the work being delayed. A financial penalty clause was added. If the work was not finished on time, Stephens had the right to fine Casseembhy Rs. 20 per day until it was completed. This fine, interestingly, is equal to the total fine a magistrate could impose if a 'fraudulent' mason was punished. We see here that the contract is not just structuring the employer-employee relationship or determining the obligations of the mason, but also encapsulating the anxieties of Stephens and the everydayness of work: wages, fines, work to be done. It is this drive to encapsulate such everyday anxieties of the work process and the uncertainty of work that would receive more attention in future contracts. We could actually read, through these contracts, the conflictual history of railway construction in modern India.

Although signed by the mason Casseembhy, the terms of the contract appear to be one-sided. These were Stephens' conditions. The two 'free' parties were clearly not *equal* parties. The contract reflected Stephens' distrust of Indian workers, embodied his interests, and legitimized his power to fine the mason outside court. While the magistrate could only fine Casseembhy Rs. 20 if he refused or neglected the terms of his contract, Stephens added another layer of pecuniary punishment (Rs. 20 per day) as part of those terms. He combined the specific performance theory with some form of the monetary damage theory. While the court ensured that the contract terms were met through the specific performance theory, the contract allowed Stephens to claim monetary damages for delays, not just specific performance with a delay. This important aspect of the contractarian ideology remains obscured if we only focus on the law of contract.

This did not mean, though, that Stephens was not equally worried about the desertion of workers or satisfactory completion of the project on time at the pre-agreed cost. Satisfaction is an elusive category and was never clearly set out in contracts. It was defined on a daily basis by Stephens, who was himself under the constant supervision of GIPR inspectors to ensure that he completed his contracts as per the guidelines of the GIPR engineer. The financial penalties stipulated by Stephens reflected the larger hierarchical contractual world of railway construction. Thus, if a contractor failed to complete his tender on time, he was liable to pay a fine of Rs. 200 per week.

Stephens makes no mention of any advance being paid to Casseembhy. Although the 1860 Act did not require such a criterion to prosecute workers for breach of contract, the practice of making an advance payment was rampant. His future contracts included a mention of the exact advance paid. But why did this change occur? First, contractors ensured that the advances paid were mentioned on paper as they were the core of business practice in a competitive labour market; and second, in the case of non-compliance by workers, contractors could approach a magistrate and demand punishment of the worker or strict performance of the clauses under one of the two Acts.

The freedom and concerns of workers were subordinated to the language used by the employer in the contract. The contract does not tell us the fears and anxieties of Casseembhy. Was he worried that Stephens might not pay his exact wages on time? We will see later that this obscuring of workers' concerns in contracts entailed ambiguities in the everyday relationship between labour and capital, which at times took a conflictual turn.

To obtain the stones on which Casseembhy worked, Stephens entered into contracts with Vaddar stone suppliers. We find drafts of four contracts on behalf of his agent Wells with four different Vaddar suppliers. Only one of them was signed. The opening and closing language of these contracts was very similar to that of the one presented earlier. The only difference between the one signed and the three unsigned contracts was as regards the advance payment made and the conditions of employment. In the contract with Cheema Suttoo Woodari, the advance mentioned was Rs. 500; for Balla Nagappa, it was again Rs. 500; for Hanumunta Luximon, it was Rs. 250; and for Bheema Hanumanta, it was Rs. 125. Wells signed the contract with Hanumunta Luximon, although his advance was not the lowest. Perhaps Luximon was more reliable than the others and provided decent stones. However, in his contract, there was an additional clause that did not appear in the other three. This may have been an important reason why Stephens selected Luximon.

> It is further agreed that the said Hanumunta Luximan must remain on the works until his services are no longer required.[53]

Was Stephens at liberty to add any clause he liked to the contract? It appears so, although only on the basis of negotiations with the workers. Contracts, for him, became legal documents and means by which he navigated the terrain of everyday work, not just the overall structuring of the labour-capital relationship. In his correspondence, Stephens never complained of a short supply of labour or material, but rather of late delivery of services or labour and the quality of the work. Intense competition for hard-working and reliable labourers and good materials, and uncertain working conditions (rain, disease, drought, famine, rural areas being cut off), forced contractors to draft highly unequal contract terms and to go with those suppliers who took a relatively small advance and provided unlimited supplies as per their demands.

Let us look at the language of contracts from 1864 1865. A contract with Shaik Alle Shaik Jullal regarding hedging between Nidungere (Nandgaon) and Jalgaon on the GIPR Contract No. 12 line, dating from 23 September 1864, included the following terms:

> The above-mentioned distance to be completed in six weeks and *if I fail to complete* the above works I agree to have the work taken out of my hands and to forfeit Rupees 1 on every ninety-six lineal yards. I have done many or may have done, or receive for the same Rupees six. The work to be executed to the satisfaction of Stephens and the Company's engineers and *fifteen per cent of the value of the work to be retained by Mr. Stephens till the completion of the contract.*[54]

Another contract dated 7 November 1864, with Fukera Yemma and Bicka Beiro, the rubble stone suppliers, stressed that they would supply stones for buildings on the GIPR line between Chalisgaon and Mhaswad station at the rate of Rs. 6 for every hundred stones. '*The stone had to be of a good quality* and each stone not to be less than 1/3 of a cubic foot', the contract stressed. Further, they were bound by a severe deterrent penalty of forfeiting 'one Rupee per hundred cubic feet of all stone delivered in case they stop delivering before they have 5000 cubic feet of stone delivered should that quantity be required.'[55]

The contract with Shaik Alle Shaik Jullal speaks of the everyday nature of work patterns at these construction sites. First, punctual delivery of the work/services was critical. Second, easy removal of the defaulting party and monetary recovery of any losses incurred were ensured before the work commenced, Third, wages were fixed beforehand for the work to be done in the future. Fourth, wages/costs were only to be paid after the double-layer inspection carried out by Stephens and the GIPR's engineer. And finally, to ensure that all these were achieved smoothly, 15 per cent of the wages/costs were to be withheld until the work had received final approval. The latter was of great significance because of the contractual nature of railway construction in this period. In the event that the company engineer found Stephens' work unsatisfactory, Stephens could force the worker to redo it as per the terms of his contract at no extra cost. Withholding of wages was a popular practice adopted by European and Indian employers to bind, discipline, and coerce workers in factories, plantations, and workshops. Stephens' growing experience of projects informed his negotiations with Indian workers and suppliers, and this, in turn, was reflected in his contracts.

In his contract with Fukera Yemma and Bicka Beiro, Stephens reserved the right not to pay the agreed rates to them if they failed to deliver 5,000 cubic feet of stones '*should they be required*'. Stephens wanted an unhindered, indefinite supply of stones, and the best thing for him was to make sure that the clause was there in the contract. However, apart from withholding of wages, a novel element was added in these two agreements that further subordinated workers. They could forfeit their wages, in full or in part, in the event of non-compliance with the contract. Robert Steinfeld shows that in nineteenth-century America, where laws did not allow the criminalization of breach of contract, employers relied on this popular device and other harsh pecuniary methods to coerce workers to complete their contracts.[56] Harsh pecuniary measures, Steinfeld remarks, were as punitive as imprisonment and could be more dangerous for workers, as they left them two choices: to continue to provide labour or to go without wages and suffer starvation ('a more disagreeable alternative to labour').[57] As pointed out earlier, Stephens applied a double layer of punitive measures—using both contracts and laws. But there is an excessive emphasis on pecuniary measures, and contracts worked as self-acting mechanisms.

In his later contracts, we find additional economic means of punishing defiant workers and suppliers. One contract signed in 1867 between Stephens' agent George Peck and the stone supplier Perajee Kerappa stated that Perajee would supply no less than 'twenty brass of good black stone', each brass comprising 100 cubic feet of stone, at the rate of 12 rupees per brass. However, in the event of him failing to do so, the contract imposed a severe monetary penalty:

> Should the said Perajee Kerappa not supply the full quality of stone above specified within one month from this date, the said Perajee Kerappa agrees to accept from the said George Peck rupees ten only per brass & this agreement will in such case be considered null & void.[58]

The power to end the contract lay with the employer, and with no risk of them suffering punitive measures. In another contract dated 23 October 1866, with the lime suppliers Rajaram Chintaman and Mahomedjee Hakimjee, Stephens devised yet another economic measure to secure his interests. Here, he demanded a third-party guarantor. The two were to supply best-quality lime to Stephens at Akola station at a fixed rate and had taken an advance. The contract included an agreement with the guarantor and stated:

> I Durjeebhoy Doorabjee hereby bind myself to become security in the sum of Rupees two hundred for the due fulfilment of the above contract.[59]

Chintaman and Hakimjee may have been new to the profession or the region, and hence a guarantee was required. Nevertheless, we have seen how Stephens' contracts tightened his grip over Indian workers and suppliers, ranging from imposing pecuniary fines to securing a guarantor, and from withholding to forfeiting of wages. We need to view these measures in the light of his relationship with workers and suppliers on the ground. This may give us some clue as to why contracts were so important in building the railway and sustaining colonial capitalism.

Contracts and Everyday Work Relations

Stephens' correspondence with his father, George, tells us that something went wrong with one of his contracts in early 1864. Consoling his son, his father wrote, 'You must be careful in future contracts to have a clause binding them to provide materials in proper time, or to pay a heavy fine in damages.'[60] It is interesting to see how a father based at a Danish university, who has never been to India, is counselling his son on how to administer his relationship with Indian workers.

In the early years, when he was working under Lee and Watson on the bridges on the Nandura—Jalamb—Alasana—Shegaon line, Stephens seems to have employed coolies, masons, and stone dressers without a written contract. If he did enter into such contracts, these have not survived in the archive. His daily jottings in his diary give an account of the relationship he had with labour contractors in the early days. The diary records that he had employed masons of the headmen Sultanbhoy and Succarams to dress stones at Jalamb quarry and workers of the headmen Yemmas, Ebrahim, Peragees, and Sapanas at the Alasana and Moregaon bridges.[61] One group produced the required stones and the other built the bridges. Uninterrupted working by the two groups was necessary for Stephens' own contract.

Stephens usually settled wages at the end of the month. He invited workers to his bungalow where he kept all his accounts. In his diary, he noted that the days wages were paid were usually full of tension and conflict. On 20 April 1863, Vaddar masons of Sultanbhoy and Succarams, who worked at the Jalamb quarry extracting and dressing stone, came to his bungalow demanding their pay. It was a bit early for their monthly wages,

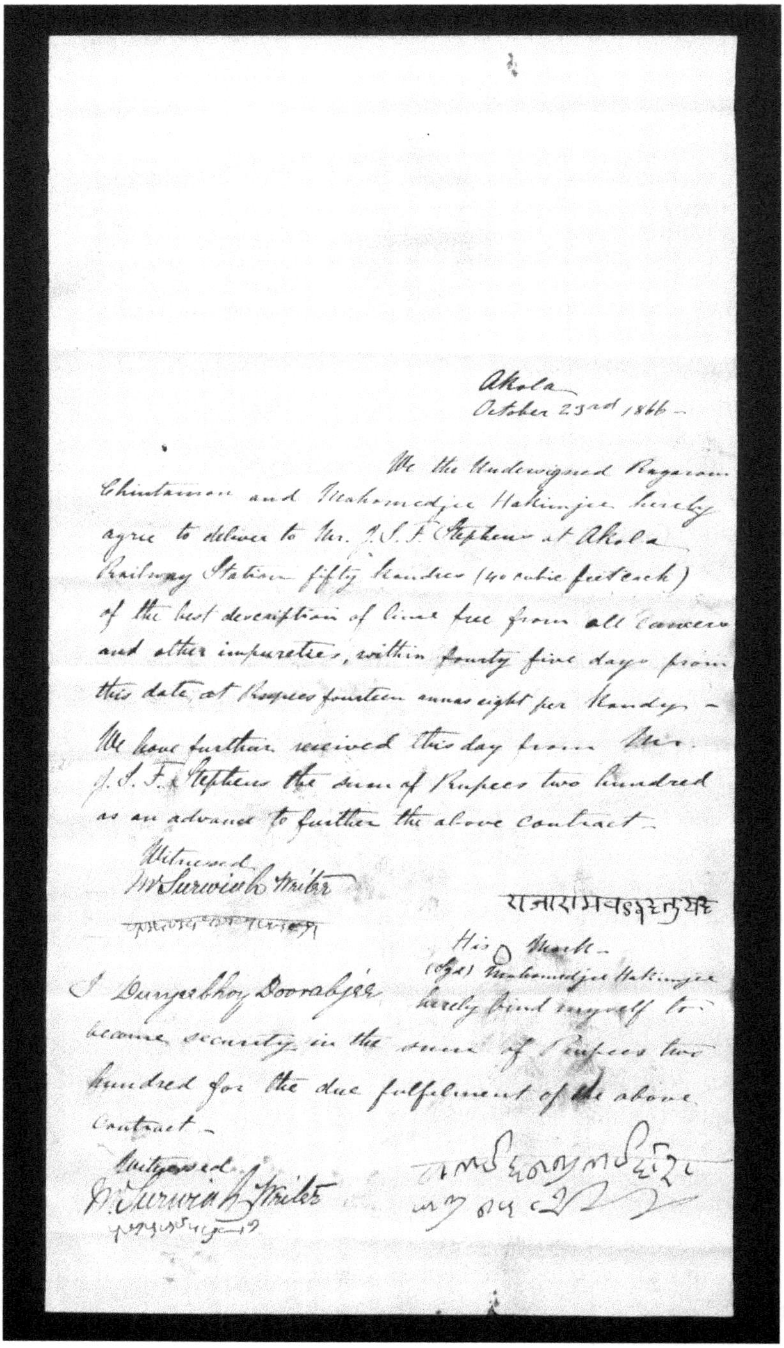

Akola
October 23rd/1866 –

We the Undersigned Ragaram Chintaman and Mahomedjee Hakimjee hereby agree to deliver to Mr. J.S.F. Stephen at Akola Railway Station fifty kandies (40 cubic feet each) of the best description of lime free from all Cancers and other impurities, within fourty five days from this date, at Rupees fourteen annas eight per Kandy. – We have further received this day from Mr. J.S.F. Stephens the sum of Rupees two hundred as an advance to further the above contract.

Witnessed
M. Surwiah Writer

His mark –
(Sgd) Mahomedjee Hakimjee

I Dunjeebhoy Doorabjee hereby bind myself to become security in the sum of Rupees two hundred for the due fulfilment of the above contract –

Witnessed
M. Surwiah Writer

Figure 2.4 Contract with lime supplier, with a third-party guarantor contract.
Source: LNU, HA, JSA, F1B:1.

but Stephens was willing to pay them. However, a wage dispute arose. He wrote that while 15 workers of Succarams took the wages offered, Sultanbhoy's workers refused to accept them.[62] It is possible that Stephens may have made deductions for absence and laziness, as records of daily attendance by workers and the amount of work done were kept by a clerk. The workers do not seem to have agreed to these deductions. Anyhow, they left his bungalow late in the night without a settlement. The next day, they did not show up for work at the quarry. 'The men have refused to work', noted a worried Stephens.[63] This was perhaps his first direct encounter with workers' protests. Although it was the day of a native festival, Stephens was sure that Sultanbhoy's men had rebelled. Succarams' men had also joined the protesters. Stephens was ill, but he was worried that work on the bridge might stop if stones did not reach the site on time. He had to seek the help of other labour contractors. A sick Stephens met Ebrahim and Yemmas and asked if they could provide men who could work at the quarry and continue to supply stones. Ebrahim and Yemmas agreed to do so.

On 23 April, however, Sultanbhoy visited Stephens' bungalow and promised to get his men back to work. Stephens cancelled the verbal contract given to Ebrahim and his men. The same evening, workers of Peragees and Sapanas who were working on the Alasana bridge came over to his bungalow demanding their wages. It was almost the end of the month for the wages, which were usually settled around the 25th. But these workers also refused to take the wages offered.[64] As before, perhaps they could not agree on the amount of work they had done, the days they had attended work, and the fines they had incurred. Next day, when Stephens went to inspect the work, he found that Peragees' and Sapanas' workers had not turned up. Workers failed to appear the next day as well.[65] It was hot, but Joseph decided to ride his horse to Jalamb (about 9 km from Alasana) to check whether Sultanbhoy's men were at work at the quarry. He reported that they were being lazy and that the work was progressing very slowly.

The matter of payment arose again on the Saturday afternoon, 2 May 1863, when Sultanbhoy's men demanded their wages. This time, after a lot of trouble, a settlement was reached.[66] The wage dispute with the Alasana bridge workers had also been settled, as they were back at work, but Stephens noted that they were being 'lazy'. On 21 May 1863, he wrote: 'Rode to the 10–4 foot culvert at Ullusna [Alasana] and gave the men a bullying about lasyness [laziness] in my absence.'[67] In the next three to four days, Joseph remeasured all the work and the quality of the stones, and paid the workers' wages.

A similar event had occurred at the Moregaon bridge site, where masons had downed tools and refused to work. It happened on a Saturday that was a holiday, but word spread that the workers had rebelled. On Monday, Sultanbhoy's men did not turn up. Stephens was forced to enter into a verbal contract with Beerubhoy to supply his men. He wrote, 'Asked Sultanbhoys men to come to work and they refused in presence of Louis [a labour agent] and one Peragies men'.[68] As much as it was an insult to Stephens, these people were key witnesses to the workers' defiance. Next day, he contacted Sultanbhoy via Louis and asked why he was not sending his men to work. Sultanbhoy told him that they had nothing to eat and were demanding wages, to which Stephens replied, 'I could not believe it to be the case but if it really was so I would gladly give his men Rs. 2 each if they would start work.'[69] Sultanbhoy said he would ask his men and get back to him in the evening, but Stephens heard nothing. Pressed for labour, Stephens sent his men to look for Sultanbhoy. The latter sent the reply that his men would not come unless they were paid full wages and their arrears. Stephens, unwilling to lose his control over them, threatened that if they did not return to work the arrears of wages would be forfeited.[70] On 20 May, Stephens secured masons from other sources. He sent Louis Pereira to Naggery (Nagzari) to look for masons, met Beerubhoy, and gave a letter of recommendation (character) to Kasebhoy in return for masons.[71] Next day, Beerubhoy's masons came to work, and Ebrahim also promised to send his, setting aside the recent last-minute cancellation by Stephens.[72] The contractor Lee accused Stephens of snatching his masons from Naggery, which means that some of the masons from there had also joined Stephens' work.[73] Work started with full force. Soon, on 23 May, Sultanbhoy visited Stephens to settle the account, demanding to have a look at his workers' attendance sheets, which Stephens refused to show him. In return, Sultanbhoy refused to hand back chisels—masonry tools provided by Stephens (Figure 2.5).[74] Stephens continued to suffer from the lack of masons until a new gang of Vaddars joined him on 8 June.[75] We should not see these conflicts as arising only between headmen and Stephens. Rather, they indicate the presence of a deeper tussle between workers and headmen, workers and Stephens, and Stephens and headmen. However, the lowest grades of workers were in a seamless web of exploitation at the hands of contractors, overseers, and muccadams. It was not only contractors who denied and cut their wages, but also muccadams who extracted a portion of workers' wages for absence and re-employment.[76]

These two incidents suggest how fluid and uncertain mofussil labour markets were, where workers had significant bargaining powers because they worked as a group and owing to a competitive labour market, and contractors like Stephens had to rely on a network of worker headmen to get their work done. References to the paper economy are also very interesting, with contractors not just writing contracts and keeping records of wages and attendance, but also writing letters of recommendation for good worker headmen. We see that workers refused unfair wages, contested the claims of employers, and threatened to desert their work. In such a scenario, stricter contracts and laws became a critical tool in controlling and subordinating the power of labour.

We also find that mere contracts, wage advances, and threats of prison and withholding of wages could not ensure a regular flow of work. Stephens

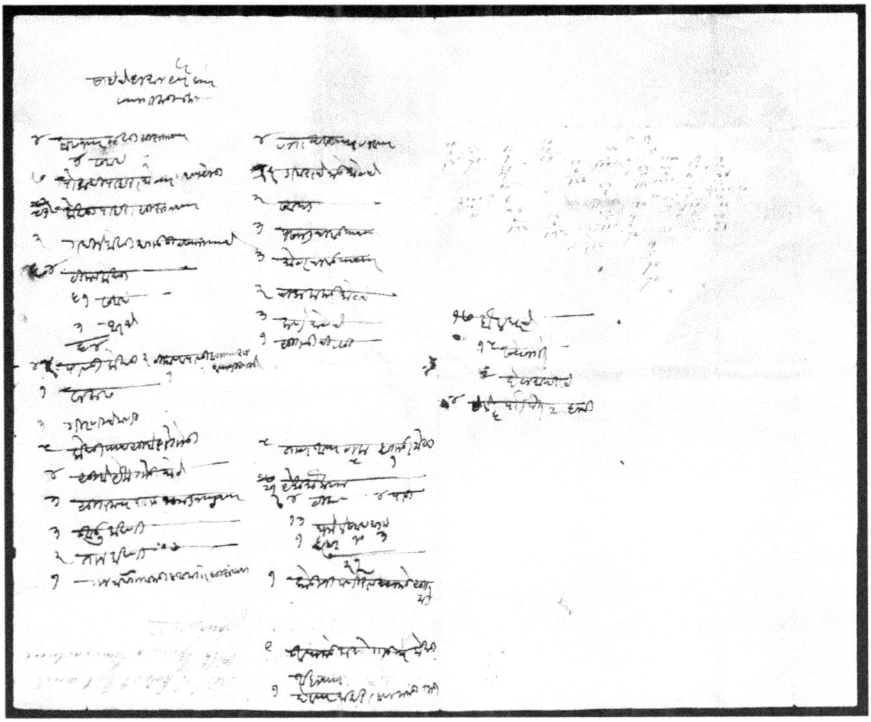

Figure 2.5 List of tools and tent and with Yemma Muccadam, January 1865.

Source: LNU, HA, JSA, F1B:1.

trained and disciplined the labour force through his daily inspections, supervisory visits, 'bullying', employing agents who supervised work, precise instructions, settling conflicts among workers, paying wage arrears on time, and sharing brandy with headmen and workers.[77] Often, he found to his surprise that workers had absented themselves without notice, and only realized this when he visited the worksite in the morning or the evening. In the afternoons, he usually took rest. The attendance registers that he kept were filled in by the native headmen, whose loyalty he had to secure by higher wages, or by a clerk. Workers absented themselves on customary holidays such as Nag Panchami, Muharrum, or Diwali, or on a rainy day without notice.[78] He often complained that workers did not work in his absence as they would do in his presence.[79] When he found that work was slow, he abused and scolded the workers. At one point, when he was experiencing labour problems due to the defiance of workers, he noted in his diary, 'Gave Saccaram a blowing up at Moorgaum for not getting on with the work.'[80]

These conflicts and negotiations must have informed young Stephens' understanding of the emerging labour-contractor relationship, as he used contracts as a tool to suppress workers' bargaining powers and resistance at work. From 1864, he put native labour contractors under agreements. We have draft copies of two such contracts. On 2 June 1865, he entered into an agreement with Garwa Jovana and Kundo Amuda Muccadams, who were to supply workmen at Amravati station and had taken an advance of Rs. 130.[81] On 12 June 1865, he drafted another agreement with Gorwapa and Kundo Amunda (already under agreement with him) to meet his growing demand for labour. The contract went:

> Mr. Gorwappa and Kundo Amunda have this day received from Mr. JSF Stephens *a further advance of Rupees one hundred as advance* to procure sixty workpeople (40 men 20 women) and hereby bind themselves to retain the above number of men if required on Mr. Stephens works at Oamrawattee as long as he may want them.[82]

The role of muccadams (headmen) was to supply the required number of workmen and to make sure that they finished the work properly. It is interesting to note the dual functions of the contract—protecting the advance offered and procuring a constant supply of labour, both male and female. Underlying these terms was the contractors' assumption that the Indian worker was dishonest.[83] While it is true that advances had become a tool used by the colonial state and employers to subordinate labour,[84] a huge advance itself needed to be protected in a competitive labour market. Williamson (probably an agent of Stephens looking over the work at Sheagaon station) wrote to Stephens on 22 October 1865, stressing that workers had been away due to Diwali and that the supplier of chunam (lime) was not responding to his repeated requests. Workers had come to his place demanding payment of wages in a dissatisfied tone. He wrote that if their wages were not paid, they would leave the work. Instead of paying the wages, he gave an advance of one rupee to unskilled workers and two rupees to skilled workers. Even after that, the workers seemed dissatisfied and did not turn up for work the next morning. We do not know whether he threatened them with legal proceedings. But in the case of the chunam supplier, he did threaten to take legal action. It was only after that he supplied the chunam.[85] Perhaps it was after this incident that he asked for a third-party guarantor for Chintaman and Hakimjee (Figure 2.4). The amount of the guarantee (Rs. 200) matched the advance paid. This innovative contract term was part of Stephens' ability to negotiate the everyday risks of the profession and the labour-capital relationship.

From Contract Laws to Actual Contracts

Let me elucidate the salient points of this essay by referring to a debate between Jairus Banaji and Neeladri Bhattacharya. We have seen that classical political economy and liberal interpretations had pushed a manufactured understanding of the contract as a voluntary engagement between two legally equal and free parties. Contracts were and are presented as a critical facilitator of the transition from slavery and coerced and forced labour to free wage labour. Employers bought labour power from workers, who sold their labour for their own survival. This buying of labour power with money was carried out with the help of a nineteenth-century legal reinvention: contracts. The worker sold his or her labour power for a limited period; otherwise, he or she would be 'converting himself [herself] from a free [wo]man into a slave, from an owner of a commodity into a commodity'.[86] As per this logic, coercion and force were inconsistent with the ideology of a contractual relationship and were a relic of the past. We have seen that this understanding had been powerfully challenged by realist and critical legal studies scholars, and by legal and labour historians such as Robert Steinfeld, Prabhu Mohapatra, and Ravi Ahuja, among others. Building upon Karl Marx, Jairus Banaji added his critique of the liberal readings of contracts. He argued that contracts are voluntary only 'in appearance'. Underneath the illusion of freedom lie coercion, unequal power relations, and inability on the part of the worker to enter into a contract on an equal footing.[87] He suggested that coercion is pervasive under capitalism, and to make sense of the reality on the ground, he distinguished 'relations of production' from 'forms of exploitation'. His understanding allows us to make sense of the presence of hired wage labour under the feudal mode of production and feudal bondage labour under capitalist relations.[88] Banaji points out that wage labour relations under capitalism were not particularly 'free', as these relations involved various forms of control over labour. Debt servitude and advance wage payments were means by which workers were integrated into capitalism and their will and labour power controlled.[89] Banaji's arguments are critical to understanding the labour relations that were developed in the construction of the GIPR railway. What was essentially happening at these construction sites was a tightening of employers' control over wage labour which, itself, was in and out of the primitive accumulation process, depending on the availability of work. When not hired, construction workers slipped back into the agrarian world to work as farmers and labourers. Ian Kerr called these construction workers semi-proletarians and semi-peasants.[90]

Neeladri Bhattacharya questioned Banaji's understanding of law, contract, and capitalism as being modular in nature, even though Banaji attempted to move out of a reductionist and fixed understanding of the labour-capital relationship. He argued that, for Banaji, as for the critical legal studies scholars, law appears to be no more than a form of deception, an illusion of freedom and rights, while underneath it reproduces the class interest of the exploiter.[91] Bhattacharya rereads Marx to suggest that law has a 'constitutive presence' and a field of 'dialogue and struggle' in which workers reconstitute the terms of their subordination and integration into capital, question their logics in everyday practice, and interpret 'the illusion of freedom' for the benefit of their own interests.[92] Bhattacharya's critique is centred on an understanding that the subordination of the worker to capital is not a given phenomenon (the model), but is historically constituted through contestation, power struggles, cultural mediation, and reinterpretation from below (the practice). This essay's findings suggest that contracts derived their meanings and contents in specific historical settings. Workers and work presented new challenges to employers, which were reflected in their contracts. The fascinating work of Z. M. S. Siddiqi shows that, although Indian labour contract laws created unfree labour relations and tied workers into slavery-like work conditions, there was always scope for a liberal interpretation of the 1859 Breach of Contract Act, and judges exercised it and dismissed employers' unjust complaints.[93]

Nevertheless, neither Banaji nor Bhattacharya refer to any specific contracts, their changing language, or ways in which workers give or are disciplined to give their assent to a new work regime or question it. When we analyse the contents of contracts, we find that their meanings were not just limited to sustaining or producing and questioning an unfree labour regime. The role of the contract appears to be wider, more complex, and more specific to local situations. The building of colonial railways without contracts would have been a slower process. Stephens completed most of his big contracts on time and got paid. Contracts and a favourable state and legal structure certainly contributed to his profits and the rise in his fortunes immediately after the launch of two powerful acts: the Act of 1859 and the Act of 1860, which criminalized desertion by workers and gave employers legal power to coerce them to fulfil their contracts as per the will of employers.

This study has drawn attention to material that forces us to move our discussion from contract laws to the actual contracts, and from there to analyse the labour-capital relationship. Contracts and contract laws did become tools of employers and the state to tie workers into unequal work conditions, restrict their autonomy, and subordinate them to the logic of capital. But there is a need to integrate contracts, laws, customs, workers' resistance, and everyday work relations into a seamless web which, at one and the same time, resolved and complicated this labour-capital relationship. When we dig deeper into the language of contracts, we find that issues such as satisfactory work, the details of wage advances, withholding of wages, security money and guarantors, employers' anxieties and fears about Indian workers, and delivery of work of good quality and on time were critical for employers. The latter were not simply interested in criminal breaches of contract; rather, they were interested in using contracts as self-acting powerful legal documents to govern the everyday work regime. Tirthankar Roy and Anand V. Swamy's arguments, discussed earlier, suggests that employers with higher cost for labour recruitment sought penal labour laws of varying degree to protect their 'upfront investment'.[94] Although the advance was not a criterion for criminal breach of contract in the 1860 Act relating to labour and services at the construction sites, their reading of contractual labour laws from the perspective and needs of business/industry (tea in this case) opens up an alternative interpretation in legal-business history. A reading of Stephen's contracts shifts our attention from laws to transaction documents, which offer a comprehensive understanding of the emerging work regime on railway construction sites and their close relationship with the contractarian ideology. His contracts refer to employers' varied concern and anxieties, which included labour insubordination, loss of wage advance, wage disputes, non-completion of projects on time, and irregular delivery of specified services and products.

The railway construction work regime of the 1860s was also supported by other mechanisms to discipline labour. Whereas the legitimacy of the contract's power as a legal document was derived from the labour laws, the laws did not alone define the scope and power of a contract. The contracts empowered employers to frame the quotidian conditions of the work, which the law was incapable of doing. As a result, employers were able to utilize both the force of the labour laws and of the contract. We see that, while Stephens and his agents relied on the ultimate threat of imprisonment and legal proceedings for completion of tasks and services, the contract itself included penalty clauses that were far harsher than the punishment laid down in the law. Such clauses, referring for example to fines for delays, the need for a guarantor who guaranteed the advance payment and punctual and satisfactory completion of the work, and withholding of a portion of wages/costs, show contracts to have been very much part of the work process, taking away the anxieties of everyday business.

Stephens' contracts also offer powerful evidence to weave into a larger history of capitalists' distrust of labour. Distrust was the subterranean logic that allowed employers to empower themselves against workers through legal and extra-legal means. The fear that workers would steal, rebel, abscond, or be lazy has guided and motivated employers throughout history to invent various mechanisms to control and discipline labour. Contracts and laws are just one of those mechanisms. Others have included withholding of wages, everyday frisking, religious and non-religious moral lessons, schooling, biometrics, and camera surveillance.[95]

Workers are recalcitrant bodies, and labour power is not easily extractable. Once contracted, workers responded to employers' expectations and behaviours in ways that challenged the terms of their contracts. The differing language of contracts suggests that workers had the power to challenge employers' expectations, defy their orders by not attending work, demand wages at unusual times, refuse to accept unfair wages, and transfer their work to other contractors. If employers did not pay wages or advances on time, workers, often collectively, demanded their wages and arrears, surrounded employers, and threatened to leave work. They demanded increases in wages even after signing their contracts.[96] And Stephens used contracts as a powerful antidote to tame these recalcitrant behaviours. However, he also used extra-legal tools such as beating, refusing to pay wages, and denying future work to insubordinate workers.

Acknowledgements

I would like to thank Professors Prabhu Mohapatra and Gunnel Cederlöf, and other participants of the workshop 'The Underbelly of the Empire: Workers, Contracts, and the Social Economy of the Industrial Turn' (December 2019) for giving their valuable feedback on this chapter. An extended discussion with Professor Mohapatra helped me to revise the chapter.

Notes

1 Michael E. Tigar and Madeleine R. Levy, *Law and the Rise of Capitalism* (New York: Monthly Review Press, 2000).
2 Ibid., ch. 17.
3 To understand the history of the evolution of the modern-day employer-employee contract relationship see, Simon Deakin and Frank Wilkinson, *The Law of the Labour Market: Industrialization, Employment, and Legal Evolution* (Oxford: Oxford University Press, 2005), pp. 41–109. They alert us to the fact that the English contract laws have medieval and early modern origins. Seeing them as inventions of capitalism is ahistorical.
4 Amy Dru Stanley, *From Bondage to Contract Wage Labor, Marriage, and the Market in the Age of Slave Emancipation* (Cambridge: Cambridge University Press, 1998).
5 Henry Sumner Maine, *Ancient Law* (London: Murray, 1861).
6 Julian S. Webb, 'Contract, Capitalism and the Free Market: The Changing Face of Contractual Freedom', *Law Teacher,* 21/1 (1987), pp. 23–31. Daniel Song, 'From Status to Contract (and Back?): A Historiography of Contract Law and the Transition to Capitalism', *Ex Post Facto*, XXII/Spring (2013), pp. 127–8.
7 M. R. Anderson, 'Work Construed: Ideological Origins of Labour Law in British India to 1918', in Peter Robb (ed.), *Dalit Movements and the Meanings of Labour in India* (New Delhi: Oxford University Press, 1999), pp. 87–120.
8 Karl Marx, *Capital: A Critique of Political Economy*, 1, trans. Ben Fowkes (London: Vintage, 1977), pp. 925–6.
9 Michel Foucault, *Discipline and Punish: The Birth of the Prison* (London: Vintage, 1995).
10 For an insightful analysis of these positions, see Song, 'From Status to Contract'.
11 Song, 'From Status to Contract', pp. 129–31.
12 Song, 'From Status to Contract'; Morton J. Horwitz, *The Transformation of American Law* (Cambridge: Harvard University Press, 1977).
13 Tigar and Levy, *Law and the Rise of Capitalism.*
14 Robert J. Steinfeld, *Coercion, Contract, and Free Labor in the Nineteenth Century* (Cambridge: Cambridge University Press, 2001), pp. 47–62. See also Deakin and Wilkinson, *The Law of the Labour Market*, pp. 75–76, who argue that although the Employers and Workmen Act (1875) had removed the criminal breach of contract clause, workers could still be sent to jail for 40 days under the 1869 Debtors Act in case they failed to pay damage to employers.
15 Ibid., pp. 74–84.
16 See Karuna Mantena, *Alibis of Empire: Henry Maine and the Ends of Liberal Imperialism* (Princeton: Princeton University Press, 2010).

17 Linnaeus University (LNU), Huseby Archives (HA), George Stephens Archive (GSA), E1:3a, Letters from George Stephens to Joseph Stephens for the year 1860–1.
18 Abbott was appointed in 1857 along with 11 other officials. The list included Edward Dangerfield (surveyor), who later supervised Joseph's work. See The British Library, India Office Records (BL, IOR), List of Agreements No. 1 (officers), L/AG/46/12.
19 LNU, HA, Joseph Stephens Archive (JSA), F1A:1, Telegram from Abbott, 27 April 1864. On the making of Joseph Stephens as a contractor, see Alexander Bubb, 'Class, Cotton, and "Woddaries": A Scandinavian Railway Contractor in Western India, 1860–69', *Modern Asian Studies*, 51/5 (2017), pp. 1369–93.
20 LNU, HA, JSA, F1A:1, Letter from Joseph Stephens, 15 February 1865.
21 Huseby Estate, Joseph Stephens' diary 1862, January 1862 entries.
22 Bubb, 'Class, Cotton, and "Woddaries"', p. 1385.
23 Ibid., pp. 1387–8.
24 Ian J. Kerr, 'On the Move: Circulating Labor in Pre-Colonial, Colonial, and Post-Colonial India', *International Review of Social History*, 51/S14 (2006), pp. 85–109; Bubb, 'Class, Cotton, and "Woddaries"'; Ravi Ahuja, 'Labour Unsettled: Mobility and Protest in the Madras Region, 1750–1800', *Indian Economic & Social History Review*, 35/4 (1998), 381–404; Ravi Ahuja, 'Labour Relations in an Early Colonial Context: Madras, c. 1750–1800', *Modern Asian Studies*, 36/4 (2002), pp. 793–826.
25 Ian J. Kerr, 'Working Class Protest in 19th Century India: Example of Railway Workers', *Economic and Political Weekly*, 20/4 (1985), pp. PE34–40.
26 Bubb, 'Class, Cotton, and "Woddaries"', pp. 1391–2.
27 See Ian J. Kerr, *Building the Railways of the Raj 1850–1900* (New Delhi: Oxford University Press, 1995); Ian J. Kerr, 'Labour Control and Labour Legislation in Colonial India: A Tale of Two Mid-Nineteenth Century Acts', *South Asia: Journal of South Asian Studies*, 27/1 (2004), pp. 7–25.
28 Kerr, 'Labour Control'.
29 Peter Robb (ed.), *Dalit Movements and the Meanings of Labour in India* (New Delhi: Oxford University Press, 1999), Introduction; M. R. Anderson, 'Work Construed: Ideological Origins of Labour Law in British India to 1918', in Robb (ed.), *Dalit Movements*, pp. 87–120; Dipesh Chakrabarty, *Rethinking Working-Class History: Bengal, 1890–1940* (Princeton: Princeton University Press, 2000).
30 Prabhu Mohapatra, 'From Contract to Status? Or How Law Shaped Labour Relations in Colonial India 1780–1880', in Jan Breman et al. (eds), *India's Unfree Workforce: Of Bondage Old and New* (New Delhi: Oxford University Press, 2009), pp. 96–125.
31 Ravi Ahuja, 'The Origins of Colonial Labour Policy in Late Eighteenth-Century Madras', *International Review of Social History*, 44/2 (1999), pp. 159–95.
32 Ibid., pp. 176–7, 185–95.
33 Prabhu Mohapatra, 'Regulated Informality: Legal Constructions of Labour Relations in Colonial India, 1814–1926', in Sabyasachi Bhattacharya and Jan Lucassen (eds), *Workers in the Informal Sector: Studies in Labour History, 1800–2000* (New Delhi: Macmillan India Limited, 2005); Mohapatra, 'From Contract to Status?', pp. 96–125.
34 Mohapatra, 'Regulated Informality'.
35 Mohapatra, 'From Contract to Status?'; Prasannan Parthasarathi, *The Transition to a Colonial Economy: Weavers, Merchants and Kings in South India, 1720–1800* (Cambridge: Cambridge University Press, 2008); Nitin Varma, *Coolies of Capitalism: Assam Tea and the Making of Coolie Labour* (Berlin: De Gruyter, 2017); Hugh Tinker, *A New System of Slavery: The Export of Indian Labour Overseas 1830–1920* (London: Hansib, 1993).

36 Nitin Sinha, '"Servant Problem" and the "Social-Subaltern" of Early Colonial Calcutta', in Nitin Sinha, Nitin Varma, and Pankaj Jha (eds), *Servants' Pasts: Sixteenth to Eighteenth Century South Asia*, 1 (Hyderabad: Orient Blackswan, 2019), pp. 311–44; Nitin Sinha, 'Contract, Work, and Resistance: Boatmen in Early Colonial Eastern India, 1760s–1850s', *International Review of Social History*, 59/S22 (2014), pp. 11–43; Chitra Joshi, 'Dak Roads, Dak Runners, and the Reordering of Communication Networks', *International Review of Social History*, 57/2 (2012), pp. 169–89.
37 Mohapatra, 'Regulated Informality'.
38 National Archives of India, Delhi, Home Department, Judicial Branch, Proceedings 13 January 1863, Prog. No. 10–12, Repeal of Sec. V Regulation 7 of 1819, Letter from Sir Wemyss, Bart, Beharampur, to R. J. Scott, dated 15 August 1862, 8. I am thankful to Nitin Varma for providing me a copy of this file.
39 Ibid., Letter from Messrs. Burn and Co. Railway Contractors to S. C. Bayley, Collector and Magistrate of Shahabad, dated 25 August 1862.
40 Maharashtra State Archives, Public Works Department, Railway, 1860, Vol. 23, No. 364, File, Act IX of 1860 Regarding the speedy settlement of disputes between workmen engaged on railways and their employers.
41 Varma, *Coolies of Capitalism*, ch. 2.
42 Ibid., pp. 48–66.
43 Tirthankar Roy and Anand V. Swamy, *Law and the Economy in Colonial India* (Chicago: University of Chicago Press, 2016), pp. 105–13.
44 Kerr, 'Labour Control'; Mohapatra, 'From Contract to Status?', pp. 116–17. For a detailed analysis of master—servant relations in Britain and contracts in the nineteenth-century Anglo-American world, see Steinfeld, *Coercion, Contract, and Free Labor*.
45 Kerr, 'Labour Control'.
46 Ramkrishna Chatterjee, 'Masters and Servants: Their Relations in Early Industries—A Case Study', *Proceedings of the Indian History Congress*, 41 (1980), pp. 585–92.
47 Kerr, 'Labour Control', pp. 19–21.
48 Mohapatra, 'From Contract to Status?', p. 121.
49 Bubb, 'Class, Cotton, and "Woddaries"'. See also the chapter by Radhika Krishnan in this volume.
50 LNU, HA, JSA, F1B:1, Contract dated 19 September 1862.
51 Mohapatra, 'From Contract to Status?', p. 119.
52 See also Ahuja, 'Origins of Colonial Labour Policy'; Nitin Sinha, 'Contract, Work, and Resistance: Boatmen in Early Colonial Eastern India, 1760s–1850s', *International Review of Social History*, 59/S22 (2014), pp. 11–43.
53 LNU, HA, JSA, F1B:1, Contract dated 29 September 1862.
54 Ibid., Contract dated 23 September 1864, emphasis mine.
55 Ibid.
56 Steinfeld, *Coercion, Contract, and Free Labor*, p. 17.
57 Ibid., pp. 17–19.
58 LNU, HA, JSA, F1B:1, Contract dated 20 May 1867.
59 Ibid., Contract dated 23 October 1866.
60 LNU, HA, GSA, E1:3a, Letter from George Stephens to Joseph Stephens, 7 March 1864.
61 Huseby Estate, Joseph Stephens' diary 1863, 20, 22, and 23 April 1863.
62 Ibid., 20 April 1863.
63 Ibid., 21 April 1863.
64 Ibid., 23 April 1863.
65 Ibid., 25 April 1863.
66 Ibid., 2 May 1863.

67 Ibid., 12 May 1863.
68 Ibid., 18 May 1863.
69 Ibid., 19 May 1863.
70 Ibid., 19 May 1863.
71 Ibid., 20 May 1863.
72 Ibid., 21 May 1863.
73 Ibid., 1 June 1863.
74 Ibid., 22 May 1863.
75 Ibid., 8 June 1863.
76 Ibid., 14 March 1863.
77 Ibid., 24 May 1863. Bubb mentions 'cherry-merry' being given by Stephens to placate workers and reward loyal ones. Bubb, 'Class, Cotton, and "Woddaries"', p. 1392.
78 Huseby Estate, Joseph Stephens' diary 1863, 12 August, 19 August, and 11 November 1863.
79 Ibid., 10 March 1863.
80 Ibid., 29 August 1863.
81 LNU, HA, JSA, F1B:1, Contract dated 2 June 1865, Pachora.
82 Ibid., Contract dated 12 June 1865, Bhuswal.
83 For a richer analysis of how colonial officials characterized Indian workers, which to some extent was informed by English notions of class morals, see Ahuja, 'Origins of Colonial Labour Policy', pp. 66–73.
84 Mohapatra, 'From Contract to Status?', p. 120.
85 LNU, HA, JSA, F1A:1, Letter from Williamson to Joseph Stephens, 22 October 1865.
86 Marx, *Capital*, pp. 270–1.
87 Jairus Banaji, 'The Fictions of Free Labour: Contract, Coercion, and So-Called Unfree Labour', *Historical Materialism*, 11/3 (2003), pp. 69–95.
88 Jairus Banaji, *Theory as History: Essays on Modes of Production and Exploitation* (Leiden: Brill, 2010).
89 Banaji, 'Fictions of Free Labour', pp. 79–80.
90 Kerr, 'Working Class Protest'.
91 Neeladri Bhattacharya, 'Lineages of Capital', *Historical Materialism*, 21/4 (2014), pp. 19–20.
92 Ibid., pp. 20–1.
93 Z. M. S. Siddiqi, 'Sanctions for the Breach of Contracts of Service (1843–1925)', *Journal of the Indian Law Institute*, 25/3 (1983), pp. 359–71. For a rough number of convictions and acquittals under various breach of contract laws, see National Archives of India, Delhi, Home Department, Judicial Branch, Proceedings 13 January 1863, Prog. No. 10–12, Repeal of Sec. V Regulation 7 of 1819.
94 Roy and Swamy, *Law and the Economy in Colonial India*, 105–14.
95 Marx, *Capital*; E. P. Thompson, 'Time, Work-Discipline, and Industrial Capitalism', *Past and Present*, 38 (1967), pp. 56–97.
96 Huseby Estate, Joseph Stephens' diary 1863, 9 March 1863.

References

Ahuja, Ravi, 'Labour Relations in an Early Colonial Context: Madras, c. 1750–1800', *Modern Asian Studies*, 36/4 (2002), pp. 793–826.

Ahuja, Ravi, 'Labour Unsettled: Mobility and Protest in the Madras Region, 1750–1800', *Indian Economic & Social History Review*, 35/4 (1998), pp. 381–404.

Ahuja, Ravi, 'The Origins of Colonial Labour Policy in Late Eighteenth-Century Madras', *International Review of Social History*, 44/2 (1999), pp. 159–95.

Anderson, M. R., 'Work Construed: Ideological Origins of Labour Law in British India to 1918', in Peter Robb (ed.), *Dalit Movements and the Meanings of Labour in India* (New Delhi: Oxford University Press, 1999), pp. 87–120.
Banaji, Jairus, 'The Fictions of Free Labour: Contract, Coercion, and So-Called Unfree Labour', *Historical Materialism*, 11/3 (2003), pp. 69–95.
Banaji, Jairus, *Theory as History: Essays on Modes of Production and Exploitation* (Leiden: Brill, 2010).
Bhattacharya, Neeladri, 'Lineages of Capital', *Historical Materialism*, 21/4 (2014), pp. 11–35.
Bubb, Alexander, 'Class, Cotton, and "Woddaries": A Scandinavian Railway Contractor in Western India, 1860–69', *Modern Asian Studies*, 51/5 (2017), pp. 1369–93.
Chakrabarty, Dipesh, *Rethinking Working-Class History: Bengal, 1890–1940* (Princeton: Princeton University Press, 2000).
Chatterjee, Ramkrishna, 'Masters and Servants: Their Relations in Early Industries—A Case Study', *Proceedings of the Indian History Congress*, 41 (1980), pp. 585–92.
Deakin, Simon and Frank Wilkinson, *The Law of the Labour Market: Industrialization, Employment, and Legal Evolution* (Oxford: Oxford University Press, 2005).
Foucault, Michel, *Discipline and Punish: The Birth of the Prison* (London: Vintage, 1995).
Horwitz, Morton J., *The Transformation of American Law* (Cambridge: Harvard University Press, 1977).
Joshi, Chitra, 'Dak Roads, Dak Runners, and the Reordering of Communication Networks', *International Review of Social History*, 57/2 (2012), pp. 169–89.
Kerr, Ian J., *Building the Railways of the Raj 1850–1900* (New Delhi: Oxford University Press, 1995).
Kerr, Ian J., 'Labour Control and Labour Legislation in Colonial India: A Tale of Two Mid-Nineteenth Century Acts', *South Asia: Journal of South Asian Studies*, 27/1 (2004), pp. 7–25.
Kerr, Ian J., 'On the Move: Circulating Labor in Pre-Colonial, Colonial, and Post-Colonial India', *International Review of Social History*, 51/S14 (2006), pp. 85–109.
Kerr, Ian J., 'Working Class Protest in 19th Century India: Example of Railway Workers', *Economic and Political Weekly*, 20/4 (1985), pp. PE34–40.
Maine, Henry Sumner, *Ancient Law* (London: Murray, 1861).
Mantena, Karuna, *Alibis of Empire: Henry Maine and the Ends of Liberal Imperialism* (Princeton: Princeton University Press, 2010).
Marx, Karl, *Capital: A Critique of Political Economy*, I, trans. Ben Fowkes (London: Vintage, 1977).
Mohapatra, Prabhu, 'From Contract to Status? Or How Law Shaped Labour Relations in Colonial India 1780–1880', in Jan Breman et al. (eds), *India's Unfree Workforce: Of Bondage Old and New* (New Delhi: Oxford University Press, 2009), pp. 96–125.
Mohapatra, Prabhu, 'Regulated Informality: Legal Constructions of Labour Relations in Colonial India, 1814–1926', in Sabyasachi Bhattacharya and Jan Lucassen (eds), *Workers in the Informal Sector: Studies in Labour History, 1800–2000* (New Delhi: Macmillan India Limited, 2005).

Parthasarathi, Prasannan, *The Transition to a Colonial Economy: Weavers, Merchants and Kings in South India, 1720–1800* (Cambridge: Cambridge University Press, 2008).

Robb, Peter (ed.), *Dalit Movements and the Meanings of Labour in India* (New Delhi: Oxford University Press, 1999).

Roy, Tirthankar, and Anand V. Swamy, *Law and the Economy in Colonial India* (Chicago: University of Chicago Press, 2016).

Siddiqi, Z. M. S., 'Sanctions for the Breach of Contracts of Service (1843–1925)', *Journal of the Indian Law Institute*, 25/3 (1983), pp. 359–71.

Sinha, Nitin, 'Contract, Work, and Resistance: Boatmen in Early Colonial Eastern India, 1760s–1850s', *International Review of Social History*, 59/S22 (2014), pp. 11–43.

Sinha, Nitin, '"Servant Problem" and the "Social-Subaltern" of Early Colonial Calcutta', in Nitin Sinha, Nitin Varma, and Pankaj Jha (eds), *Servants' Pasts: Sixteenth to Eighteenth Century South Asia*, 1 (Hyderabad: Orient Blackswan, 2019), pp. 311–44.

Song, Daniel, 'From Status to Contract (and Back?): A Historiography of Contract Law and the Transition to Capitalism', *Ex Post Facto*, XXII/Spring (2013), pp. 127–38.

Stanley, Amy Dru, *From Bondage to Contract Wage Labor, Marriage, and the Market in the Age of Slave Emancipation* (Cambridge: Cambridge University Press, 1998).

Steinfeld, Robert J., *Coercion, Contract, and Free Labor in the Nineteenth Century* (Cambridge: Cambridge University Press, 2001).

Thompson, E. P., 'Time, Work-Discipline, and Industrial Capitalism', *Past and Present*, 38 (1967), pp. 56–97.

Tigar, Michael E., and Madeleine R. Levy, *Law and the Rise of Capitalism* (New York: Monthly Review Press, 2000).

Tinker, Hugh, *A New System of Slavery: The Export of Indian Labour Overseas 1830–1920* (London: Hansib, 1993).

Varma, Nitin, *Coolies of Capitalism: Assam Tea and the Making of Coolie Labour* (Berlin: De Gruyter, 2017).

Webb, Julian S., 'Contract, Capitalism and the Free Market: The Changing Face of Contractual Freedom', *Law Teacher*, 21/1 (1987), pp. 23–31.

3 Bureaucracy and Ideologies of Control in British India

Social and Professional Networks and the 'Contract System' in Railway Building

Radhika Krishnan

Historians and economists working on the Indian railways refer to what they term the 'railway mania' of Britain in the 1840s, resulting ultimately in two principal achievements of the industrial revolution (the steamship and the steam engine) being brought to the colonies.[1] Multiple rationales have been offered to explain the spread of this 'mania' to India. Recounting the debate around the Indian railways, Bipan Chandra reminds us of the 'strong political and economic pressure' from textile manufacturers in Lancashire, who wished to access the vast supplies of cotton and wheat in India.[2] Apart from being a source of opulent raw materials, India could also become a huge consumer of textile and other products manufactured in Britain, Daniel Thorner points out.[3] In addition to the commercial and economic advantages, once put in place, the railways could be used to transport military personnel from one part of the vast colony to another in a relatively short time.[4] These economic and political justifications apart—many of which have been dealt with in great detail by a number of scholars of colonial India—we are left with the undeniable fact that railway construction remained a crucial endeavour of colonial rule in British India. The first passenger railway line in India, covering 34 km between Bori Bunder (Bombay) and Thane, was opened to traffic on 16 April 1853, barely 28 years after the world's first successful train ran between Stockton and Darlington in England in 1825. This was one of the first railway lines in the country. Before passenger trains were introduced, there were a few trains used to transport stone and other material, such as on the Red Hill line in Chennai in South India. The first short lines were followed by a rapid escalation of railway construction.[5] In Ian Kerr's estimate, by 1870, 'excluding Russia (and thus Russian Asia), fifty-five per cent of all operating railway mileage in Africa, Asia, and Latin America combined was located in India'. The fact that neither China nor Japan had operating lines at the time stresses the unique nature of railway construction in India.[6]

During these initial tumultuous years, the railway building project was held together by the 'contract' system. This was designed to protect private capital investment and to underwrite losses, and remained in place for

DOI: 10.4324/9781003317227-3

three-quarters of a decade from 1849.[7] Despite serious concerns being raised regarding the efficacy of this system (some details of which I will discuss in later sections of this chapter), the British administration decided to continue with it into the late 1860s. Scholars of railway history have by and large used an economic lens to explain this decision. In this study, I will contribute other rationales that go beyond economic rationalization of the work process to explain why the contract system remained in place for such a long time in India. The letters, correspondence, contracts, pay sheets, diaries, and accounts of the Anglo-Scandinavian entrepreneur Joseph Stephens allow us to look at the daily lived experiences of various actors within this system.[8] I use insights from this archive to argue that the social and economic relations that kept the contract system together were incompatible with utilitarian justifications of colonial rule in India. In other words, the nature of social and economic networks and relationships on the railway lines would have made their incorporation within direct colonial governance a difficult proposition. A distance, convenient perhaps, between the colonial administration and the everyday world of railway contracts had to be maintained. The roots of the contract system can thus be located not merely in the 'economic' sphere, but also equally in the social and political spheres.

'Contracts' in Railway Building: 'Macro' and 'Micro' Views

Scholars unravelling the complex history of railway building find themselves confronted with multiple archives. For years, historians and sociologists have pored over documents, in the process slowly piecing together various elements of the railway script along with its many different actors. The details are known to every student of Indian railway history: the nature of the first railway contracts, which were heavily premised on private enterprise; the state underwriting the possible losses of the railway companies; and the government's extensive supervision of railway policy and operations. In order to ensure private investment in railway construction and infrastructure, railway companies were guaranteed a return of 5 per cent per year on the capital they agreed to invest in India. In addition, the imperial government provided them with all the land they required, free of charge. In return, the state retained the right to stringently control and supervise the companies' affairs. The contracts typically ran for a period of 25 years, after which the government gave itself the option of buying back the lines from the private companies. As historical records and scholarship inform us, railway companies (such as the Great Indian Peninsula Railway (GIPR), on whose lines Joseph Stephens was awarded contracts) were successful in expanding the scale of railway lines across the country.[9]

To achieve this expansion, however, serious hurdles had to be overcome. Even as engineers employed by the railway companies and government employees supervising construction were dealing with the formidable material and technical challenges of building bridges and viaducts in decidedly difficult topographical and geological conditions, tensions between the various players routinely emerged. There were tussles over recruitment of labour, over the quality of materials used and the final construction, and over the apportionment of blame for delays and failed constructions.[10] Daniel Thorner, for instance, speaks of an 'inevitable' clash inherent in a situation where private contractors were intent on making 'handsome profits' from limited resources, while the state sought to ensure speedy, efficient, and high-quality construction using a minimum of resources.[11]

These tensions apart, however, the contracts signed between railway companies and the imperial government remained relatively simple in their essential design. It was, in a way, a matter of socializing losses and privatizing profits. When W. N. Massey, ex-Finance Minister of India, commented acerbically that 'it was immaterial to him [the English capitalist] whether the funds that he lent were thrown into the Hooghly or converted into brick and mortar,' he was possibly expressing the prevailing sentiment.[12] After all, excessive guarantees had been provided, thus vastly reducing the pressure on the railway companies to ensure profits. By the mid-1860s, as the time to rethink the original contracts drew closer, critical voices emerged. It was argued, even at the highest levels of government, that the state should take complete control of railway construction. This would make eminent economic sense, the argument went. Yet despite these vociferous criticisms of private investment in the railways and of the system of issuing contracts, the British secretary of state to India chose *not* to do away with the system. This is precisely the conundrum I seek to understand in this study. Why did the colonial state choose to continue with the contract system, at a time when the latter's limitations were obvious?

This question has certainly intrigued economic and railway historians of colonial India. Thorner, recapitulating the debate around private contracts, claims that the secretary of state negotiated new contracts with all the private railway companies except the Eastern Indian Railways on terms even more favourable to them than before. This, he further argues, was a source of great disappointment to the imperial government:[13]

> For three-quarters of a century after 1849, one or another variant of this 'semi-public' guaranteed interest system dominated the railway field . . . the *performance* of the railways . . . was markedly unsatisfactory. Yet, the slogan of 'private enterprise' was so compelling, particularly when bolstered by the political power of railway interests in London.[14]

Thorner, emphasizing the economic logic, argues that part of the reason lays in the imperial and economic demands on the colonial state, and the necessity to fund and fight a war in Afghanistan even as famines vastly diminished the state's resources. These arguments have in fact been echoed and validated by several scholars of railway history, who see pressing and increasing demands on the colonial government's stressed exchequer as an obstacle to self-financing and management of the Indian railways.[15] In other words, historians have essentially constructed what is primarily an economic argument to account for the curious continuance of the contract system.

In contrast, I seek to find answers in the social and professional worlds of the private contractors, rather than simply in the economic considerations of the colonial state. Sabyasachi Bhattacharya, tracing what he calls the 'financial foundations' of the British Raj, encourages us to identify the intricate web of often conflicting ideas and interests that underlie the policy making process.[16] He argues that the colonial state was subject to pushes and pulls exerted by several stakeholders, both within and without the colonial administrative machinery. Bhattacharya's work urges us to move beyond the idea of purely homogenous groups with neatly knit-together and carefully synchronized interests. He points out three types of 'pressure groups' that vary in terms of the 'homogeneity of interests, organisation and depth of consolidation, and specificity of objectives', which reveal complex dynamics between various actors.[17] Even though Bhattacharya observes their influence on public finances and policy, this is surely also a useful framework to understand railway building in colonial India. The contractors involved here were by no means a homogenous group, but they presented an instance of how local interests and social networks played a role in larger economic projects. Their concerns, lived experiences, machinations, and deliberations were integral parts of the larger dynamic in the imperial railway construction project.

Radhika Singha investigates labour recruitment in the decidedly different context of the First World War and explains the need to resort to formal and informal means of coercion and persuasion.[18] However, contractors working on the railway lines, unlike labour recruiters for the Imperial Army, could not utilize the state's formidable administrative reach to meet their labour requirements. For instance, prisoners in colonial jails could not be enlisted by private contractors for construction work on the railway lines. Nevertheless, much like their counterparts involved in military recruitment, they too had to resort to advance payments and bribes to ensure the continued presence of labour. It is here that the Joseph Stephens Archive (JSA) provides us with insights. As discussed in Chapter 1, the young Joseph Stephens was a small cog in the large wheel that was the contract system of Indian railway construction in the 1860s, and his documents provide us with an unusual view of exactly what railway building looked like to those who were most intimately involved with it. This archive, in a sense, provides a new lens through which to view the contract system. Writing railway history till now largely depended on what can be seen as a 'macro' view, in which the researcher has allowed official documents to speak. These documents were primarily Public Works Department files, letters between GIPR officials and the imperial government in London, long inspection reports detailing construction work on railway lines, details of inquiries into various complaints that cropped up from time to time on the railway lines, and police records. Between them, they have provided accounts of railway policy and railway construction by engineers and government officials.

Take, for instance, the familiar episode of the sudden collapse of the Mhow-ke-Mullee viaduct on the Bhor Ghat on 19 July 1867. While this was the 'most spectacular' accident on the GIPR lines, as Kerr puts it, such failures could hardly be dismissed as mere aberrations.[19] In the early years, 2,000 thousand bridges, buildings, and other masonry structures collapsed, all of these incidents being meticulously recorded and discussed at great length by the colonial administration:

> some of the early failures of railway bridges were caused by engineers not knowing how to prevent high water flows after the rainy season from scouring bridge foundations until they collapsed. On the other hand, some bridge failures, especially those involving masonry bridges or viaducts, were attributed to corrupt practices or 'scamping' to use the nineteenth century term when contractors cut corners in order to increase their profits. One member of the Governor-General's Executive Council (General Mansfield, the Commander in Chief of the Army) wrote in a minute dated 2 November 1867 that when he, Mansfield, 'was in Bombay Presidency, I used to hear a great deal of this bad scamping work'.[20]

This is a decidedly macro view of the situation, focusing on the official angst over railway building, with all its trials and tribulations. While it introduces us to the voice of the contractor, we are not privy to the day-to-day functioning of the contract system. The JSA, on the other hand, has the potential to shed new light on this official view. These documents, taken together, offer a counter-view to the official records, and consequently help us to access new and fascinating elements so necessary to the railway story. A letter to Joseph Stephens from his inspector, Mr. Peck, writing immediately after the Mhow-ke-Mullee disaster, is a case in point:

> But for the rain and difficulty in getting carpenters would have finished. . . . The Engineers in future will be very strict as regards material. A large bridge on the Bhoreghaut came down bodily the other day owing to inferior mortar. The papers have taken the matter up and are pitching into the Engineers with a vengeance.[21]

Clearly, there is potential in combining the government archives with the JSA to nuance and revise the historiography. In the process, this chapter seeks to explore additional dimensions to powerful railway narrative(s) in Indian history.

Exploring Social and Professional Networks on the Railway Lines

> In his No. 238/1056 of 29th June Captain Foord . . . applied for permission to let his work at a rate very considerably above that estimate to some European Contractors, which was refused by Major Price, then Public Works Department Secretary. . . . I who relieved Major Price in October, was consequently under the impression that the work was being carried out departmentally, or on the petty contract system and at the authorised rate. . . . I received in reply . . . in which not a hint regarding a Contractor is given, until in February I learnt while inspecting the work at Akola that it was being executed by a large Parsee Contractor who had been brought up from Bombay by Captain Foord . . .. he forwarded me a lengthy detailed contract specification under which Mr. Manoojee was working, unaccompanied by any Schedule of the Rates at which work was to be executed and giving little or no explanation.[22]

The aforementioned passage is an excerpt from a letter written in 1868 by Captain C. J. Mead (officiating secretary to the resident at Hyderabad in the Public Works Department) to the secretary of the Public Works Department of the Government of India. Mead wishes to highlight a breach of rules which in his opinion would have the effect of causing the cost of Halting Barracks, then under construction at Akola, Maharashtra, to escalate considerably from the sum anticipated and sanctioned by the government. Kerr, as he sets out to map various facets of railway building in India in the nineteenth century, speaks of 'mistakes, mismanagement', and even 'malfeasance', that were to be found on the railway lines.[23] Colonial documents in the British Library and the National Archives of India (NAI) describe scandals and tales of transactions, euphemistically termed 'informal', that all too often characterized the ambitious colonial railway project. The above-quoted excerpt from documents in the NAI, for instance, speaks of a somewhat unsavoury episode in which a large contract was quietly and dubiously handed over to a Parsi contractor. However, when documents at the NAI speak of impropriety in transactions, the JSA adds crucial detail and texture to the narratives. As I have shown elsewhere, the latter deepens our understanding of the nature of the social, professional, and economic relations operating on the GIPR works in western India.[24]

Joseph Stephens' early diary entries, those for 1860–1 forming part of the JSA and those for 1862–3 to be found in the library at Huseby, make clear the deeply social and personal roots of his future professional and economic relationships. From the very beginning of his stay in India, Stephens' career was bolstered by these largely informal social networks. The JSA reveals that from his first job offer to the initial contracts and partnerships he later procured, his social connections with British men employed in the GIPR and the British government (connections built over long horse rides, hunting sessions with fellow Europeans, dinners, and parties) played a key role. Social interactions among Europeans were interspersed with professional dealings and continued when Stephens had become well entrenched in the world of GIPR contracts. One finds the social mingling seamlessly with the professional, as complex networks formed within the European community.

Exchanges between Europeans in the larger railway network took on various forms. At one point, a police case was filed against two cartmen employed by Stephens. His inspector who supervised his work, Louis Pereira, informed him of the crisis, and suggested that he intervened. Stephens immediately wrote to Captain Bushby (presumably the person in charge in the local administration) and requested him to 'oblige' by releasing the men, since Stephens' works were 'being detained'.[25] Little is known of what subsequently transpired, but it is likely that these exchanges indicate access to powerful officers in the British administration which European contractors were able to make use of. They also point to the informal manner in which conflicts could be managed. In addition, there were informal, barter-like exchanges between contractors, such as when Stephens lent his donkeys for ballasting at a viaduct in exchange for a chain and some drills.[26]

Image 3.1 Engineers, contractors, and other visitors to the Bhor Ghat works on the Great Indian Peninsular Railways, 1856

Source: Photograph by Alice Tredwell, courtesy Huseby Bruk AB.

There were requests too, such as the one from a Parsi Indian contractor, Dadabhai Dorabjee, asking Stephens not to employ a 'native Maistry' (labour recruiter and leader of gang labour) whom he had discharged. This is an interesting indication of the camaraderie of the contractor (Indian or European) vis-à-vis the 'other', that is the worker.[27] 'Your old carpenter Ithoba . . . [and the discharged Maistry] both of them have formed partnerships. Oblige me by not letting them have any work further by you,' writes Dorabjee. He is attempting here to overcome the cultural, Orientalist othering of the non-European by invoking the necessity of solidarity between contractors against the coming together of workers.[28] Occasional bickering and even intense competition over the procuring of labour and railway contracts apart, routine, casual exchanges remained a defining characteristic of these relationships. Insults, raging verbal battles and occasionally physical ones, and threats of litigation (some carried out, some not) among the Europeans in the railway network were not unheard of.[29] Both the GIPR and British government officials were called upon to arbitrate on relevant cases. In March 1867, for instance, Stephens wrote to R. F. Stack, an assistant engineer at the GIPR, relating an episode in which his workers had approached him with a complaint regarding a European inspector, Mr. Harris. He was said to have misbehaved towards the workers on a worksite. Responding to the complaints against Harris, the GIPR at first refused to condone his violent behaviour, but then reiterated that he was indeed in the right to interfere in Stephens' work when he was carrying out contracts for the GIPR. He was even appreciated for doing so.[30]

In the correspondence of Stephens' inspectors who were in charge of engaging labour, the inspectors claim that they faced a perpetual shortage of labour and funds to get the work done. They routinely talk of the need to pay advances to engage labour—the money 'of course' being below the amount due.[31] 'You will see . . . that I have paid some 8 annas and some 7 annas and no one less than 6. I have cut a day or two from a good number of them which answers as well as giving a lower rate . . . I think the men are better satisfied,' writes Peck, indicating some of the processes of clerical manoeuvring involved in drawing up the pay sheets and ensuring profits.[32] Much wheedling and negotiation occur over advances and payments, while dissatisfaction with labour also appears as a recurring theme.[33]

This cajoling and convincing took on many interesting, often informal forms. In August 1862, Stephens adds in his meticulously maintained accounts several entries for 'cherimerry' (a small gift in the form of money or in kind) given to two cartmen. Records of 'gifts' of 'cherimerry' to the workmen are found quite often, as are records of goats presented to the Vaddars ('Woodaries') who broke stones for Stephens. In yet another instance, Stephens mentions that he gave the Vaddars 'a bottle of brandy [to] cheer them up'.[34] The workmen were disappointed with their payments, having been told that they were all in debt, and they finally left with the bottle of brandy. Blacksmiths, cartmen, Vaddars—all received these gifts of brandy.

One can thus trace a strategy of inducement to ensure that work continued. Moreover, widely differing wage rates between individuals and between sites appear in the pay sheets. Masons, for instance, are paid anything between 8 and 16 annas per day. Dhiraj Kumar Nite, who has systematized the wage sheets, argues in this volume that wage rates were negotiated by workers, and were thus often a function of their 'social identity'.[35] Social custom, he states, continued to play a role in how labour relations were negotiated.

Another interesting episode tells us much about the dynamics of labour on the railway lines. In February 1863, Stephens writes in his diary of an accident on one of the worksites: a small boy broke one of his legs when a lot of earth fell on him. Some days later, Stephens mentions that the boy 'died and was buried and the father and mother made a great noise over him'.[36] A sum of Rs. 6 had to be handed over to the parents, which 'quietened' them, Stephens adds.[37] What strikes us here is the informal nature of negotiations at play. Many aspects of work agreements on the railway line were informal, such as compensation paid after accidents on the worksite. There is scant evidence of written assurances of compensation; and the actual amount of compensation paid could well have been the result of micro-negotiations and entreaties.

Cooperation, competition, and conflict thus played out in multiple ways as contractors, engineers, supervisors, and Indian labour worked with often differing interests towards building the railways. Complex and interwoven networks were formed, human contacts (both social and professional) were built, the latter perhaps being as crucial to the railway project as the physical infrastructure that was simultaneously 'constructed'. In fact, some of these networks and connections proved to be enduring, as is made apparent for instance by Stephens' communications with the GIPR's resident engineers Edward Dangerfield and Alex Mackenzie after he settled in Sweden following his purchase of an ironmaking and agrarian estate, Huseby, in 1867. Stephens, now running the estate, continued to invoke his previous professional relationship with Dangerfield and Mackenzie, offering to sell iron and timber to the GIPR.[38] His relationship with Mackenzie is the most telling. The JSA is replete with acerbic exchanges between the two. Yet social and professional connections are not so fragile, and Stephens attempted to maintain his earlier personal and work-related association with Mackenzie long after withdrawing from work on the railway lines in India.

Bureaucracy and Ideologies of Control in British India

In this final section, I shall return to the question that I raised at the beginning of the chapter. Why did the colonial administration decide to continue with the contract system in railway construction, despite there being strong views against it amongst its officials? The officials were of the opinion that the contracts were quite a heavy burden on the exchequer. The government had to 'make good the deficit' that arose from the need to ensure guarantees to the railway companies operating in India.[39] Despite what seems to be an overwhelming body of opinion, the very same colonial state decided to continue with the contract system for three-quarters of a decade. The answer to this seeming conundrum, I will argue, had to do with the nature of the colonial state and the manner in which it went about addressing matters of governance, as much as it was mired in economic concerns.

In the preceding section, we got a glimpse of Joseph Stephens' everyday life as a railway contractor. We saw the networks that were strung together by contractors such as Stephens—networks which connected a range of actors in the elaborate script that was railway construction in 1860s India. The working of these formal and informal networks required negotiations between the various actors, negotiations that sought to address labour shortages, disputes over wages, and resentment over compensation for accidents and the like. It was not uncommon to see the individual contractor and his associates deal with these problems directly. The colonial administration was called upon to arbitrate on some of these episodes (as the fracas over the European inspector Harris's behaviour, for instance, indicates). However, the JSA suggests that many of the problems arising on the railway lines, especially related to recruiting and managing labour, were resolved by individual contractors without the active intervention of the colonial administration. The colonial state is somewhat absent from the daily travails of constructing a railway line. One could argue that in effect it had contracted out not only railway construction but also much of the business of dealing with the day-to-day problems arising from it.

Contractors such as Stephens drew upon social and professional networks as they sought to address obstacles that appeared on a routine basis. These networks were the very bedrock of the railways, as both the engineers' and the contractors' success depended on them. Arranging labour, dealing with a dispute amongst contractors or between workers and their employers, and negotiating wages and compensation all required these networks. The process of managing and recruiting labour, for instance—which included dealing with disgruntled workers and various problems that routinely arose on the worksite—required the invocation of these networks and the informal arrangements they were embedded in. In the JSA, we get a sense that the framework of these networks remained largely informal. Managing dissatisfied workers and negotiating payments took place through informal communications and settlements, without the formal intervention of the colonial state.

It was perhaps in the management of labour that these networks were most often called upon. It is worth mentioning at this point that the imperial administration had put in place a series of legislative enactments (the Railway Acts of 1854, 1869, and 1890) to deal with recalcitrant workers and their demands. Laura Bear, Ian Kerr, and others have usefully introduced us to the dynamics of the British railway bureaucracy.[40] Bear, commenting on the nature of labour in the Indian railways project, usefully describes the framework in which labour was framed and perceived by the empire, and consequently by the colonial railway administration. She tells us that the labour management regime was characterized by punitive fining, racial employment hierarchies, instability of service, and arbitrary practices of dismissal.[41] In response to this regime, Ian Kerr speaks of simultaneous deference and defiance amongst workers. As he looks at several dimensions of workers' engagement with the railways project, ranging from recruitment, work, and working conditions to workers' resistance, he discusses not just the 'oppression, exploitation, brutality and harsh conditions at work-sites', but equally the lack of passive acceptance of these conditions.[42] Resistance, he points out, appeared in 'many forms', as 'inaction', as 'direct' and even violent action, even as 'subtle and complex methods to control a work process'.[43]

Contractors, in turn, were called upon to respond to these 'subtle and complex' methods. As we have seen, they did so in multiple ways. For the colonial state and its officialdom, the contract system allowed these issues to be outsourced into a domain which was not within their immediate, everyday purview. It was an attempt to distance the administration from the complexity of everyday governance. The system, for all its financial porosity and inefficiency, also allowed the colonial state to remain at a distance from its own subjects. While financially unprofitable, the contract system thus persisted owing perhaps in part to the possibility it offered of governing from a distance. At this juncture, the wider historical context needs to be kept in mind. In the early 1860s, the colonial empire in India was recovering from the jolt to its authority arising from the 1857 'mutiny' (or the first 'War of Independence', as the revolt against the British saw it). The empire not only had successfully squashed the fiery rebellion from its colonized subjects but had also been alerted by it to the need for a more sensitive acknowledgement and reception of colonized Indians and their practices, especially in matters that could provoke social and religious sentiments.

If we look at the construction and management of railway lines as a problem of governance for the colonial state, it may not be very surprising that the British retained the contract system for this purpose, in defiance of the economic logic. It would be useful here to examine the broad ideological contours of British governance in India. Eric Stokes, as we know, delineated the philosophical foundations of colonialism, tracing for us the role utilitarianism played in establishing a popular discourse around and rationale for it.[44] Several other scholars have spoken of the utilitarian ideal and its embedding within colonial policy. The impact of initiatives driven primarily by utilitarian motives—even with the distortions that accompanied their implementation—was considerable. Indian society could be 'reformed' and 'transformed' through legislation, and through the imposition of 'legal' law and order administered by the colonial state, went this argument. At the heart of the argument was a deep sense that Indians were to be taught the virtues of governance and efficient civil administration. The application of utilitarianism meant deeply ingrained notions of 'the rule of law applied aggressively by an efficient judiciary' and of the cult of 'efficiency'. Moreover, the means were more important than the ends and needed to appear blameless, thus necessitating 'administrative and legal rationalism'. It was through this application of morally justifiable means that the 'world of chaos' and 'uncultivated society' that was India, to quote James Mill, would be rid of political and religious despotism. We find the roots of a powerful discourse that sought to continuously make a case for 'just governance', untainted by embarrassing tales of vile behaviour, crass profiteering, dubious deals, and rampant corruption. Mistakes as well as deliberate deviations from principles might have marred this grand utilitarian project.[45] Nevertheless, imperial governance was arguably based on the ideological foundations of having to demonstrate 'justness', morality, and legality.

How were these values of morality and legality to be showcased on the railway lines? Ian Kerr mentions in his detailed and well-argued book on mismanagement in early railway construction how the government repeatedly tried to safeguard itself against what it saw as massive scandals.[46] As scholars of colonial India have pointed out, implementing ideas of the rule of law, based on 'just' and 'rational' principles, was not an easy task. More often than not, colonial officials realized that governing and the 'rule of law' were embedded in processes of daily negotiations and contestations. The system that was put in place was highly centralized, but the manner of its implementation was deeply embedded in context.[47] I suggest that the decision to continue with the contract system in the construction of railway lines was shaped not only by the immediate post-Revolt contingency of keeping a distance from the daily lives of the population, but also by the larger problem of governance. The colonial state realized that governance on the railway lines involved daily negotiations and contestations, as much as it did formal rules and legislation. The colonial state in a post-Revolt scenario was, I suggest, more than happy to let the private contractor do the haggling, bargaining, and negotiating.

A Network of Contracts and Contractors

The contract system employed by the British for the purpose of railway construction emerges not just as a set of financial transactions, but also as a system that is embedded in informal and professional networks comprising workers, contractors, and colonial officials. These networks, while allowing us to see the everyday functioning of the contract system at work, also permit us to offer a more complex picture of the history of railway building in colonial India. The colonial state was conscious of the fact that it was overriding economic logic in retaining the contract system, but as we have seen, this decision was not shaped by economics. The networks built and cultivated by contractors such as Joseph Stephens allowed the British to both control and at the same time remain at a distance from the day-to-day tribulations of railway construction. Social responsibilities and patronage become embedded within the contract system. Stephens (and other European contractors) now had to negotiate with their workers on a range of matters—paying compensation when accidents occurred, and resorting to informal coercion and manipulation of pay sheets to retain labour and contain resentment, for instance. These relationships, as I have noted, simultaneously exposed the ideological challenges and dilemmas which confronted the British administration.

Railway building in India in the 1860s, grounded in formal as well as deeply informal social and professional networks and transactions, was a challenge for the imperial government to deal with. 'Official' records in Mumbai, Delhi, Kolkata, and London speak of the infuriating frustrations faced by representatives of the Raj in dealing with the inherent lack of order and precision in daily transactions. In the 1860s, the colonial state was consolidating itself; in the process, it was putting in place several structures that were compatible with this process of consolidation. On the railway lines, governance via the contract system (rather than direct governance through a vast bureaucracy) emerged as one of the means to that end. Given the specific post-'Mutiny' social and economic context of the 1860s and early 1870s, the imperial state could well have decided not to enter the everyday world of railway building in the manner that it did later. Instead, it chose to pursue a policy of benign ignorance and acceptance (as far as possible) in dealing with problems on the railway lines, allowing the system to function as long as the work was delivered.

The potential and the strength of the Joseph Stephens Archive probably lie in the help it gives us in answering the conundrum of why the contract system was retained (in some form or other) for three decades, despite the obvious economic concerns involved. To conclude, I suggest that the nature of the informal networks on the railway lines was a reason for the British to continue with this system. Having to deal with the underlying need to justify means as well as ends, the British possibly found it judicious to construct a carefully maintained (and convenient) distance between themselves and the messy, everyday world that constituted the contract system of railway building.

Notes

1 See, for instance, Daniel Thorner, 'Capital Movement and Transportation: Great Britain and the Development of India's Railways', *Journal of Economic History*, 11/4 (1951), pp. 389–402.
2 Bipan Chandra, 'Economic Nationalism and the Railway Debate, Circa 1880–1905', in R. Srinivasan, M. Tiwari, and S. Silas (eds), *Our Indian Railway: Themes in India's Railway History* (New Delhi: Foundation Books, 2006), p. 78.
3 Daniel Thorner, 'The Pattern of Railway Development in India', in Ian Kerr (ed.), *Railways in Modern India* (New Delhi: Oxford University Press, 2001), p. 81.
4 Ian J. Kerr, *Engines of Change: The Railroads that Made India* (Westport: Praeger, 2007), pp. 17–18.

5 As Thorner points out in 'Capital Movement and Transportation' (p. 391), by 1868 approximately 6,000 km of railway lines had been opened. The number rose to 16,000 km by 1882 and around 40,000 km by the turn of the century. Between 1845 and 1875, about 95 million pounds sterling (£) was invested in the Indian railways, representing what according to W. P. Macpherson, 'Investment in Indian Railways: 1845–1875', *The Economic History Review*, New Series, 8/2 (1955), p. 177, is arguably the single largest injection of British capital in India. Stuart Sweeney, in *Financing India's Imperial Railways, 1875–1914* (London: Routledge, 2016), p. 1, estimates that the railways accounted for an overwhelming 80 per cent of Britain's industrial investments in India. By 1868, £80 million had been invested, increasing to £135 million by 1882 and £236 million by 1902, according to Thorner's calculations (op. cit., p. 391).

6 Ian J. Kerr (ed.), *Railways in Modern India* (New Delhi: Oxford University Press, 2001), p. 1.

7 Thorner, 'Pattern of Railway Development', p. 95.

8 Kept in the Joseph Stephens Archive (JSA) at the Linnaeus University, Sweden.

9 Kerr, *Engines of Change*, p. 25.

10 Ian J. Kerr, *Building the Railways of the Raj: 1850–1900* (New Delhi: Oxford University Press, 1995), pp. 10–11.

11 Thorner, 'Pattern of Railway Development', p. 84.

12 Chandra, 'Economic Nationalism', p. 80.

13 Thorner, 'Pattern of Railway Development', p. 86.

14 Ibid., p. 95.

15 See, for instance, Saraswathy Rao, *The Railway Board: A Study in Administration* (New Delhi: S. Chand & Company Ltd., 1978); G. S. Khosla, *Railway Management in India* (Bombay: Thacker & Co. Ltd., 1972).

16 Sabyasachi Bhattacharya, *The Financial Foundations of the British Raj: Ideas and Interests in Reconstruction of Indian Public Finance, 1858–1872* (New Delhi: Orient BlackSwan, 2005).

17 Ibid., pp. 5–14.

18 Radhika Singha, *The Coolie's Great War: Indian Labour in a Global Conflict 1914–1921* (New Delhi: Harper Collins India, 2020).

19 Ian J. Kerr, 'The Dark Side of the Force: Mistakes, Mismanagement and Malfeasance in the Early Railways of the British Indian Empire', in Srinivasan, Tiwari, and Silas (eds), *Our Indian Railway*, p. 190.

20 Ibid.

21 Linnaeus University (LNU), Huseby Archives (HA), Joseph Stephens Archive (JSA), F1A:5, Letter from G. B. Peck to Joseph Stephens, 24 July 1867.

22 National Archives of India, PWD Proceedings July 1868, Railways Department, 'Memo by Captain C. J. Mead Officiating Superintendent Engineer, Hyderabad Circle date 19/5/1868' [manuscript], (New Delhi: Government of India, 1868), p. 550.

23 Kerr, 'Dark Side of the Force', pp. 187–212.

24 See R. Krishnan, 'Contracting and Sub-contracting in British India: Exploring the Dynamics of Railway Building through Joseph Stephens', in K. Myrvold and S. Billore (eds), *India: Research on Cultural Encounters and Representations at Linnaeus University* (Gothenburg: Makadam, 2017), pp. 50–73, for an account of the social and professional networks forged by Europeans involved in construction of the railway grid, and the role of these networks in addressing the professional challenges of railway building in the 1860s. See also R. Krishnan, 'Constructing the Indian Railways: Locating Perception and Self-perception in "Native" Responses', in M. Petersson (ed.), *Huseby in the World* (Lund: Arkiv Academic Press, 2018).

25 LNU, HA, JSA, F1A:4, Letter from Louis Pereira, 9 December 1866; F1A:8, Letter from Joseph Stephens, 10 December 1866.

26 Huseby Estate, Joseph Stephens' diary 1862, 17 January 1862.
27 LNU, HA, JSA, F1A:3, Letter from Dadabhai Dorabjee, 12 January 1868.
28 Edward Said conceptualizes the Orientalist 'Other' as irrational, weak, depraved, childlike, and 'different' from the European. See Edward Said, *Orientalism* (London: Penguin, 2003), p. 40.
29 LNU, HA, JSA, F1A, Letter to J. P. Vansittart, 16 April 1868.
30 LNU, HA, JSA, F1A, Letter from R. F. Stack, First Class Assistant Engineer, GIPR Akola, 8 March 1867.
31 LNU, HA, JSA, F1A:5, Letter from G. B. Peck, 10 August 1865.
32 LNU, HA, JSA, F1A:5, Letter from G. B. Peck, 14 February 1867.
33 Anna, a coin valued at one-sixteenth of an Indian rupee. LNU, HA, JSA, F1A:5, Letters from G. B. Peck, 4 September and 16 October 1865.
34 Huseby Estate, Joseph Stephens' diary 1863, 24 March 1863.
35 Nite, 'Labour Practices and Well-Being: Construction Workers in 1860s Western India', chapter 5 in this volume.
36 Huseby Estate, Joseph Stephens' diary 1863, 28 February 1863.
37 'Rs' here refers to the Indian currency, rupees. In the 1860s, Rs. 6 was approximately equivalent to the wages earned for 5–8 days of 'skilled' work, such as carpentry or masonry.
38 LNU, HA, JSA, F1A:8, Letter to Alex Mackenzie, 12 March 1868; ibid, Letter to Edward Dangerfield, 20 September 1869; E1:2, J. Stephens to G. Stephens 1860–9; E1:3a, G. Stephens to J. Stephens 1858–75.
39 Chandra, 'Economic Nationalism', p. 80.
40 See Laura Bear, *Lines of the Nation: Indian Railway Workers, Bureaucracy, and the Intimate Historical Self* (Columbia: Columbia University Press, 2007); Kerr, *Building the Railways*; Laura Bear, 'An Economy of Suffering: Addressing the Violence of Discipline in Railway Workers' Petitions to the Agent of the Eastern Indian Railway, 1930–47', in S. Pierce and A. Rao (eds), *Discipline and the Other Body: Correction, Corporeality, Colonialism* (London: Duke University Press, 2006), pp. 245–8.
41 Bear, 'Economy of Suffering', pp. 246–8.
42 Kerr, *Building the Railways*, p. 169.
43 Ibid., p. 170.
44 Eric Stokes, *The English Utilitarians and India* (New Delhi: Oxford University Press, 1959).
45 See, for instance, Sugata Bose and Ayesha Jalal, *Modern South Asia: History, Culture, Political Economy* (London and New York: Routledge, 1998); Sumit Sarkar, *Modern Times: India 1880s–1950s, Environment, Economy, Culture* (Ranikhet: Permanent Black, 2014); Bernard Cohn, *An Anthropologist among the Historians and Other Essays* (New Delhi: Oxford University Press, 1990); Radhika Singha, *A Despotism of Law: Crime and Justice in Early Colonial India* (New Delhi: Oxford University Press, 1998).
46 Kerr, 'Dark Side of the Force', p. 211.
47 Cohn, *Anthropologist Among the Historians*, p. 479.

References

Bear, Laura, 'An Economy of Suffering: Addressing the Violence of Discipline in Railway Workers' Petitions to the Agent of the Eastern Indian Railway, 1930–47', in S. Pierce and A. Rao (eds), *Discipline and the Other Body: Correction, Corporeality, Colonialism* (London: Duke University Press, 2006).

Bear, Laura, *Lines of the Nation: Indian Railway Workers, Bureaucracy, and the Intimate Historical Self* (Columbia: Columbia University Press, 2007).

Bhattacharya, Sabyasachi, *The Financial Foundations of the British Raj: Ideas and Interests in Reconstruction of Indian Public Finance, 1858–1872* (New Delhi: Orient BlackSwan, 2005).

Bose, Sugata, and Ayesha Jalal, *Modern South Asia: History, Culture, Political Economy* (London; New York: Routledge, 1998).

Chandra, Bipan, 'Economic Nationalism and the Railway Debate, Circa 1880–1905', in R. Srinivasan, M. Tiwari, and S. Silas (eds), *Our Indian Railway: Themes in India's Railway History* (New Delhi: Foundation Books, 2006), pp. 77–120.

Cohn, Bernard, *An Anthropologist Among the Historians and Other Essays* (New Delhi: Oxford University Press, 1990).

Kerr, Ian J., *Building the Railways of the Raj: 1850–1900* (New Delhi: Oxford University Press, 1995).

Kerr, Ian J., *Engines of Change: The Railroads That Made India* (Westport: Praeger, 2007).

Kerr, Ian J., (ed.), *Railways in Modern India* (New Delhi: Oxford University Press, 2001).

Kerr, Ian J., 'The Dark Side of the Force: Mistakes, Mismanagement and Malfeasance in the Early Railways of the British Indian Empire', in R. Srinivasan, M. Tiwari, and S. Silas (eds), *Our Indian Railway: Themes in India's Railway History* (New Delhi: Foundation Books, 2006).

Khosla, G. S., *Railway Management in India* (Bombay: Thacker & Co. Ltd., 1972).

Krishnan, R., 'Constructing the Indian Railways: Locating Perception and Self-perception in "Native" Responses', in M. Petersson (ed.), *Huseby in the World* (Lund: Arkiv Academic Press, 2018).

Krishnan, R., 'Contracting and Sub-contracting in British India: Exploring the Dynamics of Railway Building Through Joseph Stephens', in K. Myrvold and S. Billore (eds), *India: Research on Cultural Encounters and Representations at Linnaeus University* (Gothenburg: Makadam, 2017), pp. 50–73.

Macpherson, W. P., 'Investment in Indian Railways: 1845–1875', *The Economic History Review*, New Series, 8/2 (1955), pp. 177–86.

Rao, Saraswathy, *The Railway Board: A Study in Administration* (New Delhi: S. Chand & Company Ltd., 1978).

Said, Edward, *Orientalism* (London: Penguin, 2003).

Sarkar, Sumit, *Modern Times: India 1880s–1950s, Environment, Economy, Culture* (Ranikhet: Permanent Black, 2014).

Singha, Radhika, *A Despotism of Law: Crime and Justice in Early Colonial India* (New Delhi: Oxford University Press, 1998).

Singha, Radhika, *The Coolie's Great War: Indian Labour in a Global Conflict 1914–1921* (New Delhi: Harper Collins India, 2020).

Stokes, Eric, *The English Utilitarians and India* (New Delhi: Oxford University Press, 1959).

Sweeney, Stuart, *Financing India's Imperial Railways, 1875–1914* (London: Routledge, 2016).

Thorner, Daniel, 'Capital Movement and Transportation: Great Britain and the Development of India's Railways', *Journal of Economic History*, 11/4 (1951), pp. 389–402.

Thorner, Daniel, 'The Pattern of Railway Development in India', in Ian Kerr (ed.), *Railways in Modern India* (New Delhi: Oxford University Press, 2001).

4 Social Capital and Its Limits in Fortune Making

Joseph Stephens' Enterprises in India and Scandinavia, 1859–69

Dhiraj Kumar Nite

> I have now decided on coming home. I will not say much about what I could do if I remained. There are lots of contracts to be let daily at the present time, which can only be taken up by men with experience and capital; therefore, I have no doubt that I should get something if I was trying for it; but as to how much I could make in two or three years, it is impossible to say. The chances are in favour of doing well, but so much depends on circumstances local and general that I may make very little or worse lose health and life and lead the life of a slave, which I have now led so many years that I am quite tired of it. I have made up my mind to give it up and come home with what I have got, which ought to be quite enough for me, as I am not an extravagant and also allow me to follow pursuits in which I take an interest and pleasure, which one cannot take in anything in India, where the whole and sole interest is to get done with it as soon as one can and pocket the proceeds.[1]

The foregoing excerpt from a letter of Joseph Stephens, written from Murtizapur (India) on 17 December 1868 to his father, provides us with a snippet of his demanding, adventurous experience of life and business. Stephens, a Scandinavian man, was one of several such adventurers, European as well as non-European, who travelled around the world in the nineteenth century in pursuit not just of a livelihood, but of wealth.[2] A successful workman, he grew to become a contractor in the construction sector in the Bombay-Nagpur region in 1860s India. He secured a fortune to the tune of over Rs. 332,000 (more than £33,200, or Rs. 25 million in today's money), equivalent to over 600,000 Swedish riksdaler (or 34 million Swedish krona today), over the period January 1860–February 1869.[3] This fortune earned in India enabled him in 1867 to purchase and subsequently operate the substantial Huseby Estate in Sweden, consisting of about 6,000 hectares of agricultural and forest land, an iron foundry, a sawmill, a corn-grinding mill, and a manor house with furniture and other fittings.[4]

In the course of making his fortune, he lived a hard, itinerant life, endured illness, and was without what he described as any proper means

DOI: 10.4324/9781003317227-4

of amusement and intellectual stimulus in India.[5] This chapter analyses the circumstances which, over the period 1859 to 1869, enabled Stephens to successfully make his fortune in India and were responsible for him relocating his venture to Sweden. It studies his experience of life in colonial India in the 1860s in order to explain his entrepreneurial agency and identify the implications for our understanding of business models.

Stephens' drive to make a fortune was one of the cogs in the advancement of commerce, industry, and transportation in later nineteenth-century world. The phenomenon of modern managerial industrial enterprises with their organizational capabilities and managerial hierarchy, as conceptualized by Chandler, was yet to emerge even in industrially prosperous countries.[6] The Great Indian Peninsula Railway (GIPR), a British joint-stock company, was one of the large firms involved in the construction and operation of railways in southern India in the 1850s–60s. However, it subcontracted the work of construction to a couple of medium-sized European and Indian contractors, which in turn usually subcontracted to a number of petty subcontractors. This web constituted a hierarchy of construction firms, and its members functioned as 'merchant intermediaries'. They became part of a business network, reflecting shared business attitudes, aspirations, and goodwill, and maintained it through contracts, partnership arrangements, and shareholdings.[7] It is not self-evident from the thesis of business networks, as per its conceptualization by Casson and Rose,[8] how members of such a network recognize opportunities, mobilize and allocate resources, work out necessary improvisation and innovation in the organization of factors of production, distribution, and firms, and legitimize their undertakings. Here, the study of Joseph Stephens' enterprise offers us a few clues. Stephens joined the business web, earned, and profited.

Stephens arrived with virtually no financial capital and exemplified the rise and growth of a business person from a subaltern background.[9] From the vantage point of the business elite, his firm was a small player; while in comparison with several Indian subcontractors—who worked for him, and supplied labourers as well as raw materials—his was a medium-sized enterprise. Stephens' business was not exceptional. The rise and growth of petty capitalists and small firms was widespread, bringing the economies of flexibility, informality, and labour-intensive methods in early modern, colonial, and postcolonial countries. Some of these petty capitalists originated from the humble background of productive classes.[10] This chapter also underscores the significance of this phenomenon for our understanding of business history.

My analysis of Stephens' business practices critically engages with four viewpoints offered by the literature dealing with the business approaches necessary to gain a fortune. First, entrepreneurs swiftly capitalized on and adjusted to the emerging pattern of accumulation in the 'open world economy' of the nineteenth century. They improvised where necessary to maximize profits, hedged uncertainties, displayed a preference for diversification,[11] and, at times, engaged in manipulation of prices and raw materials, in place of any commitment to an optimal level of efficiency in nineteenth-century colonial India.[12] As argued by Bubb and Kerr, the early decades of railway construction were a fluid moment of profiteering by all sorts of players in later nineteenth-century India.[13] I outline instances of higher prices, 'average to inferior' descriptions of construction, and improvisation in the organization of work.

Second, the use of professional skills and commercial intelligence by business persons and the improvisation and innovation in which they engaged in their business, along with the structure of firms, contributed to cost-effectiveness, diversification, and higher growth potential.[14] Proficiency in skills of trade and hard work were important attributes of capitalists rising from a subaltern background.[15] This chapter demonstrates how skills and toil were converted into cultural and symbolic capital.

Third, the pragmatic use of a reliable and fruitful social network, including family and community bonds and, at times, inter-ethnic relationships, led to a reduction in transaction costs, mobilization of funds, and an advantageous flow of information.[16] Claude Markovits, further, argues that a racial and communal mix and partnership characterized the socio-economic world and was responsible for less discrimination and less antagonism. This social situation, he continues, contributed to the growth and dynamism seen in the economic subsystem of Bombay (western India) as compared to that of Calcutta (eastern India).[17] In another account, cosmopolitanism and community networks together were a general feature of the nineteenth-century business world of India.[18] My discussion discourages any notion that Stephens' social and cultural capital was pre-existing and constant. It describes how and on what terms he built up the necessary social and cultural resources. It considers the ways in which he deployed his social network and what were its benefits and limitations.

Fourth, imperial patronage, racial favour, and a collective oligopolistic organization of businesses defined European expatriate enterprises and their higher profits in colonial India. A neo-mercantilist ethos and racial partisanship were some of the components of the colonial form of accumulation, which as a whole did not generally promote a revolutionizing of the method of production.[19] Maria Misra argues that, unlike the official British in India, British expatriate businessmen maintained rigid racial and social hierarchies. The latter were an expression of the social codes and economic conditions of colonial society. Imperial businessmen were committed to centralized control of the firm, a non-professional conception of social hierarchy, and the significance of character rather than intellect. Misra further argues, however, that a close, collusive rapport between the colonial state and European people in business did not yield any undue favour to the expatriates.[20] I find that there was greater scope for social bonds amongst official and non-official Europeans, which in turn meant that greater opportunities could be secured from the state by Europeans as compared to Indians, even in western India.

My discussion below presents a case in which Joseph Stephens succeeded as a fortune maker despite lacking the necessary initial financial capital. He fruitfully deployed his social and cultural resources: these included his tireless toil, professional skills (cultural capital and symbolic capital), and social networks (social capital) with the local team of European engineers and officials. He turned them into something that partially filled certain gaps in his business stride. This explains the acceptance of his tenders at the local level despite their prices frequently being on the high side, even though other tenders he put in for bigger projects were rejected at the higher level of the Bombay office. Similarly, he negotiated over the complaints made by the railway engineers about the unsound quality of construction carried out by his company.

Simultaneously, he undertook a certain amount of innovation in the organization of his business. He pursued an equity- and utility-oriented approach to the Indian labour agents and material suppliers. This helped him achieve control over the workforce and secure their efficient performance, a crucial variable in a labour-intensive enterprise. He devised a flexible combination of subcontractors working on his behalf and a directly hired workforce, thereby gaining cost advantages and preserving profit margins. His alertness to the emerging opportunities to maximize income and the diversification needed to hedge risk was most remarkable of all. Guided by this entrepreneurial drive, Stephens made a timely relocation of his enterprise to the Huseby Estate and avoided the mounting pressure on his business arising from his higher prices and what critics described as the 'unsatisfactory' quality of his construction.

Professional Skill and Symbolic Capital

Stephens was one of approximately 46,000 non-official Europeans living in India in 1861 of whom 15,000 were of British origin. These numbers rose to 70,000 and 22,000, respectively, by 1871. They were not by any stretch of the imagination more than a tiny segment of the total population of the country, which numbered 256 million in 1871.[21]

The fortune Stephens made in India was bigger than that secured by several other official and non-official Europeans. A non-official European, having retired from the positions of business partner and covenanted assistant in a managing agency firm, could have saved between £30,000 and £60,000 after serving for 28–30 years in India.[22] Such a European would have been hired after his college education, at a salary of £350–£500 per annum and with an additional 25 per cent bonus for the first four years. This was far more than an equivalent clerk might have earned in a commercial house in Great Britain: a young man with a similar education received about £75–£100 per annum. Furthermore, in India, such a position included one fully paid return passage every four years to Britain, where the assistant usually spent around six months at 50–70 per cent of his Indian salary. The salary levels and associated perquisites of assistants in commercial firms were higher than those of equivalent Indian Civil Service (ICS) officers at every level. At the turn of the twentieth century, senior assistants, after 20 years of service, received Rs. 2,500–3,500 per month (£3,500 per annum). Thus, by the age of 40, many would have achieved either this or a partnership and the prestige and wealth that went with it. Usually, a partner would then spend another eight to 10 years in India, with the last few years as a senior resident partner, after which he could return permanently to Britain. He often worked in the London or Scottish office of the firm and assumed paid directorships of a variety of British and India-based companies. Many used their fortunes to buy substantial property in the home counties and Scotland or pursued a career in public life.[23] The salary of a senior ICS officer (bureaucrat: e.g., a Cotton Commissioner) was Rs. 3,000 per month in 1867, whereas a first-class railway engineer earned Rs. 650–800 a month and a second-class assistant engineer, Rs. 550 per month. None of them could manage to accumulate savings out of their salaries to a level anywhere close to what Stephens did in the space of nine years.

Stephens spent his formative nine years in the Indian subcontinent over the period January 1860–February 1869. Born in the family of an academic, George Stephens, and his homemaker wife, Mary Bennet, in Scandinavia (Stockholm) on 13 July 1841, he sailed to India from Copenhagen in search of a promising career within the British Empire in December 1859. Stephens began his professional life as a multitasking overseer on a railway construction project of the Wythes and Jackson Construction Company, in the Deccan region between Igatpuri and Bhusawal. His responsibilities included surveying, inspection, supervision, record keeping, and disbursal of wages to workers. He was also a civil engineering apprentice with his brother-in-law, John Hallen Abbott, a British civil engineer employed by the GIPR.[24] He quickly rose to a better position when he accepted an offer by the contractor E. W. Winton of the post of Inspector (surveyor, supervisor, payment clerk) in January 1861. His salary increased from Rs. 100 to Rs. 120 a month, and further to Rs. 250 a month in 1862, when he was working on the Igatpuri–Bhusawal line.[25]

Stephens partnered with his colleague, John Smith Wells, on a small subcontract from a bigger railway contractor, the Lee, Watson, and Aiton Construction Company, for railway construction between Bhusawal and Badnera on the Nagpur extension line from June to July 1862. Alongside responsibility for the duties listed earlier, Stephens also started looking after the procurement of materials, such as different sizes of stone, timber, iron, and tiles, tools, and labour from the suppliers. Stephens became a subcontractor of this project, though in the formal capacity of an agent of Wells, from November 1863. Wells gave him 'the sole charge of the plate-laying and fencing and the whole of the profits of the same, but Mr. Harkness to have half the profits of the platelaying'.[26] In December 1863, he launched his own construction business, when he also completed his apprenticeship to become a civil engineer.[27] His firm, Joseph Stephens Construction Company, executed several small tenders for the construction of railway tracks, fences, pipelines, pump houses, engine pits, culverts, viaducts, railway stations, railway cottages, and houses, all of them for the GIPR. At the same time, his firm executed other contracts to build three cotton ginning and pressing factories for the Mofussil Cotton Press and Ginning (MCPG) Company, official bungalows, and the like.

Setting his sights on a higher goal, Stephens sought to acquire both the necessary accounting and engineering skills and business techniques. The space in which he learned, experimented, and executed what he learned was the construction site itself. A certain amount of reading and practice at home, and instructional exchanges with the railway engineer, were a normal part of the process. He read the book by W. D. Haskell on the engineering of railway buildings; practised graph, chart, and design making; and studied Hindustani grammar. Such activities usually took place on Sundays and other holidays when the Indian workers celebrated religious festivals, resulting in work stoppages. One of his senior colleagues, A. J. Barker (a surveyor), lent him his level-measuring device and guided him on how to use it to take levels in the initial years.[28]

He learned by a method of trial and error. The engineers of the GIPR and the construction company normally prepared and provided contractors with a design of the structure to be built. They provided them with the centre, that is, geometrical details on the ground, and inspected how the work was progressing. It was common for contractors to make mistakes in implementing these designs. For instance, an error occurred in the execution of a construction project on 29–30 October 1862 when Stephens set out the masonry for two piers of the Mass Nullah (viaduct) and found that he had made a serious mistake in setting out the excavations. 'He had to secure a good deal to get the masonry in without letting the E. Maistry know that we were erring'. He worked with J. H. Wells, his senior colleague and partner subcontractor, until midnight on 30 October 1862 in order to finish the job and take measurements of the work done, so as to be able to send a certificate (bill) to Watson.[29] Similarly, Stephens rushed to the worksite at Alasana in the evening of 24 August 1863, despite having been unwell for the last two days, to correct an error. His writer, an employee, informed him that R. F. Stack, a GIPR engineer, had been at Alasana viaduct and 'made a great noise about *chunam* (lime) being bad'. Stephens went to the bridge after taking a large dose of quinine and found that the sand being used by the workmen was very poor, half of it being soil. He rode to the Morgaon Nullah looking for better sand.[30]

Now and then, railway engineers and another agent of a project drew Stephens' attention to issues related to the quality of lime and sand, on the one hand, and their ratios in mortar, on the other. Alex Mckenzie, an inspector of the MCPG Company, and its manager, H. Macaulay, refused to accept the application of mortar made of sand and lime in the ratio of 3:1 at the

Khamgaon site. Macaulay thrust the end of his umbrella into one portion of a wall, which fell without any resistance, to demonstrate the inferiority of the mortar used. They demanded a ratio of 2½:1, or much better 2:1, to ensure a sound masonry structure.[31] J. P. Vantilart, a railway engineer, complained that the lime being used and prepared for a wall at Borgaon Tank and House was composed of two parts sand to one part of lime, and that the lime contained lots of unburnt *kunker* (small pieces). He asked that mortar be prepared in a proportion of 1½ parts sand to 1 of lime, and that the lime be properly ground and burnt.[32]

The design and planning of construction structures became an instrument of instruction, in the form of complaints on some occasions. J. R. Sandford, a GIPR engineer, found at the Kajgaon Engine Pit that 'what I said would be the case has already occurred: its giving way when tested by the weight and vibration of passing trains'. This, Sandford continues, was entirely owing to the poor quality of the work—the stones used being too small and the lime having no more strength than so much *muttee* (soil). 'I shall not, therefore, be able to certify the work being done till this is put right', he emphatically conveyed to Stephens.[33] On another occasion, Sandford drew Stephens' attention to shortcomings in another construction project:

> I notice that you are building the roof of the gate lodges at Nandgaon much too steep. The slope should not be greater than two to one, that is, if the place is 12 feet broad outside to outside the top of the ridge piece should not be more than three feet and 2½ inches above the wall plates at the sides.[34]

Similarly, Vantilart wrote to Stephens that the arch of the door of the Borgaon Tank House was 'two inches out of thumb' and must be put right.[35]

The acquisition of both engineering and accounting skills by Stephens is what Bourdieu calls educational capital qua cultural capital.[36] This contributed to his ability to perform the tasks of design, survey, and execution of plans. Joseph Stephens Construction Company, could therefore afford not to hire an engineer. At times, his cultural capital enabled him to take up the challenge of defending his enterprise against scathing criticism from railway engineers. One such episode unfolded in January–March 1867:

> I have now carefully examined also the work on the Superintendent Bungalow at Sheegaum [Shegaon] and *cannot agree with you as to the bad quality of the work. Lime most complained of is the same as has been used in the Drivers Cottage and in my opinion has set well and will bear comparison with mortar in other buildings* at Sheegaum. . .. I had no further complaint regarding the work till you spoke to me about mortar at Nargaum [Nandgaon], when I was somewhat taken by surprise. . . . After you spoke to me at Nargaum, the masonry at Sheegaum was stopped for several days, until I got a fresh supply of lime which

> was burnt at Sheegaum and was packed in the presence of my Inspector. This lime was being used at the time you asked Mr. Sharpe [GIPR inspector] to send you a sample, but I am informed that the sample he sent you was some of the mortar that had been prepared before the building was commenced and previously to sand being cleaned, and had been lying a long time in the sun without being watered and was quite perished having been put on one side as not fit to put into the work, and was not intended to be used without being grounded a second time and fresh lime added to it.[37] (Emphasis mine)

Stephens continues:

> I also carefully examined the joints in all the corners of the door and window openings and failed to discover in any case *a straight joint from top to bottom of frame*, and *I think in no case as I notice a straight joint for more than 18 inches in height and considering the difficulty there is in building with rubble corners, where the face is only from 15 inches to 18 inches wide. I think it not so very bad.* As regards the band between the walls, my masons tell me that there is a stone in every alternate course overlapping each wall from 6 inches to 8 inches . . . the outside walls, which are not to be bad were, and having been allowed on one or two occasions previously in cases of emergency to do so.[38] (Emphasis mine)

In this case, however, his combative defence was not convincing enough to persuade Edward Dangerfield, Resident Engineer of the GIPR.

Over time, his educational capital qua cultural capital also functioned as what Bourdieu terms symbolic capital: the source and sign of honourability and respectability.[39] It helped him secure respect and recognition, particularly in the offices of the state administration. The latter addressed him as a railway contractor-cum-civil engineer. They sanctioned a plan of Stephens to dig up stones from the foundations of walls around Akola. Quarrying stone in the bed of the river would have been very slow and expensive. The district commissioners declared that the objection raised by the local Tahsildar (revenue officer) was undue interference in Stephens' works.[40] One wonders whether such a favourable response from the district bureaucracy and such very easy access to its offices were as much a part of the experience of other contractors and subcontractors!

Stephens' reputation as a railway engineer remained advantageous to him in Sweden, where he helped to realize the scheme to construct a railway between Vislanda and Karlshamn. Initially, he was disappointed with the investment of his entire savings in the purchase of the Huseby Estate. Within a few months of his arrival at Huseby, Stephens called for a meeting of local landowners over lunch on 23 July 1869. The meeting was attended by 200 people, who decided to construct a railway line from Karlshamn to Vislanda. Stephens argued that 'this poor country [Småland province] suffers more from the want of communications than anything else.' 'All the landowners would buy shares of the railway construction company even if the government investment did not come. They would offer land, labour and material in return for their shares.'[41] His swift involvement in efforts to modernize and develop this region of Sweden, and the lead he took in this regard, were a reflection of the entrepreneurial predisposition he had acquired in India. The same could be said about his interest in the communication and transportation infrastructure and the treatment meted out to farm tenants. However, his symbolic capital as a railway engineer from India had already travelled to the region before he took this initiative. Both his symbolic and his cultural capital appear to have been at work in impressing the need for speedy execution of a new railway project on the Swedish landowners.

Social Connections and 'Sleeping Partners' in Business

The business world was impregnated with the significance of social connections, what Bourdieu describes as social capital. Stephens benefited from his social identity as a member of Abbott's family. While he inherited some contacts from Abbott, he also cultivated intra-ethnic bonds with other Europeans, who occupied engineering positions in the GIPR and populated the world of professionals and other businessmen in western India. All this occurred as an outcome of both his unconscious and his deliberate efforts. In India, his social life and business networks were intertwined. His hobbies, besides gardening, were reading and writing, bird watching and hunting. Many railway engineers and other Europeans, mostly in their twenties and thirties, shared the last two of these hobbies. Stephens mentions the names of Brereton, Merrett, Manning, Darke, Winton, Hawkes, Mennie, Stack, Wells, Hunt, Ker, Abbott, and Glover, and joined them on hunts on several Sundays. They hunted black buck, waterfowl, deer, *langur*, blue bull (*nilgai*), and wild buffalo.[42] Stephens regularly brought back birds and deer and consumed them for breakfast or dinner. The companionship formed on such adventures was consolidated when they assembled for regular Sunday champagne dinner parties, hosted mostly by railway and government engineers at their tents.[43]

Social connections qua social capital were not always sufficient, and the use of 'sleeping partners' was an additional necessity to facilitate business transactions. This is plainly evidenced by the letter which J. H. Davies wrote to Stephens in reply to the latter's request for a favour. He advised Stephens to meet Mr. Bapty to secure a contract on the double-track line between Bombay and Bhusawal.

> I think you can make convenient to see Mr. Bapty and come to terms. He will find the Board either for a percentage, or he will be a sleeping partner. It may be necessary because J. H. Abbott is in England.[44]

In this case, it appears either that Stephens did not succeed in securing Bapty's involvement, or else that Bapty was unable to muster enough influence with the GIPR Board. None of the contracts tendered for by Stephens for the double line came through from the Bombay office. On another occasion, J. S. Wells, with whom Stephens worked in 1861–3, brought a proposal to Stephens related to the No. 2 and No. 3 contracts on the Shoolapoor line. Wells proposed to furnish the security money and the initial investment of Rs. 50,000 towards the company's works. To secure Abbott's support for the project, Abbott and Stephens were promised half of the profits accruing from the contract.[45] In this case, Abbott did not succeed in moving the Board in favour of Wells' tender. Nonetheless, Wells gave Rs. 1,000 to Ingeborg Abbott in March 1865.[46] He had paid a certain amount of money to Abbot to clear his bills for about 11,000 cubic yards of ballasting done between Nandgaon and Challesgaon. The contract in question had fallen into some dispute in September 1862, and was then referred to Abbott. At a rate of 9 annas (Rs. 0.56) per cubic yard, the total value of the bills was about Rs. 6,200, while Wells 'bribed' Abbott at the rate of Rs. 500 per 2,500 cubic yards in return for clearing the bills.[47] Stephens, similarly, paid engineers like Abbott and Sandford for a certain contract.[48] The use of sleeping business partners and bribes paid to helpful officials were some of the constituents of what Chatterjee describes as 'the practice of power' seen in the late eighteenth and nineteenth centuries, when Europeans established their domination in colonial India.[49]

The social capital and availability of sleeping business partners also proved helpful to Stephens in securing livelihoods, business deals, and approval of contract bills. Stephens got most of his construction contracts from the local railway office at Munmar (Manmad), and they were sanctioned by Abbott in his capacity as Resident Engineer of the GIPR from 1864 onwards. Some other tenders were approved by railway engineers, including William Mennie, T. E. Darke, Edward Dangerfield, and the agent of the MCPG Company, Major W. D. Ker, who were either Abbott's close friends or mutual friends of both. Stephens enjoyed privileged access to tender notices from such familial and cultivated friendships. Furthermore, the notice of tender included a clause as follows: 'The chief resident engineer does not bind himself to accept the lowest or any tender.'[50] Evidently, Stephens' tenders were accepted despite his quoting a higher price compared, in particular, with the Parsi (Indian) contractors. The latter usually quoted a price about one-half of Stephens'.[51] Following rejection of their tenders, some Indian contractors joined Stephens as subcontractors to execute portions of his contract at a price about one-third to two-fifths lower than what Stephens received.

The efficacy of Stephens' social capital was, however, confined to the local offices of the GIPR in the Deccan region (Manmad, Akola, Bhusawal, and Nagpur), which were headed by his kin and benefactors. This helped to secure acceptance at these offices for the higher prices in his tenders, but could not achieve the same endorsement in the Bombay office of the GIPR. Indeed, Stephens' very dependence on his locally effective social network for tenders also seems to have been a handicap when he attempted to branch out and compete for contracts at the higher level of the Bombay office. For

Table 4.1 Profitability situation in rupees (Rs.)

Type of construction work	*Rates paid to Joseph Stephens Construction Company*		*Rates Stephens paid to Indian subcontractors*		*Difference (Rs. and %)*
Earthworks	0.375/Cyd	0.35/Cyd	0.25/Cyd	0.1875	0.10 (29%) to 0.13 (33%) to 0.19 (50%)
Slope earthworks			0.25/Cyd		
Embankments	0.375/Cyd	0.285 Cyd for making up			0.13 (33%) to 0.19 (50%) to 0.097 (34%)
Signal works			0.25/Cyd		
Ballasting	0.625/Cyd	0.5/Cyd	0.25/Cyd		0.38 (60%)
Excavation	0.5/Cyd				
Excavation in rock	2/Cyd				
Platelaying	1/Lin yd		0.5/Cyd		0.5 (50%)
Laying points and crossings	2/Lin yd				
Fixing semaphores	60 each				
Fences (milk bush)			8/per 12 rail length both sides		
Masonry	0.094/Cyd		0.05/Cyd		0.044 (46%)
Masonry (rubble with cornered face)	11/Cyd	10/Cyd	8.313/Cyd		2.69 (24%) to 1.69 (17%)
Masonry (blocking course)			16/Cyd		
Masonry (ashlar)			1.3125/Cft	Re. 1/Cft	
Tiling			2.75/Sq. ft. roof		
Donkey men	35/per 50 Cyd				
Average (rough)					39.17% to 46.7%

Sources: Huseby Estate, Joseph Stephens' diary 1863, 6 February and 13 October 1863. LNU, HA, JSA, F1A:1, J. S. Wells and Stephens, 16 September 1862, 27 September 1865; F1A:2, Stephens to Abbott, 9 June 1866; F1A:3, R. Stack to Stephens, 13 April 1867, and Stephens to a subcontractor in Penambla, 8 May 1867; F1C:2, Tender for the doubling of line between Kalyan and Karjat, 12 October 1866; F1B:1, Bago Kundo signed an agreement with Stephens, 15 April 1865, Sastwa Rama and Ruggo Yesso signed a contract with Stephens, 2 October 1865, and Bappa Mokinda signed an agreement with Stephens, 7 December 1865. Cyd = cubic yard. Cft = cubic foot.

instance, J. R. Manning, Resident Engineer of the GIPR (Bhusawal), wrote to a Mr. Victor on 21 December 1865:

> Mr. Stephens, a friend of mine having finished his contracts on this part of the line is anxious to try his work in your part of the world. I can recommend him and shall be glad if we can do something to help him.[52]

However, his recommendation was to no avail when Stephens tendered for the double line project at the Bombay office:

> I got your letter but am afraid I can do nothing for you in the way of doubling. Coleman and Company have got the last length and Wells and Hover no. 5 Chalisgaum [Chalisgaon] to Mhyjee [Maheji]. They are both very low in prices and can not, I think, make much out of it. I do not hear anything of the Parsi contractor, but as he does the work between.[53]

None of the tenders submitted by Stephens to the Satara office for an irrigation project, the Poona office for a masonry bridge project, and the Bombay office for a double line project was accepted. Nor did his tenders for the construction of cotton press and ginning factories, apart from those which Major Ker offered him, succeeded.[54] His higher quotes, locally fruitful social networks, and the limited financial capital in his possession proved a major constraint to his expansion as a bigger, competitive builder.

Joseph Stephens was highly successful in leveraging his social connections to deal with disputes over his bills and the 'unsatisfactory description' of his construction. Some of his contracts for railway works and for the construction of two cotton ginning and press factories at Shegaon and Khamgaon were cancelled at the end of 1865. Some field engineers of the GIPR and the manager of the MCPG Company were dissatisfied with the slow progress and 'unsound' quality of his work. Nonetheless, Stephens' firm had no problems getting measurement of the works done and receiving payment for these unfinished projects. Mennie rescued him on several 'unsound' works done on the Nandgaon-Chalisgaon-Bhusawal line in 1865. Dangerfield played the same role in 1867–8 with regard to his works between Bhusawal and Badnera. Major Ker saw to it that Stephens received payment for his unfinished work on the Shegaon and Khamgaon factories in 1866. Moreover, Stephens' firm won some lucrative railway contracts on the Bhusawal and Nagpur route in 1866–8.

Let us consider one particular instance of a dispute over billing to understand the manner in which this leverage operated. One bill of the Stephens Company, for Rs. 3,636 and 10 annas, was stuck at the office of J. R. Rushton (Chief Resident Engineer, GIPR Akola) from April 1867. Rushton refused to certify the bills, relating to Budnaira (Badnera) station, from April to September because of some dispute over the account. Some prices claimed by Stephens in the bills were not sanctioned or were not mentioned in the schedule of prices agreed when the tenders were approved. The total cost exceeded the approved amount. Further, some items mentioned in a few bills required prior approval, as they were not mentioned in the schedule of prices drawn up at the time of the tender. Extra work undertaken, beyond the quantities estimated in the project plan, required an explanation. Rushton had, moreover, objected to the manner in which a portion of the work was measured in connection with the addition of a structure to Badnera station by Stephens. Stephens had been away from India visiting his parents in Scandinavia in June–December 1867 and therefore could not promptly handle the disputed matters, nor could his deputy, G. B. Peck. Meanwhile, the higher authority, in this case Dangerfield (Chief Resident Engineer, GIPR Nagpur), appointed R. F. Stack, another engineer, to carry out measurements for verification.[55]

Stephens approached Dangerfield for his support over this matter. Dangerfield's reply was both professional and empathetic. The matter had gone to the Chief Resident Engineer in the Bombay office, who had found it unacceptable to pay for the use of old materials pulled down from station buildings to which Stephens had been adding an extension. Abbott denied having made any promises regarding Stephens' use of and payment for the old materials. Then there were some issues of measurement.[56] Stephens now looked for help from his old friend T. E. Darke, who had retired from the GIPR and been back in London. Darke promised to endorse his viewpoint:

> With reference to old work, it was certainly understood that you were to have the old materials pulled down but you were not to be paid for the labour in pulling them down; and it was also understood that you should be treated with reference to measurements, specification, etc. in the same way as had been customary with Mr. Lee, Watson and Aiton. I have not heard from Mr. Rushton on the subject but if he refers to me, I shall, while no longer connected with the GIPR, be most happy to communicate with him.[57]

The Bombay office, finally, cleared Rs. 1,799, 6 annas, and two pies, half the value of his actual bill, in Stephens' favour in November 1870.[58]

Stephens' purchase and management of the Huseby Estate at a favourable price in 1867–9 similarly reflected the influence of his Scandinavian family and social connections, such as Hyltén-Cavallius, Fingal von Sydow (younger brother-in-law, a naval captain), and Mr. Wallenberg (brother-in-law of Sydow, a Stockholm banker).[59]

Business Conduct and Profit Margins

The manner in which Stephens conducted his business was an adoption of the business-as-usual approach, as well as an improvisation on existing business ethics. The business-as-usual approach involved a prioritization of maximum returns on effort, manipulation of raw materials and quality, and adherence to a quality of construction defined as an 'average standard'.

Stephens adopted two methods for executing construction tenders: the use of Indian subcontractors and the use of hired workers. He sublet a portion of his tender to several Indian subcontractors. There was a pattern to this. The assignments' sublet during the early years of his business included earthworks, embankments, excavation, ballasting, and fencing. Stephens subcontracted many of these works to Indian (Vaddar and Maratha) (sub) contractors, including Gorwa Savana and Kundo Ancenda Muccadams, Chimma Bappa Wuddar, Chimma Yankoo Wudaree, Bago Kundo, Sastwa Rama and Ruggo Yesso, Ismael Hakem, Khader Shaik, Kasabhoy, Chimma Patel, Khaderbhoy, Bapa Darkoo, Lotan Patel, Hunmmanta Cowjee, and Perajee Herappa Woddaree (the supplier of stone, sand, and ballasting). These Indian subcontractors were the *muccadams*, the heads of labouring gangs, known for executing the labour-intensive earthworks. They mobilized their gang members, brought their own work tools, and supervised the workers' performance. They received payment based on the task assigned or on a piecework basis. Stephens' inspectors measured the latter together with the subcontractors.[60]

Reliance on these subcontractors gave Stephens a profit margin comparable to that provided by the use of hired workers during the early years. A comparison of the figures presented in Table 4.1 with Table 4.2 is evidence of this. The real attraction of the first of these methods appears to have been that it relieved Stephens of the demanding responsibility for recruitment, control, and supervision of workers employed on the more labour-intensive components of his tenders. Stephens occasionally complained of the laziness shown and slow work performed by workers in his absence. Sometimes he scolded and threatened them for such work behaviour, and he had occasional rows with them.[61] Furthermore, he appears to have taken into account the fact that the relevant component of his tender required the kind of technical input which Indian (sub)contractors were able to provide, even without the direct presence of Stephens and his inspectors.

During the later years, especially after 1865, masonry, tiling, platelaying, and signal work were also sublet, among others to Reembhoy Casseembhoy, Sastwa Rama and Ruggo Yesso, Bago Kundo, Bappa Mokinda, NowroJee Pestrery, and the like, who were *maistries* (masons' headmen) and Parsi subcontractors. These Indians delivered the sublet assignments, which required technical inputs, under arrangements similar to those worked out with the previous category of Indian subcontractors.[62] As is shown below, the greater reliance on Indian subcontractors was a response to a rise in the wages paid to directly hired workers. The latter economic development resulted in the diminution of the profit margins available to Stephens using hired labour.

Stephens had also relied on directly employing workers, in the range of 200 to 450, for construction activities to execute certain portions of his

Figure 4.1 The contractor Mr. Clowser at his workshop at Oonee village. Constructions at Bhor Ghat.

Source: Most likely photograph by Alice Tredwell, courtesy Huseby Bruk AB.

tenders, normally those involving greater technical inputs. He proactively sought to expand access to working people and to establish greater control over the workforce. His strategy for recruiting and monitoring labour was adjusted to some of the existing practices. Apart from some European platelayers, construction workers came from several places in southern India. They included men, women, and children. Men worked in skilled professions, like masonry, blacksmithing, carpentry, and well digging, while they were joined by women and children in other sweat-labour jobs. All of them worked in different gangs headed and monitored by the labour recruiter-cum-gang leader, known as the *maistry* or the *muccadam*. The maistry and the muccadam received wage rates that were usually anything from one-third higher than to double those paid to their gang members. Workers frequently received advance payments upon recruitment, which the employer largely adjusted for in their monthly earnings. Such adjustments were not made in the case of the maistry and muccadam, an exception that seems to have been made in recognition of their services in overseeing advances or the debt dependency relationship, and guaranteeing employers the compliance of their gang members.

Workers belonged to a variety of caste, ethnic, and religious groups. Stephens' firm introduced an innovation when it negotiated the payment of differential wage rates corresponding not just to the skill hierarchy of workers but also to their social status in the locality. The Tapkir and Nawguna, for instance, received rates about one-third and one-fifth higher, respectively, than other 'coolies' and 'baggarees', although they usually performed the same jobs. This is an indication of the existence of a segmented labour market, and of the ability of the Nawguna and Tapkir to claim higher, respectable wage rates. These caste groups were known as the cotton workers (Nawguna) from Dharwar and tobacco cultivators (Tapkir) from Khandesh. Another innovation by Stephens included a monetary incentive called 'cherimerry' (a present of money: *baksheesh*), regularly paid to the labouring gangs in the initial years (1860–3) and aimed at securing workers' loyalty to their employer.[63]

Initially, Stephens entered into verbal agreements with Indian subcontractors and labour agents, but suffered losses when they did not deliver their subcontracts. Subsequently, from 1863 to 1864, he sought to have written contracts, containing penalty clauses in the event of failure or delay. Signed receipts for payments between them were also introduced to formalize the agreements. According to Roy, such a mechanism for contract enforcement was a new economic institution that was gradually emerging in the Indian subcontinent.[64]

Stephens was relatively successful in his endeavour to secure the supply of working people and mobilize labour to meet exigencies. His success also depended on a utility-oriented and equity-bound approach that he adopted in his exchanges with Indian labourers and suppliers. Some episodes recorded in his diaries exemplify this. Stephens reported to E. N. Mutow, the agent of Wythes & Jackson Construction Company, about an encounter which took place between Mr. Smith (Commander of Marines) and some masons on 27 March 1861. The former brought the case for trial before the magistrate, Mr. Tyler. Stephens considered that 'Smith has been at fault in the matter'. Mutow wrote back to Stephens:

> No doubt as you say, Smith has been at fault in the matter. I cannot help wishing that the magistrate will decide in his favour, even though at the expense of justice. For it is morally certain that if the natives get best off, there will be no holding them afterwards.[65]

Mutow expressed a racist, colonial view of the relationship between the imperial British and the colonial natives, which increased in the aftermath of the large uprising in 1857, the brutal repression that followed and the re-organization of British rule under the crown on the subcontinent.[66] Stephens seems, however, to have remained aloof from such an outlook. When his waterman was arrested by his security guard (*ramosy*) for stealing grass, he did not want him imprisoned for three months. Instead, on 26 February 1862, he got the case settled and the person let off.[67] Barry's cook stole Stephens' gun and many other things on the night of 10 June 1862. They chased the cook and found several things on the road and at his hut. The gun remained untraceable. Stephens did not push for the cook to be punished.[68] Furthermore, he presented a gift of a *puggery* (turban or headgear) and scarf worth Rs. 10 to some of his (sub)contractors, including Chimma Wooddary. Here, Stephens recognized the respectability of these Indian (sub)contractors, as well as establishing a patronage network with them.[69] He fostered a business network with the Parsi and other Indian materials suppliers and subcontractors, necessary for the construction business, according to a principle that was distinguishable from his sense of social belonging with his European friends.

How can Stephens' equity-bound, utility-oriented approach be explained? Bubb describes it as a display of cultural sensitivity towards and accommodative arrangements with the 'natives'. It reflected, argues Bubb, the effect of the 1857 rebellion against British rule in India, which left an impression on the Europeans that their meddling with the native's culture was provocative.[70] As against this, my research suggests that Stephens' father, George Stephens, a Methodist and pan-Scandinavian, had impressed on his son the need to deal with both European and Indians in a magnanimous manner for his own self-advancement:

> advise you [Joseph] to be a noble English employer of labour—the feudal Baron or petty Prince of our times—who always should be the father and protector of all under you, English or native born, for whatever their faults, they are all our brethren. The natives are so in a way you little imagine. There is no doubt, as far as history and language and tradition can prove anything, that the English are descended from the same stock as the Hindoo, that there was a time when the fathers of each of these races were dwelling in the same tents, encamped in the same Indian woodland, the cradle of our Indo-European family. The difference has been the work of time, migration, climate, teaching and above all of debasing heathenness, on the one hand, and soul-lifting heart-purifying Christianity, on the other.[71]

The correspondence between father and son during the period 1860–3 contains vignettes of such ethical teaching offered by the professorial father to his struggling son based in a distant land. The former repeatedly admonished the young Stephens 'that he ought to read as much as possible on Sunday. He should treat all people alike in business'.[72] Another source of inspiration in Joseph Stephens' dealings with the Vaddars, in particular, was Wells. The latter impressed upon him the need to keep in the good books of the industrious community of earthworkers, especially the Vaddars, for the speedy execution of construction work.[73] Stephens brought this paternalist, utility-oriented approach to the Huseby affair as well. In July 1869, he reported to his father that he offered the same food to the peasants on the Huseby Estate as he had served to the dignitaries attending the meeting of landowners.[74]

This judicious mix of business acumen and an equity-based approach towards the native labourer and (sub)contactor enabled Stephens to achieve early success in his endeavours. During the early years, Stephens' share in the total value of tenders executed under the method of hired labour was over two-fifths, after the deduction of payments to workers, to his inspectors, and for materials. This share slowly dwindled as the cost of labour surged from the latter half of 1862 and 1863 onwards.[75] Table 4.2 presents an indicative estimate of profit margins under this arrangement for the period 1862–7. This economic scenario of diminishing returns provided the context for Stephens' view, quoted at the beginning of this book, in November–December 1868. His new opinion sprang from anxious mixed feelings about his business prospects in India, as well as from self-deprecating reflection on his life in India.

Stephens' business dealings were associated with a quality of construction that was variously termed as of 'an average standard' or 'of inferior description'. The issue of quality reflected as much the profit consideration as the notion of an acceptable standard of construction itself. Several cases of 'unsound construction' executed by Stephens drew sharp criticism from the railway engineers: there were the collapses of viaducts in 1862 and 1867, an engine pit in 1865, the slovenly manner of raising embankments and building fences in 1867, and the substandard construction of cotton ginning and press factories in 1865. By the late 1860s, over 2,000 GIPR bridges, buildings, and other masonry structures had failed amidst accusations that some of the original work had been of a poor quality.[76] The matter of quality flared up even before a scandalous spate of collapses of railway structures and consequent accidents that occurred in 1867–8.[77]

Let us consider one such case. Dangerfield accepted a report submitted by Stack, the District Assistant Engineer, and Sharpe, the GIPR Inspector, which found several construction works executed by Stephens at Shegaon on the Nagpur extension line to be of 'unsound description'. They complained about the use of poor mortar, inferior and imperfectly burned lime, a ratio of sand to lime higher than 1½ to 1, dirty sand, and improperly designed masonry.[78] Dangerfield went as far as to state that:

> I cannot, therefore, consent to accept it for the company, . . . I would also refer to the nature of the work which . . . I have observed in other parts of the line where you have buildings in construction. I instance the addition to the booking office at Akolah [Akola] and the goods shed at Sheegaum Station where neither the masonry nor woodwork is up to the mark.[79]

Stephens' reply to the charge of inferior construction perturbed and amazed the critical official. The contractor defiantly and confidently argued that this

Table 4.2 Monthly share (Rs.) in the monetary value of output: An indicative estimate (around the Bhusawal—Nagpur railway) during 1862–7

Year	*Labour productivity (yds) (A)*	*Average rate Rs./yd (B)*	*Average rate (Rs./mile (C))*	*Output (Yds/month (D))*	*Rate Rs./ month (E)*	*Share of production workers (F)*	*Total share of workers, supervisors, and writers (G)*	*Total business cost, including materials and capital (H)*	*Profit margin: Stephens' share (I)*	*Stephens' share (in %) (J)*
1862	11.73	2.5	4,400	7,040	17,600	6,165	6,329	9,493.5	8,106.5	46
1863	11.73	2.5	4,400	7,040	17,600	6,315	6,930.26	10,395.38	7,204.618	41
1864	11.73	2.5	4,400	7,040	17,600	8,280	7,588.63	11,382.94	6,217.06	35
1865	11.73	2.5	4400	7,040	17,600	8,160	8,309.55	12,464.32	5,135.68	29
1866	11.73	2.5	4,400	7,040	17,600	8,280	9,098.96	13,648.43	3,951.57	22
1867	11.73	2.5	4,400	7,040	17,600	10,500	9,963.36	14,945.04	2,654.96	15
1868	11.73	2.5	4,400	7,040	17,600	10,680	10,909.88	16,364.81	1,235.19	07

Source: Over six years between 1862 and 1867, the GIPR constructed the Nagpur extension line between Bhusawal and Nagpur, covering a distance of nearly 244 miles. The average monthly progress of the work was four miles. An estimate by Kerr and Derbyshire informs us that, on average, 150 workers were employed on the construction of each mile (1,760 yards) of the railway, including bridges, tunnels, and other structures. Table 4.1 presents the rates for different construction activities paid to Stephens, which form the basis for calculating the rate (in money terms) paid to a contractor like Stephens for the construction of 4 miles a month (Column E):

= Σ[{0.375 (earthworks)+0.625 (ballasting)+0.5 (excavation)+2 (excavation in rock)+1 (platelaying)+2 (laying points & crossings)+11 (masonry of rubble with cornered face or blocking course))/7}*1760*4].

Tables in my other chapter on 'Labour Practices and Well-Being' present the wages paid to the different categories of workers and other employees, which form the basis for the estimate of the share of production workers and other employees (Column G):

= Σ[{F: Σ(150*4)*(((coolie 1+coolie2)/2+women/boys+cartman/wellsman/driller+1.5*(mason 1+mason 2)/2+0.5*(carpenter+blacksmith)/2)/5))}+2*(inspe ctor)+2*(writer)].

Column H is based on the assumption, as suggested by the Cobb-Douglas production function, that the share of labour in the production cost of a labour-intensive production process is two-thirds, and that of capital one-third, that is, 50 per cent of the workers' share.

Sources: For the period 1861–8, see LNU, HA, JSA, F1E:1 and F1E:2, Pay lists and pay sheets. Kerr, *Building the Railways*. Ian Derbyshire, 'The Building of India's Railway: The Application of Western Technology in the Colonial Periphery 1850–1920', in Ian J. Kerr (ed.), *Railways in Modern India* (New Delhi: Oxford University Press, 2005), pp. 268–304. Paul H. Douglas, 'The Cobb—Douglas Production Function Once Again: Its History, Its Testing, and Some New Empirical Values', *Journal of Political Economy*, 84/5 (1976): 903–16.

construction 'will bear comparison with the mortar in the other buildings' and that 'I think it not so very bad'.[80] Dangerfield, disturbed by his response, answered Stephens:

> I regretted not so much on account of its being opposed to my own, as that you should have pained me to understand that you considered work so evidently bad to be of a fair standard quality. . . . I am aware of the great trouble there is in procuring material of good description in Berar, but am afraid that the concession which has at times been made on this account have [*sic*] been disastrous to the company. . .. I must also bear in mind that your prices will well allow you to pay the company thoroughly good work.[81]

Stephens was neither the first nor the only contractor who attempted to justify the quality of his construction based on a notion of an average standard of quality. Rather, he harped on about and extended what had already been a business ethic for some time. In reply to the complaints about substandard quality, A. Watson, one of the owners of the Lee, Watson, and Aiton construction company, responsible for the Nagpur extension line and for subletting a portion of it to Wells and Stephens, had offered the latter the following guidance:

> Mr. Watson says that he does not want us [Wells &Stephens] to put in better work than what was previously put in by them and will back us in any case that there might be a dispute about, if our work was as good as theirs. My [Wells] wish is that no dispute may arise through our work being inferior to the former works.[82]

The business ethic of substandard construction or an acceptable average standard was an entrenched facet of railway building. It was an expression of what Kerr describes as 'mistakes, mismanagement and malfeasances that characterized the pioneering decades of railway construction (1853–1870)'.[83] Two more factors proved conducive to this situation. First, railway construction took place under the scheme of a guaranteed 5 per cent return on capital investment in the 1850s–60s, resulting in an attitude of disregard for the cost.[84] Second, following the government's controversial decision to assist the GIPR in funding reconstruction, what had begun as a 'tragedy' had become a 'gigantic swindle'.[85] We can juxtapose this scenario with another construction contract, which Joseph Stephens Construction Company carried out for the MCPG Company. Accused of inferior quality, it was confronted with the cancellation of a tender for cotton press and ginning factories that were under construction in Khamgaon and Shegaon.[86] Stephens' firm was as much a beneficiary of the prevalent business ethic as a victim of it. From December 1868, the GIPR moved onto a departmental method of construction in order to regain the advantage in terms of quality and cost. Consequently, the opportunities for a contractor like Stephens were whittled down.

Stephens was ever alert to emerging economic opportunities. He undertook some financial innovation in the form of a diversification of his business. He partnered with H. Swan in exporting cotton from India to England during the American Civil War (1861–5). Cotton prices had increased exponentially in India. We do have one piece of evidence which tells us that Stephens pocketed £368 3s (Rs. 3,680.3) from one of his cotton export transactions.[87] He was a risk-averse businessman and careful of speculative activity. He withdrew from speculative investment in the cotton trade as soon as he received word of an end to the civil war and reduced profit margins on exports of Indian cotton. He thus staved off the fate suffered by several Indian speculators in the wake of the sudden end to the cotton boom in June 1865 and the subsequent financial collapse in Bombay in the later 1860s.[88]

Joseph Stephens invested a sum of Rs. 3,368 and 6 annas in six shares of the Elphinstone Land and Press Company in Bombay.[89] He sold these shares at a price of Rs. 4,740 on the eve of his departure from India in 1868.[90] Meanwhile, he received dividends on his shares in the order of 4.5 to 5 per cent half-yearly. The rate of the dividend was higher than the bank rates of 2 to 3 per cent, respectively, paid by the Oriental Bank Corporation (Bombay) on current and fixed-deposit accounts.[91] He moved funds between his two current and fixed-deposit accounts with the Oriental Bank, transferring savings to the fixed-deposit accounts for three months at a time.

Once in possession of the Huseby Estate in Sweden, Stephens attempted to sell sleeper timber and ballast iron from Huseby to the Indian railways and Swedish dynamite, a recent invention of Alfred Nobel, more widely on the Indian market. On his way back to Sweden in February 1869, he met A. Roberts, a GIPR engineer based on the Poona line, as a fellow passenger on the ship. He befriended the latter in order to secure a contract for the supply of sleepers for the GIPR.[92] He was possibly the first person to import dynamite into India. His shipping agent, Henry Rogers, tested it on the waterfront at Bombay: 'Captain Ducat was thunderstruck . . . it was just as great success underwater as out of it.' 'I have already had two men offering me anything I liked to ask for it', Rogers added, but sadly the reluctance of the customs authorities to allow the powerful explosive to be unloaded put this venture on hold.[93] Undeterred, Joseph placed an order for five tonnes of dynamite from Stockholm through his younger brother-in-law, Sydow. The latter reported that 'no ships would be ready to carry such high amount because it raises the insurance cost'.[94]

The business scenario discussed in this chapter was an expansive one, and yet far short of what Chandler calls the modern, managerial industrial enterprise. Railway construction in later nineteenth-century colonial India was characterized by a hierarchical network of enterprises, which fostered business networks based on contracts, partnerships, and shareholdings. They forged a business culture defined by shared commercial attitudes and aspirations. Joseph Stephens and his enterprise were some of the smallest cogs in the wheel, but well interwoven into this scheme of things. He undertook innovation and improvisation in the organization of work and trade in order to secure profitability and, in turn, contributed to the growth potential of the entire business network in the short term.

This chapter has thus presented a case in which Joseph Stephens emerged as a fortune maker from a subaltern background. For this to happen, the context of an open economic world in nineteenth-century India was not sufficient. Stephens' entrepreneurial agency and ability to secure and fruitfully deploy social, cultural, and symbolic capital played a crucial part. Although he lacked the initial financial capital and affirmed a mercantilist attitude in the pursuit of maximum profit, he enthusiastically and perseveringly positioned himself to seize opportunities to generate income in the 1860s. He harnessed his strength through his relentless endeavours to develop the cultural as well as the symbolic value of his professional (accounting and engineering) skills and his untiring involvement in his businesses. He fostered an advantageous social network with the engineers and officials, who were essentially European. He was primarily able to efficaciously muster such social capital, however, in the local offices in the Deccan interior, rather than the Bombay office. Stephens also pursued a certain equity-bound and utility-driven approach to both Indian subcontractors and material suppliers. His racially accommodative, patronizing approach reflected both the context of a racially mixed business world in western India and his father's advocacy of a paternalist and utility-oriented treatment of everyone.

Stephens' manner of conducting business was an adaptation of the business-as-usual approach, according to which he prioritized the returns on his effort and associated himself with a quality of construction defined as an 'average standard' in the region. This remained financially viable and profitable in the context of a 5 per cent return on capital investment in the railways, including repair costs, guaranteed by the colonial state until the late 1860s. Finally, Stephens was ever alert to the emerging economic opportunities, undertaking financial innovation in the form of diversification of his business, and embracing a risk-averse attitude to speculation with a view to safely increasing his overall fortune. Meanwhile, the advantage of social connections in the local offices and a reputation for delivering construction of an 'unsatisfactory description', and charging relatively high prices, proved unhelpful in expanding his enterprise. Guided by his alertness to new opportunities and his desire to hedge risk, Stephens successfully relocated his venture from colonial India to Sweden.

Notes

1 Linnaeus University (LNU), Huseby Archive (HA), Huseby Estate Archive (HEA), E1:2.
2 Stephens' parents lived in Copenhagen (Denmark), and after his career in India he relocated to Sweden.
3 This estimate is based on the correspondence between Joseph Stephens and George Stephens. LNU, HA, HEA, E1:2, Letters of J. Stephens to G. Stephens,

1860–9; E1:3a, Letters of G. Stephens to J. Stephens, 1858–75; E1:12a, Miscellaneous incoming correspondence of Joseph Stephens, 1859–1900. For the currency conversions, see www.historicalstatistics.org/Currencyconverter.html, accessed on 14 December 2016. Indian silver rupees have first been converted to pounds sterling for the period of 1860–9, and then pounds sterling to Swedish riksdaler and kronor. For the period 1860–9, I have used the exchange rates provided by Piatt Andrew, 'Indian Currency Problems', *Quarterly Journal of Economics*, 15/4 (1901), p. 505.

4 LNU, HA, HEA, E1:2, E1:3a, and E1:12a.

5 LNU, HA, Joseph Stephens Archive (JSA), E1:2, Stephens to M. Bennet, 10 December 1868.

6 Alfred D. Chandler, Jr, *Scale and Scope: The Dynamics of Industrial Capitalism* (Cambridge: Harvard University Press, 2004 [1990]).

7 Mark Casson and Mary B. Rose, 'Institutions and the Evolution of Modern Business', *Business History*, 39/4 (1997), pp. 1–10.

8 Ibid.

9 Swati Chattopadhyay and Bhaskar Sarkar, 'Introduction: The Subaltern and the Popular', *Postcolonial Studies*, 8/4 (2005), pp. 357–63.

10 Mario Rutten and Carol Upadhya (eds), *Small Business Entrepreneurs in Asia and Europe: Towards a Comparative Perspective* (London: SAGE, 1997); Sharad Chari, *Fraternal Capital: Peasant Workers, Self-Made Men, and Globalisation in Provincial India* (New Delhi: Permanent Black, 2004); Barbara Harriss-White, *India Working: Essays on Society and Economy* (Cambridge: Cambridge University Press, 2003).

11 Tirthankar Roy, *A Business History of India: Enterprise and the Emergence of Capitalism from 1700* (Cambridge: Cambridge University Press, 2018); Lakshmi Subramanian, *Three Merchants of Bombay: Business Pioneers of the Nineteenth Century* (London: Portfolio, 2016); Thomas A. Timberg, *The Story of Indian Business: The Marwaris, From Jagat Seth to the Birlas* (London: Penguin Books, 2014); Dwijendra Tripathi and Jyoti Jumani, *The Concise Oxford History of Indian Business* (New Delhi: Oxford University Press, 2007).

12 R. Chandavarkar, 'Industrialisation in India before 1947: Conventional Approaches and Alternative Perspectives', *Modern Asian Studies*, 19/3 (1985), pp. 623–68; O. Goswami, 'Sahibs, Babus and Banias: Changes in Industrial Control in Eastern India', in Rajat K. Ray, *Entrepreneurship and Industry in India, 1800–1947* (New Delhi: Oxford, 1993), pp. 233–56.

13 Alexander Bubb, 'Class, Cotton and "Woddaries": A Scandinavian Railway Contractor in Western India, 1860–69', *Modern Asian Studies*, 51/5 (2017), pp. 1369–93; Ian J. Kerr, *Engines of Change: The Railroads that Made India* (Westport, CT: Praeger Publishers, 2007).

14 Claude Markovits, *Merchants, Traders and Entrepreneurs: Indian Business in the Colonial Era* (London: Palgrave Macmillan, 2008), p. 210; Carol Matheson Connell, 'Jardine Matheson & Company: The Role of External Organisation in a Nineteenth-Century Trading Firm', *Enterprise & Society*, 4/1 (2003), pp. 99–138; Timberg, *Story of Indian Business*; Tripathi and Jumani, *Concise Oxford History of Indian Business*; Ritu Birla, *Stages of Capital: Law, Culture and Market Governance in Late Colonial India* (Durham; London: Duke University Press, 2009).

15 Chari, *Fraternal Capital*; Ian J. Kerr, *Building the Railways of the Raj 1850–1900* (New Delhi: Oxford University Press, 1995).

16 Roy, *Business History of India*; Subramanian, *Three Merchants of Bombay*; Robert Lee (ed.), *Commerce and Culture: Nineteenth-Century Business Elites* (New York: Routledge, 2016); Bishnupriya Gupta, 'The Rise of Modern Industry in

Colonial India', in Latika Chaudhary, Bishnupriya Gupta, Tirthankar Roy, and Anand V. Swamy (eds), *New Economic History of Colonial India* (New York: Routledge, 2016), pp. 67–83; Timberg, *Story of Indian Business*; Markovits, *Merchants, Traders and Entrepreneurs*; Tripathi and Jumani, *Concise Oxford History of Indian Business*; Kerr, *Building the Railways*, pp. 59–67.

17 Markovits, *Merchants, Traders and Entrepreneurs*, pp. 144–8. See also Subramanian, *Three Merchants of Bombay*.

18 Roy, *Business History of India*. The findings of other scholars regarding eastern India are contrary to what Roy has maintained. The scope for pragmatic collaboration between Indian and expatriate entrepreneurs deteriorated in eastern India from the 1820s and generally from the late 1840s. See Tony Webster, 'An Early Global Business in a Colonial Context: The Strategies, Management and Failure of John Palmer and Company of Calcutta 1780–1830', *Enterprise and Society*, 6/1 (2005), pp. 98–133; Shubhra Chakrabarti, 'The English East India Company and the Indigenous Sloop Merchants of Bengal: Ankrur Dutta and his Family, 1757–1857', *Studies in History*, 20/1 (2004), pp. 131–57; Blair B. Kling, *Partner in Empire: Dwarkanath Tagore and the Age of Enterprise in Eastern India* (Berkeley: University of California Press, 1976).

19 Amiya Kumar Bagchi, *Capital and Labour Redefined: India and the Third Worlds* (London: Anthem Press, 2002), pp. 3–114; Sabyasachi Bhattacharya, *The Colonial State: Theory and Practice* (New Delhi: Primus, 2016), pp. 96–114. Sabyasachi Bhattacharya, *The Financial Foundation of the British Raj: Ideas and Interests in the Reconstruction of Indian Public Finance 1858–1872* (New Delhi: Orient Longman, 2005 [1971]), pp. 23–4, 66.

20 Maria Misra, *Business, Race, and Politics in British India 1850/1960* (New York: Oxford University Press, 1999).

21 Ibid., p. 36.

22 Ibid., p. 33.

23 Ibid.

24 J. H. Abbott worked for the GIPR from 1857 to 1884. He had also become an engineer through an apprenticeship, under the senior engineer Sir Charles Fox in 1850–2. See www.gracesguide.co.uk/John_Hallen_Abbott, accessed 13 September 2020. An apprenticeship, as part of the old system of guild pupillage, was a popular route in engineering in the British Empire until the later nineteenth century. Engineering colleges were few and far between, while hands-on learning was regarded as the principal method. See Ajantha Subramanian, *The Caste of Merit: Engineering Education in India* (Cambridge: Harvard University Press, 2019), p. 32.

25 LNU, HA, JSA, F1F:1, Diary 1860–1, 4 January 1861. LNU, HA, HEA, E1:2, J. Stephens to G. Stephens, 22 January 1861.

26 Huseby Estate, Joseph Stephens' diary 1863, 5 November 1863. LNU, HA, JSA, F1A:4, Wells to Stephens. 22 December 1863.

27 LNU, HA, HEA, E1:12a. The Article of Agreement for Apprenticeship was signed by his father and sister on 5 December 1863. It was designed to help Stephens become a civil engineer over a period of three years from 19 February 1860. The witnesses were White at Kundewaree (Kundewadi) in 1860, Stephens' sister, Ingeborg Abbott, and George Stephens. The completion of his apprenticeship in December 1863 seems to have been occasioned by the fact that J. S. F. Stephens now took up his own subcontract for railway construction from the bigger company, Lee, Watson, and Aiton Construction Company, building the railway infrastructure for the GIPR, and that the former wanted the bills signed by an engineer. See LNU, HA, JSA, F1A:4, Watson to Stephens, 26 October and 19 December 1863.

28 LNU, HA, JSA, F1A:1, Barker to Stephens, 12 September 1861.
29 Huseby Estate, Joseph Stephens' diary 1862, 30 October 1862.
30 Ibid., Joseph Stephens' diary 1863, 24 August 1863.
31 LNU, HA, JSA, F1A:1, G. Williamson to Stephens, 29 August 1865.
32 Ibid., F1A:3, Vantilart to Stephens,1 July 1868.
33 Ibid., F1A:1, Sandford to Stephens, 22 November 1865.
34 Ibid., F1A:1, Sandford to Stephens, 7 September 1865.
35 Ibid., F1A:3, Vantilart to Stephens, 1 July 1868.
36 Pierre Bourdieu, *Distinction: A Social Critique of the Judgement of Taste*, trans. Richard Nice (Cambridge: Harvard University Press, 1996 [1984]), pp. 13–14, 23.
37 LNU, HA, JSA, F1A:3, Stephens to Dangerfield, 16 March 1867.
38 Ibid.
39 Bourdieu, *Distinction*, pp. 282, 286, 291.
40 LNU, HA, JSA, F1A:2, A. H. Macaulay, Deputy Commissioner of Akola District, to Stephens, 11 May 1866; J. Fitz Gerald, Assistant Commissioner of Amravati District, to Stephens, 30 August 1866.
41 LNU, HA, HEA, E1:2, J. Stephens to G. Stephens, 23 July 1869.
42 Ibid., J. Stephens to G. Stephens, 22 January 1861.
43 Huseby Estate, Joseph Stephens' diary 1862, 23 February 1862; ibid., Joseph Stephens' diary 1863, 4 February, 28 June, and 26 July 1863; LNU, HA, JSA, F1A:2, Sandford to Stephens, 8 October 1866.
44 LNU, HA, JSA, F1A:1, Davies to Stephens, 27 April 1865.
45 Ibid., F1A:4, Wells to Stephens, 7 January 1865.
46 LNU, HA, HEA, E1:3a, G. Stephens to J. Stephens, 20 March 1865.
47 LNU, HA, JSA, F1A:1, Wells to Stephens, 21 December 1862.
48 Ibid., F1A:2, Sandford to Stephens, 8 October 1866.
49 Similar observations are made in studies of business enterprises in early nineteenth-century eastern India: Partha Chatterjee, *The Black Hole of Empire: History of a Global Practice of Power* (Princeton: Princeton University Press, 2012); Webster, 'An Early Global Business'; Bhattacharya, *Colonial State*.
50 LNU, HA, JSA, F1A:1: Abbott to Stephens, 27 April 1864; Tender notice (W. Mennie), 19 April 1865; Mennie to Stephens, 5 May and 2 November 1865; ibid., F1A:2, Abbott to Stephens, 25 April and 13 July 1866; F1D:1, Contract No. 13, July 1866.
51 Ibid., F1A:2, G. Shepherd to Stephens, 8 December 1866; J. R. Manning to Stephens, 13 December 1866.
52 Ibid., F1A:1, Manning to Stephens, 21 December 1865.
53 Ibid., F1A:2, Manning to Stephens, 13 December 1866.
54 Ibid., F1A:1, Satara Collectorate to Stephens (tender for an irrigation works), 4 February 1864, and Stephens to R. S. Sellon (tender for a river bridge in Poona), 15 February 1865; F1C:2, Stephens to Siegfried Company (tender for a press house in Khamgaon), 14 September 1868; Tender for Kherwady station: booking office platform, wooden house for booking office, and Tender for residence of store clerk, store room, and store office at Munmar station, 26 April 1866; and Tender for the doubling of line between Callian and Kurjut, 12 October 1866; F1A:2, Secretary to the GIPR Agent to Stephens, 15 and 23 November 1866; F1A:3, Julles Siegfried & Com, Bombay to Stephens, 28 September 1868.
55 Ibid., F1A:3, Dangerfield to Stephens, 8 July and 30 September 1867.
56 Ibid., F1A:3, Dangerfield to Stephens, 15 January 1868.
57 Ibid., F1A:3, Darke to Stephens, 30 December 1867.
58 Ibid., E1:12a, Miscellaneous incoming correspondence, 18 November 1870.
59 LNU, HA, HEA, E1:3a; E1:2; E1:12a.
60 LNU, HA, JSA, F1B:1, Contract papers; F1E:1, Pay lists.

61 Huseby Estate, Joseph Stephens' diary 1863, 12 May and 7 July 1863.
62 LNU, HA, JSA, F1B:1, Contract papers; F1E:1, Pay lists.
63 LNU, HA, JSA, Diary 1860–1 and pay sheets; Huseby Estate, Joseph Stephens' diaries 1862 and 1863.
64 Tirthankar Roy, *Company of Kinsmen: Enterprise and Community in South Asian History 1700–1940* (New Delhi: Oxford University Press, 2010). Tirthankar Roy and Anand V. Swamy, *Law and the Economy in Colonial India* (Chicago: University of Chicago Press, 2016).
65 LNU, HA, JSA, F1A:1, Mutow to Stephens, 28 March 1861.
66 Bhattacharya, *The Financial Foundation of the Raj*, p. 53.
67 Huseby Estate, Joseph Stephens' diary 1862, 26 February 1862.
68 Ibid., 10 June 1862.
69 LNU, HA, JSA, F1C:1, Puggery [turban or headgear] for Chimma Wooddary, 11 May 1863.
70 Bubb, 'Class, Cotton and "Woddaries"'.
71 LNU, HA, HEA, E1:3a, G. Stephens to J. Stephens, 5 February 1862. In this observation, nineteenth-century Indians were regarded as debased and in need of soul-lifting Christianity.
72 Ibid., 3 July 1861 and 21 July 1862.
73 Huseby Estate, Joseph Stephens' diary 1863, 14 February 1863. As far as the relationship between Stephens and his Indian subcontractors was concerned, it was patterned on the kind of reciprocal partnership between imperials and colonials that was occasionally found in the Bombay Presidency in nineteenth-century India. Businesspersons like Trawadi Arjunji Nathji and Jamsetjee Jejeebhoy epitomized it in the early part of that century and Premchand Roychand and Jamshedji Dorabji (a major railway contractor) later in the same century. These episodes fit well with the viewpoint maintained by Markovits in *Merchants, Traders and Entrepreneurs*: A racial and communal mix and partnership played a significant role in the growth and dynamism of the economic subsystem of Bombay Presidency. The latter witnessed less discrimination and less antagonism on the part of the imperials towards the colonials. It was a product of the fact that western India fell under British colonial control relatively late compared with the Bengal and Madras regions. This circumstance, as well as the fact that a good number of princely states were located in this region, was conducive to the control exercised by Indian merchants over the channels of information and knowledge related to the trades.
74 LNU, HA, HEA, E1:2, J. Stephens to G. Stephens, 23 July 1869.
75 I have examined wage relations in the construction sector in a separate chapter, titled 'Labour Practices and Well-Being'. The factors responsible for a steep rise in money wages paid to workers were an increase in the cost of living, the workers' struggles for higher wages, and increased competition for workers in the expanding economy of 1860s Deccan.
76 Kerr, *Engines of Change*, p. 28.
77 Bubb, 'Class, Cotton and "Woddaries"'.
78 LNU, HA, JSA, F1A:3, Dangerfield to Stephens, 8, 21, and 26 March 1867, 1 July 1868.
79 Ibid., Dangerfield to Stephens, 8 March 1867.
80 Ibid., Stephens to Dangerfield, 16 March 1867.
81 Ibid., Dangerfield to Stephens, 27 March 1867.
82 LNU, HA, JSA, F1A:4, Wells to Stephens, 9 August 1862.
83 Kerr, *Engines of Change*, pp. 19–36.
84 This financial policy was the product of an ideology of empire. Its followers believed in the need to encourage capital investment in a social overhead for the promotion of exports of useful primary commodities from the colony. The

scheme needed state guarantees or some form of subsidy. The government was inclined to aid the capitalists indirectly, rather than playing an entrepreneurial role. J. S. Mills emphasized this role of government in a backward economy. James Wilson, the Gladstonian Finance Member, felt that the foremost duty of the colonial government was to provide public works and roads with a view to increased production of exportable raw materials, like cotton. The railway companies lobbied for the government to support India in performing a special role, supplying raw materials. See, Bhattacharya, *The Financial Foundation of the Raj*, pp. 40–4.

85 Quoted in Bubb, 'Class, Cotton and "Woddaries"—British Library, India Office Records (IOR)/L/PWD/3/66 [railway letter no. 118 and accompanying letter]. The one dissenting vote on the Viceroy's Council came from General Mansfield, who testified to the 'bad, scamping work' which he had 'heard a great deal of' in the Bombay Presidency.

86 LNU, HA, JSA, F1A:1, G. Williamson to Stephens, 29 August 1865; Alex Mackenzie to Stephens, 29 September and 5 October 1865; H. Macaulay (manager of the Mofussil Press and Ginning Company) to Stephens, 29 December 1865; F1A:2, Major Ker to Stephens, 26 February 1866.

87 Ibid., F1A:2, Budden Jennings to Swan, 2 February 1866; Swan to Stephens, 6 June 1866.

88 Markovits, *Merchants, Traders and Entrepreneurs*, pp. 132–7.

89 LNU, HA, JSA, F1A:2, Oriental Bank to Stephens, 6 December 1866.

90 Ibid., F1A:3, Letter of the sale of Stephens' share, 11 August 1868.

91 Ibid., F1A:3, Elphinstone Land and Press Company Ltd, balance sheet, 30 June 1868; F1A:8, Stephens to Oriental Bank, Bombay, 27 March 1867.

92 LNU, HA, HEA, E1:2, J. Stephens to G. Stephens, 26 February 1869.

93 LNU, HA, JSA, F1A:7, Rogers & Co. to Stephens, 11 January 1868.

94 LNU, HA, HEA, E1:3a, G. Stephens to J. Stephens, 2 April 1868.

References

Bagchi, Amiya Kumar, *Capital and Labour Redefined: India and the Third Worlds* (London: Anthem Press, 2002).

Bhattacharya, Sabyasachi, *The Colonial State: Theory and Practice* (New Delhi: Primus, 2016).

Bhattacharya, Sabyasachi, *The Financial Foundation of the British Raj: Ideas and Interests in the Reconstruction of Indian Public Finance 1858–1872* (New Delhi: Orient Longman, 2005 [1971]).

Birla, Ritu, *Stages of Capital: Law, Culture and Market Governance in Late Colonial India* (Durham; London: Duke University Press, 2009).

Bourdieu, Pierre, *Distinction: A Social Critique of the Judgement of Taste*, trans. Richard Nice (Cambridge: Harvard University Press, 1996 [1984]).

Bubb, Alexander, 'Class, Cotton and "Woddaries": A Scandinavian Railway Contractor in Western India, 1860–69', *Modern Asian Studies*, 51/5 (2017), pp. 1369–93.

Casson, Mark, and Mary B. Rose, 'Institutions and the Evolution of Modern Business', *Business History*, 39/4 (1997), pp. 1–10.

Chakrabarti, Shubhra, 'The English East India Company and the Indigenous Sloop Merchants of Bengal: Ankrur Dutta and His Family, 1757–1857', *Studies in History*, 20/1 (2004), pp. 131–57.

Chandavarkar, R., 'Industrialisation in India before 1947: Conventional Approaches and Alternative Perspectives', *Modern Asian Studies*, 19/3 (1985), pp. 623–68.

Chandler, Alfred D., Jr, *Scale and Scope: The Dynamics of Industrial Capitalism* (Cambridge: Harvard University Press, 2004 [1990]).

Chari, Sharad, *Fraternal Capital: Peasant Workers, Self-Made Men, and Globalisation in Provincial India* (New Delhi: Permanent Black, 2004).

Chatterjee, Partha, *The Black Hole of Empire: History of a Global Practice of Power* (Princeton: Princeton University Press, 2012).

Chattopadhyay, Swati, and Bhaskar Sarkar, 'Introduction: The Subaltern and the Popular', *Postcolonial Studies*, 8/4 (2005), pp. 357–63.

Connell, Carol Matheson, 'Jardine Matheson & Company: The Role of External Organisation in a Nineteenth-Century Trading Firm', *Enterprise & Society*, 4/1 (2003), pp. 99–138.

Derbyshire, Ian, 'The Building of India's Railway: The Application of Western Technology in the Colonial Periphery 1850–1920', in Ian J. Kerr (ed.), *Railways in Modern India* (New Delhi: Oxford University Press, 2005), pp. 268–304.

Douglas, Paul H., 'The Cobb—Douglas Production Function Once Again: Its History, Its Testing, and Some New Empirical Values', *Journal of Political Economy*, 84/5 (1976), pp. 903–16.

Goswami, O., 'Sahibs, Babus and Banias: Changes in Industrial Control in Eastern India', in Rajat K. Ray (ed.), *Entrepreneurship and Industry in India, 1800–1947* (New Delhi: Oxford, 1993), pp. 233–56.

Gupta, Bishnupriya, 'The Rise of Modern Industry in Colonial India', in Latika Chaudhary, Bishnupriya Gupta, Tirthankar Roy, and Anand V. Swamy (eds), *New Economic History of Colonial India* (New York: Routledge, 2016), pp. 67–83.

Harriss-White, Barbara, *India Working: Essays on Society and Economy* (Cambridge: Cambridge University Press, 2003).

Kerr, Ian J., *Building the Railways of the Raj 1850–1900* (New Delhi: Oxford University Press, 1995).

Kerr, Ian J., *Engines of Change: The Railroads that Made India* (Westport, CT: Praeger Publishers, 2007).

Kling, Blair B., *Partner in Empire: Dwarkanath Tagore and the Age of Enterprise in Eastern India* (Berkeley: University of California Press, 1976).

Lee, Robert (ed.), *Commerce and Culture: Nineteenth-Century Business Elites* (New York: Routledge, 2016).

Markovits, Claude, *Merchants, Traders and Entrepreneurs: Indian Business in the Colonial Era* (London: Palgrave Macmillan, 2008).

Misra, Maria, *Business, Race, and Politics in British India 1850/1960* (New York: Oxford University Press, 1999).

Piatt Andrew, Abram, 'Indian Currency Problems', *Quarterly Journal of Economics*, 15/4 (1901), pp. 483–516.

Roy, Tirthankar, *A Business History of India: Enterprise and the Emergence of Capitalism From 1700* (Cambridge: Cambridge University Press, 2018).

Roy, Tirthankar, *Company of Kinsmen: Enterprise and Community in South Asian History 1700–1940* (New Delhi: Oxford University Press, 2010).

Roy, Tirthankar, and Anand V. Swamy, *Law and the Economy in Colonial India* (Chicago: University of Chicago Press, 2016).

Rutten, Mario, and Carol Upadhya (eds), *Small Business Entrepreneurs in Asia and Europe: Towards a Comparative Perspective* (London: SAGE, 1997).

Subramanian, Ajantha, *The Caste of Merit: Engineering Education in India* (Cambridge: Harvard University Press, 2019).

Subramanian, Lakshmi, *Three Merchants of Bombay: Business Pioneers of the Nineteenth Century* (London: Portfolio, 2016).
Timberg, Thomas A., *The Marwaris: From Jagat Seth to the Birlas* (London: Penguin Books, 2014 (1978)).
Tripathi, Dwijendra, and Jyoti Jumani, *The Concise Oxford History of Indian Business* (New Delhi: Oxford University Press, 2007).
Webster, Tony, 'An Early Global Business in a Colonial Context: The Strategies, Management and Failure of John Palmer and Company of Calcutta 1780–1830', *Enterprise and Society*, 6/1 (2005), pp. 98–133.

5 Labour Practices and Well-Being

Construction Workers in 1860s Western India

Dhiraj Kumar Nite

Even as they helped connect the Indian subcontinent through the railways, what life opportunities were made possible by the wages paid to the humblest construction workers in colonial India? My study draws upon the documents, including pay sheets (also referred to as pay lists), contract documents, and private diaries, of one of the subcontractors who became a contractor, Joseph Stephens, who carried out construction projects in the Deccan region of India in the 1860s. This chapter provides a comprehensive view of the wage relations and economic conditions of construction workers in this region, which have received little attention until now.

One of the leading scholars of construction of the railways in India, Ian Kerr, has lamented the paucity of wage data for the study of the economic conditions of railway building workers. According to him, railway companies usually hired labour agents to recruit, supervise, and distribute wages among construction workers. As far as we know, the pay sheets of these labour recruiters mostly never made their way into the archives, making the Stephens' documents a rare and valuable source.[1]

In Indian historiography, the period of the 1850s–70s saw some definitive socio-economic developments. The progress of railway construction in this period led to both the emergence and the integration of labour markets. As argued by Kerr, this development helped workers to regain bargaining power in the economy, which they had lost in the first half of the nineteenth century.[2] Other scholars share a similarly optimistic view of the recovery of per capita income overall and the real income of the productive classes.[3] My study pays close attention to this narrative of recovery. It offers a more nuanced understanding of the circumstances responsible for the new bargaining power and wage gains secured by construction workers during the 1860s.

My enquiry brings to the fore five key features which are particularly relevant to observe: (1) the real income of workers improved; (2) the 'subsistence ratio'—the ratio of total income to the cost of the subsistence basket of sweat labourers—remained less than unity; (3) the element of a constraining contract characterized the work relationship; (4) these workers secured an income sufficient for basic household subsistence only by increasing

DOI: 10.4324/9781003317227-5

the supply of total family labour in the labour market and agitating for improvements in wages; and finally, (5) women and children received a wage increase far below that of adult males. The study traces the factors responsible for this scenario for the economic life of construction workers.

As this study shows, the coercive and constraining institution of labour control and contract enforcement, used by contractors and subcontractors on the Great Indian Peninsula Railway (GIPR), was an essential feature of contractual employment and the commercialized economy on the railway lines connecting central India with the metropolitan cities. It aimed to control labour recruits, both their mobility and their demands for enhanced welfare. Simultaneously, some of the subcontractors and contractors paid relatively attractive wage rates to workers to secure better labour efforts and achieve results. In this contractual system of employment, workers secured an increase in real wages. We therefore need to modify a perspective that has highlighted the use of unfree, coerced, and dependent labour to depress the pay of labourers below the market-clearing wage available in a free labour market.[4] This study underscores that, in railway construction in the 1860s, the use of coerced labour, on the one hand, and a policy of competitively attractive wages, on the other, were not mutually exclusive, but can be explained by the prevailing circumstances.[5]

The material situation of workers was built partly on the macroeconomic conditions of railway construction in India. The state guaranteed attractive returns for the railway companies on their capital investment, while keen competition for labour power among contractors was at work as the economy expanded. In the case of contractors like the Joseph Stephens Construction Company and their management of labour, the microeconomic effects proved relatively favourable for the workers, owing to a policy of offering competitive and attractive wages in return for regular, efficient performance.

As this investigation shows, the workers' material conditions rested partly on their ability to bargain collectively for improved wages. The wage levels they aspired to were set to match price changes and household budgets. Workers looked for a wage structure that would enable them to achieve the respectable status of a male earner, whereas women and children generated a supplementary income for the household. As a social custom, this precluded the articulation of any question of a comparable increase, let alone an equal wage for women. The social tradition of a nexus between caste, race, and gender, on one side, and occupations, on the other, maintained significant wage inequality.

One of the perspectives on labour practices and their connection with welfare returns to workers maintains that enhanced welfare for the productive classes in the latter half of the nineteenth century was a product of a marketization of labour as part of economic growth, labour mobility, and a reduction in the transaction costs of labour power. The marketization of labour as part of a commercialization of the economy led to institutional change, that is, from custom- and status-based employment arrangements to contractual employment. This resulted in a fall in transaction costs and was also connected to labour mobility.[6] Here, the problem of the relatively 'depressed' standards of living for working people has been attributed to a combination of factors, such as excess labour, low productivity, and imperfect or inadequate institutional settings for contract design, and enforcement. Imperfect or inadequate institutional settings such as the 'tenancy laws' were responsible for low productivity in agriculture, while the Breach of Contract Act was responsible for some of the problematic consequences of labour relations. This perspective also argues that constraining institutions such as the Penal Labour Act and the Breach of Contract Act were 'a cruel solution to the contractual problem' in the form of the 'opportunism' of working persons, without necessarily being injurious to welfare returns to those persons.[7]

This position underestimates the coercive and constraining element of many contractual employment arrangements and the 'adverse' effects it was claimed to have on welfare outcomes and labour mobility. The nature of these contracts therefore requires an in-depth study—which this chapter attempts—to prevent erroneous conclusions about macro- and microeconomic trends. Furthermore, the perspective described overlooks the root of the imperfect or inadequate institutional framework. The imperfect institutional matrix may be attributed to the power structure implicit within it and, more so, the fact that it was preferred on account of its cost-effectiveness in achieving surplus extraction, political stability, and labour control. The connection between labour relations, the institution of contract enforcement, and economic performance was never frictionless, and this study intends to clarify these intermeshed processes.[8]

Construction Work

In the first All-India Census in 1872–3, 'labourers' make up 12.3 per cent of a total population of 238.8 million, and the number of construction workers is estimated at about 0.9 million.[9] This low figure for construction workers seems to have included only masons, who were all men. One decade earlier, in 1861, the construction of railways in its initial phase employed over 250,000 men, women, and children.[10] An average of 150 workers were engaged on each mile (1.67 km) of railway line under construction in nineteenth-century India. This average included those who were engaged in bridge construction, tunnelling, and platelaying. There were, however, significant seasonal variations in daily employment levels, with work most intense during the winter months when bridge-building and brickmaking peaked. Depending on the landscape through which the line passed, between one and five miles of railway track could be built in a month.[11]

The workers in our study were largely engaged in the construction of railway structures between Egatpoora (Igatpuri) and Duskheda, covering about 211 miles, and between Bhusawal and Badnera, a distance of approximately

149 miles. The structures built included railway tracks, bridges, culverts, railway stations, engine pits, fences, water tanks, and other railway buildings. These workers were also involved in the construction of four cotton presses and ginning factories in Amravati, Akola, Shegaon, and Khamgaon.

The construction workers recorded in Stephens' accounts performed various tasks. Both adult and experienced workers and adolescent, inexperienced, and aged workers were classified as coolie (or 'cooly' in the accounts). Their gang headman was listed as a *muccadam*. The same division was also applied to the masons, whose headman was titled *maistry*. The accounts also included carpenters and blacksmiths. In addition, we find the positions of cartman, housekeeper, horsekeeper, *ramosy* (guard), *carcoon* (clerk), a writer who kept attendance and accounts, and the inspector who acted as a manager. The class of coolie also included workers who were classified by their caste identity, such as the Nowguna, Tapkir, Sopkar, and Baggarie. One set of masons described by their caste identity was the Goundy.

Such an occupational and social profile of the workforce can be gleaned from Stephens' pay list of September 1862, detailing the workers involved in the construction of two viaducts at Ulusana (now: Alasana) and Jullumb (Jalamb). The 435 workers were listed under 16 categories, which were representative of such work.

Women constituted about 16 per cent of the total workforce and over 25 per cent of the total coolie labour force (including Cooly, Tapkir, and Nowguna). Boys made up less than 5 per cent of the total coolie workforce. A possible reason for this low percentage was the fact that males of

Table 5.1 Occupational pattern

Number of individuals	*Work category*
4	Maistries
53	Masons
2	Watermen
10	Muccadams
24	Tapkirs (tobacco cultivators from Khandesh)
91	Nowgunas (cotton cultivators and packers from Dharwar)
80	Coolies
13	Boys
5	Storekeepers
7	Blacksmiths
1	Carpenter
61	Drillers
72	Women
1	Nightwatchman
9	Cartmen
2	Guntun and Batta (weighmen)

Source: Pay list kept by Joseph F. Stephens, September 1862, Alasana and Jalamb.[12]

the age of 15 and females of the 'cohabitation' age of 13 were regarded as adults. Only those below the age of 13 were counted as children.[13] However, the All India Census of 1872–3 shows an adverse sex ratio of 940 females per 1,000 males. A very small number of girls were occasionally listed in the pay sheets, in a way that indicates that, unlike boys, they would have shouldered responsibility for kitchen and household work, and for minding toddlers.[14] The occupational and social make-up of the workforce differed on earth-moving, ballasting, and platelaying sites. The first two were generally subcontracted to Indian petty contractors or subcontractors. Among these, Ismael Hakem, Khader Shaik, Chimma Patel, Khadar Bhoy, and Hunmmanta Cowjee were noted down in Stephens' accounts. Their names indicate that they were Muslim, Hindu, as well as Parsi, belonging to the well-off echelons of their respective communities. Coolies were mostly engaged in moving earth and ballasting. For these heavy 'unskilled' tasks, women and children formed nearly half of the total labour force.

The workers' pay sheets allow us to compile statistical data on their earnings. In these, an adjustment of the money wages for price levels in the subsistence basket shared by workers reveals the trend in real wages over time. The labour market was not fully integrated in the 1860s. This means that workers received different wage rates from the same employer and for the same type of work at the different worksites. In addition, prices varied in the different markets for food grains and clothing, the two principal items forming the workers' subsistence basket.

Workers on the new construction sites received wages in cash. The pay sheets indicate that most of them received monthly wages. They generally received certain advance payments upon recruitment and *cherimerry* (gifts of cash) during the working month. Such advances and cherimerry were to some extent adjusted in the worker's monthly wage payment.

The wages paid differed according to the skill premium, profession, gender, age, experience, and social identity of the workers. The wage tables (Tables 5.2–5.4) show that, amongst male sweat labourers, customarily called coolies, rates varied to the tune of 14–43 per cent between experienced adult workers, on the one hand, and the young, aged, and what Stephens described as the 'lazy', on the other. Between men and women, wages differed by between 33 and 57 per cent. The wages paid to Nowgunas and Tapkirs were substantially higher than those of experienced coolie men. There could be a twofold explanation for this wage differentiation amongst sweat labourers. Nowgunas and Tapkirs were migrants from the Dharwar and Khandesh regions. They may have charged a higher rate to cover the costs of migration and a temporary stay in thatched huts close to the project sites. It also appears that they negotiated a wage rate in accord with their social identity as cotton workers and tobacco cultivators, thereby remaining socially superior to the coolies who had a degraded status.[15]

The *muccadam* invariably received a wage rate nearly two-thirds higher than the members of his gang. He acted as a labour agent or middleman between workers and contractors. He was responsible for the actual recruitment of coolies on behalf of contractors, the daily mobilization of coolies, and frontline supervision on the worksites. Two other factors contributed to raising his total earnings. The pay sheets reveal that advance money paid to individual gangers was frequently left unadjusted in his monthly earnings: it is not captured in the wage tables below. At the same time, pay sheets show that he worked for 26 to 30 days in a month, whereas other coolies worked an average of 24 days a month.

Significantly, construction work took place on all days. Workers themselves chose to rest on Sundays; hence, the latter became unpaid weekly holidays.[16] The same scenario occurred on a day following the monthly pay day. The cartmen were the only group working on all six days in a week, and thus 26 days a month. All of them worked from sunrise to sunset, ranging from 10 to 12 hours a day, regularly enjoying breaks for breakfast and lunch at the worksites. They absented themselves on festivals, including Dussehra, Diwali, Holi, Nagpanchami (half-day leave), Eid, and Muharram. They took breaks from the work schedule to meet other familial calls and suffered interruptions caused by sickness, monsoon showers, and storms. During the monsoon months of July and August, workers lost nearly half of their typical working days.[17]

Amongst masons, the *maistry* (their gang headman) was the counterpart of the *muccadam*, except for the fact that the difference in wage rates paid to the maistry and the masons was not more than 40 per cent at best.

Wages paid to sweat labourers, described as unskilled coolies, and masons showed a substantial increase from September 1862, in excess of the price index. Hence, their real earnings (purchasing power) rose. The biggest

Table 5.2 Wages (Rs.-As-Pies). (1 Re = 16 As, 1 As =12 Pies)

Sweat labourer 1

Year	*Coolie 1*		*Coolie 2 (adolescent, aged, inexperienced)*		*Women and boys*		*Muccadam*	
	As/day	*Rs/month*	*As/d*	*Rs/mth*	*As/d*	*Rs/mth*	*As/d*	*Rs/mth*
1830–50	2.67	4	2	3	1.33	2		
1861–August 1862	3	4.50	2.5	3.75	2	3.00	5.5	8.94
Sept–Dec 1862	5	7.50	3	4.50	3	4.50	8	13.00
1863	4.5	6.75	3.5	5.25	2.5	3.75	10	16.25
1864	6	9	5	7.50	4	6.00	9	14.63
1865	7	10.50	4	6.00	3	4.50	12	19.50
1866	6	9	5	7.50	3	4.50	13	21.13
1867	7	10.50	4	6.00	3	4.50	12	19.50
1868	7	10.50	6	9.00	3	4.50	12	19.50

Table 5.3 Wages

Skilled									
Year	*Mason 1*		*Mason 2 (adolescent, aged, inexperienced)*		*Blacksmith*		*Carpenter*		*Writer*
	As/day	*Rs/month*	*As/d*	*Rs/mth*	*As/d*	*Rs/mth*	*As/d*	*Rs/mth*	*Rs/mth*
1830–50	10	15			10	15	10	15	
1861–August 1862	10	15	4	6	10	15	6	9	12
Sept.–Dec. 1862	14	21	6	9	14	21	9	13.5	22
1863	14	21	6	9	14	21	10	15	25
1864	14	21	10	15	12	18	10	15	20
1865	16	24	8	12	16	24	16	24	12
1866	14	21	8	12	16	24	16	24	20
1867	20	30	10	15	20	30	20	30	20
1868	20	30	10	15	20	30	20	30	30

Source: From 1861 to 1868, see LNU, HA, JSA, F1E, Pay lists and pay sheets.

Table 5.4 Real wages in terms of the price of monthly subsistence in base year 1861 (Pb) [MW/(Pt/Pb). MW—Money wage. Pt—price in current year. Pb—price in base year]

Year	*Coolie 1*		*Coolie 2 (adolescent, aged, inexperienced)*		*Women and boys*	
	As/day	*Rs/month*	*As/d*	*Rs/mth*	*As/d*	*Rs/mth*
1830–50	3.75	5.62	2.81	4.21	1.87	2.81
1861–Aug 1862	3.00	4.50	2.50	3.75	2.00	3.00
Sept–Dec 1862	4.43	6.64	2.66	3.98	2.66	3.98
1863	3.59	5.38	2.79	4.19	1.99	2.99
1864	4.16	6.25	3.47	5.21	2.78	4.16
1865	5.08	7.62	2.90	4.35	2.18	3.26
1866	4.27	6.40	3.55	5.33	2.13	3.20
1867	5.48	8.22	3.13	4.70	2.35	3.52
1868	6.07	9.11	5.21	7.81	2.60	3.71
	Compound growth rates (CGR) of real wages 1861–8 [(V(tn)/V(to))^1/(tn-to)- 1]					
		10.60		11.05		3.10

increase, in the order of 8–12 compound annual rates of growth, was seen for male coolies and masons over the period 1861–8. Among them, the second grade of coolies and masons received a larger increase. This suggests there was greater demand for the low-paid employees. It could also

Table 5.5 Real wages in terms of the price of monthly subsistence in 1861 (Pb). (MW/(Pt/Pb))

Year	*Mason 1*		*Mason 2 (adolescent, aged, inexperienced)*	
	As/day	*Rs/month*	*As/day*	*Rs/month*
1830–50	14.05	21.07		
1861–Aug 1862	10.00	15.00	4.00	6.00
Sept–Dec 1862	12.39	18.59	5.31	7.97
1863	11.16	16.74	4.78	7.18
1864	9.72	14.58	6.94	10.41
1865	11.61	17.41	5.80	8.70
1866	9.95	14.93	5.69	8.53
1867	15.66	23.50	7.83	11.75
1868	17.35	26.03	8.68	13.01
Compound growth rates (CGR) of real wages 1861–8				
		8.19		11.70

Source: J. A. Robertson, *Prices and Wages in India* (Calcutta: Government Printing, 1905), pp. 10–86. The figures for prices are also adjusted from Allen, 'India in the Great Divergence'. See also R. C. Allen and Roman Studer, 'Prices and Wages in India, 1595–1930', 12 September 2009, gpih.ucdavis.edu/files/**India_Allen-Studer**_v2,pl.xls, accessed 18 October 2016. Cloth prices from Roy, 'Consumption of Cotton Cloth', pp. 22–3. For food grain prices, see also Sumit Guha, *The Agrarian Economy of Bombay Deccan* (New Delhi: Oxford University Press, 1985).

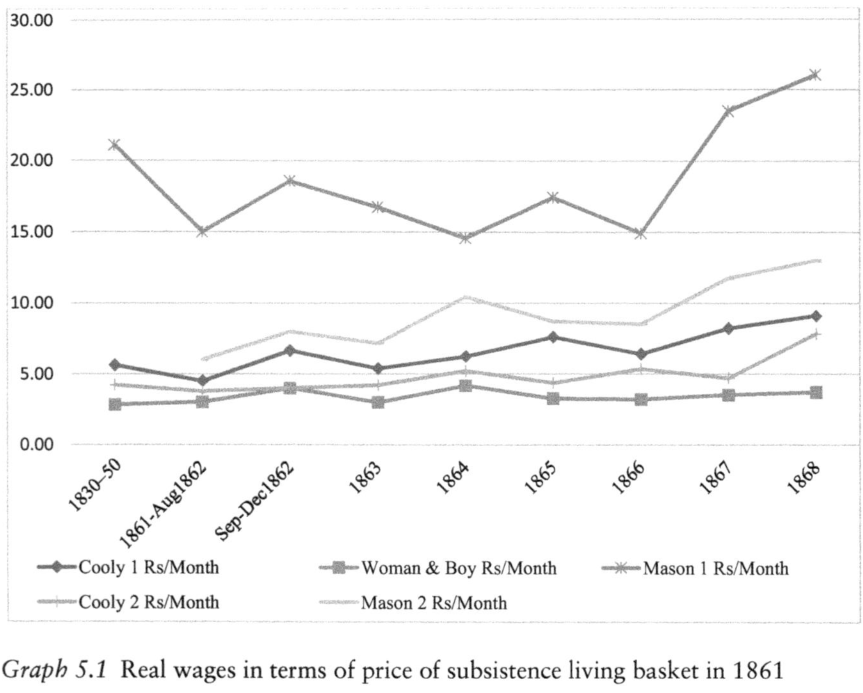

Graph 5.1 Real wages in terms of price of subsistence living basket in 1861

imply that the second-grade employees improved their skills at work and sought commensurate returns on them. Women and boys received the smallest increase. This could indicate an abundant supply of such workers for the work of loading and carrying, within a rigidly gendered labour market. It could also have been a result of the belief that women and boys were only earning a supplementary income for their families.[18]

The improvements in wages secured by construction employees were favourable compared with those of agricultural and other sweat labourers. Agricultural labourers earned in the range of As (annas) 2–4 per day and Rs. 30–67 a year in the 1860s, with some improvement secured up to the early 1870s. Subsequently, their earnings first shrank and then hovered around Rs. 45–60 a year—Rs. 4–5 a month—from the mid-1870s onwards. Their pay was often on the low side, although in addition they usually received some food and cloth from employers.[19] The increase in real wages secured by male construction workers hired directly by Stephens was bigger compared, for instance, with postal runners employed in the Deccan and central India, who received from Rs. 5 to Rs. 6.5 a month over the period 1860–70.[20] The improvement in real earnings of construction employees during the 1860s confirms a historical description, which suggests that the real income of working persons rose in the last third of the nineteenth century. Around this period, some scholars have suggested, working people attained the same standard of living which they had had at the turn of the nineteenth century.[21]

Skill Premium

The skill premium, that is, the higher remuneration for numeracy and literacy skills, as paid to the writer and the *carcoon* (clerk), seems small in comparison with the experienced mason, blacksmith, and carpenter. At the same time, it was significant in relation to the second grade of masons (see Table 5.6).[22] Writers and clerks worked every day of the month. It is also to be noted that the salary paid to European writers, such as Hant Louis, W. H. Ferriss, and Butter, was in the order of 50–90 per cent higher than that of their native counterparts, such as Sattoba Peragooh, Bittoba Peeraju, and Ugoonath Sueraraw. The wages of Indian writers were close to those of second-grade masons and far lower than those of first-grade masons. Here, three factors seem to have played a role. European writers received a premium on their command of the English language, and in recognition of their relatively high standard of living and their racial affinity with their employer.[23]

The wage distribution amongst different occupational groups also underwent a notable shift. The skill premium paid to experienced masons dwindled. By contrast, it rose for second-grade masons (see Table 5.6). Following Jan Luiten van Zanden and Pim de Zwart, the skill premium chiefly depends on interest rates and the efficiency of the capital market, arrangements for

Table 5.6 Wage distribution (inequality) ratios: Skill premium (mason/coolie, writer/mason)

Year	*Mason 1/ coolie 1*	*Mason 2/ coolie 1*	*Mason 1/ coolie 2*	*Mason 2/ coolie 2*	*Writer/ mason 1*	*Writer/ mason 2*
1830–50	3.75		5			
1861–Aug 1862	3.33	1.33	4.00	1.60	0.80	2.00
Sept–Dec 1862	2.80	1.20	4.67	2.00	1.05	2.44
1863	3.11	1.33	4.00	1.71	1.19	2.78
1864	2.33	1.67	2.80	2.00	0.95	1.33
1865	2.29	1.14	4	2.00	0.50	1.00
1866	2.33	1.33	2.80	1.60	0.95	1.67
1867	2.86	1.43	5	2.50	0.67	1.33
1868	2.86	1.43	3.33	1.67	1.00	2.00

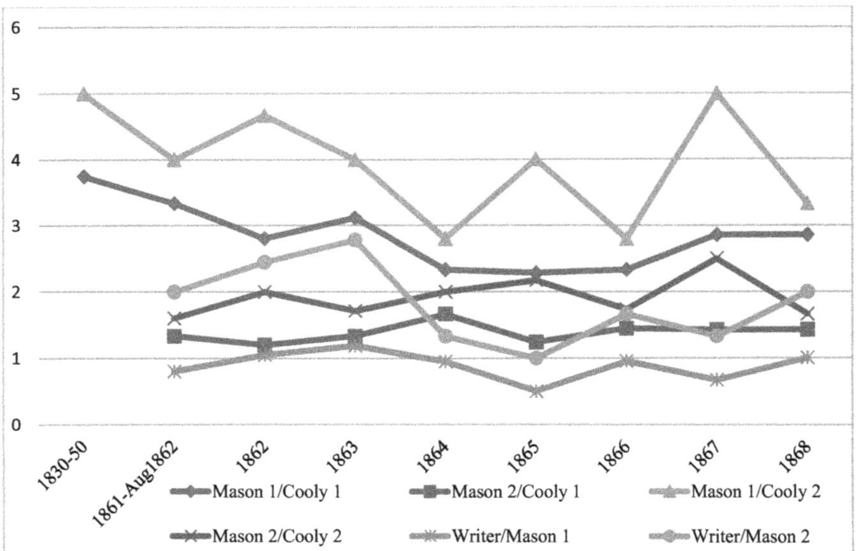

Graph 5.2 Wage inequality or distribution ratios: Skill premium

training and education, the factors shaping the demand for skill, real wages and productivity, the family pattern and its approach towards human capital formation, technological intensity, and bargaining capacity.[24] Interest rates affect the skill premium, because a low interest rate implies an efficient capital market and may allow the stakeholder to increase their investment in human capital formation (training and schooling). Interest rates on loans from the local *sowcar* (moneylender) available to peasants and workers in the Deccan were usually in the range of 24–48 per cent or even more a year. This seems exorbitant and appears to have been a source of widespread indebtedness in the productive classes. Significantly, the rate amongst moneylenders themselves, belonging to the Marwari and Bania groups, was just 6 per cent a year, and bank interest rates hovered around 8 per cent per annum in the later nineteenth century.[25] The gap in interest rates charged in India and England (4 per cent per annum) was much greater than the difference in the skill premium, Jan Lucassen and de Zwart point out.[26]

Arrangements for training showed a marked difference. In India, the caste-based mechanism for occupational training and skills transfer remained intact in the nineteenth century. Some scholars have argued that the caste system became rigid in nineteenth-century India, compared with what existed and the way it functioned in the seventeenth and eighteenth centuries. Curiously, Parthasarathi maintains that caste, rather than impeding economic activity, may have facilitated it in seventeenth- and eighteenth-century India. The rigidification of caste in the nineteenth century was a result, firstly, of the codification of new *shastric* discourse and personal laws. The latter twin developments contributed to a more rigid nexus between caste and occupation. Secondly, ruralization, peasantization, and regression in the colonial economy attenuated the scope for social and spatial mobility and caused fragmentation of the labour market.[27] This change meant that coolies and peasants could not readily insinuate themselves into the ranks of masons, blacksmiths, and carpenters and were unable to swell the supply of artisanal labour. This explains in part the rise in the skill premium and the worsening wage inequality in the nineteenth century compared with the previous two.

The marginal reduction in wage inequality between coolies and experienced masons and an increase in the same between coolies and second-grade masons also hint at a *slight* moderation of the rigid nexus between caste and occupation in the 1860s. This episode, it could be said, reflects the fact that the economy, which was *slowly* and quite *modestly* entering a new stage of commercialization, industrialization, and expansion from the 1850s onwards, still bore the retarding effect of the caste-occupation nexus. The new economy had posed few threats, however, to the constraining caste system. In the Deccan region and western India, the anti-Brahmanism movement led by Jyotiba Phule and others had begun to critique the caste system and was propagating the idea of emancipation and dignity. It sought to expand the educational opportunities of the productive classes—the subordinated castes (*Shudras* and *Ati-Shudras*)—and women from 1848 onwards.[28] One would imagine that this would have facilitated the formation of human capital and counteracted the retarding impact of the caste-occupation nexus. In the 1860s, however, its effects in terms of human capital formation, and a reduction in the skill premium and wage inequality, had still to emerge.

Factors potentially influencing the demand for skills include demographic changes and economic expansion. Sumit Guha estimates that the population of the subcontinent was 254.51 million in 1881, as against 159.14 million in 1800, a 60 per cent increase in eight decades. Similarly, the population of central India, Central Province and Berar division and Hyderabad, was 20.4 million in 1800, whereas the 1881 census counted 30.9 million inhabitants: an increase of 51 per cent. In western India (Bombay Presidency and adjacent states), the population was 12.84 million in 1800; the comparable figure for 1872 was 21.08 million, an estimated increase of 64 per cent.[29] This rise in population would, on the one hand, create a demand for housing construction and, on the other, increase the supply of sweat labourers more than skilled. This correlation would break down if per capita income, real wages, and productivity showed recognizable growth. Such growth would entail a rise in investment in human capital. By contrast, a combination of agrarian depression, deindustrialization, ruralization, and sedentarization caused the economy to contract during the first half of the nineteenth century.[30] Berar region was no exception. In this caste-stratified society, however, supplies of sweat labour and artisanal labour would be proportionate to the social stratum. We thus observe that second-grade masons, hired at a lower rate than their senior colleagues, joined the labour market in almost the same proportion as their coolie counterparts. This was reflected in comparable percentage increases in their wages.

The new spate of construction and its dynamics in the 1860s appear to have been the single most crucial factor. This expanding sector was seeking an increased number of employees and, at the same time, looking to reduce costs by showing a preference for coolies and masons of the second grade. Hence, the larger percentage increases in wages went to them.

Having established that a marked increase in wages was secured by construction workers, let us now examine the consequences of this increase by considering the standards of living workers were able to attain.

Living Standards

One indicator of living standards is the ratio of a person's total annual earnings to the cost of his or her yearly subsistence basket, what Robert C. Allen has termed the subsistence ratio.[31] This is a narrow indicator of well-being; an adequate indicator would also cover social opportunities, workplace safety, ecological integrity, security of life, freedom of participation and thought, political entitlement, and other sources of happiness.[32] Here, this narrow indicator of well-being in terms of the cost of the subsistence basket is deployed to get a sense of the degree of improvement or suffering faced by workers.

Our estimate of annual earnings takes into account the method of payment and the actual working days performed by workers. The methods of daily wages, piece rates, and task-based payments existed side by side. The number of days worked by the different occupational groups, as indicated before, varied between an average of 24 and 26 per month. The working year, excluding days away from worksites on account of interruptions caused by the monsoon and festivals, was between 288 and 264 days. Additionally, employers frequently recorded workers' performance as amounting to half or three-quarters some days and calculated wages accordingly, while the workers themselves considered such days to be full workdays. Therefore, the annual earnings of workers—wage rates multiplied by workdays—were in all likelihood lower than what we have, for the sake of convenience, roughly calculated here.

The total household income of a coolie family combined the earnings secured by both husband and wife, referred to as family labour. Earnings of boys and girls are left out in our calculation, since their overall presence in the workforce was small.

The subsistence basket is based on the consumption pattern of workers (see Table 5.7). It is larger than the 'bare bones basket' used by Allen in his comparative study of global inequality.[33] It includes an average caloric intake of 2,480 per adult in the family, that is, 2,730 for an adult man and 2,230 for an adult woman performing 'moderate work', as recommended by the National Institute of Nutrition (Indian Council of Medical Research) since 1944.[34] It also includes cloth consumption of an average of eight yards per person, which was the national average of cotton consumption in the 1860s–70s.

The basket is a conservative one from the standpoint of modern workers, who would consume and use tea, furniture, footwear, and more clothes, and spend money on a child's education and urban dwellings.[35] Doubtless, the customary subsistence necessaries of peoples, as both David Ricardo and Karl Marx noted, vary between civilizations and between classes within a civilization. They correspond to the habits and scales of moral and economic progress in societies.[36] A difference between wages and the workers' moral sense of comfort necessarily influenced both wage bargaining and management of actual household budgets.

The cost of subsistence of a worker's family is based on the view, as proposed by Guha, that a family or household in nineteenth-century India (the Deccan) consisted of an average of 4.5 persons. These families included on average 1.44 adult men and a lower proportion of women, given the skewed sex ratio of 134 men to every 100 women aged 12 and above.[37] The overall consumption size of a family would be 3.5 adults, if we assume that a child up to the age of 12 would be equivalent to 0.5 of an adult consumer (see Table 5.8).

The figures for subsistence ratios (Table 5.9 generally and Graph 5.3a in particular) reveal that none of the coolies and second-grade masons earned sufficiently to meet even the subsistence costs of their entire families in 1861–2. After that, wage increases helped second-grade masons to satisfy the prevalent social code of a respectable male earner in the artisanal community. By contrast, coolies deployed the maximum number of working members of the family, involving women and available children in wage work, in order to secure the necessary household income. Consequently, a family-labour economy was prevalent amongst coolies.[38]

Table 5.7 Subsistence basket

		Nutrients/day	
	Quantity/person/year	*Calories*	*Proteins*
Rice	93–120 kg	922.4–1,190	19.3–24.9
Jowar	94–120 kg	778.8–994.2	28.3–36.1
Beans/gram	13–19 kg	129.8–179.7	6.5–9
Meat	3 kg	21	1
Butter/ghi	3 kg	72	0
Sugar	2 kg	21	0
Salt	4 kg (11 g per day)		
Spice	2.9 kg (7.7 g per day)		
Liquor/beer/tobacco	4–5% of total expenditure		
Soap	2.6 kg		
Cotton	4–8 yds		
House	5–10% of consumer spending		
Lamp oil	2.6 kg (edible oil)		
Fuel	3 million BTU		
Mat, cot, bedding, furniture			
Kitchen and eating utensils			
Medical care			
Education and apprenticeship	Re. 1 a year per young child		
Books, newspapers, library, museum			
Recreation and amusement			
Transportation and communications			
Total		1,945–2,478	55.1–71

Source: Adapted from the table Subsistence Income: Basket of Goods, India, prepared by Allen ('India in the Great Divergence', p. 23). See also R. C. Allen and Roman Studer, 'Prices and Wages in India, 1595–1930', 12 September 2009, gpih.ucdavis.edu/files/India_Allen-Studer_v2,pl.xls, accessed 29 September 2016. The figure of four yards of cotton cloth replaces Allen's figure of 3m. The former is taken from the estimate constructed by Roy ('Indigo and Law', pp. 22–3). Jowar (sorghum) was the first-choice food grain among commoners in nineteenth-century Deccan. See Satya, *Cotton and Famine*, p. 193; Guha, *Agrarian Economy*.

Table 5.8 The cost of subsistence (Rs.). (Family size of 4.5 persons, corresponding to 3.5 adult consumers)

Year	*Person/day*	*Person/year*	*Person/month*	*Family/year*	*Family/month*
1830–50	0.058	21.16	1.76	74.08	6.17
1861	0.067	24.30	2.02	85.04	7.09
1862	0.075	27.30	2.27	95.53	7.96
1863	0.082	30.00	2.50	104.99	8.75
1864	0.097	35.23	2.94	123.29	10.27
1865	0.097	35.51	2.96	124.30	10.36
1866	0.098	35.95	3.00	125.83	10.49

Year	*Person/day*	*Person/year*	*Person/month*	*Family/year*	*Family/month*
1867	0.088	32.07	2.67	112.24	9.35
1868	0.087	31.63	2.64	110.71	9.23

Source: Price data are adjusted from Allen and Studer, 'Prices and Wages'. For the figures on household size in nineteenth-century India, see Guha, *Health and Population*, pp. 107–9.

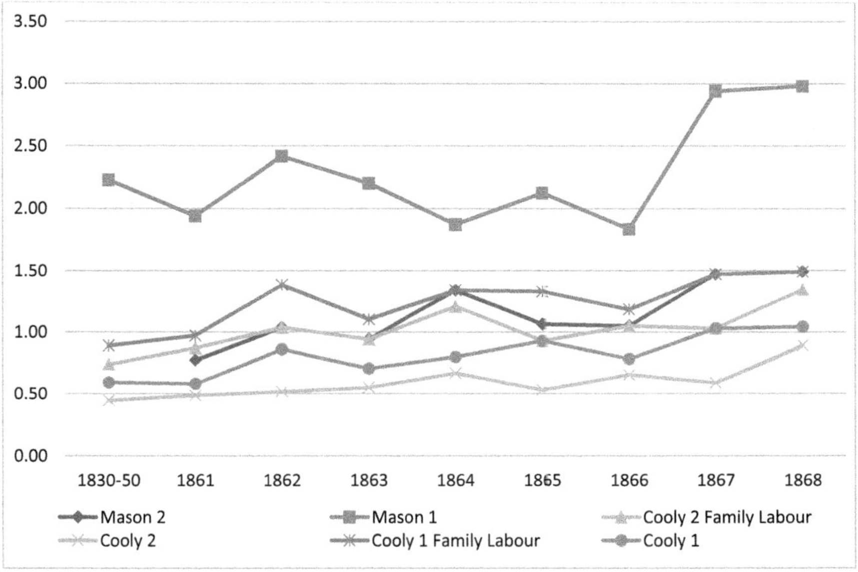

Graph 5.3a Subsistence or welfare ratios

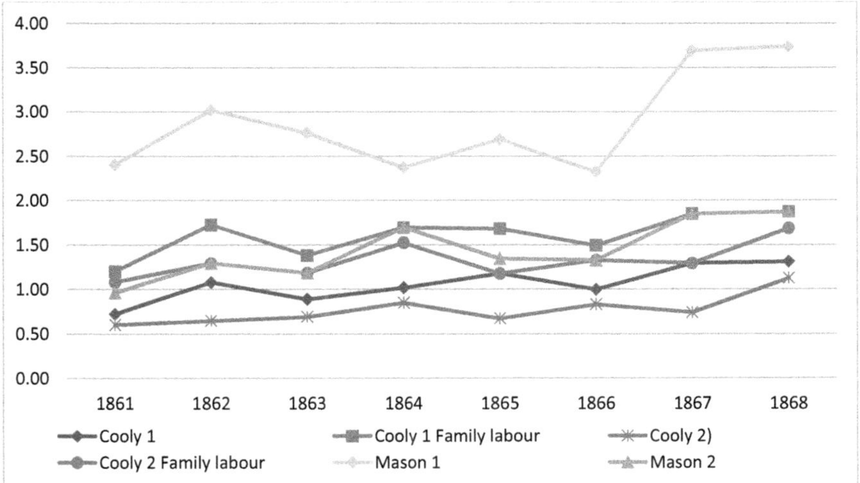

Graph 5.3b Subsistence ratios (bare-bones subsistence basket)

Table 5.9 Subsistence ratios: Annual earnings for 264 days/cost of subsistence basket

Year	*Coolie 1*			*Coolie 2*			*Mason 1*		*Mason 2*	
	Individual	*Family*	*Family Labour*	*Individual*	*Family*	*Family Labour*	*Individual*	*Family*	*Individual*	*Family*
1830s–50s	2.08	0.59	0.89	1.56	0.45	0.74	7.80	2.23		
1861	2.04	0.58	0.97	1.70	0.49	0.87	6.79	1.94	2.72	0.78
1862 (Sept–Dec)	3.02	0.86	1.38	1.81	0.52	1.04	8.46	2.42	3.63	1.04
1863	2.48	0.71	1.10	1.93	0.55	0.94	7.70	2.20	3.30	0.94
1864	2.81	0.80	1.34	2.34	0.67	1.20	6.56	1.87	4.68	1.34
1865	3.25	0.93	1.33	1.86	0.53	0.93	7.43	2.12	3.72	1.06
1866	2.75	0.79	1.18	2.29	0.66	1.05	6.43	1.84	3.67	1.05
1867	3.60	1.03	1.47	2.06	0.59	1.03	10.29	2.94	5.15	1.47
1868	3.65	1.04	1.49	3.13	0.89	1.34	10.43	2.98	5.22	1.49

Roy argues that an increase in the supply of labouring family members to the labour market had the effect of keeping wages stagnant in the long run. These depressed wages, he continues, were not necessarily a welfare loss, since the increased supply of labouring members also enabled many families to gainfully utilize surplus labour.[39] We do not have access to any alternative standpoint on the part of sweat labourers, regarding whether they regretted their inability to achieve a 'respectable' family life on a par with that of masons. Neither we know whether they were unhappy about the presence of children on worksites, either for wage work or to mind toddlers. Nor do we have any alternative opinion of women about why were they unable to bargain for an increase in wages comparable to their male counterparts.

How did the labouring poor meet exigencies such as the extra costs of marriages, funerals, sickness, festivals, and births? They devised ways to keep the cost of their consumption basket at a minimum. They consumed inferior and cheaper food grains, like jowar and bajra (millet) rather than rice.[40] Their consumption of cotton cloth remained on average four yards per person, well below the all-India average of eight yards per person in the 1860s. Their cloth consumption was the barest minimum, involving a pair of loin clothes

Figure 5.1 Railway workmen's quarters at the Great Ravine near Rajmachi Fort, 1856.

Source: Photograph by Alice Tredwell, courtesy Huseby Bruk AB.

(dhoti) for men, and a pair of sari for women. Moreover, their preference was for cheaper, coarse cotton fabrics.[41] They walked and worked barefoot. They lived in houses which the settlement surveyor and census reporter described as being of an inferior sort, constructed of mud and thatch. Migrant coolies and masons stayed in thatched huts put in place as temporary shelter in the vicinity of worksites (Graph 5.3b).[42] They had much in common with the image of the indebted cultivator. The social reformer Jotirao Phule commented critically on the neediness and anguish of the productive classes thus:

> The Malis and Kunbis labour in the fields and pay the taxes. They don't even get clothes to cover their bodies. Tiny little children tend the cattle. They have no shoes; their feet are bare. . .. He has no time to learn anything; the father is in anguish. See, he blames the gods for his misfortune.[43]

The labouring poor also frequently sought the payment of advances and cherimerry from employers. In addition, they took loans from moneylenders and gang headmen. Payment of advances was widespread. The workers negotiated advance payments on recruitment, a small part of their overall pay that was adjusted for in their monthly remuneration. Such advances were of the order of one-fifth to one-quarter of a worker's total expected monthly earnings. In many cases, the old advance was rolled over to the next month. In parallel with this transaction, workers sought cherimerry from their employers. Cherimerry related to festivals seems to have been in the form of cash gifts, called *baksheesh* (a gratuity or charitable gift), comparable to a similar custom prevalent between landowner and labourer in agrarian society. However, cherimerry paid other than on festive occasions was supplementary to advances, and was normally adjusted for in the monthly payment.[44] In a way, coolies and most masons became indebted to their employers in order to be able to afford their routine household necessaries within the temporality of work and monthly payments. Loans from *sowcars* (moneylenders) were designed to deal with other contingencies and exigencies.

The life stories of these workers seem quite close to those of small peasants, who borrowed money from moneylenders and took advances from planters and merchants for cultivation, and to meet the costs of social, religious, and other exigencies and contingencies.[45] In many of these cases, the situation of the productive classes seems to have been close to what Breman calls 'neo-bondage', what Ahuja terms 'hireling labour', and what Banaji refers to as 'coerced wage labour (formal subordination of labour to capital)'.[46] The next section dwells on the function of these kinds of economic transactions in labour relations and the appropriation of labour power.

Labour Relations From the Standpoint of Income and Subsistence

Having defined the role of wages and bonuses, we may now better understand the role of labour relations for the income and subsistence situations of labourers. Workers regularly became indebted to their employers. But what was the significance of such debt dependency as a form of neo-bondage in the labour market? How were male coolie labourers able to bargain for significant increases in their wages? Why were women and boys unable to get the same increases in pay? And why, despite the rise in wage levels, did the subsistence ratios of sweat labourers and second-grade masons remain so 'depressed'?

There were three types of working arrangement: directly employed workers, subcontracted work, and work managed by the materials suppliers, such as the Vaddars ('Woodaries') supplying stone, the tiles contractor, the chunam (lime) supplier, and the cart contractor. Within these three forms, native muccadams and maistries were invariably hired to recruit, supervise, control, and train gang members. Writers were around the worksites to maintain attendance registers (pay lists) and record the progress of work, known as taking quantities. On top of all of them, the project inspector superintended the work, gave instructions on the engineering design of the structure, known as giving levels, determined the quality of the work, made payments to all employees, procured raw materials, and secured labourers. In the case of subcontracted works, the subcontractor himself had a dual role, acting as one of the project inspectors.

Workers were hired at both time and piece rates when subcontractors and contractors employed them directly. In such cases, the vigilance maintained by the contractor and his inspectors and writers was regular and firm. Inspectors chased workers on the worksite and scolded them for any laxity in their performance.[47] The pay sheets had a section for remarks, which frequently included the comment 'lazy' for some workers, implying that it would have some bearing on their remuneration. In the case of subcontracted works, which primarily included earthworks, ballasting, quarrying, fencing, and platelaying, the native petty subcontractor received payment based on the task or a piece rate. These subcontractors paid gang members either a daily or a piece rate.

A close look at the tables of both money and real wages reveals two points at which there were significant increases: September 1862–December 1863 and 1867–8. These changes were, following the argument made by Kerr and Lucassen in other studies, partly an outcome of the bargaining power exercised by workers.[48] They went on strike, obstructed work, and withdrew their labour on many occasions in 1861–8, and particularly so in 1862–3. For instance, workers went on strike on 7 January 1862 on the site of J. S. Wells, seeking a higher wage.[49] The local masons and maistry stopped work and demanded an upward revision of the wage rate on 8–9 December 1862. John Smith Wells, a railway (sub)contractor, is known to have contemplated bringing masons from Poona. Wells believed that the Poona masons claimed relatively high rates and were suitable for arch construction. He wanted to deploy them only on the arches and keep them away from the local masons.[50] Workers on two other sites were reported to have made a noise about their wages on 28 October and 1 November 1862.[51]

Masons also went on a strike for two days on 29–30 October 1863 to demand a higher wage rate.[52]

Measurement of piecework, recording of workdays, and the corresponding remuneration, rather than wage rates, were contentious issues at times. The scenario of a strike by masons around a maistry, Sultan Bhoy, becomes evident from an account of events on 19–22 May 1863. The men refused to start work on Morgaon Bridge after the payment made on 15 May.[53] They were demanding the full payment and were reluctant to begin work despite the offer of an advance of Rs. 2 for each of them. They complained that they had nothing to eat. The dispute emerged over the time sheet maintained by Stephens. Sultan Bhoy asked for the time sheet for his men, which Stephens refused to show him. The masons complained that they were being paid for fewer days than they worked in the month. The time sheet or pay sheet reveals that the writer and inspector marked three-quarters, half, or quarter of a day for men who had supposedly arrived late at the worksite, thereby recording a smaller number of days as the total attendance than the workers believed was due.[54] Workers objected to the discrepancies in these records, resulting in 'much noise, trouble and dispute over the payment of wages'.[55]

Some other workers, in February 1863, refused to accept their monthly pay because of differences over the measurement of piecework and, hence, the amount of payment.[56] For the years after 1863, unfortunately, we do not find a daily diary of Stephens. However, some instances of workers deserting work in 1867–8 are found in the pay sheets.

Masons and coolies separately sought increases in wages. The muccadam or maistry represented them in their protests and negotiations. He was likely to have yielded to the pressure exerted by gang members, who found their wages inadequate and complained of being poorly fed despite performing hard and regular labour.[57] The caste ties among gang members helped them to forge solidarity within their occupational group, while the same factor militated against any inter-occupational solidarity between coolies and masons. Their ability to forge unity based on bonds of caste within an occupational group and to negotiate collectively for better wages also seems to have been responsible for the reinforcement of a gender-segmented labour market, in which women coolies were confined to the jobs of loader and carrier and women's wages slipped further behind those of their male counterparts. Scholars who valorize and romanticize the role of caste and community ties in popular protests aimed at economic bargaining, it could be said, overlook their adverse effect on society as a whole.[58]

What were the workers seeking to secure when they bargained for an increase in their wages? The apparent reason is generally regarded as a desire to adjust earnings in line with inflation. This does not seem a sufficiently motivating factor, however, especially for the years 1867–8, when prices moderated following the end of the cotton boom (1861–5) and despite the drought and crop failures in the Deccan during these two years.

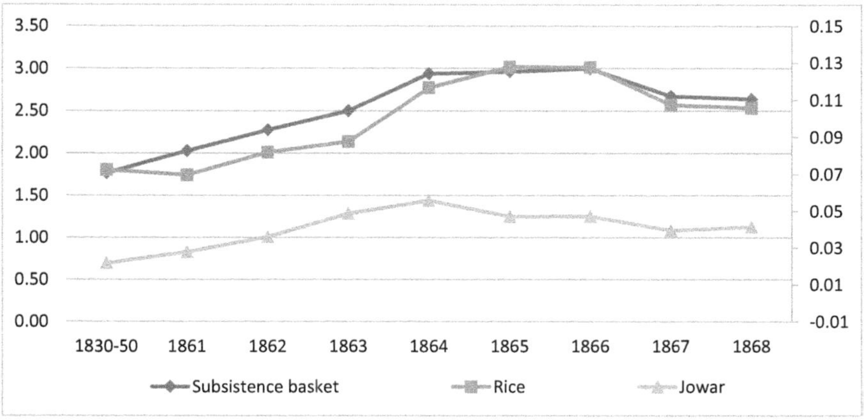

Graph 5.4 Trend in price of subsistence basket, jowar, and rice

Workers appear to have expressed a desire to raise their 'depressed' levels of subsistence and to improve their consumption basket, to include more rice than jowar, more than four yards of cloth a year, and an upgrading of their housing. Masons could spend a larger amount on all these items as compared to coolies (Figure 5.1).[59] They maintained the custom of excluding the women of their families from masonry work. Coolie men would, in all likelihood, have looked forward to becoming 'respectable earners' like their mason counterparts, by securing sufficient earnings to cover the entire household budget. In this scheme of things, therefore, coolie women were unable to assert parity in wages; they remained constrained by the image of being supplementary earners.

The wage exchange mentioned earlier took place amid an expanding economy, increased competition for labour, and a specific labour-management relationship in 1860s Deccan. Some modern centres of industry, plantations, and railway transportation sites, on the one hand, and an expansion of agriculture stimulated by rising prices of agrarian produce, on the other, both created and expanded the labour market. These developments heralded some new labour practices from the 1850s. The construction of two railway lines—Bombay to Jabalpur and Bombay to Madras from the 1850s, and the Nagpur extension between Bhusawal and Nagpur from 1862—coincided with an expansion of the cultivation of cotton in the Deccan and wheat and jowar in central India from the 1850s and, in particular, the cotton boom in 1861–5. The acreage under cultivation also increased.[60] Cotton pressing and ginning factories multiplied in Berar. Similarly, wheat processing mills were opened in central India. Landowners and district officers complained about a scarcity of labour and a land-labour ratio favourable to workers in the 1860s and 1870s.[61]

Stephens' response to the labour situation was to raise wages. Throughout the period 1860–8, Stephens did not increase the wages of his housekeepers, and on one occasion, 14 March 1861, he sacked one of them who asked for a wage rise.[62] He responded in the same way to the agitating coolies and masons until August 1862. Following this period, he succumbed to the pressure. His new wage policy aimed to attract, retain, and discipline workers by offering them a competitively attractive wage rate and linking it to proper performance. The latter was manifested in the meticulous counting of workdays and deductions of pay for late arrival at worksites. This was a period when Wells and Stephens secured a subcontract from the construction company Lee, Aiton, and Watson. They began the construction of two viaducts and a culvert, stone quarrying and some earthworks, embankment, ballasting, platelaying, and fencing between Nandura and Shegaon stations on the Nagpur extension line from July 1862. They were under pressure to finish this project before the end of 1863, which necessitated the systematic and punctual execution of the work involved. Wells, Stephens' senior partner, appeared more considerate and strategically well disposed, especially towards the coolie labour performed by the Vaddars. Vaddars were also hired for stone quarrying and supply. At times, he intervened in their disputes over wages, measurement of piecework, workdays, and amounts paid, and advised his partner and project inspector Stephens to come to terms with them, with a view to keeping the company in their good books. Initially, Stephens found such interventions by Wells—as he described it, 'Wells as usual took their part [the Vaddars']'—partisan and incomprehensible.[63] Interestingly, though, he soon saw the merit of Wells' intervention and adopted the same 'tactful' wage policy in his subsequent dealings with Vaddars.[64]

Stephens' change of heart and mind, however, needs to be understood in a broader context. Stephens was able to offer an upward revision of wages in the setting of the macroeconomic features of railway building in India in the 1850s–60s. The colonial government guaranteed the railway company a 5 per cent return on capital investment in railway building for the first 25 years. This financial arrangement proved conducive to inflating the cost of railway building, which was consequently extremely expensive in India. Kerr shows that, at an average of £18,000 per mile, the railways built in India in the 1850s–60s were costly compared with the projected figure of £12,000 a mile.[65] The private guaranteed companies had no land acquisition costs and low legal costs because the government provided the right of way. In Britain, by contrast, these items represented a substantial percentage of the cost of building railways, which was £42,500 per mile. Thus, the cost of railway construction in India was no higher than in Britain, but much higher compared with the United States.[66] Within this financial context, railway companies like the GIPR assigned the construction contracts to big companies such as Wythes & Jackson, and Lee, Aiton, & Watson. These construction companies, in turn, enlisted other medium- and small-sized contractors and subcontractors, like Jamsetji Dorabji, J. S. Wells, and J. S. F. Stephens, to execute their contracts. The (sub)contractors in question further subcontracted some portions of the business to other, native petty (sub)contractors.

Additionally, employers such as Stephens responded to the workers' demands for increased wages and the heightened competition for workers among employers with legal, extra-legal, economic, and non-economic *coercive* means of labour control. These measures coexisted with supervisory reinforcement of maximum performance by workers, aimed at both attaching workers to employers, thereby restricting their mobility, and securing labour-intensive performance. At the same time as merchants and other employers successfully persuaded the state to introduce the Workmen's Breach of Contract Act in 1859–60, railway contractors secured the passing of a similar law: the Employers and Workmen (Disputes) Act of 1860. The latter served to enforce contract terms and performance against the working classes, under threat of imprisonment and other penalties. The Joseph Stephens Construction Company made use of the new contract laws when signing agreements with labour agents, subcontractors, and suppliers.[67] Stephens' diary entries note, for instance, that labour agents like Gunapa and Kundo Aunnda (the coolie agent) and Mahdo maistry bound themselves to help tie down labour and appropriate performance from workers in the service of the company. The contract read as follows:

> 12 June 1865 at Bhusawal: Gunapa and Kundo Aunnda received from Stephens a further advance of Rs 100 to procure 60 workpeople (40 men and 20 women) and do hereby bind ourselves to retain the above number of men if required on Stephens works at Omrawattee [Amravati] as long as he may want them. Signed and thumb marked on stamp paper.[68]
>
> 23 October 1866 at Akola: Mahdo maistry signed a contract with Stephens to supply stone, sand and masons, exclusive of cooly labour supplied by Stephens, to build rubble masonry. He binds himself to put on as many masons and bring in as much material as Stephens may order and agree to have the works taken out of his hands should he not be able to carry on the works both as to speed and quality. Received advance of Rs 900. Signed and thumb marked on stamp paper.[69]

The application of contract laws to control labour does not seem to have been sufficient: their use became complementary to the established practice of employing extralegal instruments for this purpose.[70]

Both subcontractors and contractors often hired muccadams and maistries to recruit, supervise, train, and control workers. They paid a higher wage rate as well as additional advances and cherimerry to these labour agents, giving rise to an agency cost designed to tackle the transaction costs of labour control. Labour agents hailed from the same community—along the lines of caste and village or territory—as their gang members. They often occupied the position of community headman as well as master craftsman. They were careful to represent interests, such as demands for changes to wages and workloads, which gang members regarded as essential for an 'acceptable' standard of living, and sometimes led agitating members. While their authority rested partly on community ties, they drew their influence equally from their rapport with employers and, consequently, from the power delegated to them.[71] They were often responsible for the distribution of jobs, advances, payment of wages, credit, and foremanship. They assisted the writer and the inspector in maintaining the attendance register and ensuring the progress of works and specific performance of the tasks required. This mechanism ensured that intensive labour continued even on days when a project inspector did not visit the worksite.

In contrast to penal contract labour on the plantations and bonded labourers in agriculture, the available sources do not indicate that labour agents used any *physical force* to immobilize gang members.[72] They evidently resorted to pecuniary pressure on them, in the form of access to advance payments, jobs, and credit with them. Coolies and second-grade masons were usually the labouring poor, without sufficient income to cover the family's consumption. Access to advances and credit helped them to survive in an interim period before their monthly payment, and also to meet exigencies, especially sickness and consequent joblessness. Particularly noteworthy is the fact that rates of morbidity and mortality were extremely high when inadequate nutrition was a feature.[73] While the workers' dependence on advances and credit did not necessarily constrain their capacity for collective bargaining for wages, it did nonetheless facilitate the creation of attached, dependent labourers. The use of hireling labour or dependent labour and labour agents, advances, and coercive labour laws, taken together, thus effectively secured the appropriation of labour power and specific performance.

The depressed subsistence ratios and the deprived, vulnerable state of well-being shared by most construction workers were wedded to the practices of labour dependency and coerced wage labour. Such labour practices were, in turn, a product of broader Indian poverty and the availability of labouring poor. The latter, for their part, were victims of the backwardness of agriculture, which made up over 70 per cent of the economy, and of underdevelopment in general.

The macroeconomic context was an expression of factors that included resource abundance, a low capital-labour ratio, predominance of the rent-seeking agrarian elite, the stultifying effect of imperial preference, and a despotic colonial polity.[74] The nexus between caste, gender, and occupations restricted the democratization of remunerative occupational skill. Surplus extraction took place with no revolutionization of the means of accumulation, but through perpetual use of labour-intensive performance. These factors generally led to low productivity, depressed wage income, high wage inequality, and the custom of a family-labour economy. The efforts of political society, namely the colonial state and its ruling classes, were far from conducive to removing the ratchet. All these factors combined were responsible for a literacy rate of 3.3 per cent, low human capital formation, a mortality rate of 37, life expectancy of 28 years in all India, 27 in the Deccan, and 26 in Berar region, and a sex ratio of 940 females per 1,000 males in 1872.[75] These were signs of abject deprivation, vulnerability, and misery. More precisely, they reveal the human cost of the existing economic and political institutions and their impacts on working people.

From this study, which focuses on the link between the material living standards of construction workers and labour practices, we should note in particular that the real wages of workers engaged in railway and other construction work in 1860s Deccan did improve. The subsistence ratios of sweat workers, however, mostly remained below unity, and labour practices were marked by the presence of coerced, dependent labour. The labouring poor secured their basic family consumption by increasing the supply of family labour on the labour market and agitating for higher wages. Here, women and boy coolies were far from receiving anything like the wage rises paid to their male and adult counterparts.

This scenario as regards the economic living standards of workers was surely associated with the marketization of labour and emergence of contractual employment that were part of the expanding and commercializing economy of later nineteenth-century India. What is equally noticeable is that the coercive and constraining institutions of labour control and contract enforcement were essential features of the new contractual basis for employment and the commercialized economy. Through these instruments, employers sought to control and discipline labourers. They were much more than a cruel solution to the contractual problem; rather, they were a means of counteracting the pressure of labour costs and competition for labourers. Alongside this, employers like Stephens paid competitive wages to secure proper labour efforts from the workers recruited. The case studied here indicates that the constraining instrument of labour control, on the one hand, and economic incentives to work harder, on the other, were not mutually exclusive; rather, these instruments of profit maximization worked in tandem in 1860s Deccan.

The material living of workers was partly built on the macroeconomic conditions of railway building in India, that is, the attractive state-guaranteed returns on capital investment, as Kerr argues,[76] and keen competition among (sub)contractors for labour power in the Deccan. The microeconomic particulars of the Joseph Stephens Construction Company and their labour-management relationship proved relatively favourable to workers, with the company's policy of competitively attractive wages for proper labour efforts. Furthermore, their material standards of living rested partly on their ability to engage in collective bargaining for improved wages.[77] Workers were seeking a wage structure that would enable them to achieve the respectable status of a male earner, while women and children generated a supplementary income for the household budget. This social custom prevented a comparable increase, let alone equality, in the wage rates paid to women. The social tradition of a nexus between caste, gender, and race, on one side, and occupations, on the other, proved conducive to significant wage inequality.

Notes

1 Kept at Linnaeus University (LNU) in Sweden, Huseby Archives (HA), Huseby Estate Archive (HEA) and Joseph Stephens Archive (JSA). Ian J. Kerr, *Building the Railways of the Raj 1850–1900* (New Delhi: Oxford University Press, 1995).
2 Kerr, *Building the Railways*, pp. 125–6; Ian J. Kerr, *Engines of Change: The Railroads that Made India* (Westport, CT: Praeger Publishers, 2007), p. 39.
3 Stephen Broadberry and Bishnupriya Gupta, 'Indian Economic Performance and Living Standards, 1600–2000', in Latika Chaudhary, Bishnupriya Gupta, Tirthankar Roy, and Anand V. Swamy (eds), *A New Economic History of Colonial India* (New York: Routledge, 2016), pp. 15–32.
4 Prabhu P. Mohaptra, 'From Contract to Status? Or How Law Shaped Labour Relations in Colonial India, 1780–1880', in Jan Breman, Isabelle Guerin, and Assem Prakash (eds), *India's Unfree Workforce: Of Bondage Old and New* (New Delhi: Oxford University Press, 2009), pp. 96–125; Chitra Joshi, 'Fettered Bodies: Labouring on Public Work in Nineteenth-Century India', in Marcel van der Linden and Prabhu P. Mohapatra (eds), *Labour Matters: Towards Global Histories* (New Delhi: Tulika Books, 2009), pp. 3–21. Kali Chittibabu, *Patterns of Labour Migrations in Colonial Andhra* (Cambridge: Cambridge Scholars Publishing, 2015).
5 Jan Lucassen has similarly noted the function of a wage policy geared towards productivity-driven payment of a relatively higher wage to workers at the Ichapur Gunpowder Factory in late nineteenth-century Calcutta. Jan Lucassen, 'Working at the Ichapur Gunpowder Factory in the 1790s, Part I', *Indian Historical Review*, 39/1 (2012), pp. 19–56, and 'Working at the Ichapur Gunpowder Factory in the 1790s, Part II', *Indian Historical Review*, 39/2 (2012), pp. 252–71.
6 Tirthankar Roy, 'The Growth of a Labour Market in the Twentieth Century', in Chaudhary et al. (eds), *New Economic History*, pp. 179–94; Tirthankar Roy and Anand V. Swamy, *Law and the Economy in Colonial India* (Chicago; London: University of Chicago Press, 2016), pp. 104–22; Tirthankar Roy, 'Indigo and Law in Colonial India', *Economic History Review*, 64 (SI, 2011), pp. 60–75; Anand V. Swamy, 'Law and Contract Enforcement in Colonial India', in Chaudhary et al. (eds), *New Economic History*, pp. 218–32.
7 Ibid.
8 For an elaboration of some of these critical viewpoints, see Karin Hofmeester and Pim de Zwart (eds), *Colonialism, Institutional Change, and Shifts in Global Labour Relations* (Amsterdam: Amsterdam University Press, 2018); Jan Breman, *Mobilising Labour for the Global Coffee Market: Profits From an Unfree Work Regime in Colonial Java* (Amsterdam: Amsterdam University Press, 2015); Marcel van der Linden, Karl Heinz Roth, and Max Henninger (eds), *Beyond Marx* (Leiden and Boston: Brill, 2014); Jairus Banaji, *Theory as History: Essays on Modes of Production and Exploitation* (Leiden: Brill Press, 2010); Ravi Ahuja, *Pathways of Empire: Circulation, Public Works and Social Space in Colonial Orissa, c. 1780–1914* (Hyderabad: Orient Blackswan, 2009); Rana P. Behal,

One Hundred Years of Servitude: Political Economy of Tea Plantations in Colonial Assam (New Delhi: Tulika Books, 2014).

9 The population of Indian territory directly ruled by the British was 190.5 million and that of the whole of India 239 million. *Report of the Census of India 1872–73*, by Henry Waterfield (Calcutta: Government Press, 1875), p. 32; A. Heston, 'National Income', in Dharma Kumar and Meghnad Desai (eds), *The Cambridge Economic History of India*, 2 (Cambridge: Cambridge University Press, 2008 [1989]), p. 396.

10 Kerr, *Engines of Change*, p. 23.

11 Ian Derbyshire, 'The Building of India's Railways: The Application of Western Technology in the Colonial Periphery 1850–1920', in Ian J. Kerr (ed.), *Railways in Modern India* (New Delhi: Oxford University Press, 2005), pp. 278–9.

12 LNU, HA, JSA, F1E:1 and 2, Pay lists and pay sheets.

13 *Census of India 1872–73*, pp. 12–13; Sumit Guha, *Health and Population in South Asia: From Earliest Times to the Present* (New Delhi: Permanent Black, 2001), pp. 8, 106. It may be noted that the Indian Penal Code and Criminal Procedure Code of 1882 had regarded 10 as the age of consent for sexual intercourse for girls. The Age of Consent Act 1891 raised it to 12. However, the Factory Act 1881 had prohibited the employment of children below the age of 7, and permitted children aged 7–12 to be employed for no more than nine hours a day in perennial factories.

14 *Census of India 1872–73*, p. 13.

15 Bidisha Dhar notices that artisans, alongside cultivators, sought to be treated as respectable poor, as compared with coolies, on the famine-relief worksites in the latter part of the nineteenth century. Bidisha Dhar, 'Mapping Artisan Labour in Lucknow, c. 1860s—1940s', in Sabyasachi Bhattacharya and Rana P. Behal (eds), *The Vernacularisation of Labour Politics* (New Delhi: Tulika Books, 2016), pp. 212–51. The racially graded labels assigned to the working person justified inferior care and harsher work and discipline for coloured and native labourers compared to white labourers as, for instance, during the First World War. See, Radhika Singha, *The Coolie's Great War: Indian Labour in a Global Conflict 1914–1921* (Noida: Harper Collins, 2020), Chapter 5.

16 The custom of Sunday worship offered to the local deity, the Khandoba, was prevalent amongst the Deccan rural population. See Rosalind O'Hanlon, *Caste, Conflict, and Ideology: Mahatma Jotirao Phule and Low Caste Protest in Nineteenth-Century Western India* (Cambridge: Cambridge University Press, 2002 [1985]), pp. 153, 157, 162.

17 LNU, HA, JSA, F1F:1, Diary 1860–1; Huseby Estate, Joseph Stephens' diaries1862 and 1863. See also LNU, HA, JSA, Pay lists and pay sheets.

18 On the gendered labour market and accumulation regime, see Maria Mies, *Patriarchy and Accumulation on a World Scale* (London: Zed Books, 2014 [1986]).

19 Laxman D. Satya, *Cotton and Famine in Berar, 1850–1900* (New Delhi: Manohar, 1997), pp. 67, 283–5; Sumit Guha, *The Agrarian Economy of Bombay Deccan* (New Delhi: Oxford University Press, 1985), pp. 80–2; V. D. Divekar, 'Regional Economy (1757–1857): Western India', in Kumar and Desai (eds), *Cambridge Economic History of India*, 2, p. 345.

20 J. A. Robertson, *Prices and Wages in India* (Calcutta: Government Printing, 1905), p. 289.

21 Robert C. Allen, 'Real Wages in Europe and Asia: A First Look at the Long-Term Patterns', in Robert C. Allen, Tommy Bengtsson, and Martin Dribe (eds), *Living Standards in the Past: New Perspectives on Well-Being in Asia and Europe* (New York: Oxford University Press, 2005), p. 124; Stephen Broadberry, Johann Custodis, and Bishnupriya Gupta, 'India and the Great Divergence: An Anglo-Indian

Comparison of GDP Per Capita, 1600–1871', *Explorations in Economic History*, 55 (2015), p. 62.

22 Chaudhary notes that working only as a postman in the colonial period was not economically superior to working as a skilled labourer, but the combination of postman and primary school teacher generated high returns to a person's human capital, ranging from 4 to 29 per cent. Latika Chaudhary, 'Caste, Colonialism and Schooling: Education in British India', in Chaudhary et al. (eds), *New Economic History*, p. 170.

23 For similar cases, see Amiya Kumar Bagchi, *Colonialism and Indian Economy* (New Delhi: Oxford University Press, 2010), p. 258; Lucassen, 'Ichapur Gunpowder Factory, I', pp. 48–55.

24 Jan Luiten van Zanden, 'The Skill Premium and the "Great Divergence"', *European Review of Economic History*, 13/1 (2009), pp. 121–53; Pim de Zwart, *Globalisation and the Colonial Origins of the Great Divergence: Intercontinental Trade and Living Standards in the Dutch East India Company's Commercial Empire, c. 1600–1800* (Leiden: Brill Press, 2016), pp. 145–9.

25 Satya, *Cotton and Famine*, pp. 106, 213–23; Guha, *Agrarian Economy,* p. 75; Crispin Bates, 'Class and Economic Change in Central India: The Narmada Valley 1820–1930', in Clive Dewey (ed.), *Arrested Development in India: The Historical Dimension* (New Delhi: Manohar, 1988), p. 257. *Banking and Monetary Statistics of India,* Bombay: Reserve Bank of India, 1954, p. 690. Amiya Kumar Bagchi, *The Presidency Banks and the Indian Economy 1876–1914* (Calcutta: Oxford University Press, 1989), pp. 125, 181, 227. A. K. Bagchi, *The Evolution of the State Bank of India: The Roots, 1806–76* (New Delhi: Penguin, 2006 [1987]), pp. 414–20.

26 De Zwart, *Great Divergence*; Jan Lucassen and Pim de Zwart, 'Poverty or Prosperity in Bengal c.1700–1875? New Evidence, Methods and Perspectives', paper presented at 11th AILH International Conference on Labour History, 21–23 March 2016.

27 Prasannan Parthasarathi, *Why Europe Grew Rich and Asia Did Not: Global Economic Divergence, 1600–1850* (Cambridge: Cambridge University Press, 2011), pp. 6, 59–60; Broadberry, Custodis, and Gupta, 'India and the Great Divergence', p. 67; Bagchi, *Colonialism and Indian Economy*, p. xxii.

28 See Sumit Sarkar, *Modern Times: India 1880s—1950s, Environment, Economy, Culture* (Ranikhet: Permanent Black, 2014), pp. 317–21; O'Hanlon, *Caste, Conflict, and Ideology.*

29 Guha, *Health and Population*, pp. 51–8. It should be noted that Guha revises the population figure for India, which some scholars consider to have been about 207 million in 1801. According to the latter estimate the rate of population growth was 0.30 per cent per annum, as opposed to Guha's estimate of 0.75 per cent, from 1801 to 1881.

30 Chaudhary et al. (eds), *New Economic History*; Binay Bhushan Chaudhuri, *Peasant History of Late Pre-Colonial and Colonial India* (New Delhi: Pearson Longman, 2008).

31 Allen, 'Real Wages', pp. 111–30.

32 See Jan Luiten van Zanden, Joerg Baten, Marco Mira d'Ercole, Auke Rijpma, Conal Smith, and Marcel Timmer, 'Global Well-Being Since 1820', in Jan Luiten van Zanden, Joerg Baten, Marco Mira d'Ercole, Auke Rijpma, Conal Smith, and Marcel Timmer (eds), *How Was Life? Global Well-Being Since 1820* (IISH: OECD, 2014).

33 Robert C. Allen, 'India in the Great Divergence', in T. H. Hatton, K. H. O'Rourke, and A. M. Taylor (eds), *The New Comparative Economic History: Essays in Honour of Jeffrey G. Williamson* (Cambridge: MIT Press, 2007), pp. 9–32; R.

C. Allen and Roman Studer, 'Prices and Wages in India, 1595–1930', 12 September 2009, gpih.ucdavis.edu/files/India_Allen-Studer_v2,pl.xls, accessed 18 October 2016.

34 National Institute of Nutrition and Indian Council of Medical Research, *Dietary Guidelines for Indians: A Manual* (Hyderabad: Indian Council of Medical Research, 1998), pp. 89, 117.

35 D. K. Nite, 'Reproduction Preferences and Wages: The Jharia Coalfield, 1895–1970', *Studies in History*, 30/1 (2014), pp. 55–87.

36 David Ricardo, *On the Principles of Political Economy and Taxation* (London: John Murray, 1975 [1821]), pp. 93–4; Karl Marx, *Capital*, I: *The Process of Production of Capital* (London: Penguin Books, 1976 [1867]), p. 275.

37 Guha, *Health and Population*, p. 55.

38 Prison costs in Bombay province in 1868 were Rs. 38.44 for food and Rs. 5.88 for clothing, or a total Rs. 44.32 a year. See Heston, 'National Income', p. 455.

39 Roy, 'Growth of a Labour Market', p. 192.

40 Satya, *Cotton and Famine,* p. 193.

41 Ibid., pp. 192, 199; Tirthankar Roy, 'Consumption of Cotton Cloth in India, 1795–1940', *Australian Economic History Review*, 52/1 (2011), pp. 23–4; David E. U. Baker, *Colonialism in an Indian Hinterland: The Central Provinces, 1820–1920* (New Delhi: Oxford University Press, 1998), p. 154.

42 *Census of India 1872–73*, pp. 11–12; *Census of Bombay Presidency 1872–73*, pp. 28–9. The better sorts of houses were usually of masonry and tiled.

43 Jotirao Phule, *Brahman Teachers in the Education Department, Satyadipika* (Pune: June 1869), p. 87. A short ballad quoted in O'Hanlon, *Caste, Conflict, and Ideology*, p. 214.

44 LNU, HA, JSA, Pay lists and pay sheets.

45 Satya, *Cotton and Famine*, pp. 204–46; Guha, *Agrarian Economy*, pp. 75–8; H. Fukazawa, 'Agrarian Relations: Western India', in Kumar and Desai (eds), *Cambridge Economic History of India*, 2, p. 194; Jairus Banaji, 'Capitalist Domination and the Small Peasantry: The Deccan Districts in the Late Nineteenth Century', in Banaji, *Theory as History*, pp. 277–332.

46 Jan Breman, *Outcast Labour in Asia: Circulation and Informalization of the Workforce at the Bottom of the Economy* (New Delhi: Oxford University Press, 2012); Ravi Ahuja, 'A Freedom Still Enmeshed in Servitude: The Unruly "Lascars" of the SS City of Manila or, A Micro-History of the "Free Labour" Problem', in Ravi Ahuja (ed.), *Working Lives and Worker Militancy: The Politics of Labour in Colonial India* (New Delhi: Tulika Books, 2013), pp. 97–133; Banaji, 'Capitalist Domination'.

47 Huseby Estate, Joseph Stephens' diaries 1862 and 1863.

48 Kerr, *Engines of Change*; Kerr, *Building the Railways*; Jan Lucassen, 'The Brickmakers' Strikes on the Ganges Canal in 1848–1849', in Rana P. Behal and Marcel van der Linden (eds), *India's Labouring Poor: Historical Studies, c. 1600–2000* (Cambridge: Cambridge University Press and New Delhi: Foundation Books, 2007), pp. 47–84.

49 Huseby Estate, Joseph Stephens' diary 1862.

50 LNU, HA, JSA, F1A:4, Correspondence.

51 Ibid.

52 Huseby Estate, Joseph Stephens' diary 1863.

53 Ibid.

54 Ibid.

55 Ibid., 2 May 1863.

56 Ibid., 14 and 23 February 1863.

57 Ibid., 19 May 1863.

58 One such attempt is discernible in Prasannan Parthasarathi, 'The Poonamalle Insurrection of 1796', in Bhattacharya and Behal (eds), *Vernacularisation of Labour Politics*, pp. 133–45.

59 Berar was known to import rice and wheat, regarded as luxury items, for consumption by its better-off households. Satya, *Cotton and Famine*, p. 287.

60 Ibid., pp. 184–6; Michelle Burge McAlpin, 'The Effects of Expansion of Markets on Rural Income Distribution in Nineteenth Century India', *Explorations in Economic History*, 12 (1975), p. 295; Baker, *Colonialism in an Indian Hinterland*.

61 McAlpin, 'Effects of Expansion', p. 294.

62 LNU, HA, JSA, F1F:1, Diary 1860–1.

63 Huseby Estate, Joseph Stephens' diary 1863, 14 February 1863; LNU, HA, JSA, F1A:1, Wells's letter, 21 December 1862.

64 Huseby Estate, Joseph Stephens' diary 1863, 24 March 1863.

65 Kerr, *Engines of Change*, p. 26.

66 Ibid., pp. 26, 173. In the 1850s–60s, the railway companies earned an average profit of about 2 per cent, the rest coming from the public treasury.

67 The Cornwallis Code of 1793 and the Bombay Regulation IV of 1827 were in force concerning business transactions.

68 LNU, HA, JSA, F1B:1, Contract papers.

69 Ibid.

70 We find one dispute coming to court. The action was filed, however, by a native supplier against Stephens.

71 For a convincing exposition of the functioning of this labour institution, though in the 20th-century factory setting, see Chitra Joshi, *Lost Worlds: Indian Labour and Its Forgotten Histories* (New Delhi: Permanent Black, 2005).

72 See Behal, *One Hundred Years*.

73 Baker, *Colonialism in an Indian Hinterland*, p. 160.

74 The list of relevant studies is long. Among others, see Bishnupriya Gupta, 'Falling Behind and Catching Up: India's Transition from a Colonial Economy', *Economic History Review*, 72 (3) (2019), pp. 803–27; Amiya Bagchi, *Capital and Labour Redefined: India and the Third World* (London: Anthem Press, 2002); Jeffrey Williamson, *Trade and Poverty: When the Third World Fell Behind* (Cambridge: MIT Press, 2011), pp. 75–100, 145–67.

75 *Census of India 1872–73*, pp. 13; *Census of Bombay Presidency 1872–73*, pp. 72–5, 194. England had a life expectancy of 44.2 and a mortality rate of 22.6 in 1871.

76 Kerr, *Engines of Change*; Kerr, *Building the Railways*.

77 Cf. Lucassen, *Ichapur Gunpowder Factory*; Lucassen, 'Brickmakers' Strikes'.

References

Ahuja, Ravi, 'A Freedom Still Enmeshed in Servitude: The Unruly "Lascars" of the SS City of Manila or, a Micro-History of the "Free Labour" Problem', in Ravi Ahuja (ed.), *Working Lives and Worker Militancy: The Politics of Labour in Colonial India* (New Delhi: Tulika Books, 2013), pp. 97–133.

Ahuja, Ravi, *Pathways of Empire: Circulation, Public Works and Social Space in Colonial Orissa, c. 1780–1914* (Hyderabad: Orient Blackswan, 2009).

Allen, Robert C., 'India in the Great Divergence', in T. H. Hatton, K. H. O'Rourke, and A. M. Taylor (eds), *The New Comparative Economic History: Essays in Honour of Jeffrey G. Williamson* (Cambridge: MIT Press, 2007), pp. 9–32.

Allen, Robert C., 'Real Wages in Europe and Asia: A First Look at the Long-Term Patterns', Robert C Allen, Tommy Bengtsson, and Martin Dribe (eds), *Living*

Standards in the Past: New Perspectives on Well-Being in Asia and Europe (New York: Oxford University Press, 2005), pp. 111–30.

Allen, Robert C., and Roman Studer, 'Prices and Wages in India, 1595–1930', 12 September 2009, gpih.ucdavis.edu/files/India_Allen-Studer_v2,pl.xls, accessed 18 October 2016.

Bagchi, Amiya Kumar, *Capital and Labour Redefined: India and the Third World* (London: Anthem Press, 2002).

Bagchi, Amiya Kumar, *Colonialism and Indian Economy* (New Delhi: Oxford University Press, 2010).

Bagchi, Amiya Kumar, *The Evolution of the State Bank of India: The Roots, 1806–76* (New Delhi: Penguin, 2006 [1987]).

Bagchi, Amiya Kumar, *The Presidency Banks and the Indian Economy 1876–1914* (Calcutta: Oxford University Press, 1989).

Baker, David E. U., *Colonialism in an Indian Hinterland: The Central Provinces, 1820–1920* (New Delhi: Oxford University Press, 1998).

Banaji, Jairus, 'Capitalist Domination and the Small Peasantry: The Deccan Districts in the Late Nineteenth Century', in J. Banaji (ed.), *Theory as History: Essays on Modes of Production and Exploitation* (Leiden; Boston: Brill Press, 2010), pp. 277–332.

Banaji, Jairus, *Theory as History: Essays on Modes of Production and Exploitation* (Leiden; Boston: Brill Press, 2010).

Bates, Crispin, 'Class and Economic Change in Central India: The Narmada Valley 1820–1930', in Clive Dewey (ed.), *Arrested Development in India: The Historical Dimension* (New Delhi: Manohar, 1988), pp. 241–82.

Behal, Rana P., *One Hundred Years of Servitude: Political Economy of Tea Plantations in Colonial Assam* (New Delhi: Tulika Books, 2014).

Breman, Jan, *Mobilising Labour for the Global Coffee Market: Profits From an Unfree Work Regime in Colonial Java* (Amsterdam: Amsterdam University Press, 2015).

Breman, Jan, *Outcast Labour in Asia: Circulation and Informalization of the Workforce at the Bottom of the Economy* (New Delhi: Oxford University Press, 2012).

Brereton, R. M., *Reminiscences of an Old English Civil Engineer, 1858–1908* (Portland: Irwin Hodson Company, 1908).

Broadberry, Stephen, and Bishnupriya Gupta, 'Indian Economic Performance and Living Standards, 1600–2000', in Latika Chaudhary, Bishnupriya Gupta, Tirthankar Roy, and Anand V. Swamy (eds), *A New Economic History of Colonial India* (New York: Routledge, 2016), pp. 15–32.

Broadberry, Stephen, Johann Custodis, and Bishnupriya Gupta, 'India and the Great Divergence: An Anglo-Indian Comparison of GDP per Capita, 1600–1871', *Explorations in Economic History*, 55 (2015), pp. 58–75.

Chaudhary, Latika, 'Caste, Colonialism and Schooling: Education in British India', in Latika Chaudhary, Bishnupriya Gupta, Tirthankar Roy, and Anand V. Swamy (eds), *A New Economic History of Colonial India* (New York: Routledge, 2016), pp. 161–78.

Chaudhary, Latika, Bishnupriya Gupta, Tirthankar Roy, and Anand V. Swamy (eds), *A New Economic History of Colonial India* (New York: Routledge, 2016).

Chaudhuri, Binay Bhushan, *Peasant History of Late Pre-colonial and Colonial India* (New Delhi: Pearson Longman, 2008).

Chittibabu, Kali, *Patterns of Labour Migrations in Colonial Andhra* (Cambridge: Cambridge Scholars Publishing, 2015).
Derbyshire, Ian, 'The Building of India's Railways: The Application of Western Technology in the Colonial Periphery 1850–1920', in Ian J. Kerr (ed.), *Railways in Modern India* (New Delhi: Oxford University Press, 2005), pp. 278–9.
Dhar, Bidisha, 'Mapping Artisan Labour in Lucknow, c. 1860s–1940s', in Sabyasachi Bhattacharya and Rana P. Behal (eds), *The Vernacularisation of Labour Politics* (New Delhi: Tulika Books, 2016), pp. 212–51.
Divekar, V. D., 'Regional Economy (1757–1857): Western India', in Dharma Kumar and Meghnad Desai (eds), *The Cambridge Economic History of India*, 2 (Cambridge: Cambridge University Press, 2008 [1989]), pp. 332–55.
Fukazawa, H., 'Agrarian Relations: Western India', in Dharma Kumar and Meghnad Desai (eds), *The Cambridge Economic History of India* (Cambridge: Cambridge University Press, 2008 [1989]), pp. 177–207.
Guha, Sumit, *Health and Population in South Asia: From Earliest Times to the Present* (New Delhi: Permanent Black, 2001).
Guha, Sumit, *The Agrarian Economy of Bombay Deccan* (New Delhi: Oxford University Press, 1985).
Gupta, Bishnupriya, 'Falling Behind and Catching Up: India's Transition from a Colonial Economy', *Economic History Review*, 72/3 (2019), pp. 803–27.
Heston, A., 'National Income', in Dharma Kumar and Meghnad Desai (eds), *The Cambridge Economic History of India*, 2 (Cambridge: Cambridge University Press, 2008 [1989]), pp. 376–462.
Hofmeester, Karin, and Pim de Zwart (eds), *Colonialism, Institutional Change, and Shifts in Global Labour Relations* (Amsterdam: Amsterdam University Press, 2018).
Joshi, Chitra, 'Fettered Bodies: Labouring on Public Work in Nineteenth-Century India', in Marcel van der Linden and Prabhu P. Mohapatra (eds), *Labour Matters: Towards Global Histories* (New Delhi: Tulika Books, 2009), pp. 3–21.
Joshi, Chitra, *Lost Worlds: Indian Labour and Its Forgotten Histories* (New Delhi: Permanent Black, 2005).
Kerr, Ian J., *Building the Railways of the Raj 1850–1900* (New Delhi: Oxford University Press, 1995).
Kerr, Ian J., *Engines of Change: The Railroads that Made India* (Westport, CT: Praeger Publishers, 2007).
Linden, Marcel van der, Karl Heinz Roth, and Max Henninger (eds), *Beyond Marx* (Leiden; Boston: Brill, 2014).
Lucassen, Jan, 'The Brickmakers' Strikes on the Ganges Canal in 1848–1849', in Rana P. Behal and Marcel van der Linden (eds), *India's Labouring Poor: Historical Studies, c. 1600–2000* (Cambridge: Cambridge University Press; New Delhi: Foundation Books, 2007), pp. 47–84.
Lucassen, Jan, 'Working at the Ichapur Gunpowder Factory in the 1790s, Part I', *Indian Historical Review*, 39/1 (2012), pp. 19–56.
Lucassen, Jan, 'Working at the Ichapur Gunpowder Factory in the 1790s, Part II', *Indian Historical Review*, 39/2 (2012), pp. 252–71.
Lucassen, Jan, and Pim de Zwart, 'Poverty or Prosperity in Bengal c.1700–1875? New Evidence, Methods and Perspectives', paper presented at 11th AILH International Conference on Labour History, 21–23 March 2016.
Marx, Karl, *Capital, I: The Process of Production of Capital* (London: Penguin Books, 1976 [1867]).

McAlpin, Michelle Burge, 'The Effects of Expansion of Markets on Rural Income Distribution in Nineteenth Century India', *Explorations in Economic History*, 12 (1975), pp. 289–302.

Mies, Maria, *Patriarchy and Accumulation on a World Scale* (London: Zed Books, 2014 [1986]).

Mohaptra, Prabhu, 'From Contract to Status? Or How Law Shaped Labour Relations in Colonial India, 1780–1880', in Jan Breman, Isabelle Guerin, and Assem Prakash (eds), *India's Unfree Workforce: Of Bondage Old and New* (New Delhi: Oxford University Press, 2009), pp. 96–125.

Nite, Dhiraj Kumar, 'Reproduction Preferences and Wages: The Jharia Coalfield, 1895–1970', *Studies in History*, 30/1 (2014), pp. 55–87.

O'Hanlon, Rosalind, *Caste, Conflict, and Ideology: Mahatma Jotirao Phule and Low Caste Protest in Nineteenth-Century Western India* (Cambridge: Cambridge University Press, 2002 [1985]).

Parthasarathi, Prasannan, 'The Poonamalle Insurrection of 1796', in Sabyasachi Bhattacharya and Rana P. Behal (eds), *The Vernacularisation of Labour Politics* (New Delhi: Tulika Books, 2016), pp. 133–45.

Parthasarathi, Prasannan, *Why Europe Grew Rich and Asia Did Not: Global Economic Divergence, 1600–1850* (Cambridge: Cambridge University Press, 2011).

Phule, Jyotirao, *Brahman Teachers in the Education Department, Satyadipika* (Pune, June 1869).

Ricardo, David, *On the Principles of Political Economy and Taxation* (London: John Murray, 1975 [1821]).

Roy, Tirthankar, 'Consumption of Cotton Cloth in India, 1795–1940', *Australian Economic History Review*, 52/1 (2011), pp. 3–35.

Roy, Tirthankar, 'Indigo and Law in Colonial India', *Economic History Review*, 64 (SI, 2011), pp. 60–75.

Roy, Tirthankar, 'The Growth of a Labour Market in the Twentieth Century', in Latika Chaudhary, Bishnupriya Gupta, Tirthankar Roy, and Anand V. Swamy (eds), *A New Economic History of Colonial India* (New York: Routledge, 2016), pp. 179–94.

Roy, Tirthankar, and Anand V. Swamy, *Law and the Economy in Colonial India* (Chicago; London: University of Chicago Press, 2016).

Sarkar, Sumit, *Modern Times: India 1880s–1950s. Environment, Economy, Culture* (Ranikhet: Permanent Black, 2014), pp. 317–21.

Satya, Laxman D., *Cotton and Famine in Berar, 1850–1900* (New Delhi: Manohar, 1997).

Singha, Radhika, *The Coolie's Great War: Indian Labour in a Global Conflict 1914–1921* (Noida: Harper Collins, 2020).

Swamy, Anand V., 'Law and Contract Enforcement in Colonial India', in Latika Chaudhary, Bishnupriya Gupta, Tirthankar Roy, and Anand V. Swamy (eds), *A New Economic History of Colonial India* (New York: Routledge, 2016), pp. 218–32.

Williamson, Jeffrey, *Trade and Poverty: When the Third World Fell Behind* (Cambridge: MIT, 2011).

Zanden, Jan Luiten van, 'The Skill Premium and the "Great Divergence"', *European Review of Economic History*, 13/1 (2009), pp. 121–53.

Zanden, Jan Luiten van, Joerg Baten, Marco Mira d'Ercole, Auke Rijpma, Conal Smith, and Marcel Timmer, 'Global Well-Being Since 1820', in Jan Luiten van

Zanden, Joerg Baten, Marco Mira d'Ercole, Auke Rijpma, Conal Smith, and Marcel Timmer (eds), *How Was Life? Global Well-Being since 1820* (IISH: OECD, 2014).

Zwart, Pim de, *Globalisation and the Colonial Origins of the Great Divergence: Intercontinental Trade and Living Standards in the Dutch East India Company's Commercial Empire, c. 1600–1800* (Leiden: Brill Press, 2016).

6 Circulation of Knowledge, Capital, and Goods

Scandinavia and the British Empire

Eleonor Marcussen

In Scandinavian history writing, colonialism has often been limited to minor geopolitical conquests and trading outposts of the nation states, both of which have been viewed as benign rather than violent and oppressive.[1] Only since the 1990s has research begun to examine the surge in Scandinavian exploration, scientific and religious expeditions, resource extraction in Asia, the Americas, and Africa, and 'internal colonialization' in the Arctic region during the nineteenth and twentieth centuries.[2] Scandinavian colonial settlements and business and military expeditions coincided with the expansion of the major imperial powers of Europe in the early modern period, yet assumed another form than those of the dominant military powers.[3] While the trading houses and Scandinavian states left records which, compared to conventional, enduring imperial archives, have been more complicated to track down and access owing to their short-lived character and the disruption they have suffered,[4] historical works are increasingly attempting to trace the entanglement of people, material culture, and places in order to explore how the small and grand narratives of empires intersected in the modern period. This turn in understanding Scandinavian colonialism follows a general shift in imperial and global history towards research on the circulation of knowledge, people, and commodities, rather than exchanges between geographical regions or between nation states and colonies.[5] As Patricia Purtschert and Harald Fischer-Tiné argue in the case of Switzerland's history, a general understanding of the nation's past confines it to persons, events, and social processes within its geopolitical borders.[6] In South Asian history, for instance, London has been taken as the a priori centre of empire, while relatively recent research points to Switzerland and Germany as important nodes for anti-colonial networks.[7] On the other hand, for Switzerland, a 'country without colonies', colonialism played a central role in the development of businesses that would come to represent economic interests of the nation state in the postcolonial period.[8] Building on previous research into the relationship between minor colonial nations such as Sweden and Switzerland and colonialism, this chapter argues that regions beyond the colonizers and the colonized played an important role in realizing the ambitions of imperial expansion. The Huseby Estate in southern

DOI: 10.4324/9781003317227-6

Sweden, where Joseph Stephens arrived after working in India, was one such site, where the logics of resource extraction and trading networks could be utilized in a similar manner to that found within colonial spaces. At the same time, the question arises as to the role of European imperialism in the processes of modernization in Scandinavia and Sweden at this point in history. The case of Joseph Stephens' colonial career in India in the 1860s serves to illustrate how and why imperial ambitions and wealth intersected with the development of international business and infrastructural expansion in southern Sweden.

Since the archiving of Joseph Stephens' papers related to his 'Indian period' (1860–9) was set in motion in 2008, a series of publications and a recent exhibition have contributed new perspectives on Scandinavia's role in the colonial period.[9] Fascinatingly, the newly discovered material covers the business activities of Joseph Stephens in India *before* he bought the Huseby Estate in 1867 and until the end of 1869, when he wrapped up the last business commitments of his contracting and settled at Huseby. The material from India constitutes an intriguing part of the 'Stephens period' in the large Huseby Archives, which encompasses an archive collection covering the wide-ranging business papers of the estate from the late medieval period, through its industrial development after Stephens took over, up to the end of the family's era at Huseby.[10] The Indian material, covering Stephens' work and social life in India over approximately 10 years, has proved a rare source in terms of containing a wide range of labour and construction contracts between Stephens and labourers, the railway company, and other building and railway contractors. In a colonial context, the archival holdings stand out as a rich source for understanding the everyday socio-economic lives and professional relationships of labourers, middlemen, and contractors involved in the expansion of the railway and related infrastructure.[11] At the same time, an idea has formed about the professional life of Europeans making a career out of imperial expansion: how men like Joseph Stephens acquired capital as well as skills and professional networks in colonial contexts. Building upon recent research from the Joseph Stephens Archive (JSA), this chapter provides a more comprehensive picture of how professional life and experiences in India shaped Joseph Stephens as a businessman and actor in colonial networks after settling in Sweden. The chapter, which follows an individual's life history in the context of specific historical structures and contexts, is methodologically aligned with Catherine Hall's *Civilising Subjects* and chapters in the anthology *Colonial Lives Across Empire*.[12] By providing an individual and subjective perspective on the building of a colonial career, it aims to give insights into the choices and opportunities that formed part of the larger economic and social transformations that are the concern of economic historians and histories of nation states. This is done by means of a brief sketch of the Stephens family, the socio-economic context of southern Sweden, and an analysis of Joseph Stephens' trade and interactions on the Huseby Estate from 1867 until 1874.

The chapter suggests that Stephens' business strategies should be understood and interpreted in a global context, in which the British Empire's political and territorial expansion simultaneously contributed to the development of businesses in countries that had only minor colonies.

As a case study, this chapter sets out to capture change, development, and connections between people and places during Joseph Stephens' first years on the Huseby Estate. Among the primary sources drawn upon, business and private correspondence, cash books of expenses and bank withdrawals, and receipts, from the Huseby Estate Archive (HEA) and the JSA between 1867 and 1874, are the main ones used for an analysis of the professional relations and informal networks that were part of developing the estate. In Joseph Stephens' case, his almost 10-year-long career as a contractor on the expansion of the Great Indian Peninsula Railway (GIPR) would be decisive in forging a fortune that enabled him to acquire the large landed estate in southern Sweden in 1867, at the same time as these were formative years that paved the way for his future enterprises. In that, the lives of the Stephens family provide a fascinating trajectory of how British imperialism shaped networks, professionalism, and mobility, and thereby wealth acquisition, this chapter examines the question of how countries beyond the imperial heartlands became sites of interest for colonial wealth, knowledge, and migration. The purpose is thus twofold. First, the chapter examines, through the life history of Joseph Stephens, how and why British imperialism had an impact on local and regional business development in Scandinavia. Secondly, the chapter revises the narratives of socio-economic changes in Sweden during the late nineteenth century by considering the impact of larger global transformations to a far greater extent than so far acknowledged. The chapter suggests that Stephens' experiences from his 'colonial career' can serve as an example of how and why the expansion of British imperialism would come to impact the late industrialization of southern Sweden.

Making a Career: Skills and Capital Accumulation

Joseph Stephens' career in India and return to the country of his birth, Sweden, were largely facilitated by his family's networks and ambitions. Yet his return was not to the cultured milieus of Stockholm and Copenhagen, where he was born and spent his adolescence, respectively, but to a region unfamiliar to him and at the same time 'known' by his father George Stephens (1813–95) and, not least, his godfather, Gunnar Olof Hyltén-Cavallius (1818–89). Both men proved to be instrumental in the acquisition of the Huseby Estate through a curious combination of personal relationships, economic interests, and ethnographic fieldwork.[13] To all three men involved in the transaction, the investment in a landed property represented the successful completion of what the family perceived as Joseph Stephens' hard-working years in India.[14] Not unlike the situation for Scots and Irishmen, a colonial career offered to Stephens something more than was available 'at home'. As histories of colonial lives have sought to illustrate, perceptions of the opportunities offered by such a career differed depending on where you came from, rather than being a class journey with a destination in the empire.[15]

In 1859, when Joseph Stephens ventured out to India at the age of 19, he had spent his teens in the culturally affluent circles of Copenhagen, where the family had moved from Stockholm. It is probably no exaggeration to say that his father, George Stephens, had a strong influence on his only son throughout his life. Even while Joseph was in India, involved in a professional and social sphere far removed from his father's literary and cultural urban life in Copenhagen, the relationship was continuously nurtured through letters offering advice on all aspects of life, practical and spiritual. Their correspondence indicates that George Stephens' 'cultural career', without capital to back it up, motivated or pushed Joseph Stephens into choosing the path of business.[16] Although the family moved in cultured social circles both in Stockholm and in Copenhagen, where George Stephens was a central figure in the Anglophone community and the Anglican Church,[17] finances remained an issue even after he had secured promotion to professor of English at the University of Copenhagen in 1855, the same year he became a Danish subject.[18] Stephens' senior, who himself could not afford an advanced education for lack of funds, had until then secured an income mainly by teaching English,[19] although translations, publishing articles in British scientific magazines and the daily press, and providing board for Hyltén-Cavallius, his best friend, colleague, and godfather of Joseph, also helped keep the family afloat.[20] Joseph Stephens' career path, from Copenhagen to imperial railway construction in India to the Swedish countryside, appears less erratic in the light not only of his father's career transitions, but also of the itinerant lives of all his uncles, in pursuit of careers or the promotion of religion. Moving from Liverpool to Stockholm in 1834, George Stephens had followed in the footsteps of his eldest brother, Joseph Rainer Stephens, who preached Methodism to fellow countrymen in the Swedish capital from 1826 until 1829.[21] Following the path embarked on by the eldest brother, George Stephens' other three elder brothers migrated from England to Australia in the 1830s in pursuit of money, although a missionary zeal for the Anglican Church coloured their motives to some extent.[22] Thus, as Joseph Stephens grew up, letters from his uncles nurtured the idea of migration from England. Unlike Joseph, who went for a period to make a career out of imperial expansion, their ventures as they made Australia their permanent home were framed by a settler-colonial outlook.[23]

With family experience of migration on the father's side, the marriage of Joseph Stephens' elder sister, Ingeborg Stephens (1839–1911), to the British engineer John Hallen Abbott (1831–84) provided Joseph with an opportunity to pursue a career along a similar path. The couple moved to India in 1857 after Abbott had secured a position as a third-class assistant engineer on the GIPR, and in January 1860, Joseph Stephens joined them.[24] Only a few years earlier, in 1853, the GIPR had opened the first railway for public traffic in India.[25] The couple had met while Abbott was working for the engineering and contracting firm Fox, Henderson and Co. on the construction of the Zealand railway from Roskilde to Korsør, from 1852 until its completion in 1856.[26] The building of the railways in Denmark in the 1850s and 1860s created a 'massive' demand for British expertise, as this was still a technology developed primarily by the British.[27] Subsequently, when the Danish railway project was completed, Abbott continued to India in February 1857 as the business of developing infrastructure there expanded east. Before turning to the training and skills Joseph Stephens acquired before settling at Huseby, it is worth noting how in the nineteenth century men like him embarked on colonial careers on a completely different scale compared to middle-class men at the beginning of the century. As with other transformative social changes that characterized the coming of modernity, the increase in and speed of production, transport, and communications played a pivotal role in the success of their endeavours.

Under his brother-in-law, Joseph was accepted as an apprentice for three years.[28] This apprenticeship was seen as a great opportunity, since many families paid large sums to have their sons trained as engineers according to the British and North American 'shop culture' of education that characterized the profession during this period.[29] Writing to Joseph from Copenhagen in 1865, his sister Ingeborg Abbott mused over the fact that 'everyone wants to send their sons to India'.[30] His training as a civil engineer in India appeared to imply the start of a lucrative career, where the chance of making financial gains seemed to outweigh the risks. For Joseph Stephens and his family, the colonies served as a site where a person could become something different in socio-economic terms. Venturing to India and a career built on colonial expansion underlined that 'colonialism was not a secure bourgeois project', as Ann Laura Stoler writes.[31] Rather than exporting 'middle-class sensibilities' to the colonies, colonialism was about 'the making of them', an attempt by the Stephenses to amass capital in order to buy a property.[32] Both the Stephens' siblings found themselves on the lower rungs of the middle in the European community of western India, and entered an existence that they acknowledged as precarious in terms of material gains and the physical threat of disease. Although they did not belong among the 'low and licentious' Europeans described by Harald Fischer-Tiné,[33] they nevertheless had to redefine themselves in a social hierarchy where. Given their cultural background, they could have assumed a higher standing, but lacking education, social networks, and access to capital, they found themselves placed relatively low on the ladder.[34]

When Joseph Stephens arrived at Huseby, his professional experience and training had been gained entirely in India.[35] A better understanding of the skills and training he acquired there can be gleaned partly from his family network, and partly by contextualizing it within the period of rapid British imperial expansion that had shaped Stephens' early professional years. Becoming a civil engineer involved acquiring a set of practical skills and scientific knowledge in the field of engineering, which in the middle of the nineteenth century was becoming increasingly differentiated with the rapid development of technology.[36] The early establishment of engineering colleges in England led to an overproduction of students in the field for the domestic market in the 1840s, but these technological experts became part of an imperial flow of exports to the colonies.[37] In Scandinavian history, British technology and technicians played a fundamental role in the technological transfer that begun in the 1820s through major infrastructural projects. The Göta Canal project became known as 'Sweden's oldest university of technology', since it functioned as a catalyst for establishing engineering works and a vision for industrial expansion. The development of technology in Scandinavia before the middle of the nineteenth century was in this way based on the transfer of British technology to the extent that British engineering companies provided almost complete factory packages and helped local businesses in hiring the necessary expertise.[38] Hence, compared with England and other countries in Europe, engineering education in Denmark was in its infancy.[39]

Joseph Stephens has often been referred to as an 'engineer' 'building railways in India',[40] when in fact his main occupation was that of a contractor, a profession for which engineering knowledge was indeed an asset but not an essential requirement.[41] Ironically, Lars-Olof Larsson, an authority on the social history of Southern Sweden, in trying to dispel local legends about how and why Stephens bought the Huseby Estate, managed to create another one: that of Stephens the railway engineer.[42] More recently, Ingemar Gunnarsson has devoted a chapter to charting the trajectory of Stephens' education and training, including a dismissal of family legends and public myth-making. According to Gunnarsson, Stephens' apprenticeship under his brother-in-law Abbott and his time as a contractor in India qualified him as a civil engineer, a title that made him look like a man in tune with the technological knowledge needed to modernize the Huseby Estate at the time he acquired it.[43] Before Stephens entered the apprenticeship, there are few, if any, indications of formalized learning or purposeful training for becoming an engineer.[44] Ben Marsden and Crosbie Smith note that (even) historians commonly misunderstand the professional title of 'civil engineer' as requiring book learning, when in fact practical experiments and an apprenticeship system dominated education in this field until the end of the nineteenth century.[45] Of interest here is how the title 'civil engineer' could be acquired through a range of qualifications and technical skills. Stephens studied technical literature while an apprentice under his brother-in-law;[46] subsequently, he became an agent's assistant, a subcontractor, and finally a contractor in his own right, and although he never took on major projects, he managed to amass a substantial profit. Becoming and being a contractor mainly involved being able to secure contracts and then deliver the work, which meant supervising middlemen and the progress of labour, keeping track of labourers and wages, and acquiring materials for the construction of sections and buildings.[47] In order to supervise people working and to control the quantities and quality of material on various construction sites, a considerable part of the day was spent travelling on horseback, with brief stops and detours for the main leisure activity, hunting.[48]

There was a boom in the construction not only of the railways, but also equally important of the ancillary buildings and infrastructure used to process, pack, and store the main export product of the region: cotton. The time and the place, the 1860s in the construction business and the connected export trade in raw materials from Bombay, entailed a set of conditions that proved favourable to Joseph Stephens as a contractor. The export market for cotton from Berar underwent significant changes during the Crimean War of 1853–6 and the American Civil War of 1860–4, which resulted in increased demand for Indian cotton.[49] In between the wars and post the Great Uprising of 1857–8, the colonial government began implementing a range of control mechanisms that involved the expansion into the interior of its administration, as well as of communications infrastructure and urban planning. Slow transport on bullock carts from cotton-growing regions in the interior was a long-standing issue. On the road to Bombay, the cotton deteriorated, but the speed of the railway would ensure its quality, preserving its value when it arrived at the port.[50] Raw material export of cotton was given more than a fillip from political and mercantile interests in England. It was represented in particular by the lobby of the so-called cotton M.P.s who saw to the commercial interests of the industrial towns as dependent on its supply for manufacturing.[51] In the same period, the late 1850s and early 1860s, India was to be 'developed' as an area for investment and trade where the railways and inland communication acted as stimuli.[52] In connection with the building of bridges, arches, drainage, and other essential parts of the railway, contractors like Joseph Stephens supervised the continuous construction of warehouses, ginning presses, and administrative buildings along the main line and the feeders. Stephens delivered timber and undertook construction[53] for one of the largest Bombay managing houses, Nicol & Co., which held a privileged position in terms of credit resources with the City of Glasgow Bank and connections with the Government of Bombay.[54] Europeans in general held a privileged position in business, based on a mix of factors such as access to credit, racism, and networks within the British administration.[55] Nicol & Co. was one of the most influential managing houses and had worked with other European business houses since the 1840s to eliminate Indian middlemen from the raw cotton export market.[56] After the cotton boom, the firm continued supplying wheat from the same region to London during the 1870s.[57] It managed the Mofussil Press and Ginning Company,[58] for which Stephens built cotton-processing facilities in Khamgaon and Amravati for several years.[59] Agents and managers of

Nicol & Co. remained contact points for Stephens when he settled in Sweden, as importers of raw materials and manufactured goods.[60]

Contractors like Stephens appear as shadowy, even shady figures: on the one hand, they have largely evaded official paperwork and hence archives, as they were formally detached from the government and often executed subcontracts for larger companies; on the other, they were often spoken of as untrustworthy professionally, as they had a lot to gain by using lower quality materials and exploiting labour.[61] In Stephens' case, he was frequently under pressure from the GIPR to show that progress was being made and that the works under construction were of sufficient quality.[62] According to Stephens himself in a letter to his father, the reason he had acquired substantial savings compared with others who had had the same chances was his 'talent' for keeping down costs ('if I have any talent at all it is in being able to manage things cheaply').[63] Internalized skills that he had acquired as a contractor may, however, have been less obvious to him. In line with what a civil engineer was expected to know, he navigated materials, environmental conditions, and labour skills according to the local contexts and the work to be undertaken. While he had an interest in technological innovations and the technical aspects of railways, the construction work was ordered and designed by engineers of the GIPR or firms such as the Mofussil Press and Ginning Company.[64] The prospects of continuing a career as a contractor were slim, in view of a tightening of official regulations on obtaining contracts.[65] Not only Stephens' projects, but several parts of the infrastructure along the GIPR were evaluated as poor towards the end of the 1860s, and the contract system, built essentially upon a string of subcontracts, declined in favour of a departmental system and a professionalization of engineering.[66] Stephens' deliberations in correspondence with his father reflected everyday impressions of colleagues struggling to obtain jobs or taking a stroke of bad luck, and of failing constructions. Compared with colleagues, he had been fortunate to make large sums of money and to have been spared major health issues.[67] Settling back in Denmark or Scandinavia was an obvious choice, given Stephens' family relations and his limited chances of advancing further in the contractor system.

Late Industrialization and Migration in Scandinavia

Both the region where Stephens made his money and the one where he subsequently invested it underwent major economic and social transformations during the 1860s. Bombay was a fast-growing metropolis with expanding infrastructure and a port integrated into global trade networks, where Stephens, like many Europeans, arrived at a time when opportunities were rife in the booming construction business. At the opposite end of the spectrum of economic growth and urbanization, Småland province in southern Sweden had a low level of industrial growth compared with neighbouring regions, and after years of poor harvests coinciding with an increase in population, the famine of 1867 resulted in farmhands and peasants migrating in search of an income.[68] The large number of emigrants to North America from certain areas of Småland in the 1860s has been explained by a relatively early tradition of migration from the region to that continent, in combination with dwindling job opportunities in the agricultural sector and a lack of urbanization. In southern Sweden, the lack of urban centres to absorb surplus labour from the countryside was a factor that contributed to direct migration from rural areas to North America, rather than via the towns as elsewhere in the country.[69] In addition to the dearth of income opportunities as rural employment dwindled during 1867, the 1870s were marked by a population explosion, a process noticeable as early as the 1810s.[70] Larsson points out that, even during the peak of emigration between 1870 and 1914, transatlantic emigrants constituted only 10 per cent of the total outward migration from the region, as most of it was absorbed by Stockholm. Short-distance unskilled labour migration partly escaped the attention of official registers, but between 1860 and 1899, approximately 5,000–10,000 people per decade are believed to have migrated from Kronoberg to nearby countries, mainly Germany and Denmark. However, of registered migrants, 78 per cent migrated to North America between 1850 and 1914.[71] The famine of 1867, the year Stephens bought the Huseby Estate, and the following year of want triggered a 'mass migration' over the period 1868–79.[72]

Seen in the context of migration, technological change, and new labour regimes, Stephens acquired Huseby in what can be defined as a transition period. Significantly, the outmigration of farmers coincided with an influx of foreign investors, and Stephens was thus far from the only foreigner buying property in the region. According to Larsson, the transaction that put the Huseby Estate in the hands of Joseph Stephens should be understood in the context of the sale of more than 20 agricultural holdings to foreign buyers, in Kronoberg County alone, in 1867. Stephens' decision to end his career in India and invest his profits in a landed estate coincided with falling property prices due to a depression in the agricultural economy. The trend to buy farms in the south of Sweden in the 1860s was particularly strong among Danes and George Stephens' contacts with Danish businessmen in Copenhagen may have sparked the idea. Over the 15 years from 1867, approximately 250 farms were acquired by foreign buyers in Kronoberg county.[73] Economic recession, combined with new technology and production methods, threw regional ironworks into a crisis, which the Huseby Estate, as one of the exceptions, managed to survive under its new owner.[74] Like Huseby, many of the iron-producing estates that survived the 'death of the works' in this period were bought by foreigners, mainly Danes, but also German and British investors, according to Bengt Berglund's longue durée study of regional ironworks. They made lucrative deals as ironworks and businesses were declared bankrupt or forced to sell.[75] Larsson notes how most of the investors settled in Sweden, although many did not and instead ran the small industrial plants, farms, and estates through managers. Prosperous Danish farmers who invested in farms and estates mainly remained in Denmark and saw the deals as lucrative speculative opportunities.[76]

A newspaper clipping from a Danish daily, enclosed in a letter from George in Copenhagen to Joseph at Huseby in 1869, mentioned the recent acquisitions of landed estates and sawmills by Danes in Sweden, including 'engineer Stephens' buying Huseby.[77] The news dwelled on the profitable export of sawdust to Denmark which the Swedish main line through the region made possible. Larsson refers to the 1870s as a 'golden era' for the 'timber squires' (*trävarupatroner*) after the arrival of the railways in Småland. These men exploited the timber market by buying up timber at next to no cost from the peasantry, who hauled or floated it to the steam sawmills at the railway stations, where it was turned into pulp or other forms before being exported at a handsome profit to Denmark, England, or Germany.[78] New technology for turning wood fibre into the raw material of paper was adopted in Scandinavia in 1850s and 1860s, making the region a major supplier of paper and pulp, and providing a successful route for industrialization.[79] In the national context, the developments seen in Småland corresponded to the pattern of industrialization in the 1870s: industrialization driven by export markets with the help of internal communications that connected with the then newly established main line between Skåne and Stockholm.[80] While trade and the rise of business with the imperial expansion of Great Britain sparked industrialization in that country in the mid-eighteenth century, Sweden and Scandinavia at large did not have their industrial breakthrough until the 1870s. The industrial *transformation* of Sweden began in the middle of the nineteenth century,[81] intensified in the 1870s, and reached a stage of 'revolution' from the 1890s to 1910.[82] Just as Stephens's career in India had followed a desirable path enabling him to make a substantial profit, investing the capital he had acquired there in a region where industrialization, the railways, and technological innovations had barely been introduced opened up opportunities to introduce modern means of production and doing business. The arrival of Joseph Stephens and the other foreign buyers in the region coincided with the industrial breakthrough in southern Sweden.

Foreign ownership of and investment in regional production and businesses were not a novelty at Huseby, however. Like other regional ironworks, the Huseby Estate has a long tradition of ore extraction and iron manufacture going back to the Middle Ages. The nobleman Carl Carlsson Gyllenhielm (1574–1650) is regarded as its founder, to be followed by a Dutch era at Huseby, with Arnold de Rees as its most prominent representative.[83] Until the middle of the seventeenth century, German and Dutch business interests dominated ownership, production, and investments.[84] During the eighteenth century, ownership and production were gradually transferred into the hands of Swedish noble families, notably Paul Rudebeck the Elder and the Younger and later the Counts Hamilton.[85] The nineteenth century at Huseby was characterized by the establishment of small-scale workshops as a subsidiary business to agricultural production. These businesses were dominated by people from the peasant strata and would come to have a long-term impact on the development of a regional form of small-scale business ownership. A significant drawback to them was their inability to compete with larger production units regionally and nationally. Although there had been continuous technological progress in iron production in Sweden since the early modern period, technological changes can largely be attributed to industrialization in Europe, and the 1830s and 1840s in particular saw a direct impact of British advances in iron production.[86] In the national context, pig and bar iron production in the province of Småland in the 1860s was relatively insignificant, accounting for only 5 per cent of the total. These 5 per cent derived from 20,000 tonnes of lake and bog ore and 10,000 tonnes of rock ore, most of it from the large mine at Taberg, which were turned into 10,000 tonnes of pig and bar iron at 25 regional furnaces.[87] The economic crisis in Småland in the 1860s is thus partly explained by a set of interlinked processes related to industrialization, or rather the lack thereof. In the 1870s, Stephens modernized the furnace and established a mechanical engineering workshop to replace the blacksmith's forge. Indeed, as Larsson has pointed out, the demands of industrialization markedly shaped production, with the estate in the 1880s making agricultural machines and mechanical parts rather than iron tools and simple products such as pans and handles. By the end of the 1880s, other local ironworks had merged and transferred production to larger works in central Sweden, but Huseby continued to produce pig iron until the 1930s. According to Larsson, the Huseby Estate, unlike many others that could not adapt to 'modern' production methods, was transformed by Stephens and was thus able to make it through the crisis.[88]

New Networks, New Markets

Soon after Stephens had bought Huseby, he wanted to sell it, as his engagement to his godfather's daughter had ended badly. He seems to have been convinced that he had paid too much for the estate, but as the property market declined further in 1868, referred to as the worst year of the economic crisis, it would have been financially difficult to sell as he had borrowed money to buy it.[89] During his first years at Huseby, from 1869 to the end of 1874, Stephens attempted to enter into an array of business deals involving the existing resources of the estate. His business endeavours can be divided into four categories, reflecting a combination of exploring new markets and new production methods and searching for time-saving and less costly transport routes. As will be discussed in the following, Stephens targeted two markets, one related to current developments in the industrialization of southern Sweden, the other to production in England through his private networks abroad, which had developed in India and through his family in England.

Many of Stephens' outgoing business letters during this period are concerned with establishing deals with local and regional companies interested in buying timber for industrial production, such as matchstick factories, or wood for fine goods, or with exporting iron.[90] Directly related to his attempts to export goods or find business partners in other parts of the country was the question of communications by land and sea, both of which Stephens considered too slow and costly. Diverting trade towards London and imperial markets in India, for instance, proved more expensive than at first estimated.[91] Trusting his old contacts in Bombay, Stephens offered them to export 'Swedish timber', red and white pines, and iron.[92] The Bombay firm of Rogers & Co. acted as Stephens' agents and received orders for goods and iron exported from the Huseby Estate as early as 1868.[93] While in Bombay, after he had bought the estate, Stephens claimed that pine sold in India could fetch 10 times its value in the Malmö port.[94] However, the cost of exporting goods from Sweden to Bombay was twice that sent from London. As a result, Swedish iron and timber producers sold their goods on the London market.[95] In spite of this, in 1868 and 1869, Stephens investigated the options for exporting timber to Bombay where his contacts submitted tenders to the GIPR for large consignments of sleepers.[96] His father, overseeing the business at Huseby in 1868–9 when Joseph was in India, questioned Joseph's assessment of the forests at Huseby as 'comparatively valueless.'[97] If cutting and extracting young trees instead of exporting the heavy timber Joseph aimed for, his father argued, he would make money 'without ruining the forest, of course *planting largely instead*' (emphasis in original). At the same time, at Huseby he tried quite innovative ways of making money, such as producing velocipedes or advertising 'wild shooting and fishing' in the British press, the latter resulting in a visit by a group of Englishmen who in the end did not pay the bill for their lodging and hunting rights.[98] Small-scale manufacturing of products, however, was in line with the established regional business culture: most of the iron extracted in Småland was traditionally used for manufacturing rather than exported as bar iron.[99] The prototype of a bicycle, on the other hand, was a technical innovation and, in 1867, one of the first of its kind produced in Sweden. While visiting Sweden in order to buy Huseby that year, Stephens went to the Universal Exhibition in Paris, where the velocipede had been introduced. Stephens exported 12 velocipedes to his contact Rogers & Co. in Bombay at the end of 1869,[100] and according to correspondence with a potential buyer in Malmö, Huseby had the capacity to deliver at least 16–20 of them per month. Yet only two of these velocipedes have been preserved until today.[101]

The first steam locomotives reached Småland via the main line from Stockholm to Malmö in 1862, almost 10 years after the railways were in public use in Bombay.[102] Sweden's economy in the second half of the nineteenth century was weak compared with that of Denmark, where industrial growth had taken off and the introduction of railways for public and commercial use had begun in the 1840s. As research has highlighted, Stephens played an active role in establishing the already planned Vislanda-Karlshamn railway line, together with several of the leading men of the region, who shared an interest in promoting greater connectivity for business purposes.[103] An 'opening up of the region' by the means of a railway line linking Lake Salen and Lake Åsnen with Karlshamn, Stephens calculated, would increase the value of the land and of products by at least 50 per cent, as the cost of transport would be halved compared with the route via Malmö.[104] He lobbied businessmen in Karlshamn who shared his interest in expanding railway links between the port town and the inland regions, where Ålshult, belonging to the Huseby Estate, would be one node connecting the lakes to the coast, and Älmhult another.[105] Soon, in extensive correspondence with the railway authorities, he was arguing the case for improving transport in the region and making it more cost-effective by pointing to the high charges for freight to England.[106] Deals with potential buyers in England would be less profitable as the costs of shipping and inland freight were prohibitive. Britain and its imperial markets, with which Stephens had connections, were a relatively untried route for goods from inland Småland. Larsson writes that the establishment of the main railway line close-by was a decisive factor in Stephens' decision to buy Huseby, as it helped to extract and trade in the rich natural resources and products of the estate.[107] The idea of buying a property close to the main line was strongly recommended by his godfather Hyltén-Cavallius.[108] Plans to export goods with the help of the railway were continuously reported by George Stephens in letters as Joseph Stephens returned to India in 1868, after buying the estate.[109] In 1874, the Karlshamn-Vislanda line opened for traffic and provided a more efficient route as it connected Huseby to the Southern Main Line.[110] The line passing close to the Huseby Estate connected the area with the main line to the international export ports in Malmö and would make planning and dispatching orders far more time- and cost-effective.

The prospects of establishing financially viable exports of pig iron to England depended to a great extent on transport times and the cost of freight. Compared with selling material to local ironworks such as the one at Motala, the correspondence involved, waiting times in the port at Malmö, and deciding on alternative transport routes in Germany or via the large port of Gothenburg to England were in themselves cumbersome processes, often making such exports unprofitable.[111] Regional transport to well-connected small industrial units in Jönköping and Malmö was easily agreed upon, as routes and freight costs were well established between the parties.[112] Stephens' contacts in London, however, simultaneously acted as a channel for inquiries about imports of machinery to Sweden, including locomotives for the Helsingborg-Hässleholm railway, a regional line in the far south of the country,[113] a printing press, and fine machinery such as a slotting machine for production at Huseby.[114]

Before settling at Huseby, Joseph Stephens appears to have established a personal and business relationship with the Swedish merchant Anders

Figure 6.1 Joseph Stephens (left) in a meeting at Huseby together with regional timber merchants, most prominently M. M. Warburg (next to Stephens) of Bark & Warburg, Gothenburg, and Robert Ternström (sitting with arms crossed) of Schmidt & Co, Karlshamn, 1870.

Source: Photograph by Kirchoff, courtesy Huseby Bruk AB.

Gabriel Knös (1843–1905) in London in 1868.[115] Knös had moved from Uppsala to London in 1864, and at his wedding in London in 1876, Stephens was his best man. Stephens regularly paid interest to Knös, according to the cash books from 1873 to 1876,[116] most likely as a result of his exports of timber and iron to England. In the cash books, Stephens kept track of his 'London accounts', where deposits for butter were regularly made to a number of people, presumably the commission he paid to both relatives and business partners. Coincidentally, Hyltén-Cavallius himself used the popular Swedish idiom 'for all the butter in Småland' when assuring Stephens of his best intentions in recommending him to buy Huseby in 1866.[117] The saying stems from the nineteenth century and reflects the good reputation and high output of butter production in the region, which is also known for its dairy cattle. Butter was thus a regional commodity known in markets abroad as well as nationally. Stephens saw an opportunity to profit by buying it from farms and shipping it to London,[118] as well as on a smaller scale to Copenhagen.[119] He himself argued that the linguistic advantage of being fluent in both English and Swedish gave him an upper hand in this trade. He warned his middleman in London that the latter could not get away with quoting lower prices, as Swedish newspapers published the market prices in London according to quality[120] and, to the Swedish butter sellers, Stephens promised 'special specifications' from London.[121] While the butter trade was a relatively small business, it reflects how Stephens brought together his skills and his commercial networks.

Expanding the Colonial Periphery

How much can be gleaned from the individual life histories of men like Joseph Stephens for us to understand the impact of imperialism beyond the British Empire? This chapter explores how professional experiences, networks, and the infrastructure of the British Empire fed into a 'colonial career' which continued and flourished in a rural Swedish region well after Stephens had left India. A central contribution of Stephens in the context of restarting business on the Huseby Estate was that he saw the value of communications in expanding production and reaching new markets. It was not primarily his knowledge of engineering that prompted his push for a regional railway, but the economic profits he envisaged for himself and local businesses from establishing fast access by rail to industrial centres and foreign markets. In Khandesh and Berar, he had himself encountered and been shaped by the rhetoric of the railways as the key to 'opening up' regions for resource extraction and export of materials to British imperial markets. At the Huseby Estate, when pushing for the establishment of the Karlshamn-Vislanda line, Stephens argued the case for local natural resources and goods reaching international markets via Copenhagen and London, as well as for local industries in Sweden.

The growing body of research discussed earlier in this chapter, on connections between imperialism, Scandinavian colonialism, and the rise of modernity in the region, has helped to understand entanglements and connections between seemingly peripheral regions.[122] Simultaneously, as the body of research on Stephens' period in India has grown, it has become clear that his professional activities in India were not only in 'engineering' and 'building railways', as has been argued in earlier work.[123] Like others who ventured out on 'colonial careers',[124] the experience and networks Stephens gained in India informed his approach to business and entrepreneurship. His career in India involved diverse tasks, including sourcing labour and materials and bringing down costs, which probably reflected on the Huseby Estate in his readiness to try multiple new projects simultaneously, both engaging in new production and using a network of local and British sellers and buyers for relatively minor products such as butter. It is important to note that Stephens had partly inherited and partly built up a strong professional network between England, Sweden, and colonial western India.

In addition to his own experience in India, he mainly used his networks in England to get a better idea of railway technology and its possible impact in an increasingly industrialized society in Europe. At the same time, Stephens' family connection (his British brother-in-law) helped him gain access to the colonial market in India, where he worked as a contractor and made huge profits, which in turn helped him to buy and eventually set up his business on the Huseby Estate. Further, his knowledge of the economic situation in Sweden through family networks and the added benefit of knowing the local language of the country facilitated his many entrepreneurial plans to export to foreign markets. Although he showed great curiosity for innovations and new technology, leading to the production of some of the first bicycles on Swedish soil, he also made use of the resources at hand, wherever he saw an opportunity to make money. Stephens had the entrepreneurial vision to realize that, in order to compete with the already growing industries in and around Europe, it was essential to have an economically viable communications route for the export of what he produced.

Notes

1 Magdalena Naum and Jonas M. Nordin, 'Introduction: Situating Scandinavian Colonialism', in Magdalena Naum and Jonas M. Nordin (eds), *Scandinavian Colonialism and the Rise of Modernity: Small Time Agents in a Global Arena* (New York: Springer, 2013), pp. 3–16. For a brief introduction to Scandinavian colonies, from the Viking colonies to the turning of Greenland into a county of Denmark in 1953, see Erik Gøbel, 'Colonial Empires', in E. I. Kouri and Jens E. Olesen (eds), *The Cambridge History of Scandinavia, Volume II, 1520–1870* (Cambridge: Cambridge University Press, 2016), pp. 279–309.

2 Brita Brenna, 'Clergymen Abiding in the Fields: The Making of the Naturalist Observer in Eighteenth-Century Norwegian Natural History', *Science in Context*, 24/2 (2011), pp. 143–66; Dag Avango, Louwrens Hacquebord, and Urban Wråkberg, 'Industrial Extraction of Arctic Natural Resources since the Sixteenth Century: Technoscience and Geo-Economics in the History of Northern Whaling and Mining', *Journal of Historical Geography*, 44 (2014), pp. 15–30.

3 Joachim Östlund, 'The Swedish Consulate in Tripoli and Information Gathering on Diplomacy, Everyday Life, and the Slave Trade, 1795–1844', in Mika Suonpää and Owen Wright (eds), *Diplomacy and Intelligence in the Nineteenth-Century Mediterranean World* (London: Bloomsbury Academic, 2019), pp. 17–36; Aryo Makko, 'I imperialismens kölvatten? Ett maritimt perspektiv på stormaktsspelet, kolonialism utan kolonier och den svensk-norska konsulsstaten, 1875–1905', *Historisk Tidskrift*, 134/3 (2014), pp. 499–523.

4 One contemporary example is Fredrik Thomasson's successful digitization of the Swedish and Danish official colonial documents which, owing to their fragile condition, have been off limits to researchers in the French archives in Aix-en-Provence. With a team of PhD students and in collaboration with the French archives, the process of digitization and finding an online repository has taken almost 10 years. Fredrik Thomasson, 'Den karibiska skorpionen: Om digitaliseringen av det svenska Saint Barthélemy arkivet i Aix-en-Provence', *Historisk Tidskrift*, 138/1 (2018), pp. 78–90.

5 Richard Drayton and David Motadel, 'Discussion: The Futures of Global History', *Journal of Global History*, 13/1 (2018), pp. 1–21.

6 Patricia Purtschert and Harald Fischer-Tiné, 'Introduction: The End of Innocence; Debating Colonialism in Switzerland', in P. Purtschert and H. Fischer-Tine (eds), *Colonial Switzerland: Rethinking Colonialism From the Margins* (Basingstoke: Palgrave Macmillan, 2014), p. 297.

7 Harald Fischer-Tiné, 'The Other Side of Internationalism: Switzerland as a Hub of Militant Anti-Colonialism, c. 1910–1920', in Purtschert and Fischer-Tiné (eds), *Colonial Switzerland*, pp. 221–58.

8 Patricia Purtschert, Francesca Falk, and Barbara Lüthi, 'Switzerland and "Colonialism Without Colonies": Reflections on the Status of Colonial Outsiders', *Interventions*, 18/2 (2016), pp. 286–302; Purtschert and Fischer-Tiné, 'Introduction: The End of Innocence', pp. 5–7.

9 See Gunnel Cederlöf, 'Introduction' in this volume, p. 9. 'A Chest in the Attic' ('En låda på vinden'), exhibition at Huseby by Eleonor Marcussen and Gunnel Cederlöf. This was a historical exhibition about research in the Joseph Stephens Archive, Linnaeus University Library, shown on the Huseby Estate, Grimslöv, Sweden, 11 May 2019–winter 2019: https://lnu.se/mot-linneuniversitetet/aktuellt/kalender/2019/utstallning---ladan-pa-vinden/ www.husebybruk.se/en-lada-pa-vinden/?lang=en (accessed 6 September 2020).

10 The name of J. Stephens' business venture was Joseph Stephens Construction Company. Niclas Rosenbalck, 'Förteckning över Husebyarkiven vid Linnéuniversitetet, Växjö', unpublished catalogue (PDF, 245 pp.), Växjö, 2010, p. 2.

11 Radhika Krishnan, 'Contracting and Sub-contracting in British India: Exploring the Dynamics of Railway Building Through Joseph Stephens', in Kristina Myrvold and Soniya Billore (eds.), *India: Research on Cultural Encounters and Representations at Linnaeus University* (Gothenburg: Makadam Förlag, 2017), pp. 50–73; Radhika Krishnan, 'Järnvägsbygget ur arbetarnas perspektiv', in Margareta Petersson (ed.), *Från Brittiska Indien till Huseby bruk: Järnvägen som arena för modernitet och kolonialism under lycksökaren och järnvägsentreprenören Joseph Stephens tid i Indien 1860–69* (Lund: Arkiv förlag, 2018), pp. 113–34; Dhiraj Nite, 'En lycksökares liv och affärer i Indien och Skandinavien', in Petersson (ed.), *Från Brittiska Indien*, pp. 135–65.

12 Catherine Hall, *Civilising Subjects: Metropole and Colony in the English Imagination 1830–1867* (Chicago: University of Chicago Press, 2002); David Lambert and Allan Lester, 'Introduction: Imperial Spaces, Imperial Subjects', in David Lambert and Allan Lester (eds), *Colonial Lives Across Empire: Imperial Careering in the Long Nineteenth Century* (Cambridge; New York: Cambridge University Press, 2006), pp. 1–31.

13 For a brief introduction to George Stephens' and Gunnar Olof Hyltén-Cavallius' ethnographic studies and manuscripts on Nordic folklore, see Sigurd Kværndrup and Boel Lindberg, 'Inledning', in Gunilla Byrman (ed.), *En värld för sig själv: Nya studier i medeltida ballader*, Ord & Musik & Bild: Intermediala studier 1 (Växjö: Växjö University Press, 2008), pp. 11–27.

14 Linnaeus University (LNU), Huseby Archives (HA), Joseph Stephens Archive (JSA), E1:1, G. Stephens to J. Stephens, June 1866 and 3–14 December 1867.

15 Catherine Hall, 'Epilogue: Imperial Careering at Home; Harriet Martineau on Empire', in Lambert and Lester (eds), *Colonial Lives*, p. 339.

16 Judith Flanders gives examples of similar male career choices among the upwardly mobile lower middle classes in Victorian society in England. Judith Flanders, *A Circle of Sisters: Alice Kipling, Georgiana Burne-Jones, Agnes Poynter and Louisa Baldwin* (London: Penguin Viking, 2001).

17 Lene Østermark-Johansen, 'Reading Clubs, Language Societies and Female Education in Fin-de-Siècle Copenhagen', *Forum for Modern Language Studies*, 53/3 (2017), pp. 280–1.

18 George Stephens took up an appointment as *lektor* in English at the University of Copenhagen in 1851. Before moving to Copenhagen, he and his wife, Mary Stephens, had lived and raised a family in Stockholm for 19 years, from 1834 to 1851. Andrew Wawn, 'Stephens, George (1813–1895)', ONB, https://doi.org/10.1093/ref:odnb/26383 (accessed 1 December 2019).
19 Andrew Wawn, *The Vikings and the Victorians: Inventing the Old North in Nineteenth-Century Britain* (Cambridge: D. S. Brewer, 2000), p. 222.
20 Åke Svensson, *George Stephens: Forskare, samlare, publicist, debattör* (Växjö: Sanct Sigfrids Gille, 2010), p. 4.
21 Wawn, *Vikings and Victorians*, p. 222; Svensson, *George Stephens*, p. 2.
22 John Stephens (1806–50), Samuel Stephens (1808–40), and Edward Stephens (1811–61). Margareta Petersson, 'Drömmen om Eldorado', in Petersson (ed.), *Från Brittiska Indien*, pp. 168, 184–5.
23 For a discussion of the definitions of settler colonialism, see Caroline Elkins and Susan Pedersen, 'Introduction: Settler Colonialism; A Concept and its Uses', in C. Elkins and S. Pedersen (eds), *Settler Colonialism in the Twentieth Century: Projects, Practices, Legacies* (London and New York: Routledge, 2005).
24 Margareta Petersson, 'Joseph Stephens—familjen och arkivet', in M. Petersson (ed.), *Från Brittiska Indien*, p. 18.
25 Rita P. Bhambi, *The Great Indian Peninsula Railway: A Journey Through Time (1853–1871)* (New Delhi: Bharti Publications, 2016), p. 4.
26 Abbott had gone through the shops of the engineer Charles Fox (1810–74) in Birmingham, who in turn had worked under Robert Stephenson, 'the father of the railways'. Obituary, John Hallen Abbott, in *Memoirs of the ICE*, [xx], 1885, pp. 360–1.
27 Henrik Harnow, *Den danske ingeniørs historie 1850–1920* (Århus: Systime, 1998), p. 62.
28 LNU, HA, JSA, E1:12a, signed 29 February 1860.
29 Harnow, *Den danske ingeniørs historie*, pp. 19–22.
30 Petersson, 'Drömmen om Eldorado', p. 167 (translation of quote).
31 Ann Laura Stoler, 'Cultivating Bourgeois Bodies and Racial Selves', in C. Hall (ed.), *Cultures of Empire, A Reader: Colonizers in Britain and the Empire in the Nineteenth and Twentieth Centuries* (Manchester: Manchester University Press, 2000), p. 90.
32 Ibid.
33 Harald Fischer-Tiné, *Low and Licentious Europeans: Race, Class and 'White Subalternity' in Colonial India*, New Perspectives in South Asian History (New Delhi: Orient Blackswan, 2009), p. 59.
34 For an impression of the Stephens siblings' lives in India, see Petersson, 'Drömmen om Eldorado'.
35 Ingemar Gunnarsson, 'Från lärling till "ingenjör"', in Petersson (ed.), *Från Brittiska Indien*, p. 82.
36 Ben Marsden and Crosbie Smith, *Engineering Empires: A Cultural History of Technology in Nineteenth-Century Britain* (Basingstoke: Palgrave Macmillan, 2005), pp. 161–2.
37 Ibid., p. 236.
38 Markku Kuisma, 'Industrial Expansion', in E. I. Kouri and Jens E. Olesen (eds), *The Cambridge History of Scandinavia, Volume II, 1520–1870* (Cambridge: Cambridge University Press, 2016), pp. 742–769, pp. 761–3.
39 Harnow, *Den danske ingeniørs historie*, pp. 31–3.
40 Popular perceptions of Stephens as an engineer building railways are reflected in the magazine clipping 'Vem får Huseby?', *Damernas Värld* (dated 1955), Lund University Archives (Lund, Sweden), Samling Hildebrand, 'Huseby'. The Swedish historian Lars-Olof Larsson, who has written extensively on the history of the Huseby Estate, writes that Stephens received an engineering education

in England (Larsson, *Det fantastiska Huseby: En rundvandring i tid och rum*, Växjö: Huseby Bruk, 1993, p. 21) and was engaged in railway construction undertaken by his brother-in-law (Larsson, 'Hur Stephens kom till Huseby', in *Skatelövskrönika 1978*, Grimslöv, 1986, p. 6).

41 Ian J. Kerr, *Building the Railways of the Raj, 1850–1900* (New Delhi: Oxford University Press, 1995), p. 76, and for a discussion on the roles of the contractor, cf. chapter 3 in ibid., 'Contractors, Engineers and Petty Contractors: The Varieties and Problems of Management', pp. 44–84.

42 Larsson, 'Hur Stephens kom till Huseby', p. 6. Since 1964, Lars-Olof Larsson has published numerous works on the history of the Huseby Estate in the wider context of the region, from the early medieval period until today: 'Historia kring Huseby: Epoken Stephens', in *Skatelövskrönika 1978* (Grimslöv: Skatelövs hembygdsförening, 1978); 'Hur Stephens kom till Huseby'; *Det fantastiska Huseby: En rundvandring i tid och rum* (Växjö: Huseby Bruk, 1993); and the recent, longer co-edited book by Larsson and Margareta Petersson, Åke Svensson, and Erik Wångmar, *Det levande Huseby: En värld i världen* (Växjö: Historiska föreningen i Kronobergs län, 2018). Most of Larsson's publications, however, do not address the Indian period in depth, as during the time of his research the bulk of the documents had not yet been discovered in a box in the attic of the main house at Huseby. His detailed knowledge of the development of the estate after Stephens took it over thus largely excludes Stephens's period in India.

43 Gunnarsson, 'Från lärling till "ingenjör"', pp. 70–1.

44 Ingemar Gunnarsson, *En skandinavisk järnvägskontraktörs karriär i Indien 1860–1867: ackumulering av socialt och kulturellt kapital som framgångsstrategi i en kolonial kontext*, Lnu Licentiate No. 31, Department of Cultural Sciences, Linnaeus University, Sweden (Växjö: Linneaus University Press, 2020, pp. 46–7.

45 Regarding the apprenticeship system, see Marsden and Smith, *Engineering Empires*, p. 235. For a brief idea of how the definition of an 'engineer' changed in the nineteenth century, see Harnow, *Den danske ingeniørs historie*, pp. 13–14.

46 Stephens read William Davis Haskoll in India. Gunnarsson, 'Från lärling till "Ingenjör"', p. 78. The library on the Huseby Estate contains several works on engineering with notes from the 1860s, and some are likely to have been acquired in India or Copenhagen by Joseph or John Abbott. For instance, George Stephens gifted to Joseph, in 'Chepinghaven' (Copenhagen) before the latter left for Bombay in November 1859, S. C. Brees's *The Illustrated Glossary of Practical Architecture and Civil Engineering: Comprising the Theory and Modern Practice* (London: L.A. Lewis, 1853). According to notes in the book, it appears to have belonged to Rayner Storr in 1854. Also in the Huseby Library: T. Baker, *Railway Engineering; or, Field Work Preparatory to the Construction of Railways* (London: Spottiswoode and Shaw, 1848), with a handwritten note: 'Charles Blackwell, Poona, 11 June 1860'; Charles Haslett and Charles W. Hackley, *The Mechanic's, Machinist's, and Engineer's Practical Book of Reference: Adapted to and for the Use of All Classes of Practical Mechanics, Together with the Engineer's Field Book: With a Collection of Valuable Recipes* (London: Trübner and Co., 1855). Personal visit to the Huseby Estate, 8 December 2018.

47 Stephens is listed as a 'Contractor' in Akola in 1868, in LNU, HA, JSA, F1F:2, *The 'Times of India' Calendar & Directory, Abridged Edition* (Bombay: The 'Times of India' Office, London: G. Street, 30, Cornhill, 1868), p. 193. The stages in his career are mentioned in Alexander Bubb, 'Class, Cotton, and "Woddaries": A Scandinavian Railway Contractor in Western India, 1860–69', *Modern Asian Studies*, 51/5 (2017), pp. 1371, 1375.

48 LNU, HA, JSA, F1F:1, Diary 1860–1, a Letts's Diary for 1857 (London: Letts, Son and Co., 1856), including almanacs and other reference material printed at

the front of the book. Two diaries from 1862 and 1863 are held as digital copies at LNU (not archived); the originals are kept at Huseby, referred to as 'Huseby Estate, Joseph Stephens' diary 1862', a Letts's Diary for 1862 (London: Letts, Son, and Co., 1861), and 'Huseby Estate, Joseph Stephens' diary 1863' (London: Letts, Son, and Co., 1862).

49 A. Marika Vicziany, 'The Cotton Trade and the Commercial Development of Bombay, 1855–1875', unpublished PhD thesis, SOAS, University of London, 1975.

50 Marika Vicziany, 'Bombay Merchants and Structural Changes in the Export Community 1850 to 1880', in K. N. Chaudhuri and Clive J. Dewey (eds), *Economy and History: Essays in Indian Economic and Social History* (New Delhi: OUP, 1979), p. 181.

51 Sabyasachi Bhattacharya, *The Financial Foundations of the British Raj: Ideas and Interests in the Reconstruction of Indian Public Finance 1858–1872*, 2nd ed. (New Delhi: Orient Longman, 2005 [1970]), pp. 18, 248–9.

52 Ibid., p. 231.

53 LNU, HA, JSA, F1A:6: Correspondence and orders for teak and timber stretch from 1866 to 1868, e.g., W. Nicol to J. Stephens, Bombay, 7 August 1866.

54 Vicziany, 'Bombay Merchants', p. 173.

55 Asiya Siddiqi, *Bombay's People, 1860–1898: Insolvents in the City* (New Delhi: Oxford University Press, 2017).

56 Vicziany, 'Bombay Merchants', pp. 184–5; Maria Misra, *Business, Race, and Politics in British India, c.1850–1960* (Oxford: Clarendon, 1999), ch. 1: 'The Managing Agency Houses in the Era of High Imperialism, 1860–1919', pp. 17–62; Maria Misra, '"Business Culture" and Entrepreneurship in British India, 1860–1950', *Modern Asian Studies*, 34/2 (2000), pp. 333–48.

57 Crispin Bates, 'Class and Economic Change in Central India: The Narmada Valley 1820–1930', in Clive Dewey (ed.), *Arrested Development in India: The Historical Dimension* (New Delhi: Manohar, 1988), p. 252.

58 Vicziany, 'Bombay Merchants', p. 184.

59 Bubb, 'Class, Cotton, and "Woddaries"', p. 1383.

60 LNU, HA, JSA, F1a:6, Incoming letters from Nicol & Co. in 1868.

61 Bubb, 'Class, Cotton, and "Woddaries"', p. 1372. See also Bubb's article on cultural portrayals of contractors, 'An Element of Risk: The Corrupt Contractor in Indian Fiction and Film, 1886–1983', *Cambridge Journal of Postcolonial Literary Inquiry*, 4/1 (2017), pp. 109–26.

62 Huseby Estate, Joseph Stephens' diary 1863, 2 March 1863.

63 Joseph Stephens quoted in Bubb, 'Class, Cotton, and "Woddaries"', pp. 1369–70.

64 LNU, HA, JSA, F1D:1, Drawing titled: 'Mr Flemings Press [*sic*], Mofussil Press & Ginning Company "Limited", Press Building for Shegaum', signed Thomas [undecipherable], Bombay, 30 October 1865.

65 The changing conditions for railway contracts are discussed by Bhambi, *Great Indian Peninsula Railway*, pp. 204–6.

66 Ibid., p. 206.

67 Bubb, 'Class, Cotton, and "Woddaries"', pp. 1369–70.

68 Lars-Olof Larsson, *Historia om Småland* (Växjö: Diploma, 1974), pp. 213–14.

69 Ulf Beijbom, *Amerika, Amerika: en bok om utvandringen* (Stockholm: Natur och Kultur, 1977), pp. 55–8.

70 Larsson, *Historia om Småland*, p. 194.

71 Lars-Olof Larsson, *Växjö genom 1000 år* (Stockholm: Norstedt, 1991), p. 259.

72 Ibid., p. 257.

73 Larsson, *Historia kring Huseby*, p. 83. Elsewhere Larsson mentions 200 farms, among them Bolmstads säteri, Telestad herrgård, Linnebjörke säteri and

Högnalövs gård. Lars-Olof Larsson, *Länsstyrelsen och Kronobergs län under 350 år*, Historiska föreningens i Kronobergs län skriftserie, 4 (Växjö: Länsstyrelsen i Kronobergs län, 1984), p. 106.
74 Larsson, *Historia om Småland*, pp. 190–1.
75 'Death of the works' is a literal translation of the Swedish term 'bruksdöden', referring to a historical process marked by the sharp decline or closure of estates as production and manufacturing units. Bengt Berglund, *Järn i Småland: Forskningsläge, utgångspunkter och övergripande resultat*, Småländsk järnhantering under 1000 år, 1, Jernkontorets bergshistoriska skriftserie, 34 (Stockholm: Jernkontoret, 2000), p. 59.
76 Larsson, *Länsstyrelsen och Kronobergs län*, p. 106.
77 'Svenske Landeiendomme og Savværker, som eies af Danske', newspaper cutting, *Dagstelegrafen*, 8 October 1869, LNU, HA, JSA, E1:2, G. Stephens to J. Stephens, 14 October 1869.
78 Lars-Olof Larsson, Sven-Olof Olsson, Josef Rydén, and Stig Tornehed, *Småländska strövtåg genom fem sekler* (Växjö: Diploma, 1976), p. 205.
79 Kuisma, 'Industrial Expansion', p. 748.
80 Lennart Jörberg, 'Structural Change and Economic Growth: Sweden in the 19th Century', *Economy and History*, 8/1 (1965), pp. 3–4; Jonas Ljungberg and Lennart Schön, 'Domestic Markets and International Integration: Paths to Industrialisation in the Nordic Countries', *Scandinavian Economic History Review*, 61/2 (2013), pp. 17–19.
81 Jörberg, 'Structural Change', pp. 5, 8, 14, 109–10.
82 Lars Magnusson, *An Economic History of Sweden*, Routledge Explorations in Economic History (London; New York: Routledge, 2000), pp. 106–7.
83 Larsson, *Det fantastiska Huseby*, pp. 4–5.
84 Berglund, *Järn i Småland*, p. 56.
85 Larsson, *Det fantastiska Huseby*, pp. 12–19.
86 Berglund, *Järn i Småland*, pp. 58–9, 61. Also Bengt Berglund, Per-Olof Grönberg, and Tomas Nilson (eds), *Historiska perspektiv på tekniköverföring 1800–2000* (Gothenburg: Department of History of Technology and Industry, Chalmers University of Technology, 2006).
87 Larsson, *Historia om Småland*, pp. 190–1.
88 Larsson, *Historia kring Huseby*, pp. 90–1.
89 Larson, *Växjö genom 1000 år*, p. 257. Larsson, 'Hur Stephens kom till Huseby', pp. 8, 17.
90 LNU, HA, JSA, E1:1, Correspondence, Stephens to Messrs Heinoch Pollack & Co, Malmö, 2 June 1869.
91 LNU, HA, HEA, B1, Letter book, J. Stephens to Kongliga styrelsen för Statens Jernvägstrafik (Royal Board for the State Railways), 26 February 1870.
92 LNU, HA, HEA, E1: 1, Correspondence, J. Stephens, Huseby, to A. McKenzie, Bombay, 17 November 1869. His contact Henry Rogers, owner of Rogers & Co. a chemist's firm in Poona and Bombay (22 Rampart Row, Bombay), distributed a range of goods. LNU, HA, HEA, B1: 1, J. Stephens to Mr. Rogers, 25 October 1869.
93 LNU, HA, JSA, E1:2, 8a, G. Stephens to J. Stephens, 18 March 1868.
94 LNU, HA, JSA, E1:2, J. Stephens to G. Stephens, 5 March 1868.
95 LNU, HA. JSA, E1: 2, J. Stephens to G. Stephens, 14 November 1868, 15 January 1869.
96 LNU, HA. JSA, E1: 2, J. Stephens to G. Stephens, 10 May 1868, 26 February 1869.
97 LNU, HA, JSA, E1:2, G. Stephens to J. Stephens, 25 June 1869.
98 Ibid., E1:1, J. Stephens to Godden, n.d.; ibid., E1:1, 11, Newspaper cutting, n.d. ('filed 28 May' [1869]).

99 Berglund, *Järn i Småland*, p. 56.
100 It is not stated that these products were manufactured at Huseby, but it is likely in view of the costs given. LNU, HA, HEA, B1:1, Letter book, J. Stephens to Messrs J. & R. McCracken & Co., 15 December 1869; LNU, HA, JSA, F1A:7.
101 LNU, HA, HEA, E1:1, J. Stephens to Messrs Heinoch Pollack & Co, Malmö, 2 June 1869. Gert Ekström, *Älskade cykel* (Stockholm: Prisma, 2004), p. 16.
102 Larsson, *Historia om Småland*, p. 210.
103 Nite, 'En lycksökares liv', pp. 144–5. Gunnarsson, 'Från lärling till "ingenjör"', pp. 65–82. Ingemar Gunnarsson, '"Karlshamn—Wislanda Jernväg": Maktelit och nätverk i Karlshamns stad vid banans tillblivelse 1855–1874', unpublished MA dissertation, School of Humanities, Växjö University, 2003, pp. 43–4.
104 LNU, HA, HEA, E1:1, J. Stephens to G. O. Hyltén-Cavallius, 27 June 1869.
105 Ibid., J. Stephens to Consul E. Meyer, Huseby Estate, draft, 16 June 1869.
106 LNU, HA, HEA, B1, Letter book, pp. 34–5, J. Stephens to Kongliga styrelsen för Statens Jernvägstrafik (Royal Board for the State Railways), 26 February 1870.
107 Larsson, 'Hur Stephens kom till Huseby', p. 9.
108 LNU, HA, JSA, E1:2, G. O. Hyltén-Cavallius cited in letter from G. Stephens (Copenhagen) to J. Stephens (India), 6 June 1866.
109 Ibid., G. Stephens (Copenhagen) to J. Stephens (India), 23 December 1868.
110 Larsson, *Det fantastiska Huseby*, p. 24.
111 LNU, HA, HEA, E1:1, J. Stephens to W. Ritter & Co., London, 7 October 1872; reply in LNU, HA, JSA, B1:2, Letter book, J. Stephens to Ritter & Co., 29 October 1872; to W. Ritter & Co. regarding shipment of 100 or 200 tons of pig iron, 10 January 1873.
112 LNU, HA, HEA, E1:1, Freight costs of Skånska Cement Aktie Bolag, Åkarp and Lomma (in Skåne province), 8 November 1872; Freight costs for various types of iron to Malmö (Skåne) and Jönköping (Småland), 14 October 1872.
113 LNU, HA, JSA, B1:2, Letter book, J. Stephens to J. D. Field, London, 7 June 1873.
114 LNU, HA, HEA, B1:3, Letter book, J. Stephens to J. D. Field, London, 4 and 15 February 1873.
115 Ibid., Letter book, Cleve to Lorentz and Beijer, Malmö, 26 November 1868. Knös is mentioned as the recipient of various types of iron shipped from Huseby to London. He also went under the anglicized name 'Andrew Knös'.
116 LNU, HA, JSA, G1:1, Accounts book 1873–6, months of June and November 1874. HA, HBG, E1: 1, F. Seaton Leadam, London, to J. Stephens, 6 November. 1874. Stephens ordered private consumption goods such as port wine from Knös in London.
117 Ibid., E1:3a, G. Stephens, Copenhagen, to J. Stephens, India, 6 June 1866.
118 LNU, HA, HEA, E1:1, Butter receipts, various from Rydström, Adelswärd, 1872; Butter receipts from Moheda, January 1872.
119 LNU, HA, JSA, E1:3a, G. Stephens to J. Stephens, 14 October 1869.
120 Ibid., B1:2, Letter book, J. Stephens to Lovell & Carry, 20 January 1873.
121 Ibid., Letter book, J. Stephens to E. P. Lindquist, Gothenburg, 12 January 1872.
122 See footnote 1 in this chapter.
123 See footnote 40 in this chapter.
124 For example, see Hall, 'Epilogue: Imperial Careering at Home', p. 339.

References

Avango, Dag, Louwrens Hacquebord, and Urban Wråkberg, 'Industrial Extraction of Arctic Natural Resources Since the Sixteenth Century: Technoscience and Geo-Economics in the History of Northern Whaling and Mining', *Journal of Historical Geography*, 44 (2014), pp. 15–30.

Baker, T., *Railway Engineering; or, Field Work Preparatory to the Construction of Railways* (London: Spottiswoode and Shaw, 1848).

Bates, Crispin, 'Class and Economic Change in Central India: The Narmada Valley 1820–1930', in Clive Dewey (ed.), *Arrested Development in India: The Historical Dimension* (New Delhi: Manohar, 1988), pp. 241–82.

Beijbom, Ulf, *Amerika, Amerika: en bok om utvandringen* (Stockholm: Natur och Kultur, 1977).

Berglund, Bengt, *Järn i Småland: Forskningsläge, utgångspunkter och övergripande resultat*, Småländsk järnhantering under 1000 år, 1, Jernkontorets bergshistoriska skriftserie, 34 (Stockholm: Jernkontoret, 2000).

Berglund, Bengt, Per-Olof Grönberg, and Tomas Nilson (eds), *Historiska perspektiv på tekniköverföring 1800–2000* (Gothenburg: Department of History of Technology and Industry, Chalmers University of Technology, 2006).

Bhambi, Rita P., *The Great Indian Peninsula Railway: A Journey Through Time (1853–1871)* (New Delhi: Bharti Publications, 2016).

Bhattacharya, Sabyasachi, *The Financial Foundations of the British Raj: Ideas and Interests in the Reconstruction of Indian Public Finance 1858–1872*, 2nd ed. (New Delhi: Orient Longman, 2005 [1970]).

Brees, S. C., *The Illustrated Glossary of Practical Architecture and Civil Engineering: Comprising the Theory and Modern Practice, With the Subjects of Office & Field Work, the Steam Engine, Mechanical Engineering, Surveying, Levelling, & Use of Instruments, Mining and Quarrying, Manufacture of Iron, Bricks, Lime, & Cements, Carpentry, Joinery, Bricklaying, and Masonry, Slating, Painting and Glazing, Building, etc.* (London: L.A. Lewis, 1853).

Brenna, Brita, 'Clergymen Abiding in the Fields: The Making of the Naturalist Observer in Eighteenth-Century Norwegian Natural History', *Science in Context*, 24/2 (2011), pp. 143–66.

Bubb, Alexander, 'An Element of Risk: The Corrupt Contractor in Indian Fiction and Film, 1886–1983', *Cambridge Journal of Postcolonial Literary Inquiry*, 4/1 (2017), pp. 109–26.

Bubb, Alexander, 'Class, Cotton, and "Woddaries": A Scandinavian Railway Contractor in Western India, 1860–69', *Modern Asian Studies*, 51/5 (2017), pp. 1369–93.

Drayton, Richard, and David Motadel, 'Discussion: The Futures of Global History', *Journal of Global History*, 13/1 (2018), pp. 1–21.

Elkins, Caroline, and Susan Pedersen, 'Introduction: Settler Colonialism; A Concept and Its Uses', in C. Elkins and S. Pedersen (eds), *Settler Colonialism in the Twentieth Century: Projects, Practices, Legacies* (London and New York: Routledge, 2005).

Fischer-Tiné, Harald, *Low and Licentious Europeans: Race, Class and 'White Subalternity' in Colonial India, New Perspectives in South Asian History* (New Delhi: Orient Blackswan, 2009).

Fischer-Tiné, Harald, 'The Other Side of Internationalism: Switzerland as a Hub of Militant Anti-Colonialism, c. 1910–1920', in P. Purtschert and H. Fischer-Tiné (eds), *Colonial Switzerland: Rethinking Switzerland From the Margins* (Basingstoke: Palgrave Macmillan, 2014), pp. 221–58.

Flanders, Judith, *A Circle of Sisters: Alice Kipling, Georgiana Burne-Jones, Agnes Poynter and Louisa Baldwin* (London: Penguin Viking, 2001).

Gunnarsson, Ingemar, 'Från lärling till "ingenjör"', in M. Petersson (ed.), *Från Brittiska Indien till Huseby bruk: Järnvägen som arena för modernitet och kolonialism*

under lycksökaren och järnvägsentreprenören Joseph Stephens tid i Indien 1860–69 (Lund: Arkiv Förlag, 2018), pp. 65–82.
Gunnarsson, Ingemar, '"Karlshamn—Wislanda Jernväg": Maktelit och nätverk i Karlshamns stad vid banans tillblivelse 1855–1874', unpublished MA dissertation, School of Humanities, Växjö University, 2003.
Hall, Catherine, *Civilising Subjects: Metropole and Colony in the English Imagination 1830–1867* (Chicago: University of Chicago Press, 2002).
Hall, Catherine, 'Epilogue: Imperial Careering at Home; Harriet Martineau on Empire', in David Lambert and Allan Lester (eds), *Colonial Lives Across Empire: Imperial Careering in the Long Nineteenth Century* (Cambridge; New York: Cambridge University Press, 2006), pp. 335–59.
Harnow, Henrik, *Den danske ingeniørs Historie 1850–1920* (Århus: Systime, 1998).
Haslett, Charles, and Charles W. Hackley, *The Mechanic's, Machinist's, and Engineer's Practical Book of Reference: Adapted to and for the Use of All Classes of Practical Mechanics, Together With the Engineer's Field Book: With a Collection of Valuable Recipes* (London: Trübner and Co., 1855).
Jörberg, Lennart, 'Structural Change and Economic Growth: Sweden in the 19th Century', *Economy and History*, 8/1 (1965), pp. 3–46.
Kerr, Ian J., *Building the Railways of the Raj, 1850–1900* (New Delhi: Oxford University Press, 1995).
Krishnan, Radhika, 'Contracting and Sub-contracting in British India: Exploring the Dynamics of Railway Building through Joseph Stephens', in Kristina Myrvold and Soniya Billore (eds), *India: Research on Cultural Encounters and Representations at Linnaeus University* (Gothenburg: Makadam Förlag, 2017), pp. 50–73.
Krishnan, Radhika, 'Järnvägsbygget ur arbetarnas perspektiv', in M. Petersson (ed.), *Från Brittiska Indien till Huseby bruk: Järnvägen som arena för modernitet och kolonialism under lycksökaren och järnvägsentreprenören Joseph Stephens tid i Indien 1860–69* (Lund: Arkiv Förlag, 2018), pp. 113–34.
Kuisma, Markku, 'Industrial Expansion', in E. I. Kouri and Jens E. Olesen (eds), *The Cambridge History of Scandinavia, Volume II, 1520–1870* (Cambridge: Cambridge University Press, 2016).
Kværndrup, Sigurd, and Boel Lindberg, 'Inledning', in Gunilla Byrman (ed.), *En värld för sig själv: Nya studier i medeltida ballader*, Ord & Musik & Bild: Intermediala studier 1 (Växjö: Växjö University Press, 2008), pp. 11–27.
Lambert, David, and Allan Lester, 'Introduction: Imperial Spaces, Imperial Subjects', in D. Lambert and A. Lester (eds), *Colonial Lives Across Empire: Imperial Careering in the Long Nineteenth Century* (Cambridge; New York: Cambridge University Press, 2006), pp. 1–31.
Larsson, Lars-Olof, *Det fantastiska Huseby: En rundvandring i tid och rum* (Växjö: Domänverket/Huseby Bruk, 1993).
Larsson, Lars-Olof, 'Historia kring Huseby: Epoken Stephens', in *Skatelövskrönika 1978* (Grimslöv: Skatelövs Hembygdsförening, 1978).
Larsson, Lars-Olof, *Historia om Småland* (Växjö: Diploma, 1974).
Larsson, Lars-Olof, 'Hur Stephens kom till Huseby', in *Skatelövskrönika 1986* (Grimslöv: Skatelövs Hembygdsförening, 1986).
Larsson, Lars-Olof, *Länsstyrelsen och Kronobergs län under 350 år*, Historiska föreningens i Kronobergs län skriftserie, 4 (Växjö: Länsstyrelsen i Kronobergs län, 1984).
Larsson, Lars-Olof, *Växjö genom 1000 år* (Stockholm: Norstedt, 1991).

Larsson, Lars-Olof, Margareta Petersson, Åke Svensson, and Erik Wångmar, *Det levande Huseby: En värld i världen* (Växjö: Historiska föreningen i Kronobergs län, 2018).

Larsson, Lars-Olof, Sven-Olof Olsson, Josef Rydén, and Stig Tornehed, *Småländska strövtåg genom fem sekler* (Växjö: Diploma, 1976).

Ljungberg, Jonas, and Lennart Schön, 'Domestic Markets and International Integration: Paths to Industrialisation in the Nordic Countries', *Scandinavian Economic History Review*, 61/2 (2013), pp. 101–21.

Magnusson, Lars, *An Economic History of Sweden*, Routledge Explorations in Economic History (London; New York: Routledge, 2000).

Makko, Aryo, 'I imperialismens kölvatten? Ett maritimt perspektiv på stormaktsspelet, kolonialism utan kolonier och den svensk-norska konsulsstaten, 1875–1905', *Historisk Tidskrift* (Sweden), 134/3 (2014), pp. 499–523.

Marsden, Ben, and Crosbie Smith, *Engineering Empires: A Cultural History of Technology in Nineteenth-Century Britain* (Basingstoke: Palgrave Macmillan, 2005).

Misra, Maria, '"Business Culture" and Entrepreneurship in British India, 1860–1950', *Modern Asian Studies*, 34/2 (2000), pp. 333–48.

Misra, Maria, *Business, Race, and Politics in British India, c.1850–1960* (Oxford: Clarendon, 1999).

Naum, Magdalena, and Jonas M. Nordin, 'Introduction: Situating Scandinavian Colonialism', in Magdalena Naum and Jonas M. Nordin (eds), *Scandinavian Colonialism and the Rise of Modernity: Small Time Agents in a Global Arena* (New York: Springer, 2013), pp. 3–16.

Nite, Dhiraj Kumar, 'En lycksökares liv och affärer i Indien och Skandinavien', in M. Petersson (ed), *Från Brittiska Indien till Huseby bruk: Järnvägen som arena för modernitet och kolonialism under lycksökaren och järnvägsentreprenören Joseph Stephens tid i Indien 1860–69* (Lund: Arkiv Förlag, 2018), pp. 135–65.

Østermark-Johansen, Lene, 'Reading Clubs, Language Societies and Female Education in Fin-de-Siècle Copenhagen', *Forum for Modern Language Studies*, 53/3 (2017), pp. 274–90.

Östlund, Joachim, 'The Swedish Consulate in Tripoli and Information Gathering on Diplomacy, Everyday Life, and the Slave Trade, 1795–1844', in Mika Suonpää and Owen Wright (eds), *Diplomacy and Intelligence in the Nineteenth-Century Mediterranean World* (London: Bloomsbury Academic, 2019), pp. 17–36.

Petersson, Margareta, 'Drömmen om Eldorado', in M. Petersson (ed.), *Från Brittiska Indien till Huseby bruk: Järnvägen som arena för modernitet och kolonialism under lycksökaren och järnvägsentreprenören Joseph Stephens tid i Indien 1860–69* (Lund: Arkiv Förlag, 2018), pp. 167–96.

Petersson, Margareta, 'Joseph Stephens—familjen och arkivet', in M. Petersson (ed.), *Från Brittiska Indien till Huseby bruk: Järnvägen som arena för modernitet och kolonialism under lycksökaren och järnvägsentreprenören Joseph Stephens tid i Indien 1860–69* (Lund: Arkiv Förlag, 2018), pp. 15–44.

Purtschert, Patricia, Francesca Falk, and Barbara Lüthi, 'Switzerland and "Colonialism Without Colonies": Reflections on the Status of Colonial Outsiders', *Interventions*, 18/2 (2016), pp. 286–302.

Purtschert, Patricia, and Harald Fischer-Tiné, 'Introduction: The End of Innocence; Debating Colonialism in Switzerland', in P. Purtschert and H. Fischer-Tiné (eds), *Colonial Switzerland: Rethinking Colonialism From the Margins* (Basingstoke: Palgrave Macmillan, 2015), pp. 1–25.

Rosenbalck, Niclas, 'Förteckning över Husebyarkiven vid Linnéuniversitetet, Växjö', unpublished catalogue, LNU Library (PDF, 245 pp.), Växjö, 2010.
Siddiqi, Asiya, *Bombay's People, 1860–1898: Insolvents in the City* (New Delhi: Oxford University Press, 2017).
Stoler, Ann Laura, 'Cultivating Bourgeois Bodies and Racial Selves', in C. Hall (ed.), *Cultures of Empire, a Reader: Colonizers in Britain and the Empire in the Nineteenth and Twentieth Centuries* (Manchester: Manchester University Press, 2000), pp. 87–119.
Svensson, Åke, *George Stephens: Forskare, samlare, publicist, debattör* (Växjö: Sanct Sigfrids Gille, 2010).
Thomasson, Fredrik, 'Den karibiska skorpionen: Om digitaliseringen av det svenska Saint Barthélemy arkivet i Aix-en-Provence', *Historisk Tidskrift*, 138/1 (2018), pp. 78–90.
The Times of India, *The 'Times of India' Calendar & Directory, Abridged Edition* (Bombay: The 'Times of India' Office; London: G. Street, Cornhill, 1868).
Vicziany, A. Marika, 'Bombay Merchants and Structural Changes in the Export Community 1850 to 1880', in K. N. Chaudhuri and Clive J. Dewey (eds), *Economy and History: Essays in Indian Economic and Social History* (New Delhi: OUP, 1979), pp. 163–96.
Vicziany, A. Marika, 'The Cotton Trade and the Commercial Development of Bombay, 1855–1875', unpublished PhD thesis, SOAS, University of London, 1975.
Wawn, Andrew, 'Stephens, George (1813–1895)', ONB, https://doi.org/10.1093/ref:odnb/26383 (accessed 1 December 2019).
Wawn, Andrew, *The Vikings and the Victorians: Inventing the Old North in Nineteenth-Century Britain* (Cambridge: D. S. Brewer, 2000).

7 Colonial Entrepreneurial Capital in the Industrialization of Southern Sweden

The Huseby Estate under Joseph Stephens

Erik Wångmar

When Joseph Stephens moved to southern Sweden and settled on the iron-making estate of Huseby in 1869, he was part of a wave of immigration to the province of Småland.[1] Foreign nationals were buying agricultural and forest holdings sold off by people who either chose or were forced to move to towns or to other countries to make a living. Many of the newcomers came from Denmark or Germany. Joseph had further to travel, from Bombay in British-controlled India, while his family had Copenhagen as their base. This study explores how Joseph built up his business on the estate in the light of the long-term development of Sweden's economic structure. Joseph eventually became a member of the Swedish parliament, the Riksdag, and it is interesting to see how he sought to promote his own interests as an estate owner in that context. He and his wife, Elisabeth, never had a son. When Elisabeth died in 1911, therefore, Joseph increasingly involved one of his daughters, Florence, in the management of the estate, to prepare her to take over the running of it after his death. And when he drew up his will, he had Florence in mind as its next owner. To better understand how Joseph developed and managed the estate, this chapter examines the reasons for his specific choice of Huseby and how he can best be characterized as an estate owner. It considers to what extent his choices mirrored the overall development of Swedish economic activity, and whether his time as a Riksdag member influenced conditions for estate owners in general. The major share of the inheritance left by Joseph, a widower for more than two decades, was entrusted to the care of Florence—an unusual role for a woman. This study looks at the extent to which she really became part of the management of the estate during her father's lifetime.

The countries of Scandinavia experienced far-reaching economic and demographic change in the eighteenth and nineteenth centuries. In the second half of the nineteenth century, Sweden's geographical location and late industrialization compared with other nations in north-western Europe meant that the country saw strong economic expansion, a transformation of agriculture, and a major relocation of its population. The present study examines the impact this had on the way Huseby operated

DOI: 10.4324/9781003317227-7

under Stephens' management, from 1869 to 1934. Huseby was one of the many properties in Småland that were sold to foreign buyers when crop failures caused years of hardship and many of the region's inhabitants left the country. Joseph, who had acquired a fortune as a contractor on the major colonial railway building project in British India in the 1860s, invested that fortune in Huseby, and the study focuses on how he built up and ran the estate.

Important contributions to the economic history of Sweden's agrarian and forest history have discussed the agrarian transformation and, for European conditions, the comparatively late industrial revolution. Lars-Olof Larsson's studies of the Småland province stand out for the detailed substantiation. In the course of the eighteenth century and down to 1870, the area of arable land in Sweden increased three-and-a-half-fold. Over the same period, the share of cultivated land belonging to large agricultural holdings also grew. The result was a rise in the proportion of wage earners among those who owned no or only insignificant amounts of land. The expansion of arable occurred at the expense of forest land, as forests made way for fields, meadows, and pastures. The early 1860s were prosperous times for Swedish agriculture, but the end of the same decade, especially 1867–8, saw severe crop failures, which were particularly challenging in Småland and in the north of the country. In the long term, these developments had an impact on population trends in Sweden, slowing the rate of increase. This was the last serious food supply crisis in the country. It did not cause a very marked rise in mortality, but it did trigger a surge in emigration, above all to North America. Joseph in fact bought the Huseby Estate in 1867, one of the years of failed harvests. Various interventions in the economy played a part in reshaping agriculture. The enclosures, in which small agricultural holdings had been combined into larger units, meant that farms were no longer as concentrated in villages. Drainage of wetlands and lowering of lake levels created new arable land, increasing total output, and farming implements and methods gradually became more uniform across different parts of the country. In parallel with these changes, special agricultural colleges were set up. Forestry, too, was changed by drainage and new improved methods, resulting in growth in the value of forest products. Partly as a consequence, systematic planting of forests began to be carried out. At the time Joseph bought Huseby, however, there had been no appreciable decrease in the proportion of the population employed in agriculture. That process began in earnest in the ensuing decades. Some of the reduction in demand for labour in agriculture was due to increased mechanization, for example the introduction of new steam-powered threshing machines.[2]

The total area of arable in Sweden continued to increase after 1870, but now as the result of a sharp contraction of meadowland. The area under cultivation expanded until the beginning of the twentieth century, in some parts of the country until as late as the 1940s. In southern Sweden, including Kronoberg County, it reached its greatest extent in the early decades of the twentieth century, while in parts of the north, that did not happen until around 1950.[3]

Given that the Huseby Estate included both an ironworks and extensive farming and forestry, it is important to stress that the significance of iron as a Swedish export was declining in the nineteenth century. In 1770, iron and steel had accounted for around 70 per cent of the total value of the country's exports, but by 1870, the corresponding figure was just 20 per cent. That was despite the fact that, in absolute terms, the volume of iron and steel exports had trebled since 1770. Exports of grain had also seen a relative decline over the same period, from 32 to 20 per cent of all exports. Sales of timber products to other countries, by contrast, soared. Between 1770 and 1870, they rose from 6 to 42 per cent of Sweden's total exports.[4] This meant that Huseby's prospects as an ironmaking estate were looking less bright, while there was cause for much more confidence when it came to forestry. After 1870 exports of butter from Sweden grew significantly and the United Kingdom became an important market, as its agricultural sector, unlike that of other countries, was unable to supply all the food its population required. In 1900 only 12 per cent of the labour force of Great Britain and Ireland were working in the farming sector (though with a much higher proportion in Ireland than in Great Britain). This can be compared with Sweden, where agriculture employed 55 per cent of the population, a higher figure than in the neighbouring countries of Denmark (41 per cent) and Norway (44 per cent). In Finland, an even larger share—71 per cent—worked in farming. Huseby, too, would benefit from Britain's need of agricultural produce, exporting butter to the country on a modest scale. Småland's geographical location and, from the mid-nineteenth century, increasingly widely branched railway network facilitated exports of both farm and forest products. Huseby had access to a railway in its vicinity comparatively early on, thanks to the Southern Main Line (1865) and a branch line from it with a station at Vislanda that passed close to the estate. Sweden's main lines began to be built at roughly the same time as the rail network in India. Joseph came to be much engaged in the process of getting the railway branch, passing Huseby, in place so that heavy goods could be loaded onto the coaches close to his workshop and taken to Karlshamn port on the Baltic coast. During this period, he tried to keep the contacts he had developed in India and business contacts which his family network opened up in Britain and Denmark.[5]

When Joseph bought Huseby, there were just over 390,000 agricultural and forest holdings in Sweden, of widely varying size. The number of holdings continued to rise until 1920, when it totalled almost 430,000. In this respect, Kronoberg County was broadly in step with the national trend. The increase coincided with almost the whole of Joseph's long period as owner of Huseby. The total number of cattle in Sweden continued to increase up to the end of the 1930s, while the horse population peaked around 1920. Here, Huseby diverged from the national average with its large number of horses, a point discussed further below. Tractors began to be used in the 1910s, but on an extremely modest scale, only in the 1930s did their introduction really take off, and by 1940 there were 21,000 of them. Mechanization of farming was less in evidence in Kronoberg than in other parts of the country, as large agricultural holdings like Huseby were less common in that county.[6]

The number of people gainfully employed in agriculture in Sweden reached its peak as early as around 1890, with a subsequent gradual decline of 25 per cent up to 1940, from 1.6 million to just under 1.2 million. By and large, this decrease was in line with the changes seen in most countries of western and northern Europe. Given that the total labour force increased markedly in absolute terms owing to population growth, we realize that the decline in the proportion employed in agriculture was very significant, both in Sweden and elsewhere in Europe. This reduction of the Swedish agricultural workforce was not gender-neutral. Far more women than men left the sector. The relative proportions of different occupational categories in farming also changed. While the number of agricultural labourers decreased, tenant farmers and landowners remained at a relatively constant level. Most of those who left agricultural employment were emigrants, but there were also people who moved to jobs in industry, where wages were generally higher than in farming. Birth rates, too, gradually fell in rural areas, contributing—together with the decline in employment in agriculture and a corresponding rise in industry, more of which was located in the towns—to a process of urbanization in Sweden.[7]

Huseby, an Advantageous Purchase in a Year of Crop Failure

The initiative for Joseph to buy Huseby came from a friend of his father's, who was also Joseph's godfather, Gunnar Olof Hyltén-Cavallius, who in 1864 had moved back from Stockholm to his native Småland. He soon became chairman of the county agricultural society, giving him a good insight into conditions in farming. In the autumn of 1866 he suggested to his friend George Stephens that Joseph should buy an agricultural holding in the county, as prices for such properties were falling. Joseph replied in a letter from India that he could consider buying a farm costing between 50,000 and 100,000 riksdaler.[8] A purchase could take place in the summer of 1867, when he intended to visit Sweden. Hyltén-Cavallius suggested that Joseph buy the Huseby Estate, which was soon expected to be offered for sale, and presumably at a favourable price. That summer, both George and Joseph arrived at Hyltén-Cavallius' home in Moheda. At that point, they were not fully aware of how large an estate Huseby was. They were enlightened on the matter by their host, who described the many benefits which buying the property would bring. He believed that the purchase would be financially advantageous, as the estate offered a profitable combination of agriculture, forestry, and ironmaking. Good access to forests for charcoal was crucial for an ironworks, and, in view of Joseph's technical know-how, the workshop linked to it was also important. The estate comprised 46 individual agricultural properties, totalling 6,000 hectares and extending over eight parishes. After contact had been made with the Hamilton brothers' receivers, the purchase was completed in August 1867. It ended up costing far more than Joseph had reckoned with, however. With dependent farms and movables included, he paid 600,000 riksdaler for Huseby, 150,000 riksdaler of it in cash. Another 50,000 riksdaler was to be paid in six months' time, with a further 50,000 within 12 months. To raise the money, Joseph was forced to take out large bank loans. It has been speculated that the reason Joseph agreed to buy the estate, despite it landing him in considerable debt, was that he had become engaged to Hyltén-Cavallius' daughter, Anna. But the engagement was broken off shortly afterwards on Anna's initiative; Joseph's disappointment was great, and his relationship to her father deteriorated. Soon afterwards, he returned to India and his work on the railways.[9]

Several of Joseph's relatives were critical of his precipitate purchase of the large estate, and to begin with he regretted it. The severe crop failures had left a food supply crisis in their wake. The year 1867, when harvests had failed, was followed by one that saw a further decline in land prices, and the value of Huseby fell. Joseph's acquisition of the property seems to have been partly speculative, and he decided to engage the services of lawyers to sell it as soon as possible. To begin with, he sold a few of the outlying farms. One of them went to the famous singer Christina Nilsson, who bought her childhood home, Sjöabol, in Vederslöv. In 1869, however, when Joseph wound up his involvement in India, he decided to keep Huseby after all. He himself knew little about farming and forestry, and he therefore left the management of the estate to two agents when he was in India—one was the landowner Fritz von Ekensteen, from Hurva in Skåne, and the other the Malmö-based merchant Hans Friis, who later became his brother-in-law. Both these men were in contact with George, who corresponded with Joseph in India throughout this period. Their correspondence was by no means free from conflict, particularly as Huseby's finances were not entirely sound. Once he was back at Huseby, Joseph entered in earnest into his new role as an estate owner, with George's continued support.[10]

Huseby was one of many properties in Kronoberg County that were sold to foreign citizens in the second half of the nineteenth century, mainly to individuals from Germany and Denmark. This brought new capital, initiative, and knowledge to a region which at the same time was feeling the effects of large-scale emigration to North America. Many of the properties that changed hands in the county were relatively small. Joseph's purchase was one of the largest, along with the acquisition by the German lieutenant Hans Wolf von Schönberg of Bolmstad Manor (*säteri*) in 1855.[11] At Bolmstad, von Schönberg set up one of the first steam sawmills in the county. Up to the early 1880s, Germans and Danes bought over 100 agricultural holdings, chiefly in central and western parts of the county. Two key reasons for these foreign purchases were falling prices during the years of failed harvests, and the expansion of the railways, which made the export of forest products possible on a much greater scale than before. The dominant focus of historical research into this region has long been on people in need leaving Småland for North America. Widening that focus to include a study of families who moved into this part of the country, like the Stephens family, we discover a much greater element of economic dynamism and demographic change. In that connection, we should also take into account the people with little or no land who moved to Germany or Denmark, and those who completely lacked the funds to pay for a ticket to another country and therefore answered newspaper advertisements seeking agricultural labourers in Germany, with travel expenses paid. Short-term labour migration to those countries was very common.[12]

Estate Owner and Member of the Riksdag

Huseby, with its 6,000 hectares, was a large, run-down estate, and Joseph embarked on an extensive programme to restore its fortunes. He also gradually expanded the property. The largest purchase was Torne, 12 km to the south of Huseby. The arable land was of good quality, and conditions for agriculture were improved by means of subsurface drainage, embankments, and a regrouping of farmland. Joseph introduced new farming methods, including the use of chemical fertilizers and modern machinery. Forestry, too, was improved under his management. Previously, the woods had primarily been a source of charcoal and a place for livestock to graze. Now, with growing demand for raw materials for the sawmills and pulp factories, their economic value increased. Towards the end of his life, Joseph chose to limit the volumes of timber felled, with the result that on his death in 1934, there was a great deal of mature forest ready to be harvested. In the 1920s, in the later years of his life, Huseby's woodlands represented one of the most valuable privately owned forest holdings in Småland.[13]

During Joseph's time at Huseby, agricultural work was carried out on the one hand by contract workers (*statare*)—landless labourers employed on one-year contracts and paid partly in kind—and on the other by crofters, in the form of day labour. Farming on the estate was a large-scale undertaking. In 1873, there were over 100 crofts and other dwellings belonging to Huseby, accommodating around 800 people associated with its operations. In the 1920s, when there were still no tractors on the estate, some 30 workhorses were used in its day-to-day work.[14] Former employees were allowed to go on living on the estate in their old age, and were provided with a home, milk, and firewood, saving money for the Skatelöv municipal poor relief fund. Joseph was well known for what these days would be called micromanaging, and was said to be careful, economical—perhaps stingy—and strict. He remained fully active almost until his death, despite a severe hearing impairment.[15]

Figure 7.1 At the entrance of the Huseby manor house, from left, Joseph Stephens, his daughter Florence, two unknown men, daughter Maggie, Elisabeth Stephens, daughter Mary, unknown woman, circa 1900.

Source: Courtesy Huseby Bruk AB.

One of the first things to receive attention on Joseph's return from India was the ironworks, where the blast furnace was modernized. The earlier production of cast-iron stoves was phased out in favour of more modern agricultural and household products. In the 1880s, threshing machines, chaff cutters, horse rakes, mill machinery, and crushing mills were manufactured. These were the final glory days of the Huseby ironworks, which survived longer than many others in Småland when lake ore was replaced on the market by the better rock ores. As time went by, however, farming and forestry on the estate gradually became more important than iron production. In 1930 the blast furnace was charged for the last time, once again with ore from the local lakes. That the ironworks survived for so long at Huseby can probably be attributed to Joseph's conservatism and desire to keep old production processes alive as long as possible. He also had a new turbine-driven sawmill built. The short distance to the Southern Main Line that had been built between Malmö and Stockholm made it easier to get wood products to market. During his early years at Huseby, moreover, Joseph had lent his support to the building of a railway line that passed closer to the estate and carried goods directly to the coastal town of Karlshamn to the south.[16]

Joseph was deeply conservative and very much opposed to his employees joining a trade union. He resisted every attempt to set up a branch of the Swedish Agricultural Workers' Union at Huseby, where he wanted to retain his well-established position within a patriarchal order.[17] The first ever strike by his agricultural labourers, in 1920, was aimed at securing a collective agreement with the estate and improving wages. Joseph made no attempt to oppose the formation of a local branch of the Social Democratic Workers' Party in Skatelöv in 1933, but by then he was very old. The historian Lars-Olof Larsson offers the following comment on Joseph as an estate owner:

> A strong patriarchalism had been a hallmark feature of both ironmaking estates and large manor houses as late as the turn of the century, but had since then gradually begun to be eroded. At Huseby, however, it remained almost entirely intact on Joseph Stephens' death in 1934.[18]

Joseph's integration into Swedish society reached far beyond the Huseby Estate. As soon as he had become a Swedish citizen, he began to involve himself in politics. He became active at three levels: locally in the municipality of Skatelöv, regionally on the Kronoberg county council, and as a member of the First Chamber of the Riksdag.[19] Having acquired his new citizenship in 1874, he embarked on a career in local politics at the municipal general meeting in Skatelöv in December of the same year.[20] He was a Riksdag member from 1887 to 1909, representing the protectionist wing of the Ruralist (or Conservative) Party (*Lantmannapartiet/Högern*). In 1890 he was one of 44 members of the First Chamber with the title of estate owner. They made up 30 per cent of the Riksdag's membership—a proportion that was maintained until Joseph's retirement as a member in 1909. No real change occurred until after the electoral reforms of the 1920s, when the influence of the Conservatives was significantly curtailed.[21]

Protectionist policies were most prominent during the 'tariffs battle' that was under way when Joseph entered the Riksdag.[22] He submitted his first motion in January 1887, proposing increased tariffs on iron, non-ferrous metal products, and certain agricultural products. His argument was that the competition from foreign imports was highly damaging for Swedish businesses.[23] It would then be another 10 years before Joseph tabled his second motion, in 1897, calling for the introduction of tariffs on corn oil.[24] In 1903 he presented a motion on how Sweden should respond to increased tariff rates in Germany, which could have adverse consequences for several sectors of the Swedish economy.[25] His longest motion was put forward in 1904, when he argued that steps should be taken to increase the value of and yields from state-owned forests.[26] Another motion on state forests followed in 1906.[27] On Riksdag committees, Joseph was sometimes one of the members recording a reservation against the majority recommendation, for example on the subject of reducing tariff barriers affecting agriculture and iron and steel products.[28] In 1901 he also entered a reservation against introducing a law on compensation for injuries from workplace accidents, arguing that such a scheme should apply to the labour market as a whole and not just to occupations regarded as dangerous.[29] And in 1903 he recorded his opposition to one part of the draft new forestry legislation, which posed a risk of sawmill companies having greater scope to buy up private forest estates.[30]

Joseph was no passive member of the First Chamber, participating actively in its debates. From 1888 onwards, he mostly spoke on questions relating to tariff and other barriers to trade affecting agriculture, forestry, and iron and steel products. In most cases he supported tariffs on goods that were imported to Sweden, with a view to protecting the country's own industries, not least the ones he himself was engaged in at Huseby.[31] In a few instances, however, he was not a dogmatic advocate of tariffs, as in 1898, when he wanted to avoid a tariff war with Norway, as the countries were in union. Nor did Joseph want to raise the tariff on imported embroidery.[32] In 1902 he argued against a proposal on income taxes, which were considered to put large landowners at a disadvantage.[33] And in a debate in 1907, about public bodies no longer being allowed to levy taxes on the sale of intoxicating beverages, he presumably drew on his experiences from India. He spoke of having many years' experience of countries where he claimed alcohol abuse scarcely occurred, owing to religious factors combined with a moral upbringing. In another debate in 1907—where his familiarity with railway engineering came in useful—Joseph spoke of the need to investigate accidents on the railways, though without mentioning his own earlier involvement in their construction in India.[34]

During his last decade in the Riksdag, Stephens showed a growing interest in forestry questions. His first speech on the subject was as early as 1896 when he argued that Sweden's forests were of significance for the country's exports and formed an important base for the transport of goods by rail. One problem was that, as a result, excessive felling of woodlands was occurring. In his view, a consistent policy of replanting was called for.[35] In 1903 he spoke of the need for forest owners to take greater personal responsibility for safeguarding the survival of the country's forests by ensuring good regeneration. At the same time, he did not want the county forestry boards to have too much influence over private owners.[36] In 1904 he participated in the debate arising from his own motion on the need to increase the value of state-owned forests. The same year he put the case for increased funding for forestry education.[37] Another contribution on forestry matter in 1904 concerned taxation of forest felling and sawmills. He spoke from his own experience, as he had recently bought an agricultural and forest holding from the state. He argued that the way such holdings were assessed needed to be changed, so as not to force harvesting to take place for tax reasons.[38] Joseph made his last speech in May 1907, on two items of business. One was an inquiry into the living conditions of agricultural labourers, his view being that such an inquiry was unnecessary as he believed that they had a much better working environment than industrial workers. He did not even regard the landless contract workers (*statare*) as particularly vulnerable. The other question was that of forest planting on unwooded land. Joseph was of the opinion that the newly established forestry boards in each county had to be given time to take initiatives on such matters, while at the same time stressing the personal responsibility of forest owners for replanting.[39]

For his first 13 years at Huseby, Joseph remained unmarried. Not until the summer of 1880, during a stay at the spa resort of Ronneby Brunn in Blekinge, did he get to know the woman who would become his wife: Miss Elisabeth Kreüger, the daughter of Carl-Henrik Kreüger, later a rear admiral, and his first wife, Hedvig.[40] Joseph was 39 and Elisabeth 21 when they became engaged in September of that year and were married just two months later. Among the wedding guests was King Oscar II, who was a close friend of the bride's father from their time together in the navy. Elisabeth would be Joseph's link to the royal court, where she was already known after serving as a lady-in-waiting to the queen.[41] Three daughters were born in quick succession: Florence in 1881, Mary in 1882, and Margreth (Maggie) in 1883.[42]

Joseph's three daughters came to occupy different positions in relation to the finances and management of the estate. In the absence of a son, the eldest daughter, Florence, worked most closely with Joseph, and after his death she inherited the central part of the estate. She started to assist him in the management of Huseby at the age of just 20.[43] Florence remained unmarried and continued to live on the estate for the rest of her life. Right up to Joseph's death, she was an important support to him, even though he retained ultimate responsibility for financial and technical matters. The youngest daughter, Maggie, also remained a resident of Huseby, but she was not at all involved in its management as her eldest sister was.[44]

Florence had a particular interest in legal issues, above all those relating to the regulation of lakes and rivers. In Småland, a province that had suffered economic decline, more farmland was needed, and there, as on the continent of Europe, that need was met by draining wetlands and eventually also lowering lake levels. Neither Joseph nor Florence, however, had any interest in Lake Salen, to the north and upstream of the estate, being lowered. Modern forest management combined with water management of this kind would increase the flow of water in the river Helgeån, which passed by Huseby. Joseph and Florence feared flooding when bridges were blocked from the large inflow of water to the estate. The result was a protracted dispute between Huseby and the owner of Ängaholm by Salen, who wanted to lower the lake surface to create new farmland. In the end, Florence was so unhappy with the decision that the Kronoberg county agricultural engineer felt harassed by her. According to him, Florence saw it as her mission in life to try to stop the lake being lowered. Water rights relating to Lake Åsnen, too, became an issue in the later years of Joseph's life.[45] Florence could be said to have had a concern for the environment at a time when such ideas were not particularly common or especially highly rated. She also played a part in managing agriculture and forestry on the estate, and above all livestock production, which was carried out on a large scale at that time. Her particular areas of interest were sheep and horses. Breeding and rearing horses was in fact one of her few practical talents, and she formed a strong emotional bond with the animals. But when she took over as owner after her father, the large number of horses on the estate was no longer economically viable.[46] From the accounts, we see that she also handled the selling of pig iron and was in contact with the Swedish Ironmasters' Association (Jernkontoret). She had no technical expertise in this area herself, but was keen to keep the ironworks, with its blast furnace, going for as long as possible (up to 1930), although it was not operated on a continuous basis.[47] Joseph was occasionally critical of Florence's actions. In 1917, when she had promised a large delivery of wood on her own initiative, he pointed out that the effort needed to fulfil the order would result in important agricultural work being neglected.[48]

There were other competent staffs, too, in leading positions in the management of the estate. One of them was Arvid Almskog, a comparatively young man in Joseph's later years. There were thus good prospects of him remaining in his post for many years and providing important support to Florence, enabling her to own Huseby and run it well the day her father was no longer alive.[49] Joseph and Elisabeth Stephens wrote a joint will in 1908, three years before Elisabeth died, setting out among other things the three daughters' shares in the inheritance. The estate was divided into three parts, with Huseby the largest. Mary inherited the estates of Torne and Lästad, and Maggie that of Ålshult. The justification for making Huseby the largest share was the high cost of running the industrial operations. Joseph left property worth a total of 3,458,075 kronor and debts of 51,435 kronor. In a letter to the sisters after their father's death, the executor appealed to them to avoid any dispute over the unevenly divided inheritance.[50] But the outcome of Florence's management of the estate proved very different from what Joseph could have imagined, when unsuitable advisers became involved and large assets were sold off in an unproductive way, as the present author has discussed in another study.[51] Florence remained very much involved in the estate for her entire lifetime. On her 80th birthday in 1961, she said in a newspaper interview that, since the age of 15, she had had only one major interest in life, namely Huseby.[52]

As for his second daughter, Mary, Joseph's attitude was often critical.[53] Her marriage to Gunnar Liepe, entered into in 1901, gradually became less and less harmonious. In October 1922 she moved to Torne, which was owned by Joseph. Her divorce from her husband took legal effect in April 1923.[54] Regarding his youngest daughter, Maggie, Joseph's view was one of concern over her many and long spells of illness, both physical and mental.[55]

Joseph's wife Elisabeth died in June 1911, aged 52, after quite a long period of uncertain health. The couple had been married for just over 30 years. An inventory of Elisabeth's estate was drawn up in July 1911, showing net assets of 950,130 kronor. Joseph's and Elisabeth's joint will provided that all the assets were to go to the surviving spouse, with the exception of the statutory shares of the three daughters.[56]

Joseph died on 14 February 1934, at the age of 92. His funeral took place in Skatelöv Church and he was buried in Solna Cemetery.[57] An inventory of his estate was drawn up in May 1934 and was divided into two parts, including a separate inventory of his agricultural holding of Lästad. His total net assets, including gifts to his daughters the year before, amounted to 3,320,552 kronor. The final version of his will was dated November 1933. Under it, Florence received Huseby with its industrial plants, Mary received Lästad and Torne, and Maggie received Ålshult, with its sawmill. As for other property, the basic principle was that one-third was to go to each of the daughters. However, Florence had to be ensured at least 550,000 kronor, as her share of the real estate was the most expensive to run and maintain.[58]

Huseby Against the Grain of Modernization

Joseph's purchase of Huseby in 1867 would not have come about without the active involvement of Gunnar Olof Hyltén-Cavallius. It also occurred at a time when prices of farm and forest land had started to fall in Småland and many foreign nationals were buying property in Kronoberg county. For Joseph, the purchase was primarily a means of investing the money he had earned in India. He may also have been prompted by his love for Hyltén-Cavallius' daughter Anna, to whom he was briefly engaged. In addition, the industrial side of Huseby may have interested a man with engineering expertise from his time in India. At the time he bought the estate, however, his knowledge of agriculture and forestry was virtually non-existent, which must have been a definite disadvantage to begin with. He certainly did not get off to an easy start as the owner of Huseby, not least as he had to return to India from 1867 to 1869. During that period he had serious plans to sell the estate. He seems to have regretted his precipitate purchase, which had left him in debt as the purchase price exceeded his available capital. An important reason why he did not sell after all was that property prices continued to fall as a result of the food crisis during the years of crop failures. The money had been spent, and Joseph remained at Huseby.[59]

Looking at the sum total of Joseph's achievements as an estate and ironworks owner over a longer period, we see that industrial production at Huseby continued. But while the ironworks remained in operation until 1930—the last but one in Småland to close down—it gradually became a less significant component of the estate's activities. Huseby was by no means alone in seeing a decline in ironmaking. When Joseph took over, lake ore was already succumbing to the competition from rock ore and many ironworks in Småland were closing. Agriculture and forestry now emerged as the most important activities, and Joseph extended the area belonging to Huseby, primarily by buying the estate of Torne. In his later years, Joseph became more careful about felling. All the indications are that this was to ensure that his daughters would be financially well placed the day they inherited the estate. It is interesting to observe how, compared with broader trends in the economic structure of Sweden and other countries in Europe, Huseby was moving in the opposite direction. At the national and European levels, industry was taking over from agriculture as the most important sector, while at Huseby the reverse was true. Here, farming and forestry showed very positive economic growth during Joseph's many decades as owner. They were evidently profitable, even at a time when, in the wider economy, they were gradually declining in significance—although at the time of his death they still accounted for almost half of total employment in Sweden. Huseby's development has to be seen as a reflection of Joseph's success as an entrepreneur. That success was only possible, however, because he maintained almost entirely intact an authoritarian and patriarchal approach to management which, towards the end of his life, was becoming less common in wider Swedish society. It was an approach that meant that employees' wages were kept at a relatively low level and that trade unionism met with personal opposition from Joseph.[60]

While neither a leading nor an influential figure in the Riksdag, Joseph Stephens was by no means a passive member. His contribution as a parliamentarian has to be seen alongside his role as an estate owner in the First Chamber, a large proportion of whose members were of course fellow estate owners. As a protectionist politician and a supporter of tariffs, he was able to pursue and promote his interests. He was also critical of the way the state managed its own forest holdings, and was able to argue, drawing on his own credibility as a successful forest owner, that other private owners, too, must manage their own forests effectively.

The fact that Joseph and Elisabeth Stephens only had daughters in their marriage made it necessary to train them for a future role as owner of the estate. Joseph chose to focus his efforts on the eldest daughter. Apart from her being their eldest child, there were other reasons for his choice. Mary married early, and Joseph was often critical of her lack of financial prudence. Maggie was almost always ill and she, too, was therefore unsuited to managing Huseby.[61] Unlike her sisters, Florence was involved in both the agricultural and the industrial side of the estate for several decades before her father's death. Her long apprenticeship and the support of competent staff were presumably regarded as sufficient. In his final will, Joseph chose to name Florence as heir to the main estate of Huseby, where there was still some industrial activity at the time. Mary and Maggie were left other parts of the wider estate, which were of significant economic value, though they did not represent assets quite as substantial as those Florence inherited. It is thus not difficult to see a link between Florence having actively assisted

Joseph with the management of the entire estate and her subsequently inheriting the central part of it. However, the business contacts with Joseph's partners in India and Britain were now long gone.[62]

Notes

1 The Huseby Estate is in the county of Kronoberg in Småland province.

2 The enclosure reforms carried out in Sweden included the *Storskifte* in 1749 and the *Laga skifte* in 1828. Folke Dovring, *Land and Labor in Europe, 1900–1950: A Comparative Survey of Recent Agrarian History, with a chapter on land reform as a propaganda theme by Karin Dovring* (Cham: Springer Netherlands, 1965), p. 48; Lars-Olof Larsson, 'Skogstillgång, skogsprodukter och sågar i Kronobergs län', in Olof Nordström, Lars J. Larsson, John Käll, and Lars-Olof Larsson (eds), *Skogen och smålänningen: Kring skogsmarkens roll i förindustriell tid* (Växjö: Historiska föreningen i Kronobergs län, 1989), pp. 136 ff.; Olof Nordström, 'Skog och skogsmark som försörjningskälla', in Nordström et al. (eds), *Skogen och smålänningen*, pp. 51 ff.; Staffan Högberg, 'Bondelandet i Sverige', in Birgitta Furuhagen (ed.), *Äventyret Sverige: En ekonomisk och social historia* (Stockholm: Utbildningsradion, 1993), pp. 38 ff.; Lars-Olof Larsson, 'Land och län under kristendomens millennium', in Lennart Johansson (ed.), *Landen kring sjöarna: En historia om Kronobergs län i mångtusenårigt perspektiv; Kronobergsboken 1999–2000* (Växjö: Kronobergs läns hembygdsförbund/Smålands Museum, 1999), p. 238; Carl-Johan Gadd, *Det svenska jordbrukets historia*, 3: *Den agrara revolutionen 1700–1870* (Stockholm: Natur och kultur/LT, 2000), pp. 348–60; Mats Morell, *Det svenska jordbrukets historia*, 4: *Jordbruket i industrisamhället, 1870–1945* (Stockholm: Natur och kultur/LT, 2001), pp. 11 ff.; Pablo Wiking-Faria, 'Freden, friköpen och järnplogarna: Drivkrafter och förändringsprocesser under den agrara revolutionen i Halland 1700–1900', PhD thesis, Department of Historical Studies, University of Gothenburg, 2009, pp. 319 ff.; Carl-Johan Gadd, 'The Agricultural Revolution in Sweden 1700–1870', in Mats Morell and Janken Myrdal (eds), *The Agrarian History of Sweden: From 4000 BC to AD 2000* (Lund: Nordic Academic Press, 2011), pp. 118 ff.

3 Morell, *Svenska jordbrukets historia*, 4, pp. 192 ff.; Lars Kardell, *Svenskarna och skogen*, 2: *Från baggböleri till naturvård* (Jönköping: Skogsstyrelsens Förlag, 2004), pp. 7 ff.; Wiking-Faria, 'Freden, friköpen och järnplogarna', pp. 323 ff.

4 Gadd, *Svenska jordbrukets historia*, 3, p. 361.

5 Dovring, *Land and Labor in Europe*, p. 84; Dudley Dillard, *Västeuropas och Förenta staternas ekonomiska historia* (Malmö: Liber, 1993), pp. 220–38 and 387 ff.; Lennart Schön, *En modern svensk ekonomisk historia: Tillväxt och omvandling under två sekel* (Stockholm: SNS Förlag, 2000), pp. 159 ff. and 195–206; Morell, *Svenska jordbrukets historia*, 4, pp. 93 ff.; Christopher Bayly, *The Birth of the Modern World 1780–1914: Global Connections and Comparisons* (Oxford: Blackwell, 2004), pp. 172 ff.

6 Morell, *Svenska jordbrukets historia*, 4, pp. 33 ff.; Mats Morell, Carl-Johan Gadd, and Janken Myrdal, 'Statistical Appendix', in Morell and Myrdal (eds), *Agrarian History of Sweden*, p. 297.

7 Dovring, *Land and Labor in Europe*, pp. 63 and 84; Morell, *Svenska jordbrukets historia*, 4, pp. 76 ff., 84 ff., 242 ff., and 291 ff.; Iréne A. Flygare and Mats Isacson, 'The Tension between Modernity and Reality 1945–2010', in Morell and Myrdal (eds), *Agrarian History of Sweden*, pp. 214 ff.

8 100 riksdaler = 5,868 kronor in today's currency.

9 Hyltén-Cavallius lived at Stora Målen, Moheda, from 1864 to 1871, and after that at Sunnanvik, Skatelöv. Moheda and Skatelöv are in Kronoberg county. The Huseby Estate included land in the parishes of Skatelöv, Vederslöv, Öja, Blädinge, Kalvsvik, Jät, Urshult, and Almundsryd (parishes being the smallest ecclesiastical territorial entity in Sweden). The movable property at Huseby cost 70,000 riksdaler. Nils-Arvid Bringéus, 'Gunnar Olof Hyltén-Cavallius', in *Svenskt biografiskt lexikon*, 19 (Stockholm: The Swedish National Archives, 1973), p. 554; Lars-Olof Larsson, 'Historia kring Huseby: Epoken Stephens', in *Skatelövskrönika 1978* (Grimslöv: Skatelövs hembygdsförening, 1978), pp. 80 ff.; Lars-Olof Larsson, 'Hur Stephens kom till Huseby', in *Skatelövskrönika 1986* (Grimslöv: Skatelövs hembygdsförening, 1986), pp. 40 ff.; Lars-Olof Larsson, *Det fantastiska Huseby: En rundvandring i tid och rum* (Växjö: Domänverket/Huseby bruk, 1993), pp. 20 ff.; Jonas Carlquist and Andreas Tjerneld, 'Stephens, George', in *Svenskt biografiskt lexikon*, 33 (Stockholm: The Swedish National Archives, 2011), p. 382.

10 Larsson, 'Historia kring Huseby', pp. 83 ff.; Larsson, 'Hur Stephens kom till Huseby', pp. 46–56; Larsson, *Det fantastiska Huseby*, pp. 22 ff.; Carlquist and Tjerneld, 'Stephens, George', p. 382.

11 Bolmstad in Angelstad parish, Sunnerbo district (*härad*).

12 Ulf Beijbom, 'Från utvandrar- till invandrarlän', in Johansson (ed.), *Landen kring sjöarna*, pp. 365–81; Larsson, 'Land och län', pp. 238 ff. Swedish National Archives (RA), Digital Research Room (DF), Folkräkningen (Census) 1880: Hans Wolf von Schönberg, born in 1830 in Saxony, Germany, in 1880 residing at Bolmstad, Angelstad parish, Kronoberg county. Larsson, 'Land och län', p. 249; Gunnel Cederlöf, 'Huseby och det Brittiska imperiet', in Margareta Petersson (ed.), *Från Brittiska Indien till Huseby bruk: Järnvägen som arena för modernitet och kolonialism under lycksökaren och järnvägsentreprenören Joseph Stephens tid i Indien 1860–1869* (Lund: Arkiv förlag, 2018), p. 10.

13 Larsson, 'Historia kring Huseby', pp. 88 ff.; Lars J. Larsson, *Värendsbygd: Tolv socknar blev Alvesta* (Alvesta: Alvesta kulturnämnd, 1991), pp. 205 ff.; Larsson, *Det fantastiska Huseby*, pp. 22–9; Carlquist and Tjerneld, 'Stephens, George', p. 382.

14 Larsson, *Värendsbygd*, p. 206; Larsson, *Det fantastiska Huseby*, pp. 23 ff.

15 Erik Wångmar, *Husebyfröken: En studie om Florence Stephens 1881–1979* (Malmö: Égalité, 2020), pp. 55 ff.

16 Work on the Southern Main Line was completed in 1864. The new line closer to Huseby was built between Vislanda and Karlshamn and passed through Skatelöv parish. Larsson, 'Historia kring Huseby', pp. 88 ff.; Larsson, *Det fantastiska Huseby*, pp. 22–9; Larsson, 'Land och län', p. 233; Carlquist and Tjerneld, 'Stephens, George', p. 382.

17 Larsson, *Det fantastiska Huseby*, p. 28.

18 Ibid., p. 27.

19 The First Chamber was the upper house of the Riksdag. To be eligible for election to it, a man had to own property with an assessed value of at least 80,000 kronor or have an annual income of 4,000 kronor.

20 Joseph Stephens had previously been a British citizen. Alvesta kommunarkiv, Protokoll kommunalstämman i Skatelövs kommun (Minutes of Skatelöv municipal general meeting), 31 December 1874, § 2.

21 Olle Nyman, *Tvåkammarsystemets omvandling: Från privilegierätt till demokrati, Samhälle och riksdag: Historisk och statsvetenskaplig framställning*, D III (ed. Arthur Thomson) (Stockholm: Almqvist & Wiksell, 1966), pp. 39–99; Lars Sköld and Arne Halvarson, *Riksdagens sociala sammansättning under hundra år, Samhälle och riksdag: Historisk och statsvetenskaplig framställning*, D 1

(ed. Arthur Thomson) (Stockholm: Almqvist & Wiksell, 1966), pp. 399 ff.; Torbjörn Nilsson, *Elitens svängrum: Första kammaren, staten och moderniseringen 1867–1886* (PhD thesis) (Stockholm: Almqvist & Wiksell International, 1994), pp. 55 ff.; Nils Stjernquist, *Tvåkammartiden: Sveriges riksdag 1867–1970* (Stockholm: Sveriges Riksdag, 1996), pp. 28 f. and 77; Torbjörn Nilsson, *Mellan arv och utopi: Moderata vägval under hundra år, 1904–2004* (Stockholm: Santérus, 2004), pp. 145 ff.

22 Anders Norberg and Andreas Tjerneld, *Tvåkammarriksdagen 1867–1970: Ledamöter och valkretsar, 2: Östergötlands län, Jönköpings län, Kronobergs län, Kalmar län, Gotlands län, Hallands län* (Stockholm: Almqvist & Wiksell International/Riksdagen, 1985), pp. 237 f.; Tommy Möller, *Svensk politisk historia: Strid och samverkan under tvåhundra år* (Lund: Studentlitteratur, 2007), pp. 38 f.; Leif Lewin, *Ideologi och strategi: Svensk politik under 130 år* (Stockholm: Carlssons, 2017), pp. 54–82.

23 *Motioner Riksdagens första kammare* (Motions to the First Chamber of the Riksdag), 1887, no. 23.

24 Ibid., 1897, no. 23.

25 Ibid., 1901, no. 30.

26 Ibid., 1904, no. 20.

27 Ibid., 1906, no. 5.

28 For example, *Utlåtanden Riksdagens bevillningsutskott* (Opinions of the Riksdag Ways and Means Committee), 1891, no. 1, pp. 29 ff.; 1891, no. 5, pp. 1 ff. (annex); 1892, no. 2, pp. 27 ff.; 1893, no. 7, pp. 27 ff.; 1894, no. 3, pp. 12 f.; 1894, no. 5, pp. 11 ff.; 1895, no. 1, p. 26; 1896, no. 10, pp. 5 f.; 1896, no. 21, pp. 34 ff.; 1897, no. 2, p. 7; 1897, no. 25, pp. 22 ff.; 1898, no. 14, pp. 8 ff.; 1900, no. 5, p. 7; 1900, no. 26, p. 6.

29 *Utlåtanden Riksdagens tredje särskilda utskott* (Opinions of the Third Special Committee of the Riksdag), 1901, no. 5, pp. 68–75, and no. 12, pp. 12 f. and 17 f.

30 *Utlåtanden Riksdagens andra särskilda utskott* (Opinions of the Second Special Committee of the Riksdag), 1903, no. 5, p. 293.

31 For example, *Protokoll Riksdagens första kammare* (Records of the First Chamber of the Riksdag), 1888, no. 26, pp. 17 ff.; 1888, no. 30, p. 15; 1889, no. 18, pp. 11 ff.; 1889, no. 33, pp. 29 f.; 1889, no. 36, pp. 38 ff.; 1890, no. 13, pp. 6 f.; 1891, no. 27, pp. 38 f.; 1892, no. 34, pp. 48 ff.; 1892, no. 34, pp. 60 f. and 66 f.; 1894, no. 31, pp. 32 f.; 1895, no. 11, pp. 23 ff. and 42 f.; 1895, no. 12, pp. 40 f.; 1895, no. 19, pp. 22 ff.; 1897, no. 7, pp. 53; 1897, no. 9, pp. 7 f.; 1897, no. 9, pp. 13 f. and 17 f.; 1899, no. 12, pp. 19 ff.; 1900, no. 33, pp. 37 ff.; 1901, no. 16, p. 10; 1906, no. 24, pp. 26 f.; and 1906, no. 24, pp. 64 f.

32 Ibid., 1900, no. 12, pp. 12 f. and 17 f.

33 Ibid., 1902, no. 26, pp. 51 f.

34 Ibid., 1907, no. 37, pp. 30 f., and no. 43, pp. 84 f.

35 Ibid., 1896, no. 26, pp. 15 ff.

36 Ibid., 1903, no. 50, pp. 55 ff.

37 Ibid., 1904, no. 22, pp. 37 ff., and no. 24, pp. 32 f.

38 Ibid., 1904, no. 53, pp. 13 f.

39 Ibid., 1907, no. 50, pp. 3 f., 13 f., and 33 ff.

40 Elisabeth Kreüger (1858–1911), Carl-Henrik Kreüger (1822–98), Hedvig Beata Matilda Kreüger, née Retzius (1833–67).

41 RA, DF, SCB födda, vigda, döda 1860–1949 (SCB), Vigda i Skeppsholms församling i Stockholms stad (Marriages in Skeppsholmen parish, city of Stockholm), 1880. Linnaeus University (LNU), Huseby Archives (HA), Elisabeth Stephens Archive (ESA), F1:1: 'Is invited to be present at the Marriage Ceremony between

Estate Owner Joseph Stephens and our daughter Elisabeth in Stockholm, Skeppsholmen Church, on Monday 8 November 1880 at 3 in the afternoon', signed Ingeborg Kreüger, née Sparre, and C. H. Kreüger (translated from Swedish). The Huseby Archives also contain the wedding telegrams sent to the bride and groom: LNU, HA, ESA, E1:7, Telegrams dated 8 November 1880 to Elisabeth and Joseph Stephens. The letters Joseph sent to Elisabeth in 1880 were written between 19 September and 21 October: LNU, HA, ESA, E1:2, Joseph Stephens' letters to Elisabeth Kreüger, 19 September and 21 October 1880. The letters from Elisabeth to Joseph are from broadly the same period, the last one being dated 20 October: LNU, HA, Joseph Stephens Archive (JSA), E1:1, Elisabeth Stephens' letter to Joseph Stephens, 20 October 1880. Larsson, *Det fantastiska Huseby*, p. 29; Carlquist and Tjerneld, 'Stephens, George', p. 382; Margareta Petersson (ed.), *Det levande Huseby—En värld i världen* (Växjö: Historiska föreningen i Kronobergs län, 2018), pp. 91–102.

42 RA, DF, SCB, Födda i Skatelövs församling i Kronobergs län (Births in Skatelöv parish, Kronoberg county), 1881, 1882, and 1883.

43 LNU, HA, ESA, E1:2, Joseph Stephens' letter to Elisabeth Stephens, 22 July 1905.

44 Wångmar, *Husebyfröken*, pp. 285 ff.

45 LNU, HA, Huseby Estate Archive (HEA), F31A:12, Transcript of Ivar Helin's communications to Lantbruksstyrelsen (National Board of Agriculture), 30 April and 7 May 1932. Ibid., F31B:5, Record of hearing before Söderbygden Water Rights Court at Ryd on 7 June 1928 and decision of 9 July 1928; letter from Sydsvenska Kraftaktiebolaget to Florence Stephens, 18 September 1928. Engaholm Estate Collections, HBA Sjön Salen 1933-36, F31A, 12, Afskrift skrivelse till statsråden och chefer, Kungl. Kommunikationsdepartemenetet och Kungl. Socialdepartemenetet, pp. 10–11.

46 LNU, HA, Florence Stephens Archive (FSA), E1:1, Joseph Stephens' letters to Florence Stephens, 24 February, 8 April, and 9 September 1914 and 21 February 1915. Wångmar, *Husebyfröken*, pp. 278 ff.

47 LNU, HA, JSA, E1:5, Florence Stephens' letters to Joseph Stephens, 3, 6, 12, 14, and 15 February 1930.

48 LNU, HA, FSA, E1:1, Joseph Stephens' letter to Florence Stephens, 3 August 1917.

49 Ibid., F1:1, Olof Malmquist and Esaias Westborg's communication to the King, Ö 181/1958, p. 7.

50 The executor was Jean Jacques De Geer. LNU, HA, HEA, F20:2, Jean Jacques De Geer's letter to the daughters of estate owner J. S. F. Stephens, 12 July 1934.

51 Erik Wångmar, 'Brukspatronen som blev omyndig', in Margareta Petersson (ed.), *Det levande Huseby—En värld i världen* (Växjö: Historiska föreningen i Kronobergs län, 2018), pp. 128 ff.

52 *Dagens Nyheter*, 6 October 1961.

53 LNU, HA, FSA, E1:1: for example, Joseph Stephens' letter to Florence Stephens, 11 June 1920.

54 Fingal von Sydow Archive, Saltsjöbaden, Fingal von Sydow's interview with Mary Stephens, 16 September 1979. RA, DF, Kyrkoarkiv, Västra Torsås kyrkoarkiv, Inflyttningslängd (Västra Torsås church archives, Register of new parishioners), 1922. *Sveriges dödbok 1901–2013* [DVD-ROM] (Solna: Sveriges släktforskarförbund, 2014): Stephens, Mary Ingeborg, born 20 August 1882 in Skatelöv, died 9 February 1985 in Västra Torsås. Divorced 18 April 1923.

55 LNU, HA, FSA, E1:1, Joseph Stephens' letters to Florence Stephens, 30 October and 7, 8, and 17 November 1912.

56 RA, DF, SCB, Döda i Skatelövs församling i Kronobergs län (Deaths in Skatelöv parish, Kronoberg county), 1911. Arkiv Digital (AD), Västra Värends domsagas

arkiv (Västra Värend Judicial District archives), Bouppteckningar (Estate inventories), 1911, F IIIa:10, image 4700/p. 9 and image 4710/p. 10, HT, no. 9/1911, Estate inventory drawn up on 17 July 1911 relating to Mrs Hedvig Elisabeth Ingeborg Stephens, née Kreüger, deceased on 7 June 1911, comprising the estate of the deceased belonging to Allbo district. AD, Kinnevalds häradsrätts arkiv (Kinnevald District Court archives), Bouppteckningar (Estate inventories) 1910–11, F II:41, HT, no. 44/1911, Estate inventory completed on 18 July 1911 relating to Mrs Hedvig Elisabeth Ingeborg Stephens, née Kreüger, deceased on 7 June 1911, comprising the deceased's estate belonging to Kinnevald district. LNU, HA, HEA, F20:2, Will of Mr J. S. F. Stephens and Mrs Elisabeth Stephens, née Kreüger, 20 March 1908 and 12 January 1909.

57 RA, DF, SCB, Döda i Skatelövs församling i Kronobergs län (Deaths in Skatelöv parish, Kronoberg county), 1934. *Dagens Nyheter*, 16 February 1934; *Smålandsposten*, 15 and 17 February 1934; *Svenska Dagbladet*, 15 and 17 February 1934. Larsson, *Det fantastiska Huseby*, p. 29.

58 AD, Mellersta Värends domsagas arkiv (Mellersta Värend Judicial District archives), Bouppteckningar (Estate inventories) 1934, F II:15, image 2010–2410, VT, no. 110/1911, Estate inventory completed on 14 May 1934, relating to estate owner Josef[ph] Samuel Fritiof Stephens, Knight Grand Cross, deceased on 14 February 1934, comprising the estate of the deceased belonging to Kinnevald district. AD, Västra Värends domsagas arkiv, Bouppteckningar 1934, F IIIa:33, image 2710/p. 177, VT, no. 110/1934, Estate inventory drawn up on 12 May 1934, relating to estate owner Josef[ph] Samuel Fritiof Stephens, Knight Grand Cross, Huseby, Skatelöv parish, deceased on 14 February 1934, concerning the parts of the deceased's estate belonging to Allbo district. LNU, HA, HEA, F20:2, Extract from the estate inventory record drawn up at the regular spring session of Mellersta Värend Judicial District, 30 June 1934, §§ 28 and 30. Larsson, 'Land och län', p. 253; Erik Wångmar, 'Lurifaxarnas framfart—Husebyaffären 1956–1964', in Lennart Johansson, Roddy Nilsson, and Håkan Nordmark (eds), *Småländska brott* (Växjö: Historiska föreningen i Kronobergs län, 2010), pp. 289 f.

59 Larsson, *Det fantastiska Huseby*, pp. 20 ff.; Wångmar, *Husebyfröken*, pp. 51 f.

60 Larsson, *Det fantastiska Huseby*, p. 28.

61 Malin Lennartsson, Chapter 8 in this volume.

62 Wångmar, *Husebyfröken*, pp. 271 ff.

References

Bayly, Christopher, *The Birth of the Modern World 1780–1914: Global Connections and Comparisons* (Oxford: Blackwell, 2004).

Beijbom, Ulf, 'Från utvandrar-till invandrarlän', in Lennart Johansson (ed.), *Landen kring sjöarna: En historia om Kronobergs län i mångtusenårigt perspektiv; Kronobergsboken 1999–2000* (Växjö: Kronobergs läns hembygdsförbund/Smålands Museum, 1999).

Bringéus, Nils-Arvid, 'Gunnar Olof Hyltén-Cavallius', in *Svenskt biografiskt lexikon*, 19 (Stockholm: The Swedish National Archives, 1973), pp. 552–7.

Carlquist, Jonas, and Andreas Tjerneld, 'Stephens, George', in *Svenskt biografiskt lexikon*, 33 (Stockholm: The Swedish National Archives, 2011), pp. 378–87.

Cederlöf, Gunnel, 'Huseby och det Brittiska imperiet', in Margareta Petersson (ed.), *Från Brittiska Indien till Huseby bruk: Järnvägen som arena för modernitet och kolonialism under lycksökaren och järnvägsentreprenören Joseph Stephens tid i Indien 1860–1869* (Lund: Arkiv Förlag, 2018).

Dillard, Dudley, *Västeuropas och Förenta staternas ekonomiska historia* (Malmö: Liber, 1993).

Dovring, Folke, *Land and Labor in Europe, 1900–1950: A Comparative Survey of Recent Agrarian History, With a Chapter on Land Reform as a Propaganda Theme by Karin Dovring* (The Hague: Nijhoff, 1965).

Flygare, Iréne A., and Mats Isacson, 'The Tension Between Modernity and Reality 1945–2010', in Mats Morell and Janken Myrdal (eds), *The Agrarian History of Sweden: From 4000* BC *to* AD *2000* (Lund: Nordic Academic Press, 2011).

Gadd, Carl-Johan, *Det svenska jordbrukets historia*, 3: *Den agrara revolutionen 1700–1870* (Stockholm: Natur och kultur/LT, 2000).

Gadd, Carl-Johan, 'The Agricultural Revolution in Sweden 1700–1870', in Mats Morell and Janken Myrdal (eds), *The Agrarian History of Sweden: From 4000* BC *to* AD *2000* (Lund: Nordic Academic Press, 2011).

Högberg, Staffan, 'Bondelandet i Sverige', in Birgitta Furuhagen (ed.), *Äventyret Sverige: En ekonomisk och social historia* (Stockholm: Utbildningsradion, 1993).

Kardell, Lars, *Svenskarna och skogen*, 2: *Från baggböleri till naturvård* (Jönköping: Skogsstyrelsens Förlag, 2004).

Larsson, Lars J., *Värendsbygd: Tolv socknar blev Alvesta* (Alvesta: Alvesta kulturnämnd, 1991).

Larsson, Lars-Olof, *Det fantastiska Huseby: En rundvandring i tid och rum* (Växjö: Domänverket/Huseby bruk, 1993).

Larsson, Lars-Olof, 'Historia kring Huseby: Epoken Stephens', in *Skatelövskrönika 1978* (Grimslöv: Skatelövs hembygdsförening, 1978).

Larsson, Lars-Olof, 'Hur Stephens kom till Huseby', in *Skatelövskrönika 1986* (Grimslöv: Skatelövs hembygdsförening, 1986).

Larsson, Lars-Olof, 'Land och län under kristendomens millennium', in Lennart Johansson (ed.), *Landen kring sjöarna: En historia om Kronobergs län i mångtusenårigt perspektiv; Kronobergsboken 1999–2000* (Växjö: Kronobergs läns hembygdsförbund/Smålands Museum, 1999).

Larsson, Lars-Olof, 'Skogstillgång, skogsprodukter och sågar i Kronobergs län', in Olof Nordström, Lars J. Larsson, John Käll, and Lars-Olof Larsson (eds), *Skogen och smålänningen: Kring skogsmarkens roll i förindustriell tid* (Växjö: Historiska föreningen i Kronobergs län, 1989).

Lewin, Leif, *Ideologi och strategi: Svensk politik under 130 år* (Stockholm: Carlssons, 2017).

Möller, Tommy, *Svensk politisk historia: Strid och samverkan under tvåhundra år* (Lund: Studentlitteratur, 2007).

Morell, Mats, *Det svenska jordbrukets historia*, 4: *Jordbruket i industrisamhället, 1870–1945* (Stockholm: Natur och kultur/LT, 2001).

Morell, Mats, Carl-Johan Gadd, and Janken Myrdal, 'Statistical Appendix', in Mats Morell and Janken Myrdal (eds), *The Agrarian History of Sweden: From 4000* BC *to* AD *2000* (Lund: Nordic Academic Press, 2011).

Nilsson, Torbjörn, Elitens svängrum: Första kammaren, staten och moderniseringen 1867–1886 (PhD thesis) (Stockholm: Almqvist & Wiksell International, 1994).

Nilsson, Torbjörn, *Mellan arv och utopi: Moderata vägval under hundra år, 1904–2004* (Stockholm: Santérus, 2004).

Norberg, Anders, and Andreas Tjerneld, *Tvåkammarriksdagen 1867–1970: Ledamöter och valkretsar*, 2: *Östergötlands län, Jönköpings län, Kronobergs län,*

Kalmar län, Gotlands län, Hallands län (Stockholm: Almqvist & Wiksell International/Riksdagen, 1985).

Nordström, Olof, 'Skog och skogsmark som försörjningskälla', in Olof Nordström, Lars J. Larsson, John Käll, and Lars-Olof Larsson (eds), *Skogen och smålänningen: Kring skogsmarkens roll i förindustriell tid* (Växjö: Historiska föreningen i Kronobergs län, 1989).

Nyman, Olle, *Tvåkammarsystemets omvandling: Från privilegierätt till demokrati, Samhälle och riksdag: Historisk och statsvetenskaplig framställning*, D III (ed. Arthur Thomson) (Stockholm: Almqvist & Wiksell, 1966).

Petersson, Margareta (ed.), *Det levande Huseby—En värld i världen* (Växjö: Historiska föreningen i Kronobergs län, 2018).

Schön, Lennart, *En modern svensk ekonomisk historia: Tillväxt och omvandling under två sekel* (Stockholm: SNS Förlag, 2000).

Sköld, Lars, and Arne Halvarson, *Riksdagens sociala sammansättning under hundra år, Samhälle och riksdag: Historisk och statsvetenskaplig framställning*, D 1 (ed. Arthur Thomson) (Stockholm: Almqvist & Wiksell, 1966).

Stjernquist, Nils, *Tvåkammartiden: Sveriges riksdag 1867–1970* (Stockholm: Sveriges Riksdag, 1996).

Wångmar, Erik, 'Brukspatronen som blev omyndig', in Margareta Petersson (ed.), *Det levande Huseby—En värld i världen* (Växjö: Historiska föreningen i Kronobergs län, 2018).

Wångmar, Erik, *Husebyfröken: En studie om Florence Stephens 1881–1979* (Malmö: Égalité, 2020).

Wångmar, Erik, 'Lurifaxarnas framfart—Husebyaffären 1956–1964', in Lennart Johansson, Roddy Nilsson, and Håkan Nordmark (eds), *Småländska brott* (Växjö: Historiska föreningen i Kronobergs län, 2010).

Wiking-Faria, Pablo, 'Freden, friköpen och järnplogarna: Drivkrafter och förändringsprocesser under den agrara revolutionen i Halland 1700–1900', PhD thesis, Department of Historical Studies, University of Gothenburg, 2009.

8 Doing One's Duty, Making a Future

The Ironmaster's Daughters and the Unceasing Project of Rearing a Family

Malin Lennartsson

In 1869, after 10 years as a contractor on the vast railway construction project in colonial India, Joseph Stephens returned to Europe for good. He was still a young man, just 28 years of age. A couple of years earlier, he had acquired the large but run-down ironmaking estate of Huseby in Småland in southern Sweden, and over the ensuing decade he built the estate up again and saw it grow in prosperity.[1] Not until 1880, when he was approaching 40, did he marry. The future mistress of Huseby was Elisabeth Kreüger, the daughter of an admiral who was a personal friend of King Oscar II. She was 17 years younger than her husband. The year after they married, their first child was born, a daughter Florence. The next two years saw the birth of two more daughters, Mary and Maggie. After that, there were no further additions to the family, and it must have been clear early on that the three daughters would be Joseph's heirs, Elisabeth's health having deteriorated significantly following her pregnancies and births.

Northern Europe in the nineteenth century was socially and economically mobile, and Joseph Stephens' grandparents and other relatives had been able to take advantage of this, making a class journey and travelling all over the world. Margareta Petersson, a scholar of literature, has studied this process in detail for members of the Stephens' family in the Huseby Estate Archives.[2] In economic terms, though, Joseph's branch of the family had done less well, and he was forced to make his own fortune. He arrived in India with very little financial capital to build on. The colonial activities of the British in that country, however, provided him with opportunities which, through family connections, networking, and hard work, he was able to turn to good account. On his return to Sweden, his wife's family background opened doors to the higher echelons of society, even to the royal family, and the marriage of his sister Blanche to Fingal von Sydow made Joseph and his daughters relatives at one remove of Sweden's most powerful family of financiers, the Wallenbergs. The Misses Stephens at Huseby were thus born into wealth, and with access to the highest society in the country.[3] Not only financially, but also socially, they thus seem to have had excellent prospects. The ground should have been prepared for them to succeed in life. But they had one clear handicap, namely that they were women. This study explores

DOI: 10.4324/9781003317227-8

the succession from their father, Joseph, to his daughters, with a focus on the youngest, Maggie, and considers the sisters' social opportunities and personal ability to carve out independent lives for themselves.

Figure 8.1 Florence, Mary, and Maggie Stephens, mid-1890s.

Source: Courtesy Huseby Bruk AB.

As women, the Stephens sisters had limited access to education, to a professional career, and also to legal capacity—at least if they married. In the second half of the nineteenth century, reforms were introduced in Sweden that granted unmarried women legal capacity. From 1858, an unmarried woman could apply for a declaration of majority when she reached the age of 25.[4] Five years later, in 1863 she automatically attained majority at that age. If she married, however, she lost this status. Not until 1921, when the right to vote was extended to women, did married women achieve full legal capacity. Thus, opportunities for a woman in the late nineteenth century to shape her own life were limited by legislation, by a lack of institutions, and by cultural patterns, but they were not non-existent. Educational opportunities, both formal and informal, were available, at least for women who were not without financial capital. And that, as we have seen, was something the Stephens sisters did possess. The family also had social and cultural capital, although they were ambivalent and hard to pin down. Joseph Stephens had little connection with Småland before the purchase of the Huseby estate, nor does he seem to have developed any very close friendships with other estate owners in the vicinity of Huseby. In Stockholm he should have felt more at home: he had been born there, had spent his childhood in Copenhagen, and had a Stockholm girl as his wife. His English background may have been both an obstacle and a source of status. The British Empire was at its height and perhaps lent lustre to the Stephenses, but the fact that he did not come from a Swedish family may also have given them a sense of being outsiders in Sweden. During Joseph's time in India, the emphasis had been very much on his English background, and the responsibility that rested on a Christian, a European, and an Englishman was something that was constantly repeated in the letters Joseph's father George wrote to his son in India. Joseph Stephens came from a family of Methodists, a setting that stressed the value of a good education, hard work, and honesty.[5]

The Stephens' family collected and kept things, and a large number of the letters sent between them have therefore been preserved. There are not very many to the sisters as they were growing up, however. During their childhood, the family were usually together, either at Huseby or in Stockholm, during the time Joseph was a member of the First Chamber of the Riksdag (the Swedish parliament). Their correspondence became more extensive when they lived in different places and when the sisters travelled on their own on the continent. Letters between Joseph and his daughters from the 1910s, following his wife's death, are particularly numerous. Joseph's roles as a father and an educator, and what aspects of his own life experience can be traced in those roles, will be analysed by homing in on three different periods in the material preserved. First, the daughters' childhood, to see what the correspondence has to say about the girls' education and upbringing: what was expected of them, and what opportunities were they given to gain an education and hence to shape their own lives? I then go on to examine the years after their mother's death, and after the death of their father. These were not only times of upheaval and crisis but also times when the sisters had a chance to make new life choices. How, though, did they react to the loss of their parents and to their new situation in life? The focus here is on the relationship between Maggie and Joseph. As regards her elder sisters, Joseph related to Florence as his future successor at Huseby, and to Mary as a married woman. But how did he relate to Maggie, the youngest daughter, unmarried, and the one who most clearly lacked a given role in the family and in society? We may ask what moral advice and practical admonitions did he offer when he wanted to help and protect, but also to educate and guide his daughter? How did she react to his concerns and exhortations, and how did she act when she was forced to choose a path in life? When her mother and later her father died, and not least in the face of her own death?

'But They Know Nothing'

The sisters received some instruction, but it was patchy. To begin with, it was provided by a 'reading helper',[6] and later by governesses. The impression we get is that the girls' education was sporadic and occasional, and no doubt also affected by the fact that they spent several months every year in Stockholm.

When the sisters were still very young, their Aunt Blanche reacted to the fact that they were not being encouraged to engage in learning activities. In December 1885, when they were between 2 and 4 years old, she wrote to her brother:

> They will as you say soon have to begin to learn something. When Amy was five years old last November I gave her a box of 'klossar' [wooden bricks] with letters on them and since then she has learnt all the letters in playing and can now spell her own name as well as her brothers' and sisters'. Gerda learned to read and write in the same way.[7]

Blanche had herself received an education and had worked as a teacher before she married. This was something her elder sister, Ingeborg, had envied her, as a woman who was 'happy and contented, "as she has an essential occupation" at a girls' school outside Halmstad'.[8]

A few years later, in 1888, the girls were between 6 and 8 years of age, and their grandfather, George, wrote to Joseph about his grandchildren:

> I have been thinking of the dear Children. They are getting old & growing fast. Surely the time has come for serious education, say 3 hours a day for Florence, 2 for Mary, 1 for Maggie (these hours being more *half-play* than actual lessons). The younger ones would at least learn to think a little, & to be silent and rest a little.[9]

Without the knowledge of the Bible, George believed, the girls would be incapable of fighting 'the World, the Flesh & the Devil'. If the family were to employ a governess, a 'bonne', they should choose an English one, as English was the most distinguished language, the universal one, and the one with the world's finest literature. An English girl would also, he suggested, be more honest and religious than a French or Swiss one 'accustomed to abominable French Novels'.[10]

The theme of structuring and improving the girls' education recurred in a letter from George in September 1893:

> Our darlings are now soon women. ... But they know nothing, a little Swedish, no English, and not much of anything else. Youth is the season for laying the foundation of all arts, sciences and accomplishments.[11]

Despite being in a period in life in which a person is most receptive to learning, he suggested, the sisters did not know much at all, and certainly no English. They needed a competent governess

> who will teach them *English*, conversational *French* (Grammar to be added by degrees, as they advance in easy phrases); *German* (Grammar to be added by degrees, as they advance in easy phrases). Then Music-lessons to be given in *English*. Their *Drawing*-lessons must probably be given by a Drawing-master. All *household* matters and cooking to be learned under the inspection of Dear Elisabeth and in the kitchen.[12]

The education which the girls' grandfather believed they needed was very much focused on the female sphere. Apart from languages, he suggested, they should learn to draw and to run a household.

> The children may themselves have to get their bread as Governesses. No one can tell what is in store for them 10 or 20 or 30 years hereafter. I propose an English Governess. The cost is nothing compared to the advantage of a good sound, religious education—a fair start in life.[13]

George's view that education was needed to prepare the sisters for a life in which they might have to make their own living as governesses is of interest here. Their father was, after all, a very successful estate owner, and there was nothing to suggest that the Stephens sisters would ever have to support themselves. But according to their grandfather, they needed a good education to give them a 'fair start in life'.[14]

An educated daughter was a status symbol for a family, as was having a governess.[15] However, the governesses Joseph and Elisabeth employed were a source of constant friction. The one the girls had in the autumn of 1893, when George wrote his letter, he described as 'ignorant and empty-headed'.[16] The eldest daughter Florence, in particular, came into conflict with the governesses and was insolent towards them.[17] They got no support from the parents in their education of the children, or at least not from

Elisabeth.[18] In spring 1894, one governess, a 'Miss W.', suddenly left the family,[19] and by the autumn of that year another had given notice with immediate effect, claiming she could stand it no longer. Joseph wrote that it was a good thing she was out of the house and that the children were 'glad to be rid of Miss Hagberg', although he also noted 'but now they are not learning anything'.[20] He wanted a more lasting solution—they had had enough of governesses who came and went.[21] However, no real effort was made to change the situation and offer the girls a stable education; Elisabeth simply wrote that she would hurry out into Stockholm to 'enquire about lessons for the children for the winter'.[22] Apart from these temporary governesses, they received no other formal schooling.

It was of course out of the question that the estate owner's daughters should study together with the children of his workers at the elementary school at Huseby.[23] But from the beginning of the nineteenth century, girls' schools that aimed at the daughters of the middle and upper classes had been established in Sweden's towns and cities. The half-century before the Stephens' daughters were born had seen an explosion in the number of these establishments, which had been created—as private, usually female, initiatives—as a counterpart to the government-funded grammar schools for boys.[24] In Växjö, some 20 km from Huseby, there had been a girls' high school with a good reputation since the middle of the nineteenth century.[25] The Stephens' sisters could have been provided with an education there. But for some reason, their parents chose not to avail themselves of that possibility. Perhaps an indication that the Stephens' family were not integrated in the region and, partly related to that, a reflection of the fact that they spent a great deal of time in Stockholm.

One argument that was advanced for schooling for girls was that harmonious marriages required a certain equality of education between husband and wife. A girls' school set up early on had the stated aim of turning every pupil there into 'a knowledgeable, clear-thinking, and well-educated member of society, a good spouse, and a pious housewife'.[26] The emphasis was thus on the woman's role not only as a wife and mother, but also as a member of society, although that was not taken to include membership of a profession. It was also realized, however, that there was a need for education for women to make them employable.[27] In his study concerning the seventeenth century down to 1859, Sten Carlsson, one of the first social historians in Sweden to study social mobility and marriage patterns, observed that even at that time, it was understood that not all women were able to marry, particularly not in the upper classes.[28] There was in other words a consensus in the nineteenth century about women receiving an education. The discussion, rather, was about what their studies should lead to: professional activity or marriage, public life or the home.[29] Was it a matter of training to enable them to participate in public life, for instance by working, or a general education that would allow them to conduct themselves in polite society and be a worthy wife for a husband with a career?

Besides governesses and the girls' schools just mentioned, there was a further alternative for the education of a woman from the upper classes. That was to send her to a boarding school, or *Pensionat*. Maggie spent an academic year, from September 1900 to April 1901, at such an establishment in Hannover. In her letters home to her parents, she mostly wrote about her homesickness and worries about the family's health, but in letters to Joseph she also provided a few glimpses of the instruction she was receiving. The focus in the Hanoverian boarding school was on languages, both of necessity as it was an international school, but also as school subjects. In her report for the autumn term 1900, Maggie was awarded grades in German, English, and French. Apart from these languages, the only other subject she received a grade in was needlework.[30] In October 1900, she wrote: 'I have now learnt German handwriting and must always speak German to my teachers.'[31] Two months later, in her Christmas letter home, she reported: 'I now understand some German quite well and if one of the teachers reads aloud slowly from a German book, I understand.' Since the only person she could speak Swedish to, a Norwegian, had returned home, she now had no choice but to express herself in English or German.[32] She also studied English. Towards the end of the Christmas holiday, Maggie told her family: 'Now during the holidays I have read 3 English books and understand them very well.'[33] In addition, she attended services at the English Church, and the priest taught some of the girls, including Maggie, church history.[34]

We see, then, that only one of the daughters received an education going beyond that provided by governesses. Grandfather George's verdict that 'they know nothing' was perhaps an exaggeration. He claimed, after all, that they knew no English, but as adults they corresponded in that language and seem to have had a sufficient command of others to be able to pay regular visits to spas in Germany and holiday resorts on the French and Italian Rivieras without any difficulty understanding or making themselves understood. Clearly, though, there were deficiencies in their education, and their parents realized this. This was evident, not least, from Joseph's concern about the governesses coming and going, but however concerned the parents may have been, they did nothing about it.

At the turn of the twentieth century, the three sisters were in their late teens. Maggie was spending an academic year in Germany, Mary was married in the autumn of 1901 to Gunnar Liepe, a captain twice her age, and moved to Stockholm, and Florence stayed on at Huseby and served together with her mother as her father's right hand while he was away.[35] The sisters spent part of the first decade of the new century at home at Huseby, and part of it abroad or in Stockholm, where Joseph was a Riksdag member until 1909. In the summer of 1911, disaster struck—Elisabeth died at the age of 52. All her daughters were greatly affected by her loss, but Maggie in particular found it difficult to cope with her mother's death.

'To Resign Ourselves to a Loss'

When her mother died, Maggie was at crossroads in her life. Mourning for her must have been mixed with questions about her own place and what she was to make of her life. When Elisabeth passed away, Florence's role as the heiress of Huseby became clearer and she continued to help her father with his work. As the wife of Captain Liepe, Mary also had a role, even if she had not become a mother after 10 years of marriage. But what about Maggie: what was her purpose in life? She had no education that could lead to a profession, and few of her female relatives or acquaintances had any kind of gainful employment. In the decades around the turn of the century, a very large proportion of women remained unmarried, especially in the higher ranks of society.[36] With growing demands for education and the professionalization of many occupations in the nineteenth century, the marrying age for men had risen. In the middle classes and the aristocracy, it took men until the age of 35–40 to achieve a position and an income that allowed them to support a family. And when they were able to do so, they did not marry women their own age, but considerably younger ones.[37] The same pattern is evident in Maggie's family circle. Her father had been 17 years older than her mother. Maggie's Aunt Blanche had married a man 16 years her senior, and her sister Mary, one who was 19 years older than herself. That does not mean that, at the age of 28, Maggie would have been too old for marriage.[38] But the general pattern was that many women from the upper classes remained unmarried.[39]

Maggie had not been without admirers. In the spring of 1906, when she was 23, her parents corresponded about a man from Poland who had courted her and who now wished to pay a visit to Huseby. Maggie herself claimed that she was not at all interested, and Joseph was opposed to a relationship, writing in a letter to Elisabeth that

> an alliance for life must not be entered into lightly by allowing oneself to be beguiled by fair words and flowers, especially when one is in an entirely independent position and does not need to marry to be provided for.[40]

Joseph put forward no arguments beyond the fact that the man was clearly given to using 'fair words' and that Maggie was financially independent. Interestingly, it seems as if he had no problem with the idea of her remaining unmarried. She did not need to marry to be provided for. She did not need a husband. As a daughter of Joseph Stephens and a young lady on the Huseby Estate, she had always had financial resources, although after her mother's death she had greater access to money of her own. But as she could only spend the income from her inheritance from her mother, this did not in fact make her fully independent.[41] She received enough to be able to spend money and enjoy a comfortable life, but not so much that she was able to use the money for something productive.

The correspondence between Maggie and her father, and also between Joseph and Mary, shows that for several years after her mother's death Maggie lost her footing and suffered from conditions of mental and physical origin that significantly affected her life. In the following, we shall see what forms her suffering assumed and what Joseph's attitude was to his daughter's illnesses and weariness with life.

Maggie described her grief for her mother in the most forceful terms. She saw no meaning to her life and was just waiting to be united in death with the person who was dearest to her, her 'darling', her 'dear mother'.[42] Hoping to change Maggie's train of thought, Joseph wrote to her in March 1912 about the duty every Christian has to fulfil their calling:

> Remember that God has not placed us humans in this world for no reason; we have each received our calling to achieve something useful, and duty bids us discharge that calling as well as we can, and not waste our entire life because we lack the strength to resign ourselves to a loss, even if it is very great.[43]

When Joseph wrote this in the spring of 1912, Maggie was in Rapallo in Italy on a trip with Mary. So when she penned a letter to Joseph dated three days later, she had probably not yet received his exhortations about the need to find one's calling and not waste one's life. She wrote that Mary was able to make herself at home among strangers, but she was not: 'for a pain as great as mine there is no consolation; only the hope of seeing my darling again in another, far better world makes it possible for me to endure life'.[44] Two weeks later she wrote: 'That I feel sad and wretched there is no doubt, but I probably always will without my Mama.'[45] In a letter dated 12 April, Joseph thanked her for hers

> but it would have pleased me much more still if I had found you more resigned and prepared to yield to God's will, and to submit to the sacrifices which this life requires; there is so much here to do and to think about for our fellow men and women.[46]

He himself had been alone for Easter and it had not been enjoyable, but 'as I have a lot to do and think about, and am used to submitting without grumbling to the sacrifices earthly life requires, it proved more or less easy to bear.'[47] Joseph submitted to 'this life', he wrote, and having things to do and think of made life possible to endure, but Maggie did not resign herself to God's will, she did not submit. The way she showed this, however, was not by rebelling against society's expectations of an unmarried woman heading for middle age and challenging convention. She turned the rebellion on herself.

How did Joseph view Maggie's ill health? He felt, first of all, that she had been unwell for a long time. Her history of illness had not begun with her mother's death; it had been made worse by it. He dismissed the doctors who claimed that Maggie was just 'nervous', but he did not describe any real physical causes for her ill health, although he did believe that physical activity and fresh air would get her out of the vicious circle she was in:

> Maggie ought to get up early in the mornings and take a long walk in the country in the fresh air, and have some occupation that interests her so she would have something to think about that would distract her, in order to strengthen her nerves and give her an appetite, which she now completely lacks, with the result that her body is weakened by a lack of nutrition.[48]

In this letter to Mary, there was more emphasis on Maggie's practical way of life than on the kind of existential and religious counsel and exhortations he gave directly to Maggie. He also mentioned her lack of appetite and the debilitating effects of inadequate nutrition. Joseph was upset and worried about her condition; his advice and recommendations may well have irritated his youngest daughter, but they quite clearly sprang from a concern for her. Equally clear is the way Maggie became the centre around which the family's concern, anxieties, and attention revolved.

The foremost historian on nineteenth- and twentieth-century ideals for women in Scandinavia, Karin Johannisson, has devoted several works to investigating the relationship between body, mind, and society around the turn of the twentieth century. 'Female' illnesses were often linked to eating disorders.

> The fact that in most cases self-denial began in the teens and was combined with anorectic behaviour means that we have to bring into the discussion ideas concerning a young woman's transition to adulthood: her longing for direction, attention, affirmation, comfort.[49]

The illnesses, the poor health, could in other words serve as a means of securing an identity, acquiring a role. Johannisson takes her argument a step further when she asks: 'Did the idealization of female invalidity in fact place a secret weapon in her hands—a way of dominating and controlling, at the same time as she seemed to be subordinate?'[50] What is evident, at any rate, is that Maggie managed to mobilize her entire family's interest and involvement in her illness. In the correspondence, we find expressions of Joseph's and Mary's concern, but Florence was of course also involved, especially when Maggie was at Huseby. Joseph wrote to Mary in autumn 1913 that it was not strange that Florence herself was out of sorts, 'after all the anxiety she has had for Maggie all summer'.[51]

By the spring of 1913, Maggie had recovered to such an extent that she was able to travel south with Mary. They spent a few months in Lausanne, Wiesbaden, and Baden-Baden, and the tone of her letters to Joseph was more cheerful. She was admittedly keeping track of how long it had been since their mother had died and was planning a visit 'to our darling's grave' on the second anniversary of her passing on 7 June.[52] But there was no indication that she was weary of life. When Mary travelled on to the spa town of Kreuznach, however, Maggie returned to Sweden, where both her relationship to Joseph and her health rapidly deteriorated.[53] When Joseph writes to her on 18 June and is distressed that she is seriously ill again, he comments specifically on the fact that Maggie had returned to Sweden so 'happy and well', adding that she must endeavour to keep her spirits up and remember her privileged position:

> and see life, which has so much goodness and happiness to offer you, from the bright side, and thank God for the great grace that has given you so much compared with thousands of other people, who day by day have such great anxiety about obtaining daily bread for themselves and their loved ones, and think about how much good you can do by bringing many poor fellow human beings joy through your ability to be of help to them in their need, and what satisfaction it is for you to be in so fortunate a position; and so you have a great deal to live for.[54]

Charity work was common among the privileged women of the middle and upper classes, something Joseph was encouraging here, but which neither Elisabeth nor any of the three sisters engaged in to any appreciable extent. Maggie wrote to Mary on 21 June that it would 'have been a great mercy if I had died, so contented I would be to leave this world and go to my dear mother'. She also wrote that

> Papa has asked for my forgiveness and now written to me, but I still understand that he doesn't like me, and it's always a shame to be in someone's way, but of course I never know how long my life will be.[55]

Unfortunately, the letter in question has not been preserved, so what Joseph asked for forgiveness for and how we have no way of telling. What is clear, though, is that Maggie managed to turn whatever offence it may have been to her advantage and manipulate her father. Mary, who was still on the continent, wrote to Joseph from Bad Kreuznach, saying that she had just heard of 'Maggie's sudden and severe illness'.[56] A week later, she was back in Sweden, by Maggie's side in Stockholm, after her sister had undergone a stomach operation at the Sophiahemmet Hospital. Her illness was more obviously physical in character than earlier references to it suggest. Mary reported to Joseph that the operation had gone well, but had revealed an inflamed appendix and adhesions between the intestines. She hoped that Maggie, 'now she is free from this focus of disease, which all the indications are has been present for years, . . . will feel better than before and develop a better appetite'.[57]

To begin with, then, the hope was that the surgery would cure Maggie's symptoms. A careful check was kept on her weight, and in August Mary reported to Joseph: 'The previous week she is said to have put on 700 grams, but this last week I think she has in fact lost weight again, judging from how thin and wretched she now looks.'[58] In the autumn it became clear that the hopes placed in the operations had been in vain, and Joseph urged Maggie to follow 'the prescriptions of a skilled doctor, and as much as possible avoid medicine and dangerous numbing substances'.[59] But she wrote back that 'no doctor can help me'. Although she felt that the physicians were helpless in the face of her illness, they still cost money: in the same letter, she thanked her father for the 1,500 kronor she had received to pay for doctors and medicines.[60]

Joseph warned against 'dangerous numbing substances'. It is difficult to say how extensive Maggie's use of opiates was. Clearly, though, in the early twentieth century morphine could be regarded as an entirely unproblematic medication.[61] Elisabeth recommended the use of these drugs in a letter written back in 1902: 'Morphine and opium are both excellent for this purpose.'[62] A few years later, Mary wrote to Maggie asking her to

> Give my love to dear Mama and thank her for the bottle of opium I've just received and tell her my stomach is now much better, really fine, but that I'm glad to have the opium bottle to hand when the need arises.[63]

After their mother had died, the sisters sent morphine to each other. In 1914, Maggie wrote to Mary: 'Many thanks for the morphine'.[64] Karin Johannisson describes this use of medication as part of a *marketization* of sick women:

> Not only as patients at doctors' surgeries, sanatoriums, and private clinics, but also as consumers of sedatives, tonics, and painkillers, of myriad drops, pills, and powders, and of a sea of accessories for the proper care of the body. The doctors' well-documented generosity with addictive drugs such as opium and morphine can, at least by those of a cynical disposition, be placed in this context.[65]

The year 1913 ended on an unhappy note. Just before Christmas, Joseph wrote:

> But dear Maggie, you must not always take such a gloomy view of life, but rather make the best of what God has given you, and be grateful for all the good things you have received . . . because after night comes day, and in this world we have to get used to taking the rough with the smooth, and not despair.

Once again, he stressed the need to face life with courage. He went on to give Maggie concrete advice on her health and recommended her to travel to see Dr. Westerlund and subsequently to spend the winter months in southern Europe.[66]

Ernst Westerlund was a famous doctor in Sweden in the early twentieth century who had specialized in treating mental conditions in upper-class women. Using what he termed 'work therapy', which placed demands on the patient, he managed to cure many who other doctors had dismissed as hypochondriacs.[67] But Maggie really did not want to go and see him. A visit to Dr. Westerlund had been discussed the year before, but according to a letter from Mary, Maggie had refused. She was 'absolutely determined *not* to go there'.[68] Joseph's Christmas letter of 1913 ended with the words:

> May God help you to be restored to health, that is my heartfelt prayer, and I hereby wish you a happy and pleasant Christmas and all possible good things in the coming New Year, and above all restored health and joy in life. . .. Your loving, sorrowful father J. S. F. Stephens.[69]

Maggie thanked him warmly for this letter, 'which deeply moved me', and was overwhelmed by the Christmas present she had received. She did not think she would be up to travelling abroad, but was curing herself with 'iron and arsenic'.[70] Through to the following summer, the family correspondence contained reports on her health. In spring 1914, they were still concerned about her being so thin. Mary referred in one letter to 'the long starvation' that had so diminished Maggie's strength.[71] Joseph wrote:

> It is terribly sad that Maggie is so weak, but it should not come as a surprise when, despite all our urgings, she persists in denying herself *food* and other things necessary to preserving her health.[72]

In March 1914, Maggie was again admitted to hospital in Stockholm, after being looked after by the sisters' old wet nurse, Lily, at Huseby. Mary had a cold and did not dare visit Maggie, and asked her to burn her letter to avoid any spread of infection.[73] In the late spring a trip abroad was discussed, but Joseph now felt it would be far too risky.[74] Despite his misgivings, Maggie travelled with Mary and Florence to Wiesbaden and spent part of May and June there. But that was the last foreign travel they could undertake for several years. The First World War was about to begin.

The pattern from the previous year repeated itself. The stay abroad did Maggie good,[75] but once she was back home in Sweden her condition deteriorated again, and this year, too, ended on a despondent note, as her words the day after St. Lucy's Day can serve to illustrate:

> I feel so ill that I almost believe this will be my last Christmas, and may God grant it. No one would be more grateful than I to leave this earthly life; perhaps then my tired spirit could finally find peace.[76]

In 1915, Maggie continued to be beset by illness. She was nursed at home and in hospital. Like her father, she had little confidence in the doctors: 'You can see yourself that I cannot get well, so what's the point in my going to a lot of doctors who just torment me? I just want to be left alone,' she wrote to Mary.[77] That autumn, a year into the war, Joseph urged Maggie to 'think about how much worse off thousands of people are in this conflict, and thank God that we have been spared being drawn into it'.[78] The kind of exhortation which, however reasonable it may be in its call to put our own suffering in perspective, rarely has any effect. At the beginning of December Maggie returned to Huseby, and the summary she gave after the holiday period of life there was: 'Now I've been at home for a whole month. The time is passing quite quickly, and a good thing too, because life brings me no joy.'[79]

The line between mental and physical illness is difficult to draw, and indeed perhaps does not always need to be defined. In the years following her mother's death, Maggie was afflicted with concrete physical conditions, but they were reinforced and played out in an arena that affirmed a certain form of female suffering, with a focus on the delicate and the frail, and gave the sufferer attention, understanding, and a part to play. The pattern whereby Maggie's poor health and weariness with life were activated when she was at home at Huseby is patently apparent. Her need to be seen and her lack of a meaningful occupation and a place in life were not as evident when she was travelling in new environments and making new contacts, but back home there was no denying them. According to Karin Johannisson, the cult of the ailing woman faded away at the turn of the twentieth century, after which the focus shifted to promoting healthy living.[80] That is a view shared by Anna-Karin Frih, whose research has concentrated on perceptions of young women. She finds that there was a difference between the scientific medical and the popular medical discourse. The former clung for longer to a norm of female ill health, while the latter changed more rapidly, becoming more of a health discourse in the early decades of the twentieth century. A new ideal of womanhood linked to activity, sport, and public life emerged.[81] Maggie was brought up in a culture that set great store by the delicate woman, in a family where, throughout the sisters' childhood, the mother they worshipped had been in poor health, with conditions linked to that most feminine thing of all, reproduction. Elisabeth died at the age of 52 of bleeding from a ruptured fibroid. Maggie's formative years were thus shaped by a female ideal which subsequently, as she entered adulthood, became increasingly dated, but which would characterize her entire life.

'The Injustice Is Too Great'

Joseph Stephens died on 14 February 1934, in his 93rd year. His three daughters, Florence, Mary, and Maggie, were in their early fifties and were all unmarried—Mary having divorced in 1923—and none of them had any children. Now they inherited a fortune. The Huseby complex was divided up in such a way that Florence inherited the main house of Huseby, Mary was given the house where she had already lived for many years, Torne, and Maggie received Ålshult. Their shares differed in size and, above all, the grandeur of the houses, and the differences were not entirely evened out by the personal property they inherited.[82]

There is no indication that Mary was upset at her share being so much smaller than Florence's, but for Maggie the difference in what they each inherited triggered a new crisis and an extended period of illness.

In the summer of 1934, Jean Jacques De Geer, the old family friend appointed by Joseph Stephens as his executor, sent an identically worded letter to each of the three sisters. He appealed to them to come to their senses and respect the last will of their father and mother. Their disagreement over the will had even caused an embarrassing incident at the Savings Bank, he wrote. He stressed that a child who deliberately defies her parents' wishes—even if she may formally be in the right and could succeed in legal proceedings over the matter—'will never again have any real happiness in life'. A crucial point in his letter was that

> Mr Stephens, the estate owner, acquired his large fortune entirely by his own efforts. In such circumstances, the view is often that you have less or no obligation to leave it to your heirs.[83]

De Geer pointed out that Stephens had not tried to make a name for himself—'show off in the country's newspapers'—by donating millions, but had left everything to his daughters. Should they not then be able to agree among themselves?[84]

A key consideration for De Geer, in other words, was that Joseph Stephens' wealth was of his own making. He had not inherited it; it was not family property that he was morally obliged to pass on to his children, and he could therefore have done as he chose with it, and yet had left his entire fortune to his children.[85] De Geer's letter was addressed to all the sisters, but was probably aimed primarily at Maggie; there was no hint of any complaint from Florence or Mary about their inheritance, and Maggie was after all the one who received least. Her disappointment at her share was immense. Preserved among the letters from one of her male friends, Ove Vind, the Danish Master of the Royal Hunt, there is one she wrote to him dated 26 November 1934. Either the letter was never sent or this is a copy. In her letter, Maggie described how she was under constant supervision following a suicide attempt, and how she felt she had 'been treated as if I were not a member of the family; the injustice is too great'.[86] Until her father's death, Maggie had resided at Huseby. But that house had gone to Florence and no longer felt like her home. Mary, by contrast, had lived and worked for a long time on the property she had now inherited. For her, her father's death meant that she became the owner of her home, not that she lost it. Maggie must have felt orphaned, homeless, and wronged, and it would be a long time before she created her own home at Ålshult. Most of the time she stayed with her sister Mary. In the late 1930s she was in hospital for long periods, and one of her doctors, Professor Malte Ljungdahl, wrote to her in February 1938:

> Light the fire that exists within you, or—rather—let the fire that is now lit within you burn: be something, stand strong, and give: not money,

> because that only causes harm, but inspiration, opportunities for employment, culture in the wilderness, etc. And soon enough you will be filled with happiness instead of sorrow and bitterness.[87]

The doctor thus urged Maggie to focus on what she could do, the strength she had, instead of fretting and feeling bitter. Her father had appealed to her sense of duty, work ethic, and respect for her privileged position in society. Ljungdahl entreated her to bring out the 'true' Maggie, the one that was 'very much alive'.[88] Like Joseph, he also highlighted duty and the work incumbent on her at Ålshult, the part of the Huseby Estate she had become heir to. There, he emphasized, she was in a position to create jobs and promote the arts. And that in fact was what she did. Despite only living at Ålshult for the last few years of her life, her 24 years as its owner proved very successful. From her sickbed, she gave her stewards instructions on everything from what timber prices she was prepared to accept to which horse should be covered.[89] A degree of micromanagement that can cause subordinates to rebel, but which evidently worked, perhaps because she was a woman and because it was balanced with trust in her employees.[90] Joseph Stephens had also had a tendency to micromanage. He had given detailed directions to his wife when he was away on Riksdag business, and Elisabeth meticulously reported the orders she had given to their workers at Huseby. Trust in those employees, on the other hand, had been a rarer commodity.[91]

Ålshult was a smaller and initially much more modest house than those of her elder sisters, and the sense of having been unfairly treated never left Maggie. It was a constant source of resentment, but she did manage to develop the estate and increase its value over the rest of her lifetime, and while she rarely lived at Ålshult, its development proved a force for good in her life.

Joseph Stephens had set off for India, alone, at the age of 18. He had not been entirely abandoned to the world, his sister and brother-in-law were there, but all the same he had been no more than a teenager when he started to build the fortune that would form the basis for the rest of his life and that of his daughters. This was something he stressed in a letter to Maggie in 1912:

> Remember your father who, at the age of 19, had to leave his home, parents, friends, and civilized surroundings, in order—quite alone for years in the jungles[92] of India, without so much as one European for company, often for several months at a time—to do his duty and make a future for himself[93]

It is remarkable that Joseph referred to India in this letter. It shows how anxious he was to make Maggie take his advice. Half a century after his stay in the country, his daughters were unable to relate to his experiences. Neither he nor anyone else mentioned them. A few birthday greetings from his son-in-law Gunnar Liepe are exceptions. Here he congratulates Joseph for being in such good health 'in spite of 10 years stay in India's unhealthy climate'.[94] Experiences that must have been of decisive importance for Joseph had been reduced to exoticism and India represented as a dangerous place, only meant to survive.

Joseph had been the architect of his own fortune. For him, moreover, happiness as an emotional state was something we choose and are able to create. During his betrothal, he wrote to Elisabeth, concerning happiness, that its basis lay in 'contentment', in being happy and satisfied with what we have: 'We have it in our own hands to bestow upon ourselfes and only too often refuse to do so'.[95] This was an ability Maggie lacked, according to Joseph, and he may have been right, at least when she was young. But Joseph himself, was it something he possessed? Can someone have the career he had and be a contented person by nature? Not just in his youth in India, but also as the owner of the Huseby Estate, and active in that capacity until his death in his 93rd year? Nor does a capacity for contentment go hand in hand with the other ideals he highlighted, namely the importance of doing one's duty and the joy of being useful, themes he constantly returned to in his letters to Maggie—despite her having neither work nor any other duties to perform. This was an outlook on life which Joseph Stephens was brought up on and which his father continued to inculcate in him in his letters to him during his time in India. It remained with him for the rest of his life, and was something Joseph also expressed in his letters to Elisabeth, when they had known each other for just a few months and were soon to marry: 'the Gratification of feeling that one has done ones duty to our God, our fellow men and ourselves is in my mind greater than all the so called amusements of people in general.'[96] The letters to Elisabeth had an instructive tone; however, Joseph never referred to his experiences from India. India is only mentioned once in all their correspondence. On a train on his way for parliamentary work in Stockholm, Joseph related meeting six Hindu men. They had talked with each other and Joseph had asked what brought them to Sweden. They had explained that they had come to do good. Joseph asked, 'In what way'? Their answer referred to religion. Joseph explained to Elisabeth that 'all were of a very low caste, which I could determine from their appearance'.[97] No further reflections on this meeting were made in the letter.

Joseph Stephens set great store by work and duty, but did not provide his daughters with the tools to live a life where these things were in focus: neither education nor access to the fortune which would sooner or later be theirs. In acting the way he did, he was of course the product of a culture and a society that did not give women the same chances as men. But he could have chosen another path, and so too could his daughters. The laws, rules, and culture of the nineteenth and the early twentieth centuries restricted the scope women had to shape their own lives, but that did not mean that opportunities for power, education, and independence were non-existent for them. Maggie Stephens, however, was not among those who obviously made use of those opportunities, and we can only speculate on why that was. Whether explicit or not, the sisters' background, which combined Joseph's mix of English and Danish middleclass origin and many years in India with Elisabeth's birth into high society, made it difficult to find a place for them in the Swedish society. They were not really at home anywhere. Clearly, Maggie's mental and physical afflictions, which were particularly accentuated in the years after her parents' deaths, played a major part in her life, but we can also note that until Joseph died, when the sisters were all over the age of 50, they were not given access to funds that would have enabled them to shape their own lives. At the same time, they knew that a very large inheritance awaited them, leaving them with little incentive to create something of their own. This was in stark contrast to their father, who as a mere teenager had set off for another continent in search of a livelihood not only for himself but also for his parents and his sisters.

Personality is another determining factor in a person's life. Although Maggie lacked some of the character traits and abilities which Joseph would have wished to see in her—resignation to God's will, gratitude at her lot in life, an ability to do good and fulfil her duty—she had a strength and a tenacity that made an impression on people. Maggie remained unmarried. Whether that was an active choice, a decision she made about her own future, or a cause of sorrow to her is not entirely easy to say. The surviving correspondence shows that she had a number of romantic liaisons. They tended to be with married men, and it was she who set the terms for them. When the man in question no longer paid her sufficient attention, or someone else could pay her more, she ended the relationship. This perhaps suggests that she thought like her father: if you do not need to be provided for, you do not need a husband either.

Maggie's life was more than her illnesses, and the fortune she left behind was very large, much larger than the one she had inherited. Perhaps Joseph, worrying back in the 1910s about her lack of zest for life and urging her not to let the life she had been given go to waste, would have been amazed to learn what she would one day achieve. Maybe he would have realized that she was more like him than anyone else in the family. Concealed beneath her ill health and weariness with life was a strong desire for independence. After her death, a dispute arose over her estate. Her sisters objected to her having bequeathed the lion's share of her wealth to her doctor. In response, the lawyer representing the main beneficiary claimed: 'She considered herself unfairly treated by her father compared with her sisters and strongly emphasized that she had created Ålshult herself and that no one else had anything to do with it.'[98] Maggie's view had been that she was free to leave her property to whoever she wanted, as she had been a good steward of and increased her inheritance from her father, and that was what she did. Ironically, precisely as Jean Jacques De Geer had argued that Joseph had been free to do what he liked with his fortune made in India—although, unlike her, he had waived that right and left everything to his daughters.

Notes

1 Lars-Olof Larsson, 'Det borgerliga Huseby', in Margareta Petersson (ed.), *Det levande Huseby—en värld i världen* (Växjö: Historiska föreningen i Kronobergs län, 2018), pp. 74–84.

2 Joseph Stephens' paternal grandfather, John, first worked in the mining industry and later became a minister. His son, George, became a professor. Margareta Petersson, 'Joseph Stephens—familjen och arkivet', in Margareta Petersson (ed.), *Från Brittiska Indien till Huseby bruk: Järnvägen som arena för modernitet och kolonialism under lycksökaren och järnvägsentreprenören Joseph Stephens tid i Indien 1860–1869* (Lund: Arkiv förlag, 2018), pp. 19–20. Three of George's brothers went to Australia in the 1830s, with varying success. Margareta Petersson, 'Drömmen om Eldorado', in Petersson (ed.), *Från Brittiska Indien*, pp. 168–75. The family in which Joseph Stephens grew up is defined by Margareta Petersson as 'upper middle class'. Margareta Petersson, 'A Danish Family in India: Gendered Colonial Upbringing, Everyday Life, and Cultural Encounters', in Kristina Myrvold and Soniya Billore (eds), *India: Research on Cultural Encounters and Representations at Linnaeus University* (Gothenburg; Stockholm: Makadam, 2017), p. 76.

3 One indication that they belonged to the higher stratum of society was that all three sisters were presented at court. Larsson, 'Det borgerliga Huseby', p. 120.

4 For an analysis of how changes in early nineteenth century laws improved women's rights, especially regarding property, see Maria Ågren, *Domestic Secrets: Women & Property in Sweden, 1600–1857* (Chapel Hill: University of North Carolina Press, 2009), p. 170–175.

5 Petersson, 'A Danish Family', p. 78.

6 Larsson, 'Det borgerliga Huseby', p. 118.

7 Linnaeus University (LNU), Huseby Archives (HA), Joseph Stephens Archive (JSA), E1:7, Letter from Blanche, 13 December 1885 (original in English).

8 Margareta Petersson, 'Möten över gränser', in Margareta Petersson (ed.), *Det levande Huseby—en värld i världen* (Växjö: Historiska föreningen i Kronobergs län, 2018), p. 43 (original quotation in Swedish).

9 LNU, HA, JSA, E1:3b, Letter from George, 14 August 1888 (this and other letters from George quoted here were written in English).

10 Ibid.

11 Ibid., Letter from George, 3 September 1893.

12 Ibid.

13 Ibid.

14 George's interest in his grandchildren's education may have been a product of his own childhood in a Methodist setting, where there was 'great enthusiasm for upbringing and education'. Petersson, 'Joseph Stephens—familjen och arkivet', p. 20.

15 Eva-Lis Bjurman, *Catrines intressanta blekhet: Unga kvinnors möten med de nya kärlekskraven 1750–1830* (Eslöv: Brutus Östlings Bokförlag Symposion, 1998), p. 209.

16 LNU, HA, JSA, E1:3b, Letter from George, 3 September 1893.

17 LNU, HA, Elisabeth Stephens Archive (ESA), E1:2, Letter from Joseph, 4 November 1894. Larsson, 'Det borgerliga Huseby', p. 118.

18 Larsson, 'Det borgerliga Huseby', p. 118. Examples of the often strained relations between governesses and the children's mother are also cited in Eva-Helen Ulvros, *Fruar och mamseller: Kvinnor inom sydsvensk borgerlighet 1790–1870* (Lund: Historiska Media, 1996), p. 243.

19 LNU, HA, JSA, E1:2, Letter from Elisabeth, 20 March 1894.

20 LNU, HA, ESA, E1:2, Letter from Joseph, 6 November 1894 (translated from Swedish; except where otherwise indicated, all letters from Joseph, Elisabeth,

and their daughters quoted here were written in Swedish and quotations from them have been translated).

21 Ibid., Letter from Joseph, 7 November 1894.

22 LNU, HA, JSA, E1:2, Letter from Elisabeth, 5 November 1894.

23 From 1842 the law required all children to be provided with basic education in the parish in which they lived. This education was the same for boys and girls. There had been a school at Huseby since the 1830s, and Joseph Stephens himself paid for the building of one that was opened the year he married, 1880. Ada Rydgård, *Ett år på Huseby: Kammarjungfrun berättar*, Kulturföreningen Memoria, 1999:7–8 (Växjö, 1999), p. 30.

24 Gunhild Kyle, 'Kvinnor och kunskap', in Gunhild Kyle (ed.), *Handbok i svensk kvinnohistoria* (Stockholm: Carlsson, 1987), p. 125.

25 The Graffman School in Växjö was set up in 1857. Wilhelm Sjöstrand, *Pedagogikens historia, III:2: Utvecklingen i Sverige under tiden 1809–1920* (Lund: Gleerup, 1965), p. 190.

26 Gunnar Richardson, *Svensk utbildningshistoria: Skola och samhälle förr och nu* (Lund: Studentlitteratur, 2010), p. 71 (quotation translated from Swedish).

27 Sjöstrand, *Pedagogikens historia*, p. 189.

28 Briefly, it can be said that the number of suitors in keeping with a woman's station was decreasing, at the same time as women were becoming less inclined to marry 'beneath their station'. Sten Carlsson, *Fröknar, mamseller, jungfrur och pigor: Ogifta kvinnor i det svenska ståndssamhället*, Acta Universitatis Upsaliensis, 90 (Uppsala: Uppsala University, 1977), p. 110.

29 Bjurman, *Catrines intressanta blekhet*, p. 196.

30 Her grades varied between 'rather weak' and 'very good'. LNU, HA, Maggie Stephens Archive (Maggie SA), B1:1.

31 LNU, HA, JSA, E1:4b, Letter from Maggie, 14 October 1900.

32 Ibid., Letter from Maggie, 21 December 1900.

33 Ibid., Letter from Maggie, 5 January 1901.

34 Ibid., Letter from Maggie, 14 October 1900.

35 When Joseph was occupied with Riksdag duties in the middle of the summer of 1905 because of the crisis over the union between Sweden and Norway, for example, he wrote to Elisabeth that 'Florence can surely take charge of the matter and conduct the necessary negotiations'. LNU, HA, ESA, E1:2, Letter from Joseph, 18 July 1905. A few days later he expressed the view that Florence should 'urge our people to calm down'. Ibid., Letter from Joseph, 22 July 1905.

36 In the period 1870–1920, 40 per cent of women were unmarried. Karin Johannisson, *Den mörka kontinenten: Kvinnan, medicinen och fin-de-siècle* (Stockholm: Norstedt, 1994), p. 87. In the towns, the proportion was even higher, at 50 per cent. Richardson, *Svensk utbildningshistoria*, p. 72.

37 See Sten Carlsson, *Ståndssamhälle och ståndspersoner 1700–1865: Studier rörande det svenska ståndssamhällets upplösning* (Lund: Gleerup, 1973), pp. 44–8.

38 One of her closest friends, Louise De Geer, did not marry until she was 37 and had her first and only child when she was 39.

39 The Stephens sisters belonged to a class of society known before the dissolution of the system of estates in 1860 as 'commoners of rank' (*ofrälse ståndspersoner*). It included academics and estate owners, and the growing number of daughters of this group found it difficult to marry according to their station. Carlsson, *Fröknar, mamseller*, p. 57.

40 LNU, HA, ESA, E1:2, Letter from Joseph, 11 May 1906.

41 Maggie inherited 100,000 kronor on her mother's death, and was able to use the annual income from this sum. Erik Wångmar, *Husebyfröken: En studie om Florence Stephens 1881–1979* (Malmö: Égalité, 2020), p. 72.

42 See, for example, the letters from Maggie to Mary of 6 January and 2 June 1912. LNU, HA, Mary Stephens Archive (Mary SA), E1:2.
43 Peter Koch Archive (PKA), Letter from Joseph to Maggie, 10 March 1912.
44 LNU, HA, JSA, E1:4b, Letter from Maggie, 13 March 1912.
45 Ibid., 28 March 1912.
46 PKA, Letter from Joseph to Maggie, 12 April 1912.
47 Ibid.
48 LNU, HA, Mary SA, E1:1, Letter from Joseph, 18 November 1912.
49 Karin Johannisson, *Kroppens tunna skal: Sex essäer om kropp, historia och kultur* (Stockholm: Norstedt, 1997), p. 174.
50 Johannisson, *Den mörka kontinenten*, p. 229.
51 LNU, HA, Mary SA, E1:1, Letter from Joseph, 16 September 1913.
52 LNU, HA, JSA, E1:4b, Letter from Maggie, 18 May 1913.
53 LNU, HA, Mary SA, E1:1, Letter from Joseph, 10 June 1913.
54 PKA, Letter from Joseph to Maggie, 18 June 1913.
55 LNU, HA, Mary SA, E1:2, Letter from Maggie, 21 June 1913.
56 LNU, HA, JSA, E1:4a, Letter from Mary, 23 June 1913.
57 Ibid., 30 June 1913. The condition was probably appendicitis. The case history that was attached to the record of the hearing relating to her will states that she 'Underwent appendicectomy in 1913'. Swedish National Archives (RA), Vadstena landsarkiv (VLA), Mellersta Värends domsaga (MVD), Akter i tvistemål (Records of civil cases), 1958 (translated from Swedish).
58 LNU, HA, JSA, E1:4a, Letter from Mary, 19 August 1913.
59 LNU, HA, Maggie SA, E1:1, Letter from Joseph, 22 October 1913.
60 LNU, HA, JSA, E1:4b, Letter from Maggie, 25 October 1913. 1,500 kronor was a considerable sum. From letters to Elisabeth it emerges that, eight years earlier, an agricultural contract worker (*statare*) received a cash wage of 200 kronor per year, in addition to grain and lodging, and a driver 300 kronor. LNU, HA, ESA, E1:2, Letters from Joseph, 22 July and 18 August 1905.
61 Referring to the nineteenth century, Gunnel Cederlöf writes that 'the medical effects of opium were often claimed to surpass the harmful effects of the drug', and goes on to say that it was considered to depend on the moral stature of an individual whether or not its use degenerated into abuse. Gunnel Cederlöf, 'Poor Man's Crop: Evading Opium Monopoly', *Modern Asia Studies*, 53/2 (2018), p. 13.
62 LNU, HA, Maggie SA, E1:2, Letter from Elisabeth, 30 May 1902.
63 Ibid., E1:3 Letter from Mary, 9 September 1905.
64 LNU, HA, Mary SA, E1:2, Letter from Joseph, 6 November 1914.
65 Johannisson, *Den mörka kontinenten*, p. 74.
66 PKA, Letter from Joseph to Maggie, 22 December 1913.
67 Törngren, Pehr Henrik, 'Westerlund, Ernst Otto Theodor', in Torsten Dahl and Nils Bohman (eds.), *Svenska män och kvinnor: Biografisk uppslagsbok*, 8 (Stockholm: Bonnier, 1955), p. 293.
68 LNU, HA, JSA, E1:4a, Letter from Mary, 9 November 1912.
69 PKA, Letter from Joseph to Maggie, 22 December 1913.
70 LNU, HA, JSA, E1:4b, Letter from Maggie, 25 December 1913.
71 Ibid., E1:4a. Letter from Mary. The letter is undated, but from the context it is clear that it was written in February 1914.
72 LNU, HA, Mary SA, E1:1, Letter from Joseph, 25 February 1914.
73 LNU, HA, Maggie SA, E1:3, Letter from Mary, 5 March 1914.
74 LNU, HA, Mary SA, E1:1, Letter from Joseph, 7 May 1914.
75 LNU, HA, JSA, E1:4b, Letters from Maggie, 1 and 12 June 1914.
76 LNU, HA, Mary SA, E1:2, Letter from Maggie, 14 December 1914.
77 Ibid., Letter from Maggie, 13 February 1915.

78 PKA, Letter from Joseph to Maggie, 4 October 1915.
79 LNU, HA, Mary SA, E1:2, Letter from Maggie, 10 January 1916.
80 Johannisson, *Den mörka kontinenten*, pp. 87 and 90.
81 Anna-Karin Frih, *Flickan i medicinen: Ungdom, kön och sjuklighet 1870–1930*, Örebro Studies in History, 8 (Örebro: Örebro universitetsbibliotek, 2007), pp. 179–87.
82 RA, VLA, MVD, Skriftligt svaromål nr 2. I mål T 26/58 (Written defence no. 2 in case T 26/58). Florence's share was valued at over 1.2 million, Mary's at 1,081,600, and Maggie's at 1,054,700 kronor.
83 PKA, Letter from Jean Jacques De Geer to Maggie, 12 July 1934 (translated from Swedish).
84 Ibid.
85 In Swedish law, children cannot be disinherited. In the absence of a will, the estate is divided equally between the issue of the deceased. Through a will, one child, or some other person, may be favoured, but a child is always entitled to his or her statutory share, i.e. half of what they would have received if there had not been a will. The rest can be bequeathed to others. It is also possible to give funds away before death.
86 LNU, HA, Maggie SA, E1:12, Letter from Maggie to Ove Vind, 26 November 1934.
87 Ibid., E1:8, Letter from Professor Malte Ljungdahl, 20 February 1938 (translated from Swedish).
88 Ibid., Letter from Professor Malte Ljungdahl, 5 June 1938 (translated from Swedish).
89 PKA, Letters from her steward August Johansson during the years 1934 and 1935.
90 Her good relation with her employees was pointed out in obituaries. See, for example, Carl Leuhusen, 'Maggie Stephens död', *Smålandsposten*, 10 March 1958 (Växjö, 1958).
91 For clear examples, see the correspondence between Elisabeth and Joseph in the summer of 1905.
92 The word 'jungle' did not refer to jungle as a habitat, but to environments in foreign parts associated with danger and disorder. Petersson, 'A Danish Family', p. 84.
93 PKA, Letter from Joseph to Maggie, 10 March 1912.
94 Translated from Swedish. LNU, HA, JSA, EI:9 Letter from Gunnar Liepe, 12 July 1917, see also letters dated 11 July 1916 and 12 July 1920.
95 Larsson, 'Det borgerliga Huseby', p. 97 (original letter in English).
96 LNU, HA, ESA, E1:2, Letter from Joseph, 23 September 1880 (original in English).
97 LNU, HA, ESA, EI:2, Letter from Joseph, 14 July 1905.
98 RA, VLA, MVD, Akter i tvistemål, Skriftligt svaromål från advokat Åke Wettermark (Written defence from the lawyer Åke Wettermark, translated from Swedish).

References

Ågren, Maria, *Domestic Secrets: Women & Property in Sweden, 1600–1857* (Chapel Hill: University of North Carolina Press, 2009).

Bjurman, Eva-Lis, *Catrines intressanta blekhet: Unga kvinnors möten med de nya kärlekskraven 1750–1830* (Eslöv: Brutus Östlings Bokförlag Symposion, 1998).

Carlsson, Sten, *Fröknar, mamseller, jungfrur och pigor: Ogifta kvinnor i det svenska ståndssamhället*, Acta Universitatis Upsaliensis, 90 (Uppsala: Uppsala University, 1977).

Carlsson, Sten, *Ståndssamhälle och ståndspersoner 1700–1865: Studier rörande det svenska ståndssamhällets upplösning* (Lund: Gleerup, 1973).
Cederlöf, Gunnel, 'Poor Man's Crop: Evading Opium Monopoly', *Modern Asia Studies*, 53/2 (2018), pp. 1–27.
Frih, Anna-Karin, *Flickan i medicinen: Ungdom, kön och sjuklighet 1870–1930*, Örebro Studies in History, 8 (Örebro: Örebro universitets bibliotek, 2007).
Johannisson, Karin, *Den mörka kontinenten: Kvinnan, medicinen och fin-de-siècle* (Stockholm: Norstedt, 1994).
Johannisson, Karin, *Kroppens tunna skal: Sex essäer om kropp, historia och kultur* (Stockholm: Norstedt, 1997).
Kyle, Gunhild, 'Kvinnor och kunskap', in Gunhild Kyle (ed.), *Handbok i svensk kvinnohistoria* (Stockholm: Carlsson, 1987), pp. 111–36.
Larsson, Lars-Olof, 'Det borgerliga Huseby', in Margareta Petersson (ed.), *Det levande Huseby—en värld i världen* (Växjö: Historiska föreningen i Kronobergs län, 2018), pp. 63–123.
Leuhusen, Carl, 'Maggie Stephens död', *Smålandsposten*, 10 March 1958 (Växjö, 1958), p. 7.
Petersson, Margareta, 'A Danish Family in India: Gendered Colonial Upbringing, Everyday Life, and Cultural Encounters', in Kristina Myrvold and Soniya Billore (eds), *India: Research on Cultural Encounters and Representations at Linnaeus University* (Gothenburg; Stockholm: Makadam, 2017), pp. 74–99.
Petersson, Margareta, 'Drömmen om Eldorado', in Margareta Petersson (ed.), *Från Brittiska Indien till Huseby bruk: Järnvägen som arena för modernitet och kolonialism under lycksökaren och järnvägsentreprenören Joseph Stephens tid i Indien 1860–1869* (Lund: Arkiv Förlag, 2018), pp. 167–96.
Petersson, Margareta, 'Joseph Stephens—familjen och arkivet', in Margareta Petersson (ed.), *Från Brittiska Indien till Huseby bruk: Järnvägen som arena för modernitet och kolonialism under lycksökaren och järnvägsentreprenören Joseph Stephens tid i Indien 1860–1869* (Lund: Arkiv Förlag, 2018), pp. 15–44.
Petersson, Margareta, 'Möten över gränser', in Margareta Petersson (ed.), *Det levande Huseby—en värld i världen* (Växjö: Historiska föreningen i Kronobergs län, 2018), pp. 32–62.
Richardson, Gunnar, *Svensk utbildningshistoria: Skola och samhälle förr och nu* (Lund: Studentlitteratur, 2010).
Rydgård, Ada, *Ett år på Huseby: Kammarjungfrun berättar* (Växjö: Kulturföreningen Memoria, 1999).
Sjöstrand, Wilhelm, *Pedagogikens Historia, III: 2. Utvecklingen i Sverige under tiden 1809–1920* (Lund: Gleerup, 1965).
Törngren, Pehr Henrik, 'Westerlund, Ernst Otto Theodor', in Torsten Dahl and Nils Bohman (eds.), *Svenska män och kvinnor: Biografisk uppslagsbok*, 8 (Stockholm: Bonnier, 1955), pp. 293–4.
Ulvros, Eva-Helen, *Fruar och mamseller: Kvinnor inom sydsvensk borgerlighet 1790–1870* (Lund: Historiska Media, 1996).
Wångmar, Erik, *Husebyfröken: En studie om Florence Stephens 1881–1979* (Malmö: Égalité, 2020).

Bibliography

Account of Roorkee College, Established for the Instruction of Civil Engineers, With a Scheme for Its Enlargement (Agra: Secundra Orphan Press, 1851).

Ågren, Maria, *Domestic Secrets: Women & Property in Sweden, 1600–1857* (Chapel Hill: University of North Carolina Press, 2009).

Ahuja, Ravi, 'A Freedom Still Enmeshed in Servitude: The Unruly "Lascars" of the SS City of Manila or, a Micro-History of the "Free Labour" Problem', in Ravi Ahuja (ed.), *Working Lives and Worker Militancy: The Politics of Labour in Colonial India* (New Delhi: Tulika Books, 2013), pp. 97–133.

Ahuja, Ravi, 'Labour Relations in an Early Colonial Context: Madras, c. 1750–1800', *Modern Asian Studies*, 36/4 (2002), pp. 793–826.

Ahuja, Ravi, 'Labour Unsettled: Mobility and Protest in the Madras Region, 1750–1800', *Indian Economic & Social History Review*, 35/4 (1998), pp. 381–404.

Ahuja, Ravi, *Pathways of Empire: Circulation, Public Works and Social Space in Colonial Orissa, c. 1780–1914* (Hyderabad: Orient Blackswan, 2009).

Ahuja, Ravi, 'The Origins of Colonial Labour Policy in Late Eighteenth-Century Madras', *International Review of Social History*, 44/2 (1999), pp. 159–95.

Allen, Robert C., 'India in the Great Divergence', in T. H. Hatton, K. H. O'Rourke, and A. M. Taylor (eds), *The New Comparative Economic History: Essays in Honour of Jeffrey G. Williamson* (Cambridge: MIT Press, 2007), pp. 9–32.

Allen, Robert C., 'Real Wages in Europe and Asia: A First Look at the Long-Term Patterns', Robert C Allen, Tommy Bengtsson, and Martin Dribe (eds), *Living Standards in the Past: New Perspectives on Well-Being in Asia and Europe* (New York: Oxford University Press, 2005), pp. 111–30.

Allen, Robert C., and Roman Studer, 'Prices and Wages in India, 1595–1930', 12 September 2009, gpih.ucdavis.edu/files/India_Allen-Studer_v2,pl.xls, accessed 18 October 2016.

Anderson, M. R., 'Work Construed: Ideological Origins of Labour Law in British India to 1918', in Peter Robb (ed.), *Dalit Movements and the Meanings of Labour in India* (New Delhi: Oxford University Press, 1999), pp. 87–120.

Aspengren, Henrik Chetan, 'Bombay—möjligheternas stad', in Margareta Petersson (ed.), *Från Brittiska Indien till Huseby bruk: Järnvägen som arena för modernitet och kolonialism under lycksökaren och järnvägsentreprenören Joseph Stephens tid i Indien 1860–69* (Lund: Arkiv Förlag, 2018), pp. 45–64.

Avango, Dag, Louwrens Hacquebord, and Urban Wråkberg, 'Industrial Extraction of Arctic Natural Resources Since the Sixteenth Century: Technoscience and Geo-Economics in the History of Northern Whaling and Mining', *Journal of Historical Geography*, 44 (2014), pp. 15–30.

Bagchi, Amiya Kumar, *Capital and Labour Redefined: India and the Third Worlds* (London: Anthem Press, 2002).

Bagchi, Amiya Kumar, *Colonialism and Indian Economy* (New Delhi: Oxford University Press, 2010).

Baker, David E. U., *Colonialism in an Indian Hinterland: The Central Provinces, 1820–1920* (New Delhi: Oxford University Press, 1998).

Baker, T., *Railway Engineering; or, Field Work Preparatory to the Construction of Railways* (London: Spottiswoode and Shaw, 1848).

Banaji, Jairus, 'Capitalist Domination and the Small Peasantry: The Deccan Districts in the Late Nineteenth Century', in J. Banaji (ed.), *Theory as History: Essays on Modes of Production and Exploitation* (Leiden; Boston: Brill Press, 2010), pp. 277–332.

Banaji, Jairus, 'The Fictions of Free Labour: Contract, Coercion, and So-Called Unfree Labour', *Historical Materialism*, 11/3 (2003), pp. 69–95.

Banaji, Jairus, *Theory as History: Essays on Modes of Production and Exploitation* (Leiden; Boston: Brill Press, 2010).

Bates, Crispin, 'Class and Economic Change in Central India: The Narmada Valley 1820–1930', in Clive Dewey (ed.), *Arrested Development in India: The Historical Dimension* (New Delhi: Manohar, 1988), pp. 241–82.

Bayly, Christopher, *The Birth of the Modern World 1780–1914: Global Connections and Comparisons* (Oxford: Blackwell, 2004).

Bear, Laura, 'An Economy of Suffering: Addressing the Violence of Discipline in Railway Workers' Petitions to the Agent of the Eastern Indian Railway, 1930–47', in S. Pierce and A. Rao (eds), *Discipline and the Other Body: Correction, Corporeality, Colonialism* (London: Duke University Press, 2006).

Bear, Laura, *Lines of the Nation: Indian Railway Workers, Bureaucracy, and the Intimate Historical Self* (Columbia: Columbia University Press, 2007).

Behal, Rana P., *One Hundred Years of Servitude: Political Economy of Tea Plantations in Colonial Assam* (New Delhi: Tulika Books, 2014).

Beijbom, Ulf, *Amerika, Amerika: en bok om utvandringen* (Stockholm: Natur och Kultur, 1977).

Beijbom, Ulf, 'Från utvandrar- till invandrarlän', in Lennart Johansson (ed.), *Landen kring sjöarna: En historia om Kronobergs län i mångtusenårigt perspektiv; Kronobergsboken 1999–2000* (Växjö: Kronobergs läns hembygdsförbund/Smålands Museum, 1999), pp. 365–90.

Berglund, Bengt, *Järn i Småland: Forskningsläge, utgångspunkter och övergripande resultat*, Småländsk järnhantering under 1000 år, 1, Jernkontorets bergshistoriska skriftserie, 34 (Stockholm: Jernkontoret, 2000).

Berglund, Bengt, Per-Olof Grönberg, and Tomas Nilson (eds), *Historiska perspektiv på tekniköverföring 1800–2000* (Gothenburg: Department of History of Technology and Industry, Chalmers University of Technology, 2006).

Beverley, Eric Lewis, *Hyderabad, British India, and the World: Muslim Networks and Minor Sovereignty, c. 1850–1950* (Cambridge: Cambridge University Press, 2015).

Bhambi, Rita P., *The Great Indian Peninsula Railway: A Journey Through Time (1853–1871)* (New Delhi: Bharti Publications, 2016).

Bhattacharya, Neeladri, 'Lineages of Capital', *Historical Materialism*, 21/4 (2014), pp. 11–35.

Bhattacharya, Sabyasachi, *The Colonial State: Theory and Practice* (New Delhi: Primus, 2016).

Bhattacharya, Sabyasachi, *The Financial Foundation of the British Raj: Ideas and Interests in the Reconstruction of Indian Public Finance 1858–1872* (New Delhi: Orient Longman, 2005 [1971]).
Birla, Ritu, *Stages of Capital: Law, Culture and Market Governance in Late Colonial India* (Durham; London: Duke University Press, 2009).
Bjørn, C., 'Fra reaktion til grundlov', in Olaf Olsen (ed.), *Gyldendal og Politikens Danmarkshistorie* (Copenhagen: Gyldendalske boghandel Politikens Forlag, 1988).
Bjurman, Eva-Lis, *Catrines intressanta blekhet: Unga kvinnors möten med de nya kärlekskraven 1750–1830* (Eslöv: Brutus Östlings Bokförlag Symposion, 1998).
Bose, Sugata, and Ayesha Jalal, *Modern South Asia: History, Culture, Political Economy* (London; New York: Routledge, 1998).
Bourdieu, Pierre, *Distinction: A Social Critique of the Judgement of Taste*, trans. Richard Nice (Cambridge: Harvard University Press, 1996 [1984]).
Brandis, Dietrich, 'Memorandum on the Supply of Railway Sleepers of the Himalayan Pines Impregnated in India', *Indian Forester*, 4 (1879).
Brees, S. C., *The Illustrated Glossary of Practical Architecture and Civil Engineering: Comprising the Theory and Modern Practice, with the Subjects of Office & Field Work, the Steam Engine, Mechanical Engineering, Surveying, Levelling, & Use of Instruments, Mining and Quarrying, Manufacture of Iron, Bricks, Lime, & Cements, CARPENTRY, Joinery, Bricklaying, and Masonry, Slating, Painting and Glazing, Building, etc.* (London: L.A. Lewis, 1853).
Bregnsbo, Michael, and Kurt Villads Jensen, *Det danske imperium: Storhed og fald* (Viborg: Aschehoug Banks Forlag, 2005).
Breman, Jan, *Mobilising Labour for the Global Coffee Market: Profits From an Unfree Work Regime in Colonial Java* (Amsterdam: Amsterdam University Press, 2015).
Breman, Jan, *Outcast Labour in Asia: Circulation and Informalization of the Workforce at the Bottom of the Economy* (New Delhi: Oxford University Press, 2012).
Brenna, Brita, 'Clergymen Abiding in the Fields: The Making of the Naturalist Observer in Eighteenth-Century Norwegian Natural History', *Science in Context*, 24/2 (2011), pp. 143–66.
Brereton, R. M., *Reminiscences of an Old English Civil Engineer, 1858–1908* (Portland: Irwin Hodson Company, 1908).
Brincker, Benedikte, 'A "Small Great National State": An Analysis of the Cultural and Political Factors that Shaped Danish Nationalism 1760–1870', *Journal of Historical Sociology*, 16/4, December (2003), pp. 407–31.
Bringéus, Nils-Arvid, 'Gunnar Olof Hyltén-Cavallius', in *Svenskt biografiskt lexikon*, 19 (Stockholm: The Swedish National Archives, 1973), pp. 552–7.
Broadberry, Stephen, and Bishnupriya Gupta, 'Indian Economic Performance and Living Standards, 1600–2000', in Latika Chaudhary, Bishnupriya Gupta, Tirthankar Roy, and Anand V. Swamy (eds), *A New Economic History of Colonial India* (New York: Routledge, 2016), pp. 15–32.
Broadberry, Stephen, Johann Custodis, and Bishnupriya Gupta, 'India and the Great Divergence: An Anglo-Indian Comparison of GDP Per Capita, 1600–1871', *Explorations in Economic History*, 55 (2015), pp. 58–75.
Bubb, Alexander, 'An Element of Risk: The Corrupt Contractor in Indian Fiction and Film, 1886–1983', *Cambridge Journal of Postcolonial Literary Inquiry*, 4/1 (2017), pp. 109–26, https://doi.org/10.1017/pli.2016.33.

Bubb, Alexander, 'Class, Cotton, and "Woddaries": A Scandinavian Railway Contractor in Western India, 1860–69', *Modern Asian Studies*, 51/5 (2017), pp. 1369–93, https://doi.org/10.1017/S0026749X16000251.

Carlquist, Jonas, and Andreas Tjerneld, 'Stephens, George', in *Svenskt biografiskt lexikon*, 33 (Stockholm: The Swedish National Archives, 2011), pp. 378–87.

Carlsson, Sten, 'Fröknar, mamseller, jungfrur och pigor: Ogifta kvinnor i det svenska ståndssamhället', *Acta Universitatis Upsaliensis*, 90 (1977).

Carlsson, Sten, *Ståndssamhälle och ståndspersoner 1700–1865: Studier rörande det svenska ståndssamhällets upplösning* (Lund: Gleerup, 1973).

Carr, William, and Harry Hearder, *The Wars of German Unification 1864–1871* (Boca Raton, FL: Taylor & Francis Group, 1991).

Casson, Mark, and Mary B. Rose, 'Institutions and the Evolution of Modern Business', *Business History*, 39/4 (1997), pp. 1–10.

Cedergreen Bech, Svend, *Dansk biografisk leksikon*, 3rd ed., 16 vols (København: Gyldendal, 1983).

Cederlöf, Gunnel, 'Huseby och det Brittiska imperiet', in Margareta Petersson (ed.), *Från Brittiska Indien till Huseby bruk: Järnvägen som arena för modernitet och kolonialism under lycksökaren och järnvägsentreprenören Joseph Stephens tid i Indien 1860–1869* (Lund: Arkiv Förlag, 2018), pp. 9–13.

Cederlöf, Gunnel, 'Poor Man's Crop: Evading Opium Monopoly', *Modern Asian Studies*, 53/2 (2018), pp. 1–27.

Chakrabarti, Shubhra, 'The English East India Company and the Indigenous Sloop Merchants of Bengal: Ankrur Dutta and his Family, 1757–1857', *Studies in History*, 20/1 (2004), pp. 131–57.

Chakrabarty, Dipesh, *Rethinking Working-Class History: Bengal, 1890–1940* (Princeton: Princeton University Press, 2000).

Chandavarkar, R., 'Industrialisation in India before 1947: Conventional Approaches and Alternative Perspectives', *Modern Asian Studies*, 19/3 (1985), pp. 623–68.

Chandler, Alfred D., Jr, *Scale and Scope: The Dynamics of Industrial Capitalism* (Cambridge: Harvard University Press, 2004 [1990]).

Chandra, Bipan, 'Economic Nationalism and the Railway Debate, Circa 1880–1905', in R. Srinivasan, M. Tiwari, and S. Silas (eds), *Our Indian Railway: Themes in India's Railway History* (New Delhi: Foundation Books, 2006), pp. 77–120.

Chari, Sharad, *Fraternal Capital: Peasant Workers, Self-Made Men, and Globalisation in Provincial India* (New Delhi: Permanent Black, 2004).

Chatterjee, Partha, *The Black Hole of Empire: History of a Global Practice of Power* (Princeton: Princeton University Press, 2012).

Chatterjee, Ramkrishna, 'Masters and Servants: Their Relations in Early Industries—A Case Study', *Proceedings of the Indian History Congress*, 41 (1980), pp. 585–92.

Chattopadhyay, Swati, and Bhaskar Sarkar, 'Introduction: The Subaltern and the Popular', *Postcolonial Studies*, 8/4 (2005), pp. 357–63.

Chaudhary, Latika, 'Caste, Colonialism and Schooling: Education in British India', in Latika Chaudhary, Bishnupriya Gupta, Tirthankar Roy, and Anand V. Swamy (eds), *A New Economic History of Colonial India* (New York: Routledge, 2016), pp. 161–78.

Chaudhary, Latika, Bishnupriya Gupta, Tirthankar Roy, and Anand V. Swamy (eds), *A New Economic History of Colonial India* (New York: Routledge, 2016).

Chaudhuri, Binay Bhushan, *Peasant History of Late Pre-colonial and Colonial India* (New Delhi: Pearson Longman, 2008).

Chittibabu, Kali, *Patterns of Labour Migrations in Colonial Andhra* (Cambridge: Cambridge Scholars Publishing, 2015).

Cleghorn, Hugh F. C., *The Forests and Gardens of South India* (London: W. H. Allen & Co., 1861).

Cohn, Bernard, *An Anthropologist Among the Historians and Other Essays* (New Delhi: Oxford University Press, 1990).

Connell, Carol Matheson, 'Jardine Matheson & Company: The Role of External Organisation in a Nineteenth-Century Trading Firm', *Enterprise & Society*, 4/1 (2003), pp. 99–138.

Deakin, Simon and Frank Wilkinson, *The Law of the Labour Market: Industrialization, Employment, and Legal Evolution* (Oxford: Oxford University Press, 2005).

Derbyshire, Ian, 'The Building of India's Railway: The Application of Western Technology in the Colonial Periphery 1850–1920', in Ian J. Kerr (ed.), *Railways in Modern India* (New Delhi: Oxford University Press, 2005), pp. 268–304.

Dhar, Bidisha, 'Mapping Artisan Labour in Lucknow, c. 1860s–1940s', in Sabyasachi Bhattacharya and Rana P. Behal (eds), *The Vernacularisation of Labour Politics* (New Delhi: Tulika Books, 2016), pp. 212–51.

Dillard, Dudley, *Västeuropas och Förenta staternas ekonomiska historia* (Malmö: Liber, 1993).

Divekar, V. D., 'Regional Economy (1757–1857): Western India', in Dharma Kumar and Meghnad Desai (eds), *The Cambridge Economic History of India*, 2 (Cambridge: Cambridge University Press, 2008 [1989]), pp. 332–55.

Douglas, Paul H., 'The Cobb—Douglas Production Function Once Again: Its History, Its Testing, and Some New Empirical Values', *Journal of Political Economy*, 84/5 (1976), pp. 903–16.

Dovring, Folke, *Land and Labor in Europe, 1900–1950: A Comparative Survey of Recent Agrarian History, with a chapter on land reform as a propaganda theme by Karin Dovring* (The Hague: Nijhoff, 1965).

Drayton, Richard, and David Motadel, 'Discussion: The Futures of Global History', *Journal of Global History*, 13/1 (2018), pp. 1–21.

Elkins, Caroline, and Susan Pedersen, 'Introduction: Settler Colonialism; A Concept and Its Uses', in C. Elkins and S. Pedersen (eds), *Settler Colonialism in the Twentieth Century: Projects, Practices, Legacies* (London and New York: Routledge, 2005).

Eneflo, Kerstin, and Joan Ramón Rosés, 'Coping With Regional Inequality in Sweden: Structural Change, Migrations, and Policy, 1860–2000', *Economic History Review*, 68/1 (2015), pp. 191–217.

Fischer-Tiné, Harald, 'Hierarchies of Punishment in Colonial India: European Convicts and the Racial Dividend, c. 1860–1890', in Harald Fischer-Tiné and Susanne Gehrmann (eds), *Empires and Boundaries: Rethinking Race, Class, and Gender in Colonial Settings* (New York: Routledge, 2009), pp. 41–65.

Fischer-Tiné, Harald, *Low and Licentious Europeans: Race, Class and 'White Subalternity' in Colonial India*, New Perspectives in South Asian History (New Delhi: Orient Blackswan, 2009).

Fischer-Tiné, Harald, 'The Other Side of Internationalism: Switzerland as a Hub of Militant Anti-Colonialism, c. 1910–1920', in P. Purtschert and H. Fischer-Tiné (eds), *Colonial Switzerland: Rethinking Switzerland From the Margins* (Basingstoke: Palgrave Macmillan, 2014), pp. 221–58.

Flanders, Judith, *A Circle of Sisters: Alice Kipling, Georgiana Burne-Jones, Agnes Poynter and Louisa Baldwin* (London: Penguin Viking, 2001).

Flygare, Iréne A., and Mats Isacson, 'The Tension Between Modernity and Reality 1945–2010', in Mats Morell and Janken Myrdal (eds), *The Agrarian History of Sweden: From 4000 BC to AD 2000* (Lund: Nordic Academic Press, 2011).

Foucault, Michel, *Discipline and Punish: The Birth of the Prison* (London: Vintage, 1995).

Frih, Anna-Karin, *Flickan i medicinen: Ungdom, kön och sjuklighet 1870–1930*, Örebro Studies in History, 8 (Örebro: Örebro universitets bibliotek, 2007).

Fukazawa, H., 'Agrarian Relations: Western India', in Dharma Kumar and Meghnad Desai (eds), *The Cambridge Economic History of India* (Cambridge: Cambridge University Press, 2008 [1989]), pp. 177–207.

Gadd, Carl-Johan, *Det svenska jordbrukets historia*, 3: *Den agrara revolutionen 1700–1870* (Stockholm: Natur och kultur/LT, 2000).

Gadd, Carl-Johan, 'The Agricultural Revolution in Sweden 1700–1870', in Mats Morell and Janken Myrdal (eds), *The Agrarian History of Sweden: From 4000 BC to AD 2000* (Lund: Nordic Academic Press, 2011).

Gadgil, Madhav, and Ramachandra Guha, *This Fissured Land: An Ecological History of India* (New Delhi; New York: Oxford University Press, 1992).

Goswami, O., 'Sahibs, Babus and Banias: Changes in Industrial Control in Eastern India', in Rajat K. Ray (ed.), *Entrepreneurship and Industry in India, 1800–1947* (New Delhi: Oxford, 1993), pp. 233–56.

Guha, Sumit, *Environment and Ethnicity in India, 1200–1991*, Cambridge Studies in Indian History and Society, 4 (New York: Cambridge University Press, 1999).

Guha, Sumit, *Health and Population in South Asia: From Earliest Times to the Present* (New Delhi: Permanent Black, 2001).

Guha, Sumit, *The Agrarian Economy of Bombay Deccan* (New Delhi: Oxford University Press, 1985).

Gunnarsson, Ingemar, *En skandinavisk järnvägskontraktörs karriär i Indien 1860–1867: Ackumulering av socialt och kulturellt kapital som framgångsstrategi i en kolonial kontext*, LNU Licentiate No. 31, Department of Cultural Sciences, Linnaeus University, Sweden (Växjö: Linnaeus University Press, 2020).

Gunnarsson, Ingemar, 'Från lärling till "ingenjör"', in Margareta Petersson (ed.), *Från Brittiska Indien till Huseby bruk: Järnvägen som arena för modernitet och kolonialism under lycksökaren och järnvägsentreprenören Joseph Stephens tid i Indien 1860–69* (Lund: Arkiv Förlag, 2018), pp. 65–82.

Gunnarsson, Ingemar, '"Karlshamn—Wislanda Jernväg": Maktelit och nätverk i Karlshamns stad vid banans tillblivelse 1855–1874', unpublished MA dissertation, School of Humanities, Växjö University, 2003.

Gupta, Bishnupriya, 'Falling Behind and Catching Up: India's Transition From a Colonial Economy', *Economic History Review*, 72/3 (2019), pp. 803–27.

Gupta, Bishnupriya, 'The Rise of Modern Industry in Colonial India', in Latika Chaudhary, Bishnupriya Gupta, Tirthankar Roy, and Anand V. Swamy (eds), *New Economic History of Colonial India* (New York: Routledge, 2016), pp. 67–83.

Hall, Catherine, *Civilising Subjects: Metropole and Colony in the English Imagination 1830–1867* (Chicago: University of Chicago Press, 2002).

Hall, Catherine, 'Epilogue: Imperial Careering at Home; Harriet Martineau on Empire', in David Lambert and Allan Lester (eds), *Colonial Lives Across Empire:*

Imperial Careering in the Long Nineteenth Century (Cambridge; New York: Cambridge University Press, 2006), pp. 335–59.

Hansson, Staffan, 'Tekniken som samhällsomdanare: Exemplet Norrbottens teknologiska megasystem', in Eva Landberg, Karin Rönnbäck, and Per Moritz (eds), *Norrbotten: Årsbok 2007* (Luleå: Norrbottens hembygdsförbund, 2007), pp. 26–41.

Harnow, Henrik, *Den danske ingeniørs historie 1850–1920: Danske ingenrørers uddannelse, professionalisering og betydning for den danske moderniseringsproces* (Århus: Systime, 1998).

Harriss-White, Barbara, *India Working: Essays on Society and Economy* (Cambridge: Cambridge University Press, 2003).

Haslett, Charles, and Charles W. Hackley, *The Mechanic's, Machinist's, and Engineer's Practical Book of Reference: Adapted to and for the Use of All Classes of Practical Mechanics, Together With the Engineer's Field Book: With a Collection of Valuable Recipes* (London: Trübner and Co., 1855).

Heston, A., 'National Income', in Dharma Kumar and Meghnad Desai (eds), *The Cambridge Economic History of India*, 2 (Cambridge: Cambridge University Press, 2008 [1989]), pp. 376–462.

Hofmeester, Karin, and Pim de Zwart (eds), *Colonialism, Institutional Change, and Shifts in Global Labour Relations* (Amsterdam: Amsterdam University Press, 2018).

Högberg, Staffan, 'Bondelandet i Sverige', in Birgitta Furuhagen (ed.), *Äventyret Sverige: En ekonomisk och social historia* (Stockholm: Utbildningsradion, 1993).

Horwitz, Morton J., *The Transformation of American Law* (Cambridge: Harvard University Press, 1977).

Hyslop, Jonathan, 'Making Scotland in South Africa: Charles Murray, the Transvaal's Aberdeenshire Poet', in David Lambert and Alan Lester (eds), *Colonial Lives Across the British Empire: Imperial Careering in the Long Nineteenth Century* (Cambridge: Cambridge University Press, 2006), pp. 309–34.

Johannisson, Karin, *Den mörka kontinenten: Kvinnan, medicinen och fin-de-siècle* (Stockholm: Norstedt, 1994).

Johannisson, Karin, *Kroppens tunna skal: Sex essäer om kropp, historia och kultur* (Stockholm: Norstedt, 1997).

Jörberg, Lennart, 'Structural Change and Economic Growth: Sweden in the 19th Century', *Economy and History*, 8/1 (1965), pp. 3–46.

Joshi, Chitra, 'Dak Roads, Dak Runners, and the Reordering of Communication Networks', *International Review of Social History*, 57/2 (2012), pp. 169–89.

Joshi, Chitra, 'Fettered Bodies: Labouring on Public Work in Nineteenth-Century India', in Marcel van der Linden and Prabhu P. Mohapatra (eds), *Labour Matters: Towards Global Histories* (New Delhi: Tulika Books, 2009), pp. 3–21.

Joshi, Chitra, *Lost Worlds: Indian Labour and Its Forgotten Histories* (New Delhi: Permanent Black, 2005).

Kardell, Lars, *Svenskarna och skogen*, 2: *Från baggböleri till naturvård* (Jönköping: Skogsstyrelsens Förlag, 2004).

Kerr, Ian J., *Building the Railways of the Raj, 1850–1900* (New Delhi; New York: Oxford University Press, 1995).

Kerr, Ian J., *Engines of Change: The Railroads that Made India* (Westport: Praeger, 2007).

Kerr, Ian J., 'Labour Control and Labour Legislation in Colonial India: A Tale of Two Mid-Nineteenth Century Acts', *South Asia: Journal of South Asian Studies*, 27/1 (2004), pp. 7–25.

Kerr, Ian J., 'On the Move: Circulating Labor in Pre-Colonial, Colonial, and Post-Colonial India', *International Review of Social History*, 51/S14 (2006), pp. 85–109.

Kerr, Ian J. (ed.), *Railways in Modern India* (New Delhi: Oxford University Press, 2001).

Kerr, Ian J., 'The Dark Side of the Force: Mistakes, Mismanagement and Malfeasance in the Early Railways of the British Indian Empire', in R. Srinivasan, M. Tiwari, and S. Silas (eds), *Our Indian Railway: Themes in India's Railway History* (New Delhi: Foundation Books, 2006).

Kerr, Ian J., 'Working Class Protest in 19th Century India: Example of Railway Workers', *Economic and Political Weekly*, 20/4 (1985), pp. PE34–40.

Khosla, G. S., *Railway Management in India* (Bombay: Thacker & Co. Ltd., 1972).

Kling, Blair B., *Partner in Empire: Dwarkanath Tagore and the Age of Enterprise in Eastern India* (Berkeley: University of California Press, 1976).

Krantz, Olle, 'Järnbruket som blev glasbruk: Ägarskap, tillverkning, konkurrens', in Kerstin Wickman, Hans Cogne, Gunnel Holmér, and Denise Grünstein (eds), *Orrefors: Glasbrukets Historia 1898–1998* (Stockholm: Byggförlaget-Kultur, 1998).

Krishnan, Radhika, 'Constructing the Indian Railways: Locating Perception and Self-perception in "Native" Responses', in M. Petersson (ed.), *Huseby in the World* (Lund: Arkiv Academic Press, 2018), pp. 113–34.

Krishnan, Radhika, 'Contracting and Sub-contracting in British India: Exploring the Dynamics of Railway Building through Joseph Stephens', in K. Myrvold and S. Billore (eds), *India: Research on Cultural Encounters and Representations at Linnaeus University* (Gothenburg: Makadam, 2017), pp. 50–73.

Kuisma, Markku, 'Industrial Expansion', in E. I. Kouri and Jens E. Olesen (eds), *The Cambridge History of Scandinavia, Volume II, 1520–1870* (Cambridge: Cambridge University Press, 2016).

Kumar, Arun, 'Colonial Requirements and Engineering Education: The Public Works Department, 1847–1947', in Roy M. Macleod and Deepak Kumar (eds), *Technology and the Raj: Western Technology and Technical Transfers to India, 1700–1947* (New Delhi; Thousand Oaks: SAGE, 1995), pp. 216–32.

Kværndrup, Sigurd, and Boel Lindberg, 'Inledning', in Gunilla Byrman (ed.), *En värld för sig själv: Nya studier i medeltida ballader*, Ord & Musik & Bild: Intermediala Studier 1 (Växjö: Växjö University Press, 2008), pp. 11–27.

Kyle, Gunhild, 'Kvinnor och kunskap', in Gunhild Kyle (ed.), *Handbok i svensk kvinnohistoria* (Stockholm: Carlsson, 1987), pp. 111–36.

Lambert, David, and Alan Lester, 'Introduction: Imperial Spaces, Imperial Subjects', in Lambert and Alan Lester (eds), *Colonial Lives across the British Empire: Imperial Careering in the Long Nineteenth Century* (Cambridge: Cambridge University Press 2006), pp. 1–31.

Larsson, Lars J., *Värendsbygd: Tolv socknar blev Alvesta* (Alvesta: Alvesta kulturnämnd, 1991).

Larsson, Lars-Olof, 'Det borgerliga Huseby', in Margareta Petersson (ed.), *Det levande Huseby—En värld i världen* (Växjö: Historiska föreningen i Kronobergs län, 2018), pp. 63–123.

Larsson, Lars-Olof, *Det fantastiska Huseby: En rundvandring i tid och rum* (Växjö: Domänverket/Huseby bruk, 1993).

Larsson, Lars-Olof, *Historia kring Huseby* (Grimslöv: Skatelövs Hembygdsförening, 1978).

Larsson, Lars-Olof, 'Historia kring Huseby: Epoken Stephens', in *Skatelövskrönika 1978* (Grimslöv: Skatelövs hembygdsförening, 1978).

Larsson, Lars-Olof, *Historia om Småland* (Växjö: Diploma, 1974).

Larsson, Lars-Olof, 'Hur Stephens kom till Huseby', in *Skatelövskrönika 1986* (Grimslöv: Skatelövs hembygdsförening, 1986).

Larsson, Lars-Olof, 'Land och län under kristendomens millennium', in Lennart Johansson (ed.), *Landen kring sjöarna: En historia om Kronobergs län i mångtusenårigt perspektiv; Kronobergsboken 1999–2000* (Växjö: Kronobergs läns hembygdsförbund/Smålands Museum, 1999).

Larsson, Lars-Olof, *Länsstyrelsen och Kronobergs län under 350 år*, Historiska föreningens i Kronobergs län skriftserie, 4 (Växjö: Länsstyrelsen i Kronobergs län, 1984).

Larsson, Lars-Olof, 'Skogstillgång, skogsprodukter och sågar i Kronobergs län', in Olof Nordström, Lars J. Larsson, John Käll, and Lars-Olof Larsson (eds), *Skogen och smålänningen: Kring skogsmarkens roll i förindustriell tid* (Växjö: Historiska föreningen i Kronobergs län, 1989).

Larsson, Lars-Olof, 'Studier kring järnhantering i södra Småland fram till det industriella genombrottet', in Lars-Olof Larsson and Leif Rubensson (eds), *Från blästbruk till bruksdöd*, Jernkontorets bergshistoriska skriftserie (Jönköping: Järnkontoret, 2000), pp. 11–252.

Larsson, Lars-Olof, *Växjö genom 1000 år* (Stockholm: Norstedt, 1991).

Larsson, Lars-Olof, Margareta Petersson, Åke Svensson, and Erik Wångmar, *Det levande Huseby—En värld i världen* (Växjö: Historiska föreningen i Kronobergs län, 2018).

Larsson, Lars-Olof, Sven-Olof Olsson, Josef Rydén, and Stig Tornehed, *Småländska strövtåg genom fem sekler* (Växjö: Diploma, 1976).

Lassen, Aksel, 'The Population of Denmark, 1660–1960', *Scandinavian Economic History Review*, 14/2 (1966), pp. 134–57.

Lee, Robert (ed.), *Commerce and Culture: Nineteenth-Century Business Elites* (New York: Routledge, 2016).

Leuhusen, Carl, 'Maggie Stephens död', *Smålandsposten*, 10 March 1958 (Växjö, 1958), p. 7.

Lewin, Leif, *Ideologi och strategi: Svensk politik under 130 år* (Stockholm: Carlssons, 2017).

Linden, Marcel van der, Karl Heinz Roth, and Max Henninger (eds), *Beyond Marx* (Leiden; Boston: Brill, 2014).

Ljungberg, Jonas, and Lennart Schön, 'Domestic Markets and International Integration: Paths to Industrialisation in the Nordic Countries', *Scandinavian Economic History Review*, 61/2 (2013), pp. 101–21.

Lucassen, Jan, 'The Brickmakers' Strikes on the Ganges Canal in 1848–1849', in Rana P. Behal and Marcel van der Linden (eds), *India's Labouring Poor: Historical Studies, c. 1600–2000* (Cambridge: Cambridge University Press; New Delhi: Foundation Books, 2007), pp. 47–84.

Lucassen, Jan, 'Working at the Ichapur Gunpowder Factory in the 1790s, Part I', *Indian Historical Review*, 39/1 (2012), pp. 19–56.

Lucassen, Jan, 'Working at the Ichapur Gunpowder Factory in the 1790s, Part II', *Indian Historical Review*, 39/2 (2012), pp. 252–71.

Lucassen, Jan, and Pim de Zwart, 'Poverty or Prosperity in Bengal c.1700–1875? New Evidence, Methods and Perspectives', paper presented at *11th AILH International Conference on Labour History*, 21–23 March 2016.

Macpherson, W. P., 'Investment in Indian Railways: 1845–1875', *The Economic History Review*, New Series, 8/2 (1955), pp. 177–86.

Magnusson, Lars, *An Economic History of Sweden*, Routledge Explorations in Economic History (London; New York: Routledge, 2000).

Maine, Henry Sumner, *Ancient Law* (London: Murray, 1861).

Makko, Aryo, 'I imperialismens kölvatten? Ett maritimt perspektiv på stormaktsspelet, kolonialism utan kolonier och den svensk-norska konsulsstaten, 1875–1905', *Historisk Tidskrift* (Sweden), 134/3 (2014), pp. 499–523.

Mantena, Karuna, *Alibis of Empire: Henry Maine and the Ends of Liberal Imperialism* (Princeton: Princeton University Press, 2010).

Markovits, Claude, *Merchants, Traders and Entrepreneurs: Indian Business in the Colonial Era* (London: Palgrave Macmillan, 2008).

Marsden, Ben, and Crosbie Smith, *Engineering Empires: A Cultural History of Technology in Nineteenth-Century Britain* (Basingstoke: Palgrave Macmillan, 2005).

Marx, Karl, *Capital, I: The Process of Production of Capital* (London: Penguin Books, 1976 [1867]).

Marx, Karl, *Capital: A Critique of Political Economy*, I, trans. Ben Fowkes (London: Vintage, 1977).

McAlpin, Michelle Burge, 'The Effects of Expansion of Markets on Rural Income Distribution in Nineteenth Century India', *Explorations in Economic History*, 12 (1975), pp. 289–302.

McLaren, Martha, *British India and British Scotland, 1780–1830: Career Building, Empire Building, and a Scottish School of Thought on Indian* Governance (Akron: University of Akron Press, 2001).

Meyer, William Stevenson, Richard Burn, James Sutherland Cotton, and Herbert Hope Risley, *The Imperial Gazetteer of India* (Oxford: Clarendon Press, 1908).

Mies, Maria, *Patriarchy and Accumulation on a World Scale* (London: Zed Books, 2014 [1986]).

Misra, Maria, '"Business Culture" and Entrepreneurship in British India, 1860–1950', *Modern Asian Studies*, 34/2 (2000), pp. 333–48.

Misra, Maria, *Business, Race, and Politics in British India 1850/1960* (New York: Oxford University Press, 1999).

Moberg, Vilhelm, *The Emigrants: A Novel* (New York: Simon and Schuster, 1951).

Moberg, Vilhelm, *Utvandrarna* (Stockholm: Bonniers Förlag, 1949).

Mohaptra, Prabhu, 'From Contract to Status? Or How Law Shaped Labour Relations in Colonial India, 1780–1880', in Jan Breman, Isabelle Guerin, and Assem Prakash (eds), *India's Unfree Workforce: Of Bondage Old and New* (New Delhi: Oxford University Press, 2009), pp. 96–125.

Mohapatra, Prabhu, 'Regulated Informality: Legal Constructions of Labour Relations in Colonial India, 1814–1926', in Sabyasachi Bhattacharya and Jan Lucassen (eds), *Workers in the Informal Sector: Studies in Labour History, 1800–2000* (New Delhi: Macmillan India Limited, 2005).

Möller, Tommy, *Svensk politisk historia: Strid och samverkan under tvåhundra år* (Lund: Studentlitteratur, 2007).

Morell, Mats, *Det svenska jordbrukets historia*, 4: *Jordbruket i industrisamhället, 1870–1945* (Stockholm: Natur och kultur/LT, 2001).

Morell, Mats, Carl-Johan Gadd, and Janken Myrdal, 'Statistical Appendix', in Mats Morell and Janken Myrdal (eds), *The Agrarian History of Sweden: From 4000 BC to AD 2000* (Lund: Nordic Academic Press, 2011).

Naum, Magdalena, and Jonas M. Nordin, 'Introduction: Situating Scandinavian Colonialism', in Magdalena Naum and Jonas M. Nordin (eds), *Scandinavian Colonialism and the Rise of Modernity: Small Time Agents in a Global Arena* (New York: Springer, 2013), pp. 3–16.

Nelson, A. E., *Central Provinces District Gazetteers, Akola District, Volume B, Statistical Tables (1891–1907)* (Nagpur: Government Press, 1909).

Nilsson, Torbjörn, *Elitens svängrum: Första kammaren, staten och moderniseringen 1867–1886* (PhD thesis) (Stockholm: Almqvist & Wiksell International, 1994).

Nilsson, Torbjörn, *Mellan arv och utopi: Moderata vägval under hundra år, 1904–2004* (Stockholm: Santérus, 2004).

Nite, Dhiraj Kumar, 'En lycksökares liv och affärer i Indien och Skandinavien', in Margareta Petersson (ed.), *Från Brittiska Indien till Huseby bruk: Järnvägen som arena för modernitet och kolonialism under lycksökaren och järnvägsentreprenören Joseph Stephens tid i Indien 1860–69* (Lund: Arkiv Förlag, 2018), pp. 135–65.

Nite, Dhiraj Kumar, 'Reproduction Preferences and Wages: The Jharia Coalfield, 1895–1970', *Studies in History*, 30/1 (2014), pp. 55–87.

Norberg, Anders, and Andreas Tjerneld, *Tvåkammarriksdagen 1867–1970: Ledamöter och valkretsar*, 2: *Östergötlands län, Jönköpings län, Kronobergs län, Kalmar län, Gotlands län, Hallands län* (Stockholm: Almqvist & Wiksell International/Riksdagen, 1985).

Nordström, Olof, 'Förteckning över glasbruk och hyttor i Sverige 1150–2000', *Glasteknisk tidskrift*, 54/3 (1999), pp. 77–84.

Nordström, Olof, 'Skog och skogsmark som försörjningskälla', in Olof Nordström, Lars J. Larsson, John Käll, and Lars-Olof Larsson (eds), *Skogen och smålänningen: Kring skogsmarkens roll i förindustriell tid* (Växjö: Historiska föreningen i Kronobergs län, 1989).

Nyman, Olle, *Tvåkammarsystemets omvandling: Från privilegierätt till demokrati, Samhälle och riksdag: Historisk och statsvetenskaplig framställning*, D III (ed. Arthur Thomson) (Stockholm: Almqvist & Wiksell, 1966).

O'Hanlon, Rosalind, *Caste, Conflict, and Ideology: Mahatma Jotirao Phule and Low Caste Protest in Nineteenth-Century Western India* (Cambridge: Cambridge University Press, 2002 [1985]).

Østermark-Johansen, Lene, 'Reading Clubs, Language Societies and Female Education in Fin-de-Siècle Copenhagen', *Forum for Modern Language Studies*, 53/3 (2017), pp. 274–90.

Östlund, Joachim, 'The Swedish Consulate in Tripoli and Information Gathering on Diplomacy, Everyday Life, and the Slave Trade, 1795–1844', in Mika Suonpää and Owen Wright (eds), *Diplomacy and Intelligence in the Nineteenth-Century Mediterranean World* (London: Bloomsbury Academic, 2019), pp. 17–36.

Parthasarathi, Prasannan, 'The Poonamalle Insurrection of 1796', in Sabyasachi Bhattacharya and Rana P. Behal (eds), *The Vernacularisation of Labour Politics* (New Delhi: Tulika Books, 2016), pp. 133–45.

Parthasarathi, Prasannan, *The Transition to a Colonial Economy: Weavers, Merchants and Kings in South India, 1720–1800* (Cambridge: Cambridge University Press, 2008).

Parthasarathi, Prasannan, *Why Europe Grew Rich and Asia Did Not: Global Economic Divergence, 1600–1850* (Cambridge: Cambridge University Press, 2011).

Petersson, Margareta, 'A Danish Family in India: Gendered Colonial Upbringing, Everyday Life, and Cultural Encounters', in Kristina Myrvold and Soniya Billore (eds), *India: Research on Cultural Encounters and Representations at Linnaeus University* (Gothenburg; Stockholm: Makadam, 2017), pp. 74–99.

Petersson, Margareta (ed.), *Det levande Huseby—En värld i världen* (Växjö: Historiska föreningen i Kronobergs län, 2018).

Petersson, Margareta, 'Drömmen om Eldorado', in Margareta Petersson (ed.), *Från Brittiska Indien till Huseby bruk: Järnvägen som arena för modernitet och kolonialism under lycksökaren och järnvägsentreprenören Joseph Stephens tid i Indien 1860–69* (Lund: Arkiv Förlag, 2018), pp. 167–96.

Petersson, Margareta, 'Joseph Stephens—Familjen och arkivet', in Margareta Petersson (ed.), *Från Brittiska Indien till Huseby bruk: Järnvägen som arena för modernitet och kolonialism under lycksökaren och järnvägsentreprenören Joseph Stephens tid i Indien 1860–69* (Lund: Arkiv Förlag, 2018), pp. 15–43.

Petersson, Margareta, 'Möten över gränser', in Margareta Petersson (ed.), *Det levande Huseby—En värld i världen* (Växjö: Historiska föreningen i Kronobergs län, 2018), pp. 32–62.

Phule, Jyotirao, *Brahman Teachers in the Education Department, Satyadipika* (Pune, June 1869).

Piatt Andrew, Abram, 'Indian Currency Problems', *Quarterly Journal of Economics*, 15/4 (1901), pp. 483–516.

Purtschert, Patricia, Francesca Falk, and Barbara Lüthi, 'Switzerland and "Colonialism without Colonies": Reflections on the Status of Colonial Outsiders', *Interventions*, 18/2 (2016), pp. 286–302.

Purtschert, Patricia, and Harald Fischer-Tiné, 'Introduction: The End of Innocence; Debating Colonialism in Switzerland', in P. Purtschert and H. Fischer-Tiné (eds), *Colonial Switzerland: Rethinking Colonialism From the Margins* (Basingstoke: Palgrave Macmillan, 2015), pp. 1–25.

Rajan, S. Ravi, *Modernizing Nature: Forestry and Imperial Eco-Development 1800–1950*, Oxford Historical Monographs (Oxford; New York: Clarendon Press, Oxford University Press, 2006).

Rangarajan, Mahesh, *Fencing the Forest: Conservation and Ecological Change in India's Central Provinces, 1860–1914*, Studies in Social Ecology and Environmental History (New Delhi: Oxford University Press, 1996).

Rao, Saraswathy, *The Railway Board: A Study in Administration* (New Delhi: S. Chand & Company Ltd., 1978).

Ricardo, David, *On the Principles of Political Economy and Taxation* (London: John Murray, 1975 [1821]).

Richardson, Gunnar, *Svensk utbildningshistoria: Skola och samhälle förr och nu* (Lund: Studentlitteratur, 2010).

Robb, Peter (ed.), *Dalit Movements and the Meanings of Labour in India* (New Delhi: Oxford University Press, 1999).

Rosenbalck, Niclas, 'Förteckning över Husebyarkiven vid Linnéuniversitetet, Växjö', unpublished catalogue, LNU Library (PDF, 245 pp.), Växjö, 2010.

Roy, T., 'Indigo and Law in Colonial India', *Economic History Review*, 64 (SI, 2011), pp. 60–75.

Roy, T., and Anand V. Swamy, *Law and the Economy in Colonial India* (Chicago; London: University of Chicago Press, 2016).

Roy, Tirthankar, *A Business History of India: Enterprise and the Emergence of Capitalism From 1700* (Cambridge: Cambridge University Press, 2018).
Roy, Tirthankar, *Company of Kinsmen: Enterprise and Community in South Asian History 1700–1940* (New Delhi: Oxford University Press, 2010).
Roy, Tirthankar, 'Consumption of Cotton Cloth in India, 1795–1940', *Australian Economic History Review*, 52/1 (2011), pp. 3–35.
Roy, Tirthankar, 'The Growth of a Labour Market in the Twentieth Century', in Latika Chaudhary, Bishnupriya Gupta, Tirthankar Roy, and Anand V. Swamy (eds), *A New Economic History of Colonial India* (New York: Routledge, 2016), pp. 179–94.
Roy, Tirthankar, and Anand V. Swamy, *Law and the Economy in Colonial India* (Chicago: University of Chicago Press, 2016).
Runblom, Harald, and Hans Norman, *From Sweden to America: A History of the Migration*, Acta Universitatis Upsaliensis, Studia historica Upsaliensia, 74 (Minneapolis: University of Minnesota Press, 1976).
Rutten, Mario, and Carol Upadhya (eds), *Small Business Entrepreneurs in Asia and Europe: Towards a Comparative Perspective* (London: SAGE, 1997).
Rydgård, Ada, *Ett år på Huseby: Kammarjungfrun berättar* (Växjö: Kulturföreningen Memoria, 1999).
Said, Edward, *Orientalism* (London: Penguin, 2003).
Sarkar, Sumit, *Modern Times: India 1880s–1950s, Environment, Economy, Culture* (Ranikhet: Permanent Black, 2014).
Satya, Laxman D., *Cotton and Famine in Berar, 1850–1900* (New Delhi: Manohar, 1997).
Schön, Lennart, *En modern svensk ekonomisk historia: Tillväxt och omvandling under två sekel* (Stockholm: SNS Förlag, 2000).
Siddiqi, Asiya, *Bombay's People, 1860–1898: Insolvents in the City* (New Delhi: Oxford University Press, 2017).
Siddiqi, Z. M. S., 'Sanctions for the Breach of Contracts of Service (1843–1925)', *Journal of the Indian Law Institute*, 25/3 (1983), pp. 359–71.
Singha, Radhika, *A Despotism of Law: Crime and Justice in Early Colonial India* (New Delhi: Oxford University Press, 1998).
Singha, Radhika, *The Coolie's Great War: Indian Labour in a Global Conflict 1914–1921* (Noida: Harper Collins, 2020).
Sinha, Nitin, 'Contract, Work, and Resistance: Boatmen in Early Colonial Eastern India, 1760s–1850s', *International Review of Social History*, 59/S22 (2014), pp. 11–43.
Sinha, Nitin, '"Servant Problem" and the "Social-Subaltern" of Early Colonial Calcutta', in Nitin Sinha, Nitin Varma, and Pankaj Jha (eds), *Servants' Pasts: Sixteenth to Eighteenth Century South Asia*, 1 (Hyderabad: Orient Blackswan, 2019), pp. 311–44.
Sjöstrand, Wilhelm, *Pedagogikens historia, III: 2. Utvecklingen i Sverige under tiden 1809–1920* (Lund: Gleerup, 1965).
Sköld, Lars, and Arne Halvarson, *Riksdagens sociala sammansättning under hundra år, Samhälle och riksdag: Historisk och statsvetenskaplig framställning*, D 1 (ed. Arthur Thomson) (Stockholm: Almqvist & Wiksell, 1966).
Song, Daniel, 'From Status to Contract (and Back?): A Historiography of Contract Law and the Transition to Capitalism', *Ex Post Facto*, XXII/Spring (2013), pp. 127–38.

Stanley, Amy Dru, *From Bondage to Contract Wage Labor, Marriage, and the Market in the Age of Slave Emancipation* (Cambridge: Cambridge University Press, 1998).

Steiner, Henriette, *The Emergence of a Modern City: Golden Age Copenhagen 1800–1850* (Burlington: Ashgate Publishing Company, 2014).

Steinfeld, Robert J., *Coercion, Contract, and Free Labor in the Nineteenth Century* (Cambridge: Cambridge University Press, 2001).

Stjernquist, Nils, *Tvåkammartiden: Sveriges riksdag 1867–1970* (Stockholm: Sveriges Riksdag, 1996).

Stokes, Eric, *The English Utilitarians and India* (New Delhi: Oxford University Press, 1959).

Stoler, Ann Laura, 'Cultivating Bourgeois Bodies and Racial Selves', in C. Hall (ed.), *Cultures of Empire, a Reader: Colonizers in Britain and the Empire in the Nineteenth and Twentieth Centuries* (Manchester: Manchester University Press, 2000), pp. 87–119.

Subramanian, Ajantha, *The Caste of Merit: Engineering Education in India* (Cambridge: Harvard University Press, 2019).

Subramanian, Lakshmi, *Three Merchants of Bombay: Business Pioneers of the Nineteenth Century* (London: Portfolio, 2016).

Svanberg, Ingvar, 'The Use of Wild Plants as Food in Pre-industrial Sweden', *Acta Societatis Botanicorum Poloniae*, 81/4 (2012), https://doi.org/10.5586/asbp.2012.039.

Törngren, Pehr Henrik, 'Westerlund, Ernst Otto Theodor', in Torsten Dahl and Nils Bohman (eds.), *Svenska män och kvinnor: Biografisk uppslagsbok*, 8 (Stockholm: Bonnier, 1955), pp. 293–4.

Svensson, Åke, *George Stephens: Forskare, samlare, publicist, debattör* (Växjö: Sanct Sigfrids Gille, 2010).

Swamy, Anand V., 'Law and Contract Enforcement in Colonial India', in Latika Chaudhary, Bishnupriya Gupta, Tirthankar Roy, and Anand V. Swamy (eds), *A New Economic History of Colonial India* (New York: Routledge, 2016), pp. 218–32.

Sweeney, Stuart, *Financing India's Imperial Railways, 1875–1914* (London: Routledge, 2016).

Thomasson, Fredrik, 'Den karibiska skorpionen: Om digitaliseringen av det svenska Saint Barthélemy arkivet i Aix-en-Provence', *Historisk Tidskrift*, 138/1 (2018), pp. 78–90.

Thompson, E. P., 'Time, Work-Discipline, and Industrial Capitalism', *Past and Present*, 38 (1967), pp. 56–97.

Thorner, Daniel, 'Capital Movement and Transportation: Great Britain and the Development of India's Railways', *Journal of Economic History*, 11/4 (1951), pp. 389–402.

Thorner, Daniel, 'The Pattern of Railway Development in India', in Ian Kerr (ed.), *Railways in Modern India* (New Delhi: Oxford University Press, 2001).

Tigar, Michael E., and Madeleine R. Levy, *Law and the Rise of Capitalism* (New York: Monthly Review Press, 2000).

Timberg, Thomas A., *The Marwaris: From Jagat Seth to the Birlas* (London: Penguin Books, 2014 (1978)).

The Times of India, *The 'Times of India' Calendar & Directory, Abridged Edition* (Bombay: The 'Times of India' Office; London: G. Street, 30, Cornhill, 1868).

Tinker, Hugh, *A New System of Slavery: The Export of Indian Labour Overseas 1830–1920* (London: Hansib, 1993).

Torstendahl, Rolf, *Engineers in Western Europe: Ascent—and Decline? A Profession Torn Between Technology and Economy, 1850–1990, with Outlooks to the Present* (Berlin; Heidelberg: Springer-Verlag, 2021).

Tripathi, Dwijendra, and Jyoti Jumani, *The Concise Oxford History of Indian Business* (New Delhi: Oxford University Press, 2007).

Ulvros, Eva-Helen, *Fruar och mamseller: Kvinnor inom sydsvensk borgerlighet 1790–1870* (Lund: Historiska Media, 1996).

Varma, Nitin, *Coolies of Capitalism: Assam Tea and the Making of Coolie Labour* (Berlin: De Gruyter, 2017).

Wångmar, Erik, 'Brukspatronen som blev omyndig', in Margareta Petersson (ed.), *Det levande Huseby—En värld i världen* (Växjö: Historiska föreningen i Kronobergs län, 2018), pp. 124–132.

Wångmar, Erik, *Husebyfröken: En studie om Florence Stephens 1881–1979* (Malmö: Égalité, 2020).

Wångmar, Erik, 'Lurifaxarnas framfart—Husebyaffären 1956–1964', in Lennart Johansson, Roddy Nilsson, and Håkan Nordmark (eds), *Småländska brott* (Växjö: Historiska föreningen i Kronobergs län, 2010).

Wawn, Andrew, 'Stephens, George (1813–1895)', ONB, https://doi.org/10.1093/ref:odnb/26383 (accessed 1 December 2019).

Wawn, Andrew, *The Vikings and the Victorians: Inventing the Old North in Nineteenth-Century Britain* (Cambridge: D. S. Brewer, 2000).

Webb, Julian S., 'Contract, Capitalism and the Free Market: The Changing Face of Contractual Freedom', *Law Teacher*, 21/1 (1987), pp. 23–31.

Webster, Tony, 'An Early Global Business in a Colonial Context: The Strategies, Management and Failure of John Palmer and Company of Calcutta 1780–1830', *Enterprise and Society*, 6/1 (2005), pp. 98–13.

Vicziany, A. Marika, 'Bombay Merchants and Structural Changes in the Export Community 1850 to 1880', in K. N. Chaudhuri and Clive J. Dewey (eds), *Economy and History: Essays in Indian Economic and Social History* (New Delhi: OUP, 1979), pp. 163–96.

Vicziany, A. Marika, 'The Cotton Trade and the Commercial Development of Bombay, 1855–1875', unpublished PhD thesis, SOAS, University of London, 1975.

Wiking-Faria, Pablo, 'Freden, friköpen och järnplogarna: Drivkrafter och förändringsprocesser under den agrara revolutionen i Halland 1700–1900', PhD thesis, Department of Historical Studies, University of Gothenburg, 2009.

Williamson, Jeffrey, *Trade and Poverty: When the Third World Fell Behind* (Cambridge: MIT, 2011).

Zanden, Jan Luiten van, 'The Skill Premium and the "Great Divergence"', *European Review of Economic History*, 13/1 (2009), pp. 121–53.

Zanden, Jan Luiten van, Joerg Baten, Marco Mira d'Ercole, Auke Rijpma, Conal Smith, and Marcel Timmer, 'Global Well-Being Since 1820', in Jan Luiten van Zanden, Joerg Baten, Marco Mira d'Ercole, Auke Rijpma, Conal Smith, and Marcel Timmer (eds), *How Was Life? Global Well-Being Since 1820* (IISH: OECD, 2014).

Zwart, Pim de, *Globalisation and the Colonial Origins of the Great Divergence: Intercontinental Trade and Living Standards in the Dutch East India Company's Commercial Empire, c. 1600–1800* (Leiden: Brill Press, 2016).

Publications From Research Related to the Huseby Estate and Joseph Stephens Archives

Aspengren, Henrik Chetan, 'Bombay—Möjligheternas Stad', in Margareta Petersson (ed.), *Från brittiska Indien till Huseby Bruk: Järnvägen som arena för modernitet och kolonialism under lycksökaren och järnvägsentreprenören Joseph Stephens tid i Indien 1860–69* (Lund: Arkiv Förlag, 2018), pp. 45–64.

Aspengren, Henrik Chetan, 'Fact of the Matter: Statistical Counter-Representations in India 1860s–1880s', in Kristina Myrvold and Soniya Billore (eds), *India: Research on Cultural Encounters and Representations at Linnaeus University* (Gothenburg: Makadam, 2017), pp. 29–49.

Bubb, Alexander, 'An Element of Risk: The Corrupt Contractor in Indian Fiction and Film, 1886–1983', *Cambridge Journal of Postcolonial Literary Inquiry*, 4, no. 1 (2017), pp. 109–26.

Bubb, Alexander, 'Class, Cotton, and 'Woddaries': A Scandinavian Railway Contractor in Western India, 1860–69', *Modern Asian Studies*, 51, no. 5 (2017), pp. 1369–93.

Bubb, Alexander, 'Klass, bomull och "Woodaries"', in Margareta Petersson (ed.), *Från brittiska Indien till Huseby Bruk: Järnvägen som arena för modernitet och kolonialism under lycksökaren och järnvägsentreprenören Joseph Stephens tid i Indien 1860–69* (Lund: Arkiv Förlag, 2018).

Bubb, Alexander, 'Reading by Chance in a World of Wandering Texts', in Elleke Boehmer, Rouven Kunstmann, Priyasha Mukhopadhyay and Asha Rogers (eds), *The Global Histories of Books: Methods and Practices* (Basingstoke: Palgrave, 2017), pp. 73–96.

Cederlöf, Gunnel, 'Circular Migrations, Capital, and Opportunity: A Global History of Scandinavia and India at the Industrial Turn, an Introduction', in Gunnel Cederlöf (ed.), *The Imperial Underbelly: Workers, Contractors, and Entrepreneurs in Colonial India and Scandinavia* (New Delhi: Oxford University Press), Chapter 1.

Cederlöf, Gunnel, 'Huseby och det Brittiska imperiet', in Margareta Petersson (ed.), *Från brittiska Indien till Huseby Bruk: Järnvägen som arena för modernitet och kolonialism under lycksökaren och järnvägsentreprenören Joseph Stephens tid i Indien 1860–69* (Lund: Arkiv Förlag, 2018), pp. 9–13.

Cederlöf, Gunnel (ed.), *The Imperial Underbelly: Workers, Contractors, and Entrepreneurs in Colonial India and Scandinavia* (New Delhi: Oxford University Press).

Gunnarsson, Ingemar, *En skandinavisk järnvägskontraktörs karriär i Indien 1860–1867: Ackumulering av socialt och kulturellt kapital som framgångsstrategi i en kolonial kontext*, licentiate dissertation, Department of Cultural Sciences, Linnaeus University, Sweden (Växjö: Linnaeus University Press, 2020).

Gunnarsson, Ingemar, 'Från lärling till ingenjör', in Margareta Petersson (ed.), *Från Brittiska Indien till Huseby Bruk: Järnvägen som arena för modernitet och kolonialism under lycksökaren och järnvägsentreprenören Joseph Stephens tid i Indien 1860–69* (Lund: Arkiv Förlag, 2018), pp. 65–82.

Krishnan, Radhika, 'Bureaucracy and Ideologies of Control in British India: Social and Professional Networks and the "Contract System" in Railway Building', in Gunnel Cederlöf (ed.), *The Imperial Underbelly: Workers, Contractors, and Entrepreneurs in Colonial India and Scandinavia* (New Delhi: Oxford University Press), Chapter 2.

Krishnan, Radhika, 'Contracting and Sub-Contracting in British India: Exploring the Dynamics of Railway Building through Joseph Stephens', in Kristina Myrvold and Soniya Billore (eds), *India: Research on Cultural Encounters and Representations at Linnaeus University* (Gothenburg: Makadam, 2017), pp. 50–73.

Krishnan, Radhika, 'Järnvägsbygget ur arbetarnas perspektiv', in Margareta Petersson (ed.), *Från brittiska Indien till Huseby Bruk: Järnvägen som arena för modernitet och kolonialism under lycksökaren och järnvägsentreprenören Joseph Stephens tid i Indien 1860–69* (Lund: Arkiv Förlag, 2018), pp. 113–134.

Kumar, Arun, 'The Life of Contract Capitalism and the Building of the Colonial Railway', in Gunnel Cederlöf (ed.), *The Imperial Underbelly: Workers, Contractors, and Entrepreneurs in Colonial India and Scandinavia* (New Delhi: Oxford University Press), Chapter 3.

Lennartsson, Malin, 'Doing One's Duty, Making a Future: The Iron Master's Daughters and the Unceasing Project of Rearing a Family', in Gunnel Cederlöf (ed.), *The Imperial Underbelly: Workers, Contractors, and Entrepreneurs in Colonial India and Scandinavia* (New Delhi: Oxford University Press), Chapter 8.

Marcussen, Eleonor, 'Circulation of Knowledge, Capital, and Goods: Scandinavia and the British Empire', in Gunnel Cederlöf (ed.), *The Imperial Underbelly: Workers, Contractors, and Entrepreneurs in Colonial India and Scandinavia* (New Delhi: Oxford University Press), Chapter 6.

Nite, Dhiraj Kumar, 'Social Capital and Its Limits in Fortune Making: Joseph Stephens' Enterprises in India and Scandinavia, 1859–1869', in Gunnel Cederlöf (ed.), The *Imperial Underbelly: Workers, Contractors, and Entrepreneurs in Colonial India and Scandinavia* (New Delhi: Oxford University Press), Chapter 4.

Nite, Dhiraj Kumar, 'Archives, Being and Representation: Studies Into the Formation and Usage of Grassroots Archives', *Waseda Rilas Journal*, No. 6 (October 2018), pp. 575–577.

Nite, Dhiraj Kumar, 'Construction Workers, Remuneration and Welfare Levels: The Bombay-Nagpur Region During the 1860s', in Jan Lucassen, Najaf Haider, and Radhika Seshan (eds), *Work, Labour and Wage Earners in Medieval and Modern India* (New Delhi: SAGE, forthcoming).

Nite, Dhiraj Kumar, 'En Lycksökares Liv och Affärer i Indien och Skandinavien', in Margareta Petersson (ed.), *Från brittiska Indien till Huseby Bruk: Järnvägen som arena för modernitet och kolonialism under lycksökaren och järnvägsentreprenören Joseph Stephens tid i Indien 1860–69* (Lund: Arkiv Förlag, 2018), pp. 135–65.

Nite, Dhiraj Kumar, 'Labor, Wages, and Living Standards of Working People: Early Modern and Colonial India, 1600–1870', in Kristina Myrvold and Soniya Billore (eds) *India: Research on Cultural Encounters and Representations at Linnaeus University* (Gothenburg: Makadam, 2017), pp. 131–161.

Nite, Dhiraj Kumar, 'Labour Practices and Well-being: Construction Workers in the 1860s Western India', in Gunnel Cederlöf (ed.), The *Imperial Underbelly: Workers, Contractors, and Entrepreneurs in Colonial India and Scandinavia* (New Delhi: Oxford University Press), Chapter 5.

Petersson, Margareta, 'A Danish Family in India: Gendered Colonial Upbringing, Everyday Life, and Cultural Encounters', in Kristina Myrvold and Soniya Billore (eds), *India: Research on Cultural Encounters and Representations at Linnaeus University* (Gothenburg: Makadam, 2017), pp. 74–99.

Petersson, Margareta, *Det levande Huseby: En värld i världen*, ed. Margareta Petersson, Historiska föreningen i Kronobergs län 12, 2018, pp. 37–48.

Petersson, Margareta, 'Drömmen om Eldorado', in Margareta Petersson (ed.), *Från brittiska Indien till Huseby Bruk: Järnvägen som arena för modernitet och kolonialism under lycksökaren och järnvägsentreprenören Joseph Stephens tid i Indien 1860–69* (Lund: Arkiv Förlag, 2018), pp. 167–196.

Petersson, Margareta (ed.), *Från brittiska Indien till Huseby Bruk: Järnvägen som arena för modernitet och kolonialism under lycksökaren och järnvägsentreprenören Joseph Stephens tid i Indien 1860–69* (Lund: Arkiv Förlag, 2018).

Petersson, Margareta, 'Hem och hierarki i kolonial marginal', in Kristina Hermansson, Christian Lenemark and Cecilia Pettersson (eds), *Liv, lust & litteratur* (Gothenburg: Makadam Förlag, 2014), pp. 287–298.

Petersson, Margareta, 'Joseph Stephens: Familjen och arkivet', in Margareta Petersson (ed.), *Från brittiska Indien till Huseby Bruk: Järnvägen som arena för modernitet och kolonialism under lycksökaren och järnvägsentreprenören Joseph Stephens tid i Indien 1860–69* (Lund: Arkiv Förlag, 2018), pp. 135–65.

Petersson, Margareta, 'Joseph Stephens skapar en förmögenhet i brittiska Indien', in Lars-Olof Larsson (ed.), *Det levande Huseby: En värld i världen* (Växjö: Historiska föreningen i Kronobergs län, 2018), pp. 37–48.

Petersson, Margareta, *Koloniala drömmar, kärlek och kvinnoroller i Husebyarkiven* (Gothenburg: Makadam, 2021).

Wångmar, Erik, 'Brukspatronen som blev Omyndig', in Lars-Olof Larsson (ed.), *Det levande Huseby: En värld i världen* (Växjö: Historiska föreningen i Kronobergs län, 2018), pp. 124–32.

Wångmar, Erik, 'Colonial Entrepreneurial Capital in the Industrialization of Southern Sweden: The Huseby Estate under Joseph Stephens', in Gunnel Cederlöf (ed.), *The Imperial Underbelly: Workers, Contractors, and Entrepreneurs in Colonial India and Scandinavia* (New Delhi: Oxford University Press), Chapter 7.

Wångmar, Erik, *Husebyfröken: En Studie om Florence Stephens 1881–1979* (Malmö: Égalité, 2020).

Index

Note: Page numbers in *italics* indicates figures and page numbers in **bold** indicates tables on the corresponding page.

Abbott 80; Ingeborg 5, 81, 95n27, 138–139, 184; John Hallen 5, 9, 18, 29, 76, 80–81, 84, 95n24, 138–140
agriculture, agrarian: land (farmland), India 2, 9, 11, 103, 109, 121, 124; land (farmland), Sweden 14, 17, 143–145, 161–166, 169, 173
Akola 20n11, 41, 61, 79, 81, 89, 104, 123
Allen, Robert C. 112, 113
Älmhult 147
Alvesta 15
apprentice, apprenticeship 5, 12, 15, 29, 34, 76, 95n24, 95n27, **114**, 139–140
artisan 17, 28–31, 34, 111–113, 127n15

Banaji, Jairus 46–48, 118
Bania 111
Bear, Laura 65
Berar 1–2, 6, 8–12, 18, 19n2, 29, 91, 112, 121, 125, 130n59, 141, 149
Bhattacharya, Neeladri 46–48
Bhattacharya, Sabyasachi 59
Bhor Ghat 9, 32, 60, *62*, *86*
Bhusawal 8–9, 28–29, 76, 80–81, 83, **90**, 103, 121, 123
Bombay: business 9, 97n73, 141–142, 146–147; port 1–2, *10*, 141; Presidency 8, 30–31, 74, 92, 112; railway 2, 56, 75, 80–81, 83–84, 121
Bourdieu, Pierre 78–80
British East India Company 30
British Empire 8, 137, 149, 183
Bubb, Alexander 18, 29–30, 74, 88

capitalism 26–27, 41, 47
Carlsson, Sten 186
caste 10, 29–31, 87, 102, 104, 111–112, 120, 123–124, 197
Chandra, Bipan 56
cherimerry 6, 30, 63, 87, 105, 118, 123
colonialism: British 65, 139; Scandinavian 16, 135, 149
Copenhagen 3, 5–6, 17, 29, 76, 137–139, 143–144, 149, 153n46, 162, 183
cotton: ginning, pressing 77, 83, 91, 104; market (domestic, international) 1–2, 9, *10*, 92, 113, 120–121, 141; production 8–10, 12, 19n2, 121, 141
crop failure *see* drought

Deccan 1–2, 3, 5–6, 14–15, 17, 20n11, 76, 81, 93, 97n75, 101, 109, 111, 113, 120–121, 125
Denmark 139, 143–144, 146, 161, 163, 165–166
drought: in India 39, 120; in Sweden 162, 165, 172

Elphinstone Land and Press Company, Bombay 92
entrepreneur/-ial: in India 16, 73, 75, 149; in Sweden 80, 93, 150, 173

Fischer-Tiné, Harald 135, 139
forest, forestry: forest based polities 11; production in India 11; production in Sweden 16, 146, 161–163, 165–167, 169–170, 173–174
Foucault, Michel 27
Frih, Anna-Karin 194

gender, gendered 102, 105, 109, 120, 124, 164
Germany 14–15, 135, 143–144, 147, 161, 165–166
Great Indian Peninsula Railway (GIPR) 2, 57, 73, 102, 137
Great Uprising (1857–1858) 1, 12, 66, 141
Guha, Sumit 8–9, 11, 111, 113
Gunnarsson, Ingemar 18, 140

Huseby Estate 7, 13, *14*, 16, 72, 75, 79, 84, 89, 92, 135–137, 140, 143, 146, 149, 162, 164, 175n9, 183
Hyderabad 9, 112
Hyltén-Cavallius, Gunnar Olof 14, 84, 137–138, 147–148, 164–165, 172, 175n9
Hyslop, Jonathan 15

Indian Civil Service (ICS) 76
Indian Council of Medical Research 113
industry, industrial 11, 28, 32, 73, 92, 121, 140, 142–144, 147–149, 169, 173; deindustrialization 2, 112; industrialization 111, 137, 144–145, 161; managerial 73, 92; production 1, 146, 172; revolution 56, 162
infrastructure: communication 80, 141; expansion in India 2, 141–142; expansion in Sweden 136, 140; railway 9, 12, 58, 64, 139
Institution of Civil Engineers in England 6, 20n9
iron: foundry 72; furnace 15, 168; ironworks 16–17, 142–145, 147, 163, 165, 171–172; production in Sweden 145, 147, 167

Johannisson, Karin 190, 192, 194
Joseph Stephens Archive 1, 18
Joseph Stephens Construction Company 29, 77, 78, **82**, 91, 102, 123, 125, 136

Kalmar 15
Karlshamn 17, 79, 147, 149, 163, 167
Kerr, Ian 29, 32–33, 47, 60–61, 65–67, 74, 91, 101, 119, 122, 125
Khandesh 9, 11, 29–30, 87, 105, 149
King Oscar II of Sweden 170, 182
Knös, Anders Gabriel 148, 156n115
Kronoberg (county) 13–14, 16–17, 143, 162–165, 172

labourer *see* worker
labour market: in India 29–32, 38, 44, 46, 87, 101–102, 105, 109, 111–112, 117, 120–121, 125; in Sweden 169
landowner: in India 31, 118, 121; in Sweden 79–80, 89, 164, 169
Larsson, Lars-Olof 16, 140, 143–145, 147, 162, 168
law: Assam Contract Act 1865 32; Bengal Native Labour Act III 1863 32; contract law (in general) 7, 26–28, 31–32, 46–50, 123; Employers and Workmen Act 1875 28, 51n14; Employers' and Workmen's Disputes Act IX 1860 32; Penal Labour Act 103; property law (in general) 26; Railway Acts 1854, 1869, and 1890 65; Workmen's Breach of Contract Act XIII 1859 27, 30–32, 38, 40, 48, 50n14, 53n93, 103, 123
Lee, Watson, and Aiton Construction Company 29, 76, 90, 95n27
Levy, Madeleine R. 26
Liepe, Gunnar 171, 187–188, 197
Lucassen, Jan 111, 119

Maine, Henry 26, 28
maistries (labour gang headmen) 37, 63, 77, 85, 86, 104, 106, 119–120, 123; *see also muccadams*
Malmö 146–147, 165, 167
Markovits, Claude 74
Marsden, Ben 140
Marx, Karl 27, 47, 113
McLaren, Martha 15
Methodist 88, 183, 199n14
migrants, migration 3, 14–16, 105, 137, 138, 143, 161–162, 166
Misra, Maria 74
Mofussil Cotton Press and Ginning (MCPG) Company 77
Mohapatra, Prabhu 12, 31, 33, 47
moneylender (*sowcar*) 9, 110–111, 118
muccadams (labour gang headmen) 29, 44–46, 85–86, 104–106, 119–120, 123; *see also maistries*

Nagpur 1–2, 8–9, 28–29, 32, 34, 72, 76, 81, 83–84, 89, **90**, 91, 121–122
Nashik 5–6, 9, 29
network: business 13, 16–17, 57, 73, 80–81, 88, 92, 136–137, 142; professional 44, 59, 67–68, 149–150;

social, kinship 16, 30, 61–62, 64–65, 74–75, 83, 93, 137, 139, 145, 163
Nicol & Co., Bombay 142

parliament in Sweden 17, 161, 173, 175n19, 183, 194
Parsi 61, 63, 81, 83, 85, 88, 105
Petersson, Margareta 6, 181
Phule, Jotirao 111, 118
Plateau (Deccan) 1, 2, 8
Poona 29, 83, 92, 119
Public Works Department, India 2, 13, 59, 61
Purtschert, Patricia 135

railway: college 12–13, 21n21, 95n24, 140; company 2, 57–58, 65, 101–102, 122; contract 2, 29, 39, 57, 83, 122; engineer 5–7, 12–13, 29, 32, 34, 40, 57, 60, *61*, 64, 75–78, 80–81, 93, 138–142; in Sweden 15, 144, 146–147, 163, 167, 175n16; worker (*see* worker)
Ricardo, David 113
Rogers & Co., Bombay 146
Royal Indian Engineering College, Surrey, England 12–13

Satya, Laxman D. 2, 9–10
Siddiqi, Z. M. S. 48
Singha, Radhika 59
Småland (province) 13–17, 79–80, 142–145, 162–163, 170, 172–173
Smith, Crosbie 26, 140
sowcar see moneylender
Stephens: Blanche (married: von Sydow) 181, 184, 188; Elisabeth (born: Kreüger) 17, 161, 170–173, 176–177n41, 178n56, 181, 185–188, 194; Florence 17, 161, 170–173, *182*, 187–188, 194–195; George 3–5, 41, 88, 138, 151n13, 152n18, 164, 185; Joseph 3, *4*, 6, 13–17, 28–29, 72, 95n27, 136, 161, 167–168, 181–184; Joseph Rainer 138; Maggie 18, 170–171, *182*, 187; Mary *182*
Stokes, Eric 66
Stoler, Ann Laura 139
Swedish Ironmasters' Association (*Jernkontoret*) 171

textile 2, 9–10, 31, 56
Thorner, Daniel 56, 58
Tigar, Michael E. 26–27
tobacco cultivators 87, 105
trade 5, 141, 144, 146; export from India 2, 9–10, 92, 97–98n84, 141–142, 144; export from Sweden 15–16, 146–150, 163, 165–166

Vaddar, Woddaries 29–30, 38, 41, 44, 63, 85, 88, 119, 122
Vislanda 22n31, 79, 147, 149, 163, 175n16

wage: advance payment 28–32, 38, 46, 48–49, 59, 63, 86, 105–106, 118, 120, 123–124; contract worker, Sweden 201n60; daily wage **106**, **107**, 112
Western Ghats 8–9
wetland, in Sweden 16–17, 162, 170
worker, labourer: child 13, 87, 102–103, 105, 109, 113, 117–119, 125–126, 127n13; coolie 29, 41, 87, 104–106, 111–113, 118, 120–122, 124–125; gang 37, 44, 63, 85–87, 104–106, 118–120, 124; men 87, 102–103; protest, strike, refusal to work 33, 37–38, 43–44, 49, 119–120, 168; recruitment 2, 9, 26, 30–32, 37, 48, 58, 63, 65–66, 85–86, 101–102, 105–106, 118–119, 123, 125; unfree, coerced 27–28, 31, 33, 40, 47–48, 102, 118, 124–125; union, Swedish Agricultural Workers' Union 168; women 13, 46, 87, 102–105, 109, 113, 117, 119–121, 123, 125–126
worker, trade: blacksmiths 63, 86, 104, 109, 111; carpenters 60, 63, 104, 109, 111; cotton 87, 105; earthwork 29, 85, 88, 119; fencing 29, 85, 119, 122; industrial 170; lime (*chunam*) suppliers 34, 41, *42*, 46, 77–79, 119; mason 34, 37, 41, 43–44, 64, 79, 85–87, 104, 106, 109, **110**, 111–113, 118–124; stone suppliers, stone dressers 34, 38–43, 63, 85, 119, 122, 122–123; tiling 85
Wythes and Jackson Construction Company 29, 76

Zanden, Jan Luiten van 109
Zealand Railway Company 5, 139
Zwart, Pim de 109, 111

For Product Safety Concerns and Information please contact our EU representative GPSR@taylorandfrancis.com
Taylor & Francis Verlag GmbH, Kaufingerstraße 24, 80331 München, Germany

www.ingramcontent.com/pod-product-compliance
Ingram Content Group UK Ltd.
Pitfield, Milton Keynes, MK11 3LW, UK
UKHW020141200926
475702UK00005B/858
* 9 7 8 1 0 3 2 3 2 0 9 2 2 *